Edmund Hubhouse

Church-wardens' accounts of Croscombe, Pilton, Patton, Tintinhull, Morebath and St. Michael's, Bath

1349 to 1560

Edmund Hubhouse

Church-wardens' accounts of Croscombe, Pilton, Patton, Tintinhull, Morebath and St. Michael's, Bath
1349 to 1560

ISBN/EAN: 9783337262112

Printed in Europe, USA, Canada, Australia, Japan

Cover: Foto ©Lupo / pixelio.de

More available books at **www.hansebooks.com**

Church-Wardens' Accounts

of

Croscombe, Pilton, Yatton, Tintinhull, Morebath, and St. Michael's, Bath,

RANGING FROM A.D. 1349 TO 1560.

EDITED BY

RIGHT REV. BISHOP HOBHOUSE

(*Late Bishop of Nelson, N.Z.*).

PRINTED FOR SUBSCRIBERS, BY THE SOMERSET RECORD SOCIETY.

1890.

LONDON:
HARRISON AND SONS, PRINTERS IN ORDINARY TO HER MAJESTY,
ST. MARTIN'S LANE.

Contents.

	PAGE
EDITOR'S PREFACE	ix–xxvi
WARDENS' ACCOUNTS OF SIX SELECTED PARISHES	1–228
REMARKS ON OTHER ACCOUNTS INSPECTED . . .	229–232
GLOSSARY . .	233–242
APPENDICES	243–253
INDEX . .	255–275

Contents of Editor's Preface.

History and Aim of the Work; The Parish from 1349 to 1560, p. xi; The Parish in Council, p. xi; Ways and Means, p. xii; Wardens and their Functions, p. xiv; Church-Rates, p. xvi; Sidesmen, p. xvii; Chantry-Wardens, p. xvii; Personnel of Parish, p. xviii; Parish-life, p. xx; The Church-house, p. xxi; What was Lacking, p. xxiii; Relief of Poor, and other things not named, p. xxiii.

Somerset Record Society.

REPORT.

THE losses and gains since the presentation of my last Report leave our Society one less in numbers than it was at that time.

The finances, as will be seen by the annexed account, are in a satisfactory state.

The expense of printing the third volume has been unusually heavy owing to the nature of the subject, but it is expected that our printing expenses will now return to their former level. There must, however, as I forewarned the Society last year, be an additional charge upon our funds in the coming year for transcriptions, as we shall not be able to obtain the volunteer assistance which has been so freely afforded us hitherto, and has saved the Society considerable expenditure.

Our fifth volume is now in hand. It will contain two unpublished Custumals of Glastonbury Abbey of the 13th century, with some other documents bearing upon the same subject. I am glad to be able to report that the important work of dealing with this interesting subject has been kindly undertaken by Mr. C. I. Elton, Q.C., M.P., F.S.A.

J. A. BENNETT, *Hon. Sec.*

SOUTH CADBURY RECTORY,
    BATH.

SOMERSET RECORD SOCIETY.

Account for the Year 1889.

	£	s.	d.		£	s.	d.
To Balance in Bank per last Account	135	11	4	Harrison, Printing and Binding Vol. III.	154	3	6
,, Additional Subscriptions for 1887	3	3	0	Secretary's Postage, Stationery, and Sundries	1	4	4
,, ,, ,, 1888	5	5	0	Balance ...	152	17	7
,, Subscriptions for 1889	120	14	0				
,, ,, from New Members	5	5	0				
,, ,, paid in advance	33	12	0				
,, Interest on Deposit to 31st December, 1889	4	15	1				
	£308	5	5		£308	5	5

	£	s.	d.
To Balance brought down	152	17	7

Examined and found correct,

EDWIN SLOPER, *Auditor.*

List of Subscribers.

ADLAM, W., The Manor House, Chew Magna.
ANTIQUARIES, THE SOCIETY OF, Burlington House.
ARCHÆOLOGICAL SOCIETY, THE SOMERSET, Taunton.
ARCHBOLD, W. A., 20, Albemarle Street, London.

BADCOCK, H., Taunton.
BAILWARD, H., Horsington, Somerset.
BAKER, E. E., Weston-super-Mare.
BARNARD, REV. H. J., Pucklechurch, Bristol.
BATES, E. H., Newton Surmavill, Yeovil.
BATTEN, J., Aldon, Yeovil.
BENNETT, G., 2, Whitehall Place, London.
BENNETT, REV. J. A., South Cadbury Rectory, Bath.
BIRKBECK, REV. W. J., The Vicarage, Milborne Port.
BLACKER, REV. BEAVER H., 26, Meridien Place, Clifton.
BODLEIAN LIBRARY, THE, Oxford.
BOND, T., TYNEHAM, Wareham.
BOSTON, THE PUBLIC LIBRARY, Boston, U.S.A.
BOURDILLON, E. D., Poundisford Park, Taunton.
BOUVERIE, P. P., Brymore House, Bridgwater.
BRAIKENRIDGE, W. JERDONE, 16, Royal Crescent, Bath.
BRAMBLE, LIEUT.-COL., Cleeve House, Yatton.
BROADMEAD, W. B., Enmore Park, Bridgwater.
BROOKING-ROWE, J., Castle Barbican, Plympton.
BROWNE, THE VEN. ARCHDEACON, Wells.
BUCKLE, EDMUND, 23, Bedford Row, London.
BULLEID, J. G., Glastonbury.

CARLINGFORD, RIGHT HON. LORD, The Priory, Chewton Mendip, Bath.
CARTWRIGHT, REV. H. A., Whitestaunton, Chard.
CHURCH, THE VERY REV. R. W., DEAN OF ST. PAUL'S, St. Paul's, London.
CHURCH, REV. CANON C. M., Wells.

CLARK, W. S., Street.
CLOETE, W. D., Churchill Court, Congresbury.
COLEMAN, REV. J., Cheddar.
CORK AND ORRERY, THE RIGHT HON. THE EARL OF, Marston, Frome.
COWIE, THE VERY REV. B. M., DEAN OF EXETER, The Deanery.

DAVIS, MAJOR, 55, Great Pulteney Street, Bath.
DANIEL, REV. W. E., East Pennard, Shepton Mallet.
DAUBENY, W., Stratton House, Park Lane, Bath.
DICKINSON, F. H., Kingweston, Somerton.
DODINGTON, T. MARRIOTT, Horsington, Somerset.
DUCKWORTH, REV. W. A., Orchardleigh Park, Frome.

EDWARDS, SIR G., Stoke Bishop, Bristol.
ELLIS, REV. J. H., 29, Collingham Gardens, South Kensington.
ELWORTHY, F. T., Foxdown, Wellington.

FANE, THE HON. SIR SPENCER PONSONBY, Brympton Yeovil.
FISHER, E., Abbotsbury, Newton Abbot.
FLOYD, W., 39, Russell Square, London.
FOLJAMBE, CECIL G. S., Cockglode, Ollerton, Newark.
FOXCROFT, E. T. D., Hinton Charterhouse, Bath.
FOXCROFT, Mrs., Hinton Charterhouse, Bath.
FREEMAN, E. A., D.C.L., Somerleaze, Wells.
FRY, THE RIGHT HON. LORD JUSTICE, Failand House, Long Aston, Bristol.

GEE, REV. H., St. John's Hall, Highbury.
GEORGE, W., 3, King's Parade, Clifton.
GIBBS, ANTONY, Charlton, Nailsea.
GLASTONBURY ANTIQUARIAN SOCIETY, THE.
GREEN, EMANUEL, F.S.A., Devonshire Club, St. James's.
GREENFIELD, B. W., 4, Cranbury Terrace, Southampton.

HALLETT, T. P. G., Claverton Lodge, Bath.
HARRIS, R., Wells.
HARVARD COLLEGE LIBRARY, THE, Cambridge, Mass., U.S.A.
HERRINGHAM, REV. W. W., Old Cleeve Rectory, Taunton.
HERVEY, THE RIGHT REV. LORD ARTHUR, Bishop of Bath and Wells, Wells.
HERVEY, REV. SYDENHAM, Wedmore Vicarage, Weston-super-Mare.
HICKES, REV. T. H. F., Draycot Vicarage, Cheddar.
HIPPISLEY, W. A. COX, 10, High Cross Street, Leicester.
HOBHOUSE, THE RIGHT REV. BISHOP, Wells.
HOBHOUSE, H., Esq., M.P., Hadspen House, Castle Cary.

HOLMES, REV. T. S., Wookey Vicarage, Wells.
HOOPER, HIS HONOUR JUDGE, Thorne, Yeovil.
HORNER, F., Mells Park, Frome.
HORNER, REV. G., Mells Rectory, Frome.
HOSKINS, REV. C. T., North Perrott Rectory, Crewkerne.
HOSKINS, H. W., North Perrot Manor, Crewkerne
HOSKINS, H. W. P., 5, Portman Street, London.
HOWES, REV. J. G., Exford Rectory, Taunton.
HUDD, A. E., 94, Pembroke Road, Clifton.
HUMPHREYS, A. L., 26, Eccleston Road, Ealing Dean.
HUNT, REV. W., 24, Phillimore Gardens, Campden Hill, Kensington, W.
HUSEY-HUNT, B., Compton Pauncefort.
HUTCHINGS, HUBERT, Sandford Orcas, Sherborne.
HYLTON, LORD, Ammerdown Park, Radstock.
HYSON, REV. J. B., Tintinhull Vicarage, Yeovil.

JACKSON, REV. CANON, Leigh Delamere Rectory, Chippenham.
JENKYNS, H., Riverside, East Molesey, Surrey.

KNYFTON, MRS., Uphill, Weston-super-Mare.

LEIR, REV. R. L. M., Charlton, Musgrove, Wincanton.
LEIR, REV. W. MARRIOTT, Ditcheat Rectory, Castle Cary.
LONG, COL. W., Congresbury.
LUTTRELL, G. F., Dunster Castle, Dunster.
LYTE, H. MAXWELL, C.B., 3, Portman Square, London.

MACKENZIE, REV. C. H. N., East Harptree, Bristol.
MANNING, R. G., Wells.
MASTER, REV. G. S., Flax Bourton.
MEADE, REV. DE COURCY, Bath.
MEDLEY, REV. J. B., Lullington Rectory, Frome.
MELLIAR FOSTER-MELLIAR, W. M., North Aston, Deddington, Oxon.
MILDMAY, REV. A. ST. JOHN, Hazelgrove House, Sparkford, Bath.
MITCHEL, F., Chard.
MOGG, W. REES, Cholwell House, Temple Cloud, Bristol.
MOYSEY, H. G., Bathealton Court, Wiveliscombe.

NORRIS, H., South Petherton.

PAGET, SIR R., BART., M.P., Cranmore Hall, Shepton Mallet.
PERCEVAL, CECIL H. S., Henbury, Bristol.
PHELIPS, W., Montacute House, Ilminster.

PIGOTT, C. SMYTH-, Brockley Court, West Town, R.S.O., Somerset.
PINNEY, COL., Somerton Erleigh.
PLUMPTRE, THE VERY REV. E. H., D.D., DEAN OF WELLS, The Deanery.
POYNTON, REV. F. J., Kelston Rectory, Bath.
PRANKERD, S. D., The Knoll, Sneyd Park, Bristol.

RENDELL, REV. L. T., Timsbury Rectory, Bath.
ROGERS, REV. E., Odcombe Rectory, Ilminster.
ROGERS, T. E., Yarlington House, Wincanton.

SINGER, J. W., Frome.
SKRINE, H. M., Warleigh Manor, Bath.
SKRINE, H. D., Claverton Manor, Bath.
SLOPER, E., Taunton.
SOMERVILLE, A. F., Dinder, Wells.
STEPHENSON, REV. J. H., Lympsham Rectory, Taunton.
STRACHEY, SIR E., BART., Sutton Court, Pensford, Bristol.

THOMPSON, REV. ARCHER, Milton, Wells.
THRING, REV. G., Hornblotton Rectory, Castle Cary.
TITE, C., Shutes House, Wellington.
TREVILIAN, E. B. CELY, Midelney Place, Curry Rivel, Taunton.
TYNDALE, J. W. WARRE, Evercreech, Bath.
TYNTE, COL. KEMYS, Cefn Mably, Cardiff.

UNIVERSITY LIBRARY, THE, Cambridge.

WALTERS, G., Somerleaze, Frome.
WATTS, B. H., 13, Queen Square, Bath.
WEAVER, REV. F. W., Milton Vicarage, Evercreech.
WELLS, The Cathedral Library.
WINWOOD, REV. H. H., 11, Cavendish Crescent, Bath.
WORDSWORTH, THE RIGHT REV. J., LORD BISHOP OF SALISBURY, The Palace, Salisbury.

YOUNG, REV. F. M., The School House Sherborne.

Editor's Preface.

THE documents which form the corpus of this volume are of a class so little known, and *primâ facie* so little capable of enriching history, that it needs a few words to justify their selection.

I was asked in 1883 to inspect the Tintinhull Accounts then newly brought to light. I found in them not merely dry entries of Wardens' receipts and outlay, but a picture of village life, a record of habits, views, convictions, aspirations, which surprised me; moreover, I found that they untaught me no little. The church fabric and services were not maintained by the neighbouring Priory which owned all the acreage, but by the people, highly organized for purpose of continual contribution. I found also that the "parish" was a purely religious organization, distinct in its origin, its *raison d'être*, its principles, its working, and its aims, from the manor or the tything, though composed of the same personnel, man for man.

Since that time I have had opportunities of examining other Wardens' accounts noticed below, and I have found the same picture of church-life,[1] whether in village or in town.

It seemed to be fully within the province of a Record Society to make these documents public, to rescue them from peril of perishing or oblivion, and to bring their teaching to a focus.

The collections selected for thorough examination as the basis of these remarks were six; of these, one collection, St. Michael's, Bath,[2] had been printed by the Somerset Archæological Society in 1878 and 1879, in full. Of another, Morebath, portions were printed in 1883. I have not seen these two MSS., and am therefore not answerable for the faithfulness of transcription. For the handling of the other MSS., I am primarily indebted to friends, without whose aid my eyes could not have surmounted their task. The Rev. T. S. Holmes, Vicar of Wookey, made a verbatim transcript of the whole Pilton MS., the accuracy of which I can avouch from close collation. Our unwearied Secretary, Rev. J. A. Bennett, made large extracts from the Yatton, Croscombe, Tintinhull, and Morebath originals, transcribing what

---

[1] The only important variation from the rule of raising funds by voluntary means was that of Bridgwater, where there was an involuntary rate, at least a rate enforced in "invitos" though voted by the vestry voluntarily. *See* p. 230.

[2] This collection will be designated hereafter by **B**, the others by their initial letters, **C, Y, P, T, M**. *See* below for a short introduction to each collection at the head of the Accounts.

he judged to be the normal or more instructive portions, and summarizing the remainder. I have collated the first three before presenting them in print.

I have to regret that our space would not allow us to present a transcript of the *whole* MSS. The publication of the portions will, I hope, stir up others, like the new Vicar of Morebath, to enterprise a verbatim copy, and thereby to ensure the parishes against the loss of any of the substance of their now-valued chronicles.

I regret, too, that such stores as are lying at Banwell and Bridgwater should be left half searched. There is probably matter enough in these, even if not swelled by further discoveries, to fill another volume, and to add to our knowledge of the subject.

It is probable that both at Chard, and at Wells, where the municipal authorities[1] were heads of Guilds, and as such, were closely entwined with Church administration, the Church accounts are to be found among the town records. I am therefore obliged to send forth this collection in the consciousness of its being very incomplete, but in the hope that other hands will be stirred up and other hoards opened for its completion.

I may hope, however, that this work will serve to fill in part the remaining blank in our knowledge of the social life of our forefathers. This blank has been felt by our Society as one which it ought to aim at filling, and it has already achieved some steps in the process. In Vol. I the task of illustrating the working life of a diocese (then so potent a factor in the body politic), was assigned to me to work out from the Register of Bishop Drokensford, 1309-29. In Vol. II Mr. Green has given us a sight of the forcible close in 1547 of the ritual system which had prevailed in our village churches, and which revived under Queen Mary only to die again under Elizabeth.

It remained to ascertain what that system was as developed in our villages, and to learn how far it had operated in the formation of our people's habits and customs. The present volume attempts to do this.

To illustrate the other side of the village life, its prædial and manorial sides, *i.e.*, its land tenures and husbandry; the relations between the owner and the occupier of the soil, of the lord of the manor, his customary tenants and his bondmen there must be a search into the vast store of manor court rolls, bailiffs' compoti, and custumalia which are yet extant.

Part of this search, viz., into the Glastonbury custumalia is already on foot, and will, it is believed, add to our yet scanty knowledge of the class relations of the village communities; and, if handled as we hope by one who has already manifested his knowledge of the mediæval land tenures, it may be hailed as a most effective contribution to the common aim of our Society.

---

[1] Mr. Serel, in his history of St. Cuthbert's Wells, has given "in extenso," contracts made for work in that Church in the 15th Century, the Mayor being a party, and the record remaining with the Corporation.

I now proceed to draw from the documents here edited or elsewhere inspected their teaching with regard to

The Parish, its Organisation and Condition

(Within the limits of 1349 and 1560).

[N.B. Where no other date is stated, all remarks below apply to this period.]

To reach the meaning of "Parish" antecedently to the changes which imposed civil functions on the religious community, we must be indebted, not to any later writings, but to co-temporary documents.

From them we find that the "parish" was the community dwelling in an area defined by the Church, organized for Church purposes, subject to Church authority.

The area might coincide with a manor or manors, or a piece of a manor or a tithing, or it might differ from all other defined areas. It was at times altered by Church authority.

Within this area every resident was a parishioner, and, as such, owed his duty of worship and contribution to one stated Church, and his duty of confession and submission to the official guidance of a stated pastor, entitled his Rector, or to the Rector's deputy, entitled Vicar.

There was no choice allowed.

The community was completely organized with a constitution which recognized the rights of the whole and of every adult member to a voice in self-government, but kept the self-governing community under a system of inspection, and (if need should be) restraint from central authority.

The necessary officers were (1), the Rector or his deputy; (2), the Wardens, the chosen representatives of the parishioners.

The whole adult population were accounted parishioners, and had an even voice when assembled for consultation under the Rector. Seeing that both sexes served the office of Warden, there can be no doubt that both had a vote.

The place of meeting was the Church. The name of "vestry," as applied to the Church council, nowhere appears.

It must have grown up after the date when vestry-rooms grew up, and were large enough, as at Croscombe, to contain an assembly. These must have been rare. In most country parishes the Churches served for the parishioners' council-room.

The Vestry.

The functions of the vestry (to use the later term) are gathered from the things entered as done "*coram parochianis.*" The formal acts were (1), the yearly election of Wardens; (2), audit of the outgoing Wardens' Accounts; (3), transfer of the Church goods, and of balance of cash and livestock from the outgoing to the incoming Wardens by inventory; (4), consultation on the needs of the Church fabric and ornaments, and on the methods of raising funds, with instructions to the Wardens for effecting repairs, &c.

A wide freedom in the management of the fabric and accessories seems to have been left to the parish by the Diocesan Authorities. Probably the people were duly monished when they fell short of their prescribed duties. Otherwise, they were left free in the exercise of their bounty; but it must be remembered that they were under the regular inspection of Rural-Deans and Archdeacons, who held most effective powers to enforce their monitions, and that the Wardens were sworn to the Visitatorial Court to make presentments of every defect.

The liability of the parish to maintain and furnish the House of God was uncontested. It was the settled duty of each member to help in so doing, a duty always pressed on the conscience by the Clergy in making their parishioners' wills,[1] and the duty of the collective body must needs accrue from this rule for each of its constituents.

But though the duty arose "*in foro conscientiæ*," it was, according to the mediæval methods of guiding consciences, enforceable "*in foro externo*," *i.e.*, in the Church Courts beginning with the Archdeacon's monition. Such a monition, we find, issued to St. Mary's, Bridgwater (*see* p. 231) based probably on the Vicar's presentment of some defect in the spire. The parish obeyed the monition and placed the estimated sum in the Vicar's hands for executing the repair, as ordered.

The details of the parishioners' liability were defined by papal and provincial constitutions. Archbishop Winchelsea's constitution, *circa* 1300, was in force in the middle of the 16th Century. I have given it in Appendix A, as exhibiting the authorised demands made upon lay members of the Church. They were large, but large as they were, were outstripped by the people's zeal, which went far beyond the imposed minimum in supplying the necessaries of Divine Service.

In the apportionment of the "*onera*" (*i.e.*, the requirements of the Church), between the parish and the Clergy, custom always had some variant voice, and in the apportionment between the Lay Rector and Vicar in an appropriated[2] parish, the Bishop's award was the rule. This was generally settled by a deed called "*ordinatio vicariæ*" issued at the time of appropriation, but it was subject to revision and was not seldom revised when justice to needy Vicars demanded it.

Ways and Means.

The mode of raising funds in discharge of liabilities was left to local option. Even in the rare case of a monition the parish was free to choose its own method of meeting the imperative demand. If there was no balance in hand, voluntary rates (called "setts," at M, p. 209) were sometimes made on some loose basis of rateability, and I suppose with no more attempt at enforcement than what the loss of the neighbours' good-will could effect. Special collections were more common, and of donors to these many lists survive, but one only case of a rate imposed by the majority upon the unwilling has come to light. This impost was levied at Bridgwater year after year upon the whole area of the parish, the town and the hamlets being divided into wards, and each ward visited by a collector who reported defaulters. One list of defaulters is extant, and also the charge incurred by the Wardens for entering a suit against them in the Archdeacon's Court. Even in this process of assessment the first stage was voluntary.

The parish was free to raise its funds, like all its neighbours, by the good-will of its

---

[1] The forthcoming extracts, edited by Rev. F. W. Weaver, from the oldest wills in H.M. Probate Registry, Wells, show that every dying person strove to leave something to his Parish Church, and to the mother Church of the Diocese, the Cathedral, too.

[2] *I.e.*, where the rectorial Tithe had been perpetually annexed to a religious Society or Office. Cases of revised apportionments to Vicars may be seen in Reg. Drok., fo. 265, affecting Over Stowey and Yatton.

members. It was under no compulsion to rate them according to their property, but when it chose to do so, each member was bound to discharge his obligation to the Church in the way and amount determined for him. It then became an involuntary impost.

The Bridgwater rate is the only one known (to me at least) as a clear instance of the principle (a general one in mediæval self-governing communities), of the majority binding the minority in the discharge of duties common to each member.[1]

But if it was rarely exercised, the reason is made clear by our records. The good-will of the people found the needed funds without resort either to compulsion or to any outside sources.

The modes of eliciting this good-will were various and worth studying.

1. The Church, after inhibiting the employment of labour on festal days, and requiring the people of all classes, as a sacred obligation, to attend the Church Services, busied itself to find amusements for the gathered people, thus identifying the Holy Day and the Holiday

2. The popular amusements thus provided were the occasions for drawing out the peoples' contributions. The Church Ale was, by the end of the 15th Century, the most universal Churchwardens' resort for eliciting the bounty of the parish.

3. The principle of association was also largely employed. The constituent classes of the community were banded together for the maintenance of special devotions, *e.g.*, lights, obits, the shrine of a patron saint, &c.

Each of these guilds had its festal day, its Service, and its revelry, and made its gathering of money; which, after defraying the guild-objects, was added to the Wardens' fund. This guild-system was most fully organised at Croscombe, where it must have been co-extensive with the community. *See* p. 1.

4. The popular bounty was also elicited by other incitements. The names of benefactors were written in a roll, "the bede-roll," called also Kalendar, Martilege, Liber obitalis. The names were given out to the parishioners on great[2] days and their prayers bidden in behalf of the donors, "pro bono statu" if living, "pro salute animæ," if dead.

Some of the donors specify this enrolment as a condition of their gifts, some leave a fee to the "bedeman" who should bid the prayers in their behalf. The poorest, judging by the smallest of their bequests, were anxious to be among the benefactors. An iron crock, a girdle, a ring,[3] a swarm of bees, and yet smaller gifts in kind may be found amongst the bequests of the poor, which the Wardens had to turn into money for their coffer.

5. The gifts of livestock were frequent, and of a nature which led the Wardens into farming them for the sake of annual returns. Sheep, cows, bees, were often given, and sometimes managed by the Wardens; but the management in the hands of officers changing yearly was difficult, and the stock is apt to disappear suddenly from the accounts, testifying to some

---

[1] At Wembdon a middle course was adopted in 1325. *See* Reg. Drok., fo. 248. The parishioners all agreed to a rate for rebuilding their Church. Some defaulted. This breach of faith was reported to the Bishop, who thereupon ordered the defaulters' names to be returned to him, intimating that they would be cited to Wells Consistory. The basis of this rate was *consent*, and the defaulters' offence was breach of faith.

[2] In all Churches one fixed day was celebrated as the anniversary for the Benefactors (Good-doers, C. 45), called variously, the great Dirige, the Commemoration, the Mass for the Founders.

[3] The commonest gift of all—sometimes specified as the wedding-ring.

unexplained failure. At **C**, p. 40, the contract for management of a flock of sheep may be seen. At **P**, the church-herd of cows had their own Warden, see the Key-Warden's account, p. 63. At **M**, almost every side-altar was endowed with sheep. Even St. Michael's, Bath, a city parish, had a small flock.

6. Close akin to the farming of livestock was the trade (for it was nothing less) carried on at the church-house for the benefit of the church-coffer. The growth of this institution calls for separate treatment—*see* below. It became at last the most productive of all the fiscal devices. Its fiscal success led in fact to its moral ruin and its abolition.

7. Larger gifts were common, but the larger ones did not usually swell the Wardens' credit-sheet. They aimed at securing some abiding spiritual benefit to the donor and his family, *e.g.*, by addition of a chapel with its endowed chantry and obituary services. At **B**, we can track the growth of endowments in the form of house-property given to the parish, and administered by the Wardens, for the sake of maintaining anniversaries in behalf of the donors, *see* p. 228.

The houses were endowments of the *parish* and lightened the burden on the voluntary funds, but rich donors more commonly aimed at erecting or succouring newer institutions. At **C**, the Palton chantry was enfeoffed with an estate valued in 1537 at £29 1s. 6d., charged with maintenance of four priests. At Bridgewater the Lady Wardens administered an ample revenue for the lights and services of the lady-chapel, whilst the lights of the High Cross had in 1389 a rent roll of £2 14s.

8. By religious plays. In 1451 a Christmas play was got up at **T** (p. 184), by five parishioners, who gave the nett profits to the new rood-loft. At **M**, we read of an Easter-play; in each case the events of the religious season being set forth for the teaching of the unlettered people and thus combining edification with amusement. At St. Peter's, Oxford, the Wardens kept a set of players' garments which they not only used for Christmas plays at home, but let out on hire for behoof of their funds. These plays were, I suppose, held to be so far hand-maids to the church in her teaching office as to justify their being represented in the naves of the churches—the scenery, if any, being of the simplest. The Play-Kings with their mock courts were on the other hand, altogether secular, and exhibited in the church-house with more freedom of revelry and jest. We find them performing not only at Christmas, **C** and **T**, but at three of the four seasons, in the summer at **T**, in the autumn at **B**.

They all brought funds to the Wardens, as also did the Robin Hood-exhibitions at the village butts.

Wardens.

It is evident that Wardens who had to ply such fiscal machinery had very varied functions to perform, *e.g.*, farming, trading, selling gifts in kind, housing corn, selling beef when the bull was killed, **T**, p. 183, furnishing the church-house, overseeing its brewery, its bakehouse, its entertainments.

They had besides the duty of presentment to the Archdeacon's Court, as now, of moral delinquencies in their Rector or the flock. Further they had to make many journeys, *e.g.*, to fetch a Freemason from Exeter for building St. George's Chapel at **C**, in 1508, for buying standing trees, felling and seasoning the timber, as at **Y**, p. 85.

The complex nature of the office did not deter the parishioners from selecting females.

At **M**, p. 219, Lucy Scely held the office single-handed in the most difficult times, viz., 1548. Dame Isabel Newton was Warden at **Y** in 1496–7.

The office on the other hand was wholly free from all civil functions or even eleemosynary calls.

The earlier descriptions of the Wardens *custodes bonorum, Procuratores ecclesiæ S. Margaretæ* or *Joannis*, limit the office to the narrow bounds of providing the necessaries of a system of worship at a particular church or chapel. This and no more was the actual range of the wardens' office as deputed by the parishioners, and this was the object for which voluntary funds were committed to them. Their disciplinary functions accrued to them, as Bishop's Officers, empowered in the Visitation Court.

No civil functions were cast upon them[1] until quite late in the reign of Henry VIII, when they begin to receive orders to provide harness or arms for soldiers, to relieve maimed soldiers, or otherwise to meet the public needs for which the civil government neglected to provide.

In the reign of Edward VI, 1549, the voluntary alms of the members of the church were formally and regularly demanded for the relief of the poor. In 1552, the poor man's box was set up in the church under the Archbishop's injunctions, and the Wardens were required to gather the donations of the people, and to dispense them amongst the poor.

The Wardens thus became Relieving Officers, and when the mass of poverty, which had been quickened by the dissolution of the monasteries, became too heavy for voluntary alms, and demanded the impost of a poor's rate, the Wardens needed the aid of special officers for their novel functions of levying and dispensing a rateable tax.

The establishment of the rating power wrought a great change in the functions of the Vestry, of the Wardens, and of the parish.

Henceforth it passed from an ecclesiastical organisation of churchmen for their own special purposes, to a machinery, which, in addition, could discharge various functions for the civil power.

It was used regularly through the reigns of Elizabeth and James I, for maintenance of army hospitals, for passing maimed soldiers, for relief of wayfaring Irish and others, and for equipments of volunteers. Further, as the Hundred and Manor Courts waned in their active control over the secular interests of the locality, the Vestry became the chief council of the community, and having authority to tax the whole area of the parish, it was able to provide for any dropt duties and expenses. By successive stages it became the highway

---

[1] There were two legislative attempts, but both disregarded, at least by the parishes whose records are extant. (1). The provisions of the Statute of Labourers, 1349, which required Churchwardens along with officers of boroughs and counties to aid labourers to return to their homes, seem to have been quite inoperative, though sometimes quoted as evidence of the parish being a civil institution. The earliest charge for anything not ecclesiastical, is in 1512-13, at **Y.** *see* below p. 80. In 1528 the Wardens of **Y.** take up the yearly duty of scouring the Yeo with repair of sluices for the common safety. This may have been laid upon them by a Commission of Sewers, though preceding the Act in 23rd of Hen. VIII, which gave permanence to such Commissions, or it may have been prompted by desire for the safety of the village. (2). The Act of 27 Hen. VIII, 1535-6, " for punishment of sturdy vagabonds and beggars" seems to have been as inoperative as that of 1349. It required Churchwardens or two others of every parish (under pain of forfeiting 20s. every month) to gather voluntary alms of good Christian people, with boxes, every Sunday or Holy Day in such good discretion as that impotent folk, not able to work, should be holpen, so as not to go openly in begging, and also required that the lusty should be kept in continual labour.

board appointing its waywardens, and levying its highway rates. The care of the Pound the appointment of Hayward, the repair of Stocks, and appointment of Tything men often lapsed into its hands. In the huge parishes of London it has been gradually invested by the Legislature with large powers as the Local Government Board of each parochial area; and there its civil functions have so overtopped its ancient ecclesiastical ones as to hide their origin and induce the belief that it drew its birth from the civil community, assuming to itself the care of the church, not as its original purpose, but only as a necessary incident to the union of Church and State.

It will be easier for the next generation to realize the Vestry in its original purpose. It ceased to be a Poor Law Board in 1834 by the establishment of unions. It lost its rating power by the Church Rate Abolition Act of 1867, which restored its original dependence on voluntary funds. The Local Government Act, of 1888, has begun to transfer to the larger civil community the management of the streets of London. And the rector of the London parish has no longer to preside over a body charged with vast duties of a most secular character.

The village Vestry has now ceased to spend funds on equipping soldiers, or on the slaughter of vermin. It retains the election of Overseers and Guardians of Poor, and of Waywardens, as a testimony of the length it has wandered from its original functions.

Church Rates.

Our documents show no trace of recourse to compulsory rate imposed by external authority.[1] The voluntary contributions being adequate to the needs, there was no reason for seeking other and less desirable means. We cannot conclude that compulsory power could not have been invoked "ab extra." Within the parish the principle of community-self-government was strong. It was strong enough in the Manor Courts to enforce fines and general submission to the will of the majority. At St. Michael's, Bath, the Vestry laid the Wardens under penalty, 18th Henry VIII—but I have never met with a case anywhere in Bishop's Registers of compulsion being invoked by the Church community to enforce demands, except upon those who had consented to them.

In Reg. Drok., fo. 248, we find a case where the Bishop threatened compulsion against certain parishioners of Wembdon, near Bridgwater, who *after* consenting to a voluntary rate laid "juxta valorem possessionum," for the rebuilding of their Church, had failed to pay. The Bishop desired that the list of defaulters should be sent to him with a view to their citation. *Ante* p. xiii, note.[1]

This case shows how easily a rate made by consent of a parish under monition might become compulsory, for each Churchman, who in Vestry opposed obedience to the monition, might be cited for contumacy, and when his assent had once been obtained, he was liable to be cited for breach of engagement.

The powers of compulsion were indeed ample enough, though happily little needed. In Bishop Roger de Norbury's Reg. at Lichfield, we find the Bishop on visitation in 1325 ordering the repair of the roof of Mayfield Church in Staffordshire. The parishioners pleaded that the inhabitants of the chapelry of Butterton had shirked their liability to

---

[1] The case of Bridgwater above named was one where the people by their own consent imposed a rate on themselves, and then coerced defaulters.

join in repairing the mother Church. The Bishop thereupon interdicted the Butterton people from the use of their own Chapel until they had done their duty to the mother Church of Mayfield.

The power of Interdict, *i.e.*, the excommunication of the whole community, was the weapon always ready for forcing the community into providing (1) the Church for the living, (2) the Churchyard for the dead, and (3) all the accessories of worship, if not found "aliunde."

The liability of the parish was a settled thing, but in the modes of discharging it there was ample option. In the case of disputed proportion of the liability, to be borne by the Chapelries of a mother Church, the Bishop was called in to settle it.

A decree of this kind is found in Reg. Drok., fo. 243, where the Bishop finally released the people of Wyke St. Lawrence from further liability to repair the mother Church of Congresbury, but made them liable to the exclusive maintenance of their own Chapel, Graveyard, and Services.

Sidesmen, *i.e.*, Testes Synodales.

These were occasionally appointed when ordered by the Ordinary to attend the Visitation Court as witnesses, or needed by the Wardens to support Wardens' presentments with their testimony in the Court.

The name of sidesmen does not appear, nor any formal name, nor does it appear how they were selected, but probably by the parish in whose name they were to give their evidence at the synod. The inference drawn from the documents is that this office was not a necessary or a constant part of the framework of the parish, that it was supplementary to one department of the Wardens' duties, viz., the disciplinary.

In Canon 90 of 1603 the office is treated as a perpetual one. Two or three or more discreet persons are to be chosen in *every* parish by the joint consent of minister and parish, or failing their consent, by the Ordinary. They are called sidesmen or assistants, *i.e.*, to the Wardens, and are spoken of in the title as if they had a *joint* office with the Wardens.

Chapel and Chantry Wardens.

These offices sprang up to answer the demands created almost universally during the 15th Century by the addition of chantries and chantry chapels, some endowed with lands and cattle, some maintained by guilds.

In the case of the latter, the guildsmen were sure to elect their own Wardens. They were probably responsible to the guilds only, not to the parish, or to the Visitation Court, in which they were, I presume, not sworn in—but in the case of malversation of sacred goods, they would be as individuals amenable to the censures of the Court "*pro salute animæ*."

In the case of well-endowed chantries, where the priest was presented to the Bishop and instituted, the Wardens obtained nearly even rank with the Parish Wardens. They sometimes wielded a large income, and maintained festival services in which all parishioners could join.

The secular successors of some of these guilds, the Mayors and Town Councils are still found, as in Wells and Chard, nominating a Warden to act co-ordinately with the other Wardens for the whole parish the guild-origin of the Council's right being quite forgotten

c

The existence of chantries is now brought to light in almost every church restoration by the survival of piscinæ or some other token in the East or the side wall; but even where the fabric reveals no token, and perhaps never bore one, the existence of a guild, bound to maintain some special services, either obituary for the benefit of the departed, or festal, in honour of the guild's patron, or of the guild's feast day, may be presumed in all but the smallest of fabrics. If there were no side-altar, the high altar was available, and the parish priest was remunerated out of the oblations for officiating.

The publication of Edward VI's Chantry Commissioners' Report, 1547, has helped to show the prevalence of chantry endowments, but it must be remembered that it is an incomplete record. There were many endowments, which, warned by the signs of coming spoliation,[1] vanished in the latter days of Henry VIII—some of the chantries, maintained only by the goodwill of a guild, yielded nothing to the grasp of the Commissioners—some places, where chantries are known to have existed, seem unaccountably to have escaped the visitation, *e.g.*, Mells, Leigh, Whatley, Tintinhull, Bruton and its chapels.

The Personnel

Of the average village parish was as follows—

1. Rector or Vicar invested with a permanent cure of souls. If disabled, an assistant priest, generally entitled "Capellanus."
2. A Deacon or sub-deacon, or both in the larger parishes.
3. A Clerk in minor orders, entitled—"*clericus parochialis*" and "*aquæ bajulus*" from his attending the priest with holy water. He was supported by the parishioners, by customary dues, which, if withheld, were enforced by monition.
4. A Sexton, in the modern sense, as grave-digger, and outside caretaker.
5. The Wardens, variable in number.
6. The Sidesmen—when needed.
7. The Wardens of the voluntary bodies, or of endowed chapels, or of guilds, or stores or herds.
8. The keepers of the procession-crosses.

In one of our selected parishes, **M.**, in addition to all the usual officers appears a body of men, probably exceptional, certainly supernumerary, elected by the parishioners, and recognized, though perhaps not empowered by the Ordinary. They are called each year from the number elected, the five men, or the four, or the nine, and by no other name. The reasons of their election were probably exceptional. Their action may be briefly viewed in the account rendered to the parish in 1527, p. 221, and again in p. 223, where "four honest men" are said to be "chosen to govern the parish in all causes concerning the wealth of the Church" "under orders at Visitation." They were a parochial council chosen it would seem "*pro re natâ*."

[1] The Chantry Commissioners report (p. 130) the fact of the Earl of Huntingdon, escheating the lands given by his ancestor about a century earlier for endowing a College of Priests in North Cadbury Church.

Lower Offices.

Of Deacons and Sub-deacons we hear little. That they were at times in use, the double and triple sedilia of our churches testify; but there was no endowment for them, neither any aid from the parish funds. The offices were a training for the priesthood, and to those candidates who were drawn from the lowest ranks, must have been their chief training. They were sometimes quartered in the parsonage-house[1] where they got some teaching in return for services, and they got some support from the illiterate neighbours who required their clerkly help.

Schoolmasters there were none.

The office which the parish was required to support was that of Parish Clerk, in official language, *aquæ bajulus*, the carrier of Holy Water. He was in minor orders, perhaps sometimes raised to the sub-deaconship, if unmarried. He attended the priests inside the church, and also at the visitation of the sick, and carried Holy Water and Bread at seasons to some of the houses.[2]

At **M.**, p. 223, we find the details of his duties and emoluments. In Drok. Reg., folio 156, we find at Chedzoy the Bishop removing from the "*Beneficium aquæ benedictæ*" one who was neither tonsured nor "*literatus*," and requiring the curate to admit the Bishop's nominee, duly qualified. The office was regulated by Canon-law, and was imposed upon the parish, as the Canon of 1603 testifies. Singers appear sometimes, but whether as a trained choir, or some out-of-door performers, such as waits, is not clear. At **P.**, they twice received a gratuity from the wardens.

An organist was maintained at Yatton, the earliest, Harry Organs, earning his name by his art, and bequeathing it to his posterity.

The occasional mention of organs at **C.** looks like the use of a borrowed and "portative" instrument.

Ringers received gratuities now and then. They were probably a volunteer band, taking fees, as they came, but not wages.

The clock is found in every Church, in spite of being a costly article and needing frequent repair and paid care. The caretaker was generally the clerk, but with a special fee.

The care of the crook, *i.e.*, the chief processional cross, was at **P.**, a paid office. After a time, St. Michael's guild provided a crook for themselves, with its own keeper, leaving the distinction of "High Crook," to the chief one which headed the great Paschal Procession of the whole parish.

The care of the other manifold gear, candles, lamps, candlesticks (cansticks), banners, censers, incense, surplices and minor robes, with the "folding up of the vestments" did not belong to any one office, except in parishes rich enough to maintain a sacristan. They were paid for in separate items. Hence washing, wax, melting down old wax and making it

---

[1] See Abp. Peckham's Injunctions in 1280, to Lichfield Chapter in Dugd. Mon. V. 6, where he requires the Vicar of Bakewell to keep a Deacon and Sub-deacon as "commensales" and as pupils, and the Chapter, as rectors, to allow them 20*s.* and 10*s.* for clothing.

[2] Within memory the clerks of East Somerset carried an Easter-cake to each principal house, and received a fee in return.

up anew, with scouring of metal, all form regular and weighty items. At T. the washer-women declined to take anything for their labour, leaving us an example which the Wardens did well to record, though little dreaming that it would be held up for the incitement of church people at the end of 400 years. At P., the Warden charges for "sunning the cloths," a much needed process in a church never warmed.

Having omitted it elsewhere, I will here remark on the system, which must have brought much stir and trouble to the servants of the church, of executing works on the spot with material bought by the Wardens. When books were wanted, parchment was bought, a scribe hired, a book-binder fetched and furnished with material. Clock weights and sheets of lead were cast on the spot, the metal being brought from Mendip. Even the high art required for ornate robes could be sometimes found near enough at hand to be employed on the spot by the Wardens, who had to find the materials. The grand workmanship of the rood-screen at Y. was all executed by Crosse, a carver in Cleeve within the parish, the oak being bought by the Wardens in standing trees, which they selected, felled, and seasoned. The fine bench-ends at T. were executed in the same way,

The diffusion of skilled art and of taste through the village communities is thus evidenced incontestably.

The Life of the Parish.

With the above view of the constitution of the parish, we may proceed to a view of its life.

The religious conditions of the community stood in strong contrast to the civil. The spiritual authority was strong enough to control all orders and degrees of men in their mutual relations. The Church regulated the festal and work days. It claimed for the servile population to be free from the demands of service on the days set apart as Holy Days of obligation. These days were not only the Lord's day and the great Christian Feasts, but also days of local observance, *e.g.*, the dedication day of the Parish Church, the day of the local Saint or of the principal guild-patron.

On all these days the labourer, though born in serfdom, was free, only bound to the service of his Divine master. He donned his best clothes, he joined his fellow-guildsmen, he marched under banners to the Church as the common home of the highest and the lowest.

After Divine Service, there were amusements provided at the Church-house, or on the village green. Somebody had given a tavern of ale, and invited the parishioners of the next parish that kept these social terms, or there was a return revelry at the Church-house of that parish, or the guild of Webbers or of Hogglers was holding its "ale," or Robin Hood was mustering his men at the Butts, or the young men or the maidens were keeping Hockday.[1]

The bulk of the parishioners, even the serfs, were, I conceive, engaged through their various associations in planning these amusements. They were not spectators or partakers merely, but also managers sharing in the pageant and in the costs; and thereby the bonds

---

[1] The Monday and Tuesday in the second week after Easter week. At St. Peter's, Oxford, the maidens stopped the thoroughfares on the first day, making the young men pay for passing. On the second day the young men levied toll of the maidens. The proceeds went to the Wardens.

of social fellowship were tightened, and the barrier lines between servile and free, which seem to the student of our law books to be so impassable, were melted away by the warmth of kindly fellowship.

Certain it is that in these documents no trace is found of any class disfranchised by bondage from the even enjoyment of the privileges, spiritual or social, which attached to the religious community.

If we glance at a manor court roll of the day, the condition of the civil community as there seen stands in strong contrast to the condition of the religious community, (the very same persons be it remembered) as shown in the Church accounts.

In the civil document the community is divided into sharply defined classes, the lord of the soil and his tenants, the tenants into bond and free, the villeins again sub-divided according to the size of their holdings into virgatarii, fardellarii, etc. The relative duties of class to class are sharply defined too, and are involuntary. They are all enforceable and enforced by fine and penalty. But in spite of this harsh look there are traces to be seen of a gradual blending of classes and interests, and of a continual softening of the earlier barrier lines. Though the legal distinction between the servile and the free tenant went on, it became so modified in practice that the same persons are found in the Court Roll on the list of the bondmen, and of the leasehold occupiers of farms which they obtained by payment of fine.

In Henry VIII's Valor, 1537, the monastic estates are shown to be no longer managed on the earlier system of the demesne cultivated for the lord by his serfs under a reeve, the rest of the manor in villenage. In 1537, the manor is found apportioned into farms leased to the newly-created race of renting yeomen, and worked by free labour for wages. The manorial community had become much more blended and assimilated; and wherever we can get peeps into its inward spirit and condition it was actuated by a strong *esprit de corps* which must have tended potently to fuse the stiff social partitions.

The great blending force is, I conceive, to be found in the church, not only in its masterprecepts of brotherly love and mercy, but in the peculiar form which it adopted of social action, a form which its lofty authority then enabled it to carry out. It was able to mitigate the rigour of the landlord's demands upon the servant of the soil, whom serfdom would else have doomed to an unceasing round of toil. It was strong enough to say to the master, "Thy servant shall rest on the days that are marked as holy. Thou and thy servant together shall on those days resort to the house of your Divine Master, as fellow servants, and there pay your united homage of prayer and praise."

It was in this way that the Holy Day of the Church became the Holiday of the people. The holy day and the holiday, now so different, were in origin identical, and for some time identical in meaning and in mode of observance. The growing divergence is traceable in these documents (the later of them), but it is our present business to note that they were once identical, and to measure the very wide social import of that fact.

The Church-house, being the focus of the social life of the parish (meaning by that word the Christian community), will be fitly introduced here in illustration of the above.

The growth of this institution may be traced in all its stages in T. Beginning with a bakehouse for the holy wafer, and for the holy loaf, it came to be a place of sale for the latter, and when brewing gear was added for the brewing of the holy ale, a place of sale for that also, instead of the churchyard. It had, by these facilities for baking and brewing, become a source of revenue. This revenue was enhanced by letting the oven and the brewing vessels on hire for the use of private persons.

The next step was to get possession of a dwelling-house, and to make it a place of entertainment. A house was obtained (subject only to a quit rent to the manorial lord) close to the church, in the reign of Henry VII. Agnes Cokke, *i.e.*, the cook who probably owed her surname to her calling, was placed in it to manage the complex concerns, now including cookery.

In 1533 it had reached its full development. It was a most convenient centre of sociality. Anyone who wished to forward a church object found appliances ready. He had only to proclaim an ale (*taberna* in churchwardens' latin, *i.e.*, a tavern), and the parishioners flocked to it, and gratefully brought their contributions.

With enlarged appliances, they enlarged the area of hospitality. Tintinhull invited Montacute and Stoke, Montacute and Stoke on their festal days invited Tintinhull, for an interchange not only of sociality, but of religious offices and contribution.

These *tabernæ* were, I consider, expansions of the earlier institution of the "Holy Ale," which in its simplest form was the Wardens' sale of Ale blessed by the Rector and carried home, as the holy loaf was, from the church door. The *taberna* was a social consumption of the ale. It was a revelry, and liable to sensual abuse. The abuses abounded in proportion as the power of the church to check them waned, and the religious origin of the institution was forgotten.

The Church-house, however, went on with dangerous popularity all through Elizabeth's reign,[1] and in spite of just puritan dislike. The 88th Canon of 1603, "Churches not to be profaned," only touched the evil so far as to guard consecrated places from revelry. It did not forbid the ales. In this county the civil authority interposed, and, in spite of the Bishop's (Piers) apology, succeeded in quenching them together with all the peculiar social life of the village community out of which they had sprung.

They have never revived in any form but that of a club-walk, and that institution originates in association for mutual aid, not for the furtherance of Divine Service.

The houses nevertheless had a long, though inglorious history. They became the property of the civil parish which had no funds for repairing them. They were generally used, whilst each parish was chargeable with maintaining its own poor, for housing the poorest families. When the reformed Poor Law in 1834 gathered the indoor paupers into union workhouses, the squalid tenement, once the Church-house, was sold, and the price carried as a parish contribution to the building of the central workhouse. The Church-house was, I believe, as universal an adjunct to the church, as the Sunday School-room has become in this century. Every small tenement reputed to be, or to have been parish property, lying very near to the church, may be suspected of having been once the focus of the social life of the church community, it may be under the name of our Lady House as at Pilton, or Guildhall as at Stanford, Berks.

I have spoken of the Christmas play and also of the Play-kings, amongst the means of raising church funds. There were also mumming and minstrel performances, which no doubt found a rallying place at the church-house; but I am inclined to think that they were wholly in the hands of wandering bands of laymen, owning no sober control, and not in

---

[1] The chief source of income at **T**, and elsewhere, to the end of the 16th Century.

the hands of parish officers. To judge by what survived of them within memory, their subject was always a crusading one. St. George rescuing a Christian maid from her Turkish captors was always presented, and the joy of his never-failing victory was expressed in a dance, the *morris*, *i.e.*, moorish dance. The whole was out of doors, near Whitsuntide, or at least in May.

At Y. the continual charge for minstrels at Whitsuntide points, I conceive, to a mumming performance with music and dancing. There was often a Whitsun Ale held by the Wardens at the same time.

Life in the Parish, what it lacked.

Our documents lead us, by their silence, to see what the parish of the 15th and 16th Centuries had not. It had no school or schooling within reach, no books, no readers.

The whole scholarship of the village was confined to the Clergy, and to the steward of the manor, who knew enough of technical Latin to make entries in the Court Rolls. The clergy were the chief scribes invoked for drafting agreements or reading them, or for making wills. The Wardens regularly charge for the writing of their accounts by a hired hand, and they were obliged to trust that hand for spelling, a craft then in its infancy, and enjoying the widest freedom from rule. Whether the scribe used his choice in employing English or Latin, or a mixture of both, the average Wardens were equally unable to read the result.

The use of Latin in the audit sheets, passed "*coram parochianis*," must not be taken as evidence of erudition. The same people were used in the manor[1] court to have their proceedings recorded in Latin. To those who could not read, it mattered not. They were used to resort to learned help for the solution of every record, as they did for the transmission of their most important secrets by letter. The entire unletteredness of the community told in many ways upon their habits. All tidings were passed from mouth to mouth, not only delaying the rate of progress, but ensuring distortion of the intelligence in its passage through many and unintelligent media. The village resort, whatever it was, whether ale bench, or Church-house, or the village green, was the news-room where the latest rumours could be heard and discussed. I cannot but think that one of the objects of the Church-house was to afford a kind of club-house for villagers, the general resort of all ages, ranks, and sexes, free from the uncontrolled temptations and the unbridled language of the publican's ale bench, and that it must have served a purpose of social education in promoting interchange of thought and speech between the chiefs and elders of the parish on the one side, and the poorer and younger members on the other, but of this we lack positive evidence.

Relief of Poor.

There is one department of parish life on which our documents might be expected to speak, but they are quite silent.

It is the care of the poor and disabled. There was, as we know, no State relief for

---

[1] Court Rolls were written in Latin till a very late date, long after it was abandoned by the parish. In fact, the parish was the first institution that adopted the use of English for its records. *See* Y, 1445.

the poor, no enforced provision of any kind. The parish contributed nothing. Its funds were evidently raised for other purposes, and, until they were deemed by the civil power to be a convenient resort for abating the growing poverty, they were never applied in alms. At the end of Henry the VIII's reign, when the effects of the dissolution were making themselves felt, the first items of poor relief appear, but under orders from without. The effect is well known. The violent diversion of voluntary funds from their intended purpose dried up the source in the good-will of the donors. The civil power in Edward the VI's reign tried to formalize a system of poor relief through the agency of the Church without taxation, but it was found necessary to introduce a rating system, and to support it by legal sanction. But we are here concerned with the question : What did the parish, as a Christian community, strongly feeling the brotherhood-tie, do spontaneously for the relief of the needy?

The audit sheet does not show a single eleemosynary item.

I can only suppose that the brotherhood tie was so strongly realized by the community, that the weaker ones were succoured by the stronger, as out of a family store. The brotherhood tie was, no doubt, very much stronger then, when the village community was from generation to generation so unalloyed by anything foreign, when all were knit together by one faith and one worship, and close kindred; but, further than this, the guild-fellowships must have enhanced all the other bonds in drawing men to share their worldly goods as a common stock. Covertly if not overtly, the guildsman bound himself to help his needy brother in sickness and age, as he expected his fellow-guildsman to do for him in his turn of need; and these bonds, added to a far stronger sense of the duty of children towards aged parents than is now found, did, I conceive, suffice for the relief of the poor, aided only by the direct almsgiving which flowed from the parsonage house, or in favoured localities, from the doles or broken meat of a monastery.

This latter was, of necessity, limited in area to the neighbourhood of the convent gate. The majority of parishes in the land were out of reach of it. The amount of the *stated* money doles is returned in the Valor of Henry VIII[1] as an abatement of the taxable income of the house. If spread evenly over the country it would not have gone far in relief. As it was, being given at the gate, together with broken meat, very considerable, but ungaugable in amount, it cannot have served as a reliable substitute for other means of relief throughout the breadth of the land. To take an instance.—The doles statedly given to the poor at Glastonbury are returned in 1537 at £140 16s. 8d.—a large sum, so large, probably, as to attract a body of resident beggars in waiting at the gate, but not large enough to flow beyond a few neighbouring villages whose able-bodied poor might reach the gate on the favoured days. It could not have touched the distant manors of the Abbot's vast estate. It did not touch any who could not come to fetch it. At Wells there were similar doles at Penniless Porch and at Saint John's Hospital, equally restricted to a small area. Passing from Wells northward, no other centre of almsgiving could be found nearer than Bath, Keynsham, Bristol, or going southwards and westward at the Abbeys of Muchelney, Athelney, Taunton, Cleeve, Barlynch, and St. John's Hospital, Bridgwater.

The monastic alms must have been, besides this insufficiency, far too uneven and limited in area to have eased the strain of poverty beyond their own neighbourhoods. Our

---

[1] *See* App. C, for table of eleemosynary doles charged upon monastic lands.

problem, "what did the parish do?" still remains unsolved. The manorial records are as silent as the parochial. The manor-court rolls show no entry implying that the poverty of the dependents of the manor ever came before the court except in abatement of a fine. The serfs were by theory of law (once true in fact) incapable of acquiring property, and therefore must have been by the presumption of law dependent on their Lord, and in the days of disability as wholly dependent as the slaves of Carolina on their owners. It is true that after 1349 they began, in spite of law, to acquire rights, and to earn money, but still their support in times of need or sickness was not within the cognizance of the manor-court, and seems to have been left wholly to the good-will of the lords. At least no machinery for securing their due support is now known to exist. The grand eleemosynary scheme, issued by Bishop Drokensford in 1313—see Reg. Drok., fo. 141a and App. C—for the manors of his see, is an evidence of the obligation felt by great landowners, and it may be hoped, felt by all, though not by all in an equal degree, in obedience to conscience quickened by public opinion and long-standing custom.[1]

Whatever the care taken or not taken by the owners of the soil and of the servile population, we come back to the fact that the parish, *i.e.*, the organized Christian community, as such, did nothing in the way of money-relief, and to the conclusion that long custom based on, and ever inspired anew by Christian teaching and example, bound the divers classes of the community in such close brotherhood-ties, as to ensure the relief of the neediest.

Things Unnamed.

Besides relief of the disabled there are other matters not spoken of in the records, the absence of which I cannot account for, *e.g.*, (1), the administration of the rites of Confirmation; and (2), of preaching; (3), of confession. The visits of a confirming Bishop were likely to have shown themselves in the accounts in the way of charge for his retinue; witness the charges at Y in 1486, p. 79, for entertainment of the Bishop's men at a Consecration. (2), For preaching, the pulpit was always ready, being wanted for the far more frequent use of the bedeman bidding the prayers. Preaching no doubt was not a regular part of the Sunday observances as now. It was rare, but we must not conclude from the silence of our MSS. that it never was practised.[2] Confirmation, too, must have been administered, though, perhaps, only in the larger churches. (3), The ordinance of confession probably required some convenience in the Church which the Wardens would provide for.

There is no mention of the use of the Offertory as a means of gathering the alms of a congregation. It was not in use, as in our reformed ritual. Whatever was offered on the Altar came within the designation of Altarage (*alias* Altelage) and was due to either Rector or Vicar, as his endowed right, and so altogether beyond the Warden's reach. The Alms-

---

[1] The operative strength of such forces may be more easily believed in by remarking that within memory Ireland, Scotland, and the Isle of Man, had no poor law, *i.e.*, no compulsory relief for the needy, who therefore depended on the good-will of kindred, neighbours, former employers, and the alms of the Church.

[2] Prebendary Randolph in the "Newbery House Magazine," February, 1890, quotes a presentment made by the questmen of Colyton, Devon, in 1301, complaining of the rarity of their Vicar's preaching. Of its quality they did not complain, because it was his best, and he was a good man, but he stinted quantity and he would not admit the preaching friars to eke out his insufficiency as his predecessors did.

d

box is not mentioned, and probably did not exist till ordered by the First Prayer-book of Edward VI.

Of the Friars as Village preachers we hear nothing. At T, p. 184, a Friar of Ilchester is recorded as a donor by will, which shows that the members of the begging order had slackened their founder's rule of owning nothing. At P a Frary-clerk yearly received a fee of x*d*., but who he was or what his services to the parish, is left in the dark. The activity of the Friars as that of the older Orders had probably waned by the 15th Century.

It remains now only to repeat my regrets for the insufficiency of my researches, and my hopes that short-coming as they are, they will serve as a spur to others to gather whatever of value remains hidden amongst the dry entries. I am sure there is much, and that with our increased facilities for reaching the history of our forefathers, the work of thrashing out the grains will be an easier one for after comers. There is also something besides history to be gained. In dwelling on these records of church-life, I have been led to many reflections on the theology of the past day in its practical effect on the morals and habits of the people, on the religious convictions so differing from those which now sway the popular mind, and on the methods of engaging the religious interests of those classes who were absolutely unlettered. The object of this work being historical, and not theological, I am not warranted in expressing any of my reflections, which I have felt free to express in the pulpit and elsewhere. If the absence of them should seem to savour of approval of practices which have been forbidden by the reformed Church of England, either as erroneous or inexpedient, I will beg my readers to take note that my silence is due to the limits of my position. I am set to find out and put forth things as they were, and not to express my approval or disapproval.

Thanks.

Hearty thanks are due to those good friends, without whose help I should have failed to accomplish the work, the Revs. J. A. Bennett, T. S. Holmes, H. W. Pereira. On them has fallen the largest share of the labour of transcription and preparation for the press. I must also thank those kind guardians of the original records, who have courteously entrusted them to my inspection, viz.: Mr. Penny, of Tintinhull, and the Incumbents of Yatton, Pilton, and Croscombe.

Wells, June, 1890.

CROSCOMBE:

[SPELT IN THE MSS. CORSCOMBE AND COSCOMBE.]

FISCAL SYSTEM.

The two wardens were chosen yearly by the parishioners. They held their audit on January 11th, or some day in that month, or February—once in March. The audit sheet was made out at the time of audit, after the announcement of recent gifts and bequests, and the receipt of subsidies from the guilds. The wardens then presented their bill of expenses, got their acquittance, and after choice of new wardens, handed over to them the church goods and the stock, *i.e.*, the balance of money, rings or other valuables in the box or coffer (the value always stated).

The new wardens began their administration with a sum of cash for immediate needs.

There was another fund, "dead money," not subjected to audit, though administered by the wardens. It served for maintaining lights for the departed, and for the general anniversary obit. It was fed by gifts and bequests.[1] The balance of this fund called the "Reste," was entered in the sheet.

The Guilds who presented their offerings at the audit were:—

The Young Men, or "yonglyngs."
The Maidens.
The Webbers (weavers).
The Tuckers (Fullers).
The Archers, personated by Robin Hood and Little John.
The Hogglers,[2] probably the field labourers and miners.
And once—1483-4—The Wives.

Each guild received at the outset of the year a stock (xij$d$. or so) for immediate charges, such as the maintenance of their light at one of the altars. This they supplemented by a collection on their special feast-day, and brought back to the wardens the "new and old;" "the stock and the crece," *i.e.*, increase. If anything hindered their yearly revel, they "broughte yn noughte."

The largest items of receipt were from the "Croke," *i.e.*, the processional Cross which

---

[1] The wills of the period often mention the "Ded lyght" and "Soul lyght."

[2] Wright's Provincial Dictionary gives "hoggle" as a Somerset word=to take up from the ground, like potatoes. See Glossary.

had its special keeper, as had also St. Michael's Croke. The gathering of alms was made during the procession.

At Easter a special gathering, entered separately, was made for the paschal taper, the font-taper, and the trendel.

The form of the wardens' account is descriptive of the proceedings of the audit. Each contributor is represented as coming into the church and presenting his offering, *e.g.*, "Cometh yn Roben Hod and presentyth yn," and then taking out his "stok" for the coming year's stewardship.

Probably the entire community was enlisted in one or other of these guilds, and thereby all classes associated not only in the maintenance of the church, and its services, as members of the same religious body, but also in the festivities of their holydays, which brought all classes together as members of the same social community.

THE FABRIC was maintained by the same means as the services. In no case did the wardens look beyond the parish for funds, though some gifts from outside seek them, *e.g.*, from Bishop Bekynton's executors, 1478, and an altar cloth from Dame Elizabeth Shepton, a friend now unknown.

In 1476 the fabric must have consisted of nave and chancel, both with aisles, of tower, and porch.

In 1506-7 additions were made, probably the strong rooms at the south-west angle, which served for vestry and treasure-house, and also the chapel on the north of the chancel aisle, intended for the more dignified cultus of St. George, which thenceforth became popular, and brought in large gatherings.

The payments to Carter, the Exeter Freemason, go on through 1508-9-10. He is called the "Jorgemaker," and paid specially for the setting up of the "Jorge," xxx*s.*, showing that his work was principally in the addition of this substantially-built chapel. In 1512-3 the chapel was at last completed. "The hole coste of the Jorge" is summed up at xxvij*l.* xj*s.* vj*d.*, but in spite of this large outlay, the funds were very thriving.

At the audit of 1512-3 the wardens handed on a balance of x*l.* iv*s.* vj*d.* in the chest, besides a store of rings, and of some other articles priced at x*l.*

This affluence, so unknown to modern wardens, and so enviable, was wholly due to the one-hearted zeal and bounty of the parishioners themselves.

THE ACCOUNT BOOK.

This is kept in the parish chest. It is of paper, much dogs'-eared, with a tattered remnant of its leathern binding. Of the whole volume, only 122 pages survive, the earliest and latest having been lost: the modern paging will be found noted in these transcripts.

The audits run on from 1475, with few exceptions, to 1548, when the accession of Edward VI, and the visits of his Commissioners broke the old order. Spoliation set in, 1547-8. In 1548-9, 1550-1, 1552-3, are irregular entries savouring of the unsettledness of the times. In 1553-4, after Queen Mary's accession, the wardens present to the parish an inventory of goods recovered from their hiding during the late reign.

In 1555-6, inclusive, there are entries, but no regular audit.

Circumstances of the Parish.

With an acreage of only 1,433 acres, its agricultural wealth was small. The cloth trade was its chief support, with perhaps a little lead-mining. The Palton family, whose manor house still survives in small remnant on the north side of the church, were the chief landowners up to 1449, when the last Palton died, and apparently left no resident successor.

The community must have been mainly composed of the middle and lower classes, such as are represented in the guilds. Only two families, the Mayows and the Denshyls, probably clothiers, were rich enough to give endowments.

The benefice was a Rectory in the gift of the Paltons and their successors.

The last Palton made an addition to the endowments and to the fabric, circa 1449, by enfeoffing a guild with lands and tithe at East Horrington. The enfeoffment deeds have lately come to light in H.M. Record Office. (See note on Mayow's gift, below sub anno 1483.)

These endowments were not applicable to any but their own specified purposes.

All the maintenance of the fabric, the ritual, the bells, books, and vestments, with all accessories, *e.g.*, the church house, the clerk and sexton, were drawn from the voluntary alms of the members of the church.

January mccccLxxvi. Audit for 1474–5.

A loose sheet with torn edges, the date lost. Date determined by names of wardens elect, who present the accounts in January, 1476–7, *i.e.*, the next year.

. . . The said year by Thomas . . . , Warden for yere past. . .
Comes John Joyce and William Branch, and brings in of the King's revel[1]. . .
Comes John, and bryngs in of the remayn of font-tapur and trendel . . .
Item, the rent of the last year past for Fyllocks . . .
It. The goders of Synt Collas[2] bryngs in of encrese for this year . . .
It. the Carchof[3] and a ryng of the gifte of Jone Doltyng, present in by the . . .
It. the Auter cloth of the gyfte of dam Elsabeth Shepton, present in by the Wardens . . .
It. the Wardence bryng in ayen[4] the stoke of last yere, that . . . . . ix*l.* x*d.*
Comes the Webers and bryng in their stoke xij*d.*, and more encrece xj*d.*; summa . xxiij*d.*
Comes Harry Mew and Thomas Symones and received a stoke of . . . . xij*d.*
Comes W. Branch and presents in for Synt Meghel which lyse in his hands as a stoke   iij*d.*
. . . W. B. and bryngs in the Cherche money that he . . . of ij yere ago;
  summa . . . . xviij*d.*
. . . bryng in encrece for the yere . . . . vj*d.*
Come tokers and bryngs in their stoke xij*d.*, and more encrese xj*d.*; summa . . xxiij*d.*
Comes Thomas Costrell and Rogger, and received a stoke of . . . . xij*d.*
Comes Hoglers and bryngs in there stoke ij*s.*, and more encrece x*d.*; summa . . ij*s.* x*d.*

---

[1] Probably the Christmas-tide sport, which had a wide currency under varying names and forms, centering in a King and a mock court (see Brand's Pop. Antiquities v. i, p. 259, ed. Bohn). Its abuse led to a restraining canon in Worcester Diocese, 1240. This revel brought income to the wardens thrice, viz., in 1476, 1478, 1504.

[2] Gatherers of St. Nicholas.   [3] Kerchief, a word of most variable spelling.   [4] Again.

Comes Thomas Costrell and Richard Tropenell and received a stoke of	ij*s.*
Comes yong men and bryngs ij*s.* ij*d* clere.	
Hit apers by the sa	xxx*s.* iij*d.*
So they be in the parrych det. ix*s.* ix*d.*, which they have paid.	
. . . go quit away.	
The money of the Croke of this yere comes to in the box	iij*l.* xvij*s.*
Paid to Harper for his yere's wages	v*s.*
Paid to John Joyce and Harper for the Croke kyping this yere . . .	xx*d.*
Summa of the Cherch goods, Croke, and ryngs sylver	xvij*l.* v*d.*
Comes John Hill and John Harper ayen chosen by the parrech for Wardens for this year.	
Delyvered to John Hille	vj*l.* xiij*s.* iv*d.*
So raymens in stoke in the box	x*l.* vj*s.* xi*d.*
It. There is left of dede money in the box and parson paid[1] . . .	lij*s.* vj*d.*

PAGE 1.

𝔄nno mccccl𝔵𝔵vi, *i.e.*, 1476–7 for 1475–6.

Acounte y made of the parresche church of Corscomb the xj day of Janever by John Hille and John Harper, Wardens for the yere past.

Comes Thomas Blower and John Hille and presents in xl*s.* of Roben Hod's recones (reckonings).	
Comes John Joyce and Roger and presents in of fonttapur and trendel—of encres .	iij*s.*
Comes Sowthemor and bryng in for ffyllok's rent	iiij*s.*
Comes Walter Mayow and presents in of the gyfte[2] of Isabel Mayow, 1 payer vestements of white damaske (? broidered) and delyvered into cherche.	
Comes the Weybers Harry Mewe and Thomas Symonds, and presents in xxij*d.*, and they receive a yen for a stoke	xij*d.*
Comes William Brabuck and presents in of old and new of Synt Myghel light which remayns al in his hands	vj*s.* viij*d.*
Comes the Hogglers, and presents in of old and new (Tropenel and Harper) iij*s.* x*d.*, and they received a yen for a stoke	ij*s.*
Comes young men William Coggen and Nicol Edmonds and bryng in of encres of the past iij*s.* ix*d.* that remayns in their hands delyvered to them more by Heyman of his gaderyng of old	ij*s.* ij*d.*
Comes Tokers and Roger and Costrell and presents in cler ij*s.* ij*d.*, and Roger and Braunch received a stok of xij*d.*	
Comes the maydens and bryng in of encres cler . .	ix*d*
Comes Mayster[3] John Toker and gyfes to the new legent[4] .	vj*s.* viij*d.*

---

[1] *I.e.*, after paying the priest for his services.
[2] Gyfte, and qyste, *i.e.*, bequest, are written so alike as to be hardly discernible.
[3] A master fuller.
[4] A book of Legenda Sanctorum for reading on Saints' days.

PAGE 2.

Janver Ao. mcccclxvi [sic].

Comes the Wardence and bryng in a bille of their cost done the yere past as hit
aperes by same bille . . . . xxxiijs. vijd.
Item the Wardence have paid for stoff[1] and writtyng of the new legent which is xlvi
queyres, pres per queyer iijs. ; summa . . . . . . vjl. xviijs.
So the parresch is in the det of the wardenes . . . . . xxxviijs. iijd. ob.
The money of the Crok of the yere comes to . . . . . lixs. vijd.
Paid to Harper for his yer's wages . . . . vs.
Paid to Harper for kepyng of the Croke . . . . xxd.
Summa of the cherches goods that remaynes at this contes. . . xjl. xvjs. jd.
Paid to Robart Clerk xijd., and to Loward ijd.
Comes Hille and Harper and are chossen wardens for this yere by al the parresch.
delyvered to them . . . . xlvs.
So remaynes in the Box of stock . . . . ixl. xvs. save ob.
There is left of the ded money at this cont. . . . . . xlvjs. jd.

PAGE 3.

Anno mcccclxxvii, i.e., 1477–8 for 1476–7.

Acountes y made of parresche cherch of Corscomb, the last day of Janever in said yer
by John Hille and John Harper, Wardence.
Comes Richard Downe and presents in of the gyfte of Marget Medamer for shep xijd.
Jone Fenton at her det gaf to our lady a ryng gylt.
Item, of the gyfte of John Smythe to the cherche . . . . . . xijd.
It. John Taillor, weber, gaf to the cherche . . . . xijd.
It. Of the gyfte of Maud Malleway sylver ryng gylt and a token gyrdel of sylver.
It. of the gyfte of Annes Gybons 1 sylver rynge gylte.
        John Malleway, the yonger . . . iijs. ivd.
        Thomas Webb of Chew . . . . . xijd.
        John Malleway, the elder, 4 wedors, sold for . . vijs. ivd.
        John Nelle 1 gowne of grene in kepynge of the wardence.
Comes William Branche and presents in of Synt Myghel money vijs. vd., which he
takes ayen in his owne kepyng.
Comes yong men William Coggan and Nicol Edmonds and presents in of old and
new (and a candelstok in the peler (pillar) next the fonte which cost ijs. jd.),
vijs., and the wax paid. So remayns in ther hands agen . . . . ijs. jd.
Comes William Coggan and presents in of the Kyng's revell . . . . xxs.
Comes hoglers and presents in of old and new (tropenell and harper) . . iijs. viijd.
they have received agen in stoke ijs. Costrell hath hit.
Comes the Webers, Harry Mew and Thomas Symonds, and present in of old and new
xviijd. ob. they received ayen in stoke . . . . xijd.
Comes Tokers, Roger Morris and William Bramber, and presents of old and new
ijs. ijd.—they have received the stoke ayen . . . . . . xijd.
Received of Sowthemore for fellok's . . . . ivs.

[1] Materials.

PAGE 4.

Janever Ao. mcccclxxvii. *i.e.*, Jan. 1477–8 for 1476–7.

Comes the maydence Marget Smyth and Jone Bayle and presents in, of old and new,
al things lowed . . . . ix*s.* vij*d.*
herof moste be abated for wax and makyng . . . . . . ij*s.* vj*d.* ob.
So is cler vij*s.* ob.—delyvered to them ayen . . . . . . ij*s.* vj*d.*
Comes Maister John and presents in that he hath of Synt Collas lyght, al things paid xij*d.*
Comes Hill and Harper[1] and presents in of pascal money, that they gadered on
Ester day . . . . vij*s.* ix*d.*
Ther remaynes of the dede money in the box this yere . . . . xxxix*s.* viij*d.*
The money of the Croke this yere . . . . iij*l.* x*s.*
It. alowed to Harper for his labour v*s.* and for kepyng of the croke . . . xx*d.*
Summa . . . . vj*s.* viij*d.*
John Yeng hath in his hands of the Cherche lede one cwt. dim. iiijlb.
The somma of al the Cherche goods at this acombt . . . . . xiv*l.* xiv*s.*
Comes John Hille and John Harper agen, and are chossen for this yere folloying
wardence by al the parrasch—delyvered to them same time xl*s.* So re-
maynes . . . . xij*l.* xiij*s.* j*d.*

PAGE 5.

Ao. mccccLxxviii. *i.e.*, 1478–9 for 1477–8.

Acountes y made of the parrausch cherche of Corscomb the first day of March in forsaid year by John Hille and John Harper, Wardence of the Cherche for the yere past.
Comes John Hille and bryngs in the gyfte of :—

Maister John Towker . vj*s.* viij*d.*	Annes Clerke, ryng, kerchef and aporn.	
Nicol Edmonds . . xx*d.*	Thomas Blower, 1 vyolet long gowne	
Joyce (son) . . . xvj*d.*	[2]in grayne, a ryng gold with a	
Hugh Pendleton . . iv*d.*	torcas[3] and a kerchief of [4]sypers	
John Williams . . iv*d.*	to make a corpas.	
John Abbot . . . iv*d.*	Thomas Loward, a [5]chepe, pris . . xiv*d.*	
Harrison (fadour) . . iv*d.*	Honnethron a [6]newe, pris . . xiv*d.*	
William May, an ewer, bras.	Water Crowtecote . . . vj*s.* viij*d.*	
Water Loware, a tokyng shere.	Margere Hoper, 1 sylver ryng.	

Ther is in sylver ryngs in al xvj., of which are taken owte ij. to selle.
It. there be ij golde ryngs, that were Dangvyls and Isabel Blowers.
The money of the Croke of this yere is . . . . . . iij*l.* ij*d.*

---

[1] Wardens. Their election is not noted at the last audit, but their re-election is in this. The allowance to Harper, v*s.*, is for some costly trouble, not a salary. This would have been shared by both.
[2] *I.e.*, dyed before weaving.   [3] Turquoise.
[4] Cyprus silk for a corporas cloth. "Cyprus-lawn."—*Milton.*   [5] Sheep.   [6] An ewe.

Received of Richard Sowthmore for Felloks house rent of yere past . . . xiv*s*.
Comes Harper and presents of the Kyng's revell of thes yere past . xiij*s*. j*d*.
whereof was stole away ij*s*. vij*d*. So remaynes cler . . x*s*. vij*d*.

PAGE 6.

Comes H. and H. Wardenes and bryng in a bille of expence of this yere past lviij*s*. ix*d*. Whereof rebate that Hille had at the begyneng xl*s*. Rest to the Wardenes xviij*s*. ix*d*. paid them, so quits herof.

It. Alsone More oweth for the wast of the ¹torches for her husband, xlb. price v*s*. a syned (assigned) the wardence the same v*s*. in the xl*s*. that they have in stoke.

Comes Hille and Harper and presents in of the gaderyng on Ester day for paskall and fonte taper . . . . vij*s*. x*d*.

Comes Water Mayow² and Jone his wife, and have gyf in to the cherche for the ryngeng of Courfu for ever more so much londs as shall be in valew of iv*s*. rent yerly.

Comes Hille and Harper and presents a grene gowne of the gyfte of John A'Walkeden.

Comes William Branch and presents in of Synt Meghel light viij*s*. v*d*. which remaynes in his hands.

Comes yong men William Coggan and his felow and presents in ij*s*. ix*d*. to Edward Bolle (Bull) a stok . . . . xij*d*.

Comes Hoggelers, Tropenell and Harper, and presents in iij*s*. j*d*. delyvered to them ayen . . . . ij*s*.

Harry Mew hath bought John A'Walkdences gowne for . . . . . . xviij*d*.

Comes the Webers Harry Mew and Thomas Symones and presents in old and new xxj*d*. delyvered them ayen . . . . xij*d*.

Comes the Tokeres, Roger Morrys and William Branche, presents in of old and new ij*s*. They have received the stoke ayen . . . . xij*d*.

Comes the Maydence and presents in of old and new iij*s*. clere. delyvered to Annes Beke ayen . . . . ij*s*.

Comes Plente and cnowth (acknowledges) hym dettar to the Cherche for his servant xx*d*.

Sold to Richard Maudley the gowne that was Thomas Blowes for . . . xiij*s*. iv*d*.

PAGE 7.

Item. alowed Harper for his wage for kepyng of the Croke, ... vj*s*. viij*d*.
It. ther remayns of the dede money in the box cler . . . . . xxxiij*s*.
Summa of al the cherch goods³ at this count . . . . . xvj*l*. xviij*s*. x*d*. ob.
It. the parson hath bought John Nelles gowne for . . . . . iij*s*. paid.
Summa du (*i.e.*, to parish) . . . . xvij*l*. j*s*. x*d*. ob.

Comes John Harper and William Branch and ar chossen for Wardence for this yere comyng.

Delyvered to them in stoke xl*s*.—so remains . . . xv*l*. j*s*. x*d*. ob.

---

¹ Torches kept by the wardens to serve at funerals.

² The Mayows were people of substance, probably of the parish; see W.M.'s gifts, 1480-1 and 1483-4.

³ The inventory was no doubt produced in vestry at the transfer to the new wardens, but its loss forbids our knowing what was included in "Church-goods"—probably not vestments, but only such things as had been given to sell for the maintenance of the fabric and service.

PAGE 8.

Ao. mccccľxxix. Feb. 4, 1479–80 for 1478–9.

Acont y made of the barrerch of Corscomb the iiij day of ffeverer in said yere by William Branch and John Harper, Wardence for the yere past.

Comes Branch and bryngs in of the quest (*i.e.*, bequest) of Water Bigge . . . xij*d*.
 It. a cloth of holland for the hye auter of the gyfte of bischop Bekenton (*i.e.*, his executors).
 It. received of Richard Sowthemore for fylloks house . . . . . iv*s*.
 It. Branch brought in for the ij. sylver ryngs that he had to selle . . ij*s*. iv*d*.
 It. (Branch) paid of the croke money of this yere past . . . lviij*s*. viij*d*. ob.
 It. paid to Branche for wasscheng of vestments and sorplers . . . iij*s*.
 It. of the gyfte of phelpot troge by the hands of John Hille . . . vj*s*. viij*d*.
Comes the maidence and presents cler of this yere with stoke . . . iij*s*.
 Delyver hem ayen (Annes Beke and Isabel Hoper) . . . . ij*s*. for stock.
Comes Harry Mew and Thomas Symens and presents in . . . . xx*d*.
 Delyvered them in stoke ayen . . . . xij*d*.
Comes Richard Branch, Roger Morys and presents in . . . . . ij*s*. ij*d*.
 Delyvered them in stoke ayen . . . . xij*d*.
Comes the wardence, Branch and Harper, and bryng in a byll of dyverse cost of the cherche, as it aperes by ther bill . . . . . . ix*l*. xiij*s*. iv*d*.
Ther remaynes of sed money in the box ther . . . . xxvj*s*. vj*d*.
The somma of the money clere in stok in the churche is . . . . xj*l*. vi*s*.
Comes William Branch and Harper, and are chosen for this yere comyng.
 delyvered to them in stok xl*s*. So remanes in box . . . . ix*l*. vj*s*.

PAGE 9.

mccccľxxx. *i.e.*, Jan. 13, 1480–1 for 1479–80.

Aconts y made of the parrasch of Corscomb, the xiijth day of Janever, yn ye seyd yere by William Branche and John Harper, wardenes, for the yere past.

The said Wardence bryng in a harnest gyrdel of the quest of Elner (Eleanor) Tyler, bukul and pendant, and xij barres blake torfft.[1]
 It. of the gyft of Maude Gardener xx*s*., and a golde ryng wayeng . . xvj*s*. viij*d*.
 It. received of Richard Sowthemor for Fyllok's House . . . . iv*s*.
 It. rec. of the Croke-money for the yere past . . . . . lv*s*. vij*d*.
 It. paid to Harper for his labour in the cherche and croke . . . vj*s*. viij*d*.
Comes the Maydens and presents clere of this yere with stoke . . . iv*s*. viij*d*.
 Delyvered to Jone Hill (Mor's servant) . . . . . ij*s*. in stoke.
Comes Harry Mew and Thomas Symens and presents in . . . . ij*s*.
 Delyvered to Mew ayen in stoke . . . . xij*d*.
Comes Branch and Roger Morrys and presents in . . . . ij*s*. j*d*.
 Delyvered to John Costrell ayen in stoke . . . . . . xij*d*.
Comes the Wardence and bryng a bylle of dyverse costs for the cherche as it apers be ther bille . . . . xlv*s*. ij*d*

[1] Taffeta.

Ther remaynes of ded money in the box clere	xxs. save jd. ob.
Therefore the money clere in the stoke of the cherche is	xiijl.
Comes Roger Morris and William Branch and are chosson for this yer Wardence.	
delyvered to them in stoke	ivl.
So remaynes in the box	ixl.
Also, Water Mayow hath gyf and granted to the parresch yerly for ever to the fyndyng of the lamp to four (before) the hey Auter	vjs. viijd. yerly.

PAGE 10.

Ao. mccccxxxi. *i.e.*, Audit, Saturday after Epiphany, 1481–2 for 1480–1.

A countes y made of the parresche cherch of Corscombe, the Saturday next after xijth day in forsaid yere by Roger Morris and William Branch, Wardence for the past.

First the Wardence presents in of the gyfte of Annes Down, modor	xijd.
It. same Wardence present in more of gyfte of John Tailor, Dyndo (Dinder)	xijd.
It. Rich. Southmore for Fellok's	ivs.
It. the Croke-money this year is	iijl. vs. xd.
Comes the maidens and present in clere of this yer past noght yet.	
Comes Harry Mew and Thomas Symons (weavers) and present in nought.	
Comes John Costrell, Edward Boull, and presents in	iijs. ivd.
delyvered to John Costrell ayen for next yere	xxd.
Comes Hoggelers, Thomas Costrell and his felaschep (fellowship), presents in	iijs. ivd.
del. to Costrell ayen in stoke	ijs. ijd.
Comes the yonglens[1] and presents in bolles (Bull's) hands of owed ij year past	ijs. vd.
Comes yonglens and presents in Rich. Costrell's hands, and Rich. Bolles for two yers	vjs. xd.
Comes John Halse and Roger Morris for Roben Hod's revel, presents in	xls. ivd.
Comes William Champion and presents in of levyng (levying) of the grate belle	vjs. xd.
Comes William Branch, and presents that he hath in his kepyng of the yere last past.	
Richard Costrell ryng the same yere and Jone Mede[2]	xxvjs. viijd.

PAGE 11.

Comes in W. Branch and presents that he hath in his hands of Synt Meghelles lyght for ij yere clere	ivs.

Cost of Church house. {
Comes the Wardence, Roger Mors and W. Branch, and bryng a Bille for makyng of the Cherch house of the costs in their tyme.	
ffirst paid to the carpenter Bedford	ivl. xixs.
It. paid to the massons, Horman and his felaschip	vl. xixs. vd. ob.
It. they have paid for dyverse thyngs for cherche nede, as hit aperes by their bille	xlivs. jd.
Summa hereof	xiijl. ijs. xjd. ob.
Whereof they have received at ij times	xijl.
So is rest to said Wardens	xxijs. xjd. Paid them the said rest.

[1] Younglings used in *Spenser* for lads.
[2] Their wedding-ring, probably—an offering made to the church after the wife's death.

It.	Water ¹Mayow hath paid for the yere past for the lamp	vjs. viijd.
It.	He hath paid More for Corfu ryngeng	ivs.
It.	ther remens of the dede money in the boxe (parson and lyght paid)	xiijs. vjd.
It.	paid to Branche for his ²labour in the cherche, and kepyng of the Croke	vjs. viijd
It.	gyf to Branch for his labour and tendens of the Cherche house	iijs. iiijd.

Rest remaynes in the box of cherche money xxxvs. ivd. and xxijs. ivd. and more xls. ivd.
Roben Hode money, Summa al . . . . vl. ijs. vijd.
Comes W. Branch and William Wynsor, and are chossen for this yere comyng wardens.
delyvered to them iijl. vjs. viijd., and viijd. delyvered to Will. Toyt for lyghts.
Rest due in the box, al thyngs content . . . . xxxvs.
It. remayns in John Joyse hands for John Yeng, lede . . . . vjs. vjd.

PAGE 12. *xx*³ ─────────

Ao. mcccciiii ii. Jan. 25th, 1482-3 for 1481-2.

A countes made of the parysch church of Coscomb a Synt Powell (Paul's) day in the forsayd year by W. Branch and William Wyndylsor, Wardeynes for the yere past.
First the Wardeynes present in of the gefte of Agnys Bygg a ryng of sylver, same gylte.
It. presents of the gefte of the Lady Schefton a ryng of gold with a ruby.
It. presents of the gefte of John Dyte a ryng of selver and a kerchew.
It. recd. . . of Water Mayow to helpe to a boxe . . . xxs.
reste in the boxe.
Comys (comes) the maydyngs presents in for this year nowgte.
Comys Harry Mew and Thomas Symonys and presents nowgte.
Comys J. Costrell and E. Bole and presents in . . . . iijs. vijd.
delyvered to John Costrell . . . . xxd.
Comys yonge men and presents in . . . . iijs. viijd.
delyvered ayen to Rychard at Wyll the stoke . . . . . . xijd.
Comys W. Branch and presents in that he hath in hys hande of olde and newe for Synt Mychaell . . . . vjs.
Hoglers went not⁴ this yere.
Comys in the Wardenys Bronche and his felow and bryngys in a byll . xxixs. ixd. ob.
Comys Wyndylsor and bryngys in a byll of his costs . . . iijl. xviijs. viijd.
All payd and quyte (quit).
Also Rychard Downe and oweth⁵ for a kow of quest of his dowgters . vjs. viijd.
PAGE 13.
It. remaynes of the dede money, the parson and lygte paid . . . vijs. jd. ob.
It. R. Sowthmore for Fylloks . . . . ivs.
Comys Robin Hode and presents in . . . . xxxiijs. ivd.

¹ This benefactor has not yet found an endowment for his pledged support of lamp and curfew. He therefore pays in cash. See note p. 11.
² Not as Warden, but as Keeper of the Croke or some other charge.
³ The letters ʀʀ written over thus denote scores, which must be multiplied by the units below them. The same remark applies to the c for a hundred.
⁴ I.e., did not go in procession and revel; hence no collection.
⁵ I.e., settles the price, and acknowledges the debt.

The Croke money this yere is . . . . iij*l*.
Paid to Bronch for his labour tendying to the Church and croke . . . vjs. viij*d*.
Comys W. Bronch and John Cornysh and are chosyn for thys yere wardynys ; de-
  lyvered to them . . . . xl*s*.
So reste in the box of the church money . . . . iv*l*. xviijs. x*d*.

PAGE 14.

c *xx* ————

𝔄o. 𝔇m. m iiii iiii iij. Audit, Jan. 17, 1483–4 for 1482–3.

A cont made of parrach churche of Corscomb the xvij day of Janever in the yere afore-
said by Will. Branche and John Cornyche, Wardens for the yere past.
First, the wardens present in of the gyft of Iset Cooke a kerchef and iiij*d*. in money.
It. they present more of the gyft of Wyst of the hamm¹ . . . . . xij*d*.
Rd. Sowthemore oweth for the house called felloks for the yere past . . iiij*s*.
Comes Harry Mew and Thomas Symonds and presents nougt.
Comes John Costrell and Ed. Bolle and presents in clere . . iij*s*. iv*d*.
  delyvered to John Costrell xx*d*. in stoke.
Comes Ric. Willes and Ric. Maudley and presents in . . . . .js. v*d*.
  delyvered Ric. Willes ayen in stoke . . . . xij*d*.
Comes the madens, Halses and Hilles, and presents in clere . . . ixs. vj*d*.
Comes the hoggelers and presents in clere . . . . . ivs. iv*d*.
  delyvered to Harry Mew same time . . . . ij*s*.
Ric. Willes was Roben Hode, and presents in for yere past . . . . xxiij*s*.
Alles Abbot hath bought an old Sauter (psalter) for ij*s*. Whereof she hath paid xx*d*.
  Rest iiij*d*., that she oweth.
It. of the gyft of Water Mayow to the cherche werkes v*l*. which he asyned (assigned)
  shuld be paid of Horryngdon and of lond that he lent tords the purchessyng of
  Horryngdon oute of the Kyng's Hands.²

PAGE 15.
It. there was of the croke money in the boxe of the yere past . . . xlviijs. viij*d*. ob.
W. Branch hath in his hands of Synt Meghel's money of old vj*s*., and more encrest
  this yeare . . . . xx*d*.

¹ Ham, a large wood and farm in Pilton, but close to Croscomb.
² In 1548 the Commissioners of Edward VI. report, that the Guild or Fraternity of Corscombe were possessed of lands at East Horrington, with the free Chapel there, of which they held the advowson ; also of lands in Wilts, and of houses, &c., in Shepton, by gift of Walter Mayow and wife ; valued altogether at xxvij*l*. vj*s*. viij*d*. nett, per ann. The Guild was founded to maintain four priests (two of whom survived), one of whom should minister in East Horrington Chapel ; also to maintain an annual obit with perpetual light in Croscombe Church for W. Mayow, and for nightly ringing of the curfew ; also to pay viij*d*. for repair of two almshouses ; and vij*d*. for relief of the poor.
The property at East Horrington had belonged to the Palton family. The whole of the endowments were seized by the Crown, and granted to lay owners.
"The King's hands" were probably the Royal Escheator's, demanding payment for a license to convey the land in mortmain.

summa	vij*s*. viij*d*.
Of dede money left of last yere save over	vij*s*. j*d*. ob.
paid there of to the parson	v*s*.
and paid to Branch for wax and makyng	xviij*d*.
So rest at present	vij*d*. ob.
Paid to Branch for xij lb. wax and makyng	vij*s*. iv*d*. ob.
and for wasshyng ij*s*. viij*d*. summa	ix*s*. ob.
and for skorryng (scouring) of candelsteks	xij*d*.
Branch hath in his hands of Ester gaderyng for paskall and font tapur clere	v*s*. xj*d*.
Branch hath of the wyfes[1] dansyng in his hands	vj*s*.
Paid to Branch for his labour and kepyng of croke	vj*s*. viij*d*.
It. there is in money redy lefte	xxxvj*s*.
and in Branch hands	lij*s*. j*d*.
and in Madeley's hands and Hille's	v*l*.
Whereof paid to Toyte	viij*d*.
Paid to Branch and Cornysch iij*l*. by me Ric. Maudley of said money, and Hill most pay xl*s*. save ix*d*.	
Rest in rey (ready) money with iv*s*. in Sowthmore hands	xxxix*s*. iij*d*.
Comes William Branch and John Halse for wardens for the yere comyng.	
delyver them the foresaid	xl*s*.

PAGE 16.

(A.D. Mill cccc iiii iiii, *i.e.*, Jan. 8, 1484–5 for 1483–4.

A cont made of the parach church of Corscomb the viij day of January in the yere aforesaid by William Bronche and John Halse, wardens of the yere past.

Firste the wardeynys present in the yefte of Ric. Tropnell	vj*s*. viij*d*.
It. John Perys of hame (Ham)	viij*d*.
Thomas Paty oweth for William Pew ys gyfte to the church	vj*s*. viij*d*.
Ric. Sothmor oweth for the hows callyd Vylloks for thys yere past	iiij*s*.
Comys Harry Mew and Thomas Symons and presents in nowgte.	
Comys John Costrell and Edward Bole and presents in	ij*s*. xj*d*.
delyvered to John Costrell	xx*d*.
Comys yong men and presents nowgte.	
Comes the maydyngs and presents in	xvj*s*. iij*d*. ob.
It. therof is payd to Bronch for xlb. wax and the makyng	vj*s*. iv*d*.
Comys the hogglers and presents in	iv*s*. j*d*. ob.
So reste	iij*s*. vj*d*. ob.
delyvered to Harry Mew	ij*s*.
Comys Robyn Hode and presents in	xxiij*s*. viij*d*.
It. there was of the croke money in the boxe of this yere past	xliij*s*. viij*d*.
It. the creyse (increase) of the paskall	iv*s*. vj*d*.
It. for a ryng that was sold	vij*d*.
It. Rychard Down for a kow of the yfte[2] of his dowgter	vj*s*. viij*d*.

[1] The only instance of the matrons' revel and contribution.   [2] *I.e.*, gift: given in 1482.

PAGE 17.
It. rest of the dede money . . . . xj*d*.
It. payd to Bronch for kepyng of the cloke[1] . . . . iiij*s*.
It. for wayschyng of the church gare (gear) . . . . . . v*s*. iiij*d*.
It. I payd to Toyte . . . . xij*d*.
It. payd to Bronch for hys labur . . . . vj*s*. viij*d*.
It. for skowryng of the kandylstyks . . . . xvj*d*.
So reste of the hole money . . . . v*l*. vj*s*. j*d*.
It. more John Hyll hath on hys hond to pay of Horyngdon[2] money . xl*s*. save ix*d*.
Comys Wyllyam Bronch and John Boklond for wardens of thys yere comyng, and ys
   delyveryd to them . . . . xl*s*.
So rest of the stoke . . . . iiij*l*. vj*s*.

PAGE 18.

𝕬.𝕯. mccccłxxxv. *i.e.*, Jan. 14, 1485–6 for 1484–5.

A cont made of the parisch church of Corscomb the xiiij day of Januar in the yere afor sayde by Wyllyam Bronch and John Boklonde, Wardaynes of the yere past.
First the Wardeynys comys in and presents in of the yefte of John Baker of Lamport
   (Langport) a gold rynge . . . . iij*s*. iiij*d*.
It. of the yeft of Sir Wyllyam Costrell a sirpalys (surplice) . . . . iij*s*. iiij*d*.
Also presents of the yefte of John Mallway a harnayst gurdyll with a ray-corse[3] and a
   ryng of selver.
Also of the yeft of Alys Sothemore, a ryng of sylver.
Also of the yefte of John Smyth, a ryng of sylver.
Also of the yefte of John Madokoke . . . . viij*d*.
Thomas Paty owyth for the yeft of Wyllyam Pew . . . . . . vj*s*. viij*d*.
Rychard Down for a cow of the yefte[4] of his dowgter . . . . . vj*s*. viij*d*.
Comys the Wefeyrs (Weavers) Harry Mew and Thomas Symons and presents . . vij*d*.
Comys Rychard Sothemore payth the rent of Vylloks . . . . . . iiij*s*.
Comys the Tokers John Costrell and Edward Bole and presents . . . ij*s*. viij*d*.
   delyvered to John Costrell a stoke . . . . xviij*d*.
Comys the yong men John May and Richard Mowle and presents in for the yere
   past and thys yere . . . . viij*s*. ij*d*.
So a batyde (abated) for wax and makyng of the lygth . . . . . xviij*d*.
   delyvered a stoke to John May and Rychard Mowle . . . . . xiiij*d*.

PAGE 19.
Comys Wyllyam Bronch and presents in for the font tapyr and the pascall . . vj*s*. viij*d*.
Comys the hoggelers and presents in . . . . vj*s*. ij*d*.
   delyveryd a stoke to Bronch . . . . ij*s*.
Comys the maydyns and presents in . . . . xvij*s*. iv*d*.
   delyveryd to Bronch a stoke . . . . iij*s*. iv*d*.

---

[1] The first notice of a clock.   [2] To repay Walter Mayow's Loan. See p. 11.
[3] Striped bodice attached to girdle.   [4] See 1482–3.

It. there was of the croke money of thys yere past . . . . . iv*l*. ij*s*. xj*d*.
Comyss Wyllyam Bronch and presentyth in of Synt Mychaell croke . . . iv*s*.
So reste in Bronch ys honde.
Comys Wyllyam Bronch and John Buklonde and delyveryth xxvij*s*. v*d*. of the xl*s*. that was delyveryd to them (*i.e.*, for stock) the last yere, and all thyngs ys made clere rekenyng.
To Wyllyam Bronch for kepying of the cloke . . . . iiij*s*.
It. for his labor . . . . vj*s*. viij*d*.
It. for wayschyng of the cherche gar . . . . v*s*. iiij*d*.
It. for skowryng of the candylstyke . . . . xvj*d*.
It. to Wyllyam Toyte for hys labor . . . . xij*d*.
So reste of all the hole stoke . . . . xi*l*. xvi*s*.
Comys Wyllyam Bronch and John Carter for Wardaynes of thys yere comyng and ys delyvered to them . . . . xl*s*.

PAGE 20.

𝔄.𝔇. mccccl̄xxxvi, *i.e.*, Jan., 1486–7 for 1485–6.

A cont made at parych chyrch of Coscomb the xx day of January in the year afor sayd by Wyllyam Bronch and John Carter, wardaynes of the yere paste.
Fyrst the Wardynys commys and presents in
Thomas Paty owyth for the yefte of Wyllyam Pew . . . . . vj*s*. viij*d*.
Rychard Down for a cow of the yefte of his dowgter . . . . vj*s*. viij*d*.
It. they presents of the yefte of Mayster John Wylton . . . . . vij*d*.
It. of the yefte of Wyllyam Kogan . . . . xx*d*.
It. of the yefte of Alys Frawnceys, a ryng of selver, and of money . . . iv*d*.
It. of the yeft of Robert Smyth . . . . viij*d*.
    Do.   Wyndelsor's servant . . . . iiij*d*.
    Do.   Rys Costrell's servant . . . . iiij*d*.
    Do.   Robert Browne, a sawter (psalter) and . . . . iiij*d*.
    Do.   John May . . . . xij*d*.
    Do.   Alys Bronch . . . . iiij*d*.
    Do.   John Joce ys servant . . . . iiij*d*.
    Do.   John Champyon . . . . vj*s*. viij*d*.
    Do.   Alys Tafe ij rynges, and . . . . . . iiij*d*.
    Do.   John Champyon to the bellys[1] . . . . . vj*s*. viij*d*.
    Do.   John Browne of Ham . . . . xvj*d*.
    Do.   Robert Smyth to the bellys . . . . . . xij*d*.
Comys Robyn Hode, Wyllyam Wyndylsor, and presents in for the yere paste iij*l*. vj*s*. viij*d*. ob.

PAGE 21.

Comys the maydynys and presents in . . . . . xvij*s*. iv*d*.
Comys the hoggelers and presents in . . . . . iiij*s*. x*d*.
   delyveryd a stoke to Rychard at Wyll . . . . ij*s*.
The Croke money ys . . . . . . iij*l*. xiv*s*. ij*d*.
Comys the tokers and presents . . . . . iij*s*.

[1] Bells.

Whych remaynyt in Rychard Costrel ys hand and Edward Bole.
Comys Rychard Sothemore and payth the rent of Vyrloxys . . . . iiijs.
Comys Bronch and payth the paschall money . . . . . . iiijs. vjd.
   To Bronch for hys labor . . . . vjs. viijd.
   It. for waschyng of the Chyrch gar . . . . vs. iiijd.
   It. for skowryng of candylstyk . . . . xvjd.
   It. to Toyte for hys labor . . . . xijd.
So reste of all the hole stoke, and all things clere . . . . . ixl. xvjs. jd.
Comys Wyllyam Bronch and Rychard Vowlys for Wardenys of thys yere commyng,
   and delyveryd to them . . . . xls.

PAGE 22.

A.D. mccccfxxxvii, *i.e.*, Jan. 12, 1487–8 for 1486–7.

A cont made at the parysch Cherch of Corscomb the xij day of January in the ere a for sayde by Wyllyam Bronch and Rychard Vowlys, Wardaynys of the ere paste.
Fyrst the wardaynys commys and presents in of the [ere] paste.
Thomas Paty owyth for a kow of the yefte of Wyllyam Pewe, price . . vjs. viijd.
Rychard Down for a cow of the yefte of hys dowgter, price . . vjs. viijd.
John a Dene owth for the yfte of hys syster iij selver sponys . . xxs. in money.
It. of the yefte of Rychard a Mawdeley . . . . . . iijs. iiijd.
It. of the yefte of Wyllyam Yrysch, servant of Wyllyam Champyon . . iijs. iiijd.
It. the yfte of Yevayn Thomas . . . . xijd.
It. of the yefte of Wylliam Kogan
   Do.   Harry Hoper . . . . vjd.
   Do.   Davy a Powell . . . . iiijd.
   Do.   Crystyon Cornish a ryng of sylver . . . vjs. viijd. money.
It. to the bellys . . . . xijd.
Comys the maydonys and present in . . . . . . xxijs.
   dylyveryd to . . .
Comys the hogglers and presents in . . . . vs.
   delyveryd to Rychard att Wyll . . . . ijs.
Croke money . . . . iiijl. xvijs. xd. ob.
Comys Tokers and presents in . . . . iijs. vjd.
   delyveryd to Rychard Costrell and Edward Bole . . . . xxd.

PAGE 23.

Comys vefers [weavers] and presents in nowgte.
Comys yong men and presents in . . . . . . iijs. iiijd.
   So rest in Rychard Browne ys honds and Thomas Hewys.
Comys Rychard Sothemore and bryngs in rent of Vylloks . . . iiijs.
Comys Wyllyam Bronch and presents in of the paschall . . vjs. ijd. ob.
   To Bronch for hys labor . . . . vjs. viijd.
   It. for waschyng of the Chyrch gar [gear] . . . . . vs. iiijd.
   It. for skowrynge of candylstyks . . . . xvjd.
   It. payd to Wyllyam Toyte . . . . xijd.

Comys Wyllyam Bronch and presents in of Synt Mycaell money	vjs.
So restyth in hys hands of the olde money by for [before] and this yere	viijs. xd.
It. payd to Willyam Bronch for wax to the hy¹ crose and makyng withall	iijs. xd.
It. payd to Wyllyam Bronch for kepyng of the cloke	iiijs.
It. payd to Harry Mew for kepyng of the croke	xd.
It. payd to Wyllyam Bronch	xd.
So rest and all thyngs content in money on the stoke of thys yere	ixl. xjs. vjd.
Comys Wyllyam Bronch and John Dunpayn for Wardaynys of thys yere comyng and delyveryd to them	iijl. xs. of the same mony.

PAGE 24.

A.D. mccccIxxxviii, i.e., Jan. 19, 1488–9, for 1487–8.

A cont y made at the parysh chyrch of Corscomb the xix day of January in the yere afor saide by Wyllyam Bronch and John Dunpayn, Wardenys of the yere past.
[The three first entries of Paty, Down, and John a Dene are identical with those of last year.]

It. of the yfte of John Merke a ryng of sylver, and of money	xijd.
Do. „ John Wasyn a ryng of sylver and a kerchew.	
Do. „ Davy Uphavel	iiijd.
Comys the maydyns and presents in	xxs. iiijd.
delyveryd to Elenor Boklonde for the stoke	iiijs.
Comys the hoggelers and presents in	vs.
delyvered to R. att Wyll for the stoke	ijs.
The Croke money	iijl. xvs.
Comys Tokers and presents in	iiijs.
delyveryd to R. Costrell and Edward Bole	xxd.
Comys the Wefers and presents in nowgte.	
Comys yong men and presents in	iijs. ivd.
dylyveryd to Edwarde Windsore for the stoke	xxjd.

PAGE 25.

Comys Sothemore and bryngs rent of Vylloks	iiijs.
Comys W. Bronch and presents in of the paschall	iiijs. jd.
Do. do. do of Synte Mychaell money	
Comys Robyn Hode and presents in²	iijl. vijs. viijd.
To Bronch for his labor	vjs. viijd.
It. for waschyng of Chyrch clothys	vs. iiijd.
It. for skowryng of candylstyks	xvjd.
It. for wax to the rode-lofte³	ijs. xjd.
It. for kepyng of the cloke	iiijs.
It. for kepyng of the Croke	xxd.
It. to Wyllyam Toyte	xijd.

¹ "Iligh." It stood on the rood-loft with lights burning before it. It was the most elevated and conspicuous devotional object in the church.
² An extraordinary effort. ³ Earliest mention.

It. to Wyllyam Bronch	xij*d*.
It. payd to Thomas Rogg for pleyng at orgons[1]	iij*s* iiij*d*.
So reste and all thyngs content in money in the stoke of this yere . . .	xj*l*. vij*s*.
Restyth more of the Tokers lygth in Bronch ys honds	ij*s*. iiij*d*.
Comys W. Bronch and John Honythorne for Wardens of thys yere folowyng and ys	
dylyveryd to them	iij*l*. vj*s*. viij*d*.
So restyth in the stoke	viij*l*. iiij*d*.

PAGE 26.

𝔄.𝔇. mccccłxxxix. *i.e.*, Jan. 16, 1489–90 for 1488–89.

A cont y made at the parysch chyrch of Corscomb the xvj day of January in the yere aforsayd by W. Bronch and J. Honythorne [&c.].

Thomas Paty oweth of the yfte of W. Pewe . .	vj*s*. viij*d*.
resevyd hereof	v*s*.
John a Dene [as before].	
It. of the yfte of Syr John Comb, parson of Corscomb a grette maser with a ston.	
It. of the yfte of Syr John Camell ij powchys of felewote [velvet], one of rede felewote	
and another of blake, and ij stonys of sylver and gylde.	
It. of the yfte of John Hille a synat [signet] of sylver and a tuell [towel] of twylly.	
It. of the yfte of Edyth Calow	viij*d*.
It. of the yfte of Edwarde Perys xij*d*. and to the bellys	viij*d*.
It. of the yfte of John Crytyon	xij*d*.
Comys the maydyns and presents in	xxiij*s*. iv*d*.
Wer of they have payd for wax and makyng	iiij*s*.
delyveryd to W. Bronch a stoke	iiij*s*.
Comys the hoggelers and presents in	vj*s*. ij*d*. ob.
Delyveryd to Rychard att Wyll a stoke	ij*s*.
Comys the Tokers and presents in	iiij*s*. vj*d*.
delyveryd to Edward Bole a stoke . . .	xx*d*.
Comys the Wefars and present in nowgte.	
Comys the yong men and presents in .	iiij*s*. vj*d*.
delyveryd to Rogger More . . .	xx*d*.

PAGE 27.

Comys R. Sothemore and brings in rent of Vylloks	iiij*s*.
Croke money	v*l*. v*s*. x*d*.
Comys W. Bronch and presents in of the pascall	iiij*s*.
[To W. Bronch, washing, candelsticks, cloke and croke, and W. Toyte as usual.]	
It. to Thomas More for pleyng at orgenys	vj*s*. viij*d*.
So rest, etc.	viij*l*. xv*d*.
W. Bronch and Water Jonys chosen wardens.	
Delivered to them	xl*s*.
Rest in stoke	vj*l*. xv*d*.

---

[1] Organ playing mentioned here and once only again, 1489–90. The instrument was probably portable.

PAGE 28.

A.D. mcccclxxxx, i.e., Jan. 15, 1490-1 for 1489-90.

W. Bronch and Water Jonys, Wardens, Jan. 15.
Th. Paty and John a Dene as usual.

It. of the yfte of Alys Lorayn		xij$d$
Do.	Anys Sterlyng	iij ryngs of sylver.
Do.	Edyth More	j ryng of sylver.
Do.	Alys Symons	j ryng of sylver.
Do.	Isatt Nett	j ryng of sylver.
Do.	More in money	xd.
Comys the maydyns and presentyth in		xxv$s$.
wher of they have payd vs. for wax		vs.
delyveryd to Elenor Boklonde		iiij$s$.
Comys the hoggelers and presentyth in		vs. iij$d$. ob.
delyveryd to R. att Wyll		ij$s$.
Comys the Tokers and presentith in		ij$s$. ix$d$.
delyveryd to Ed. Bole		xx$d$.
Comys the Wefars and presentith in nowgte.		
Comys the yong men		iv$s$. ij$d$.
delyveryd to John Mawdeley		xx$d$.
Croke money		iij$l$. vs. ij$d$.

PAGE 29.

Comys W. Bronch and presenteth in of the pascall	iiij$s$. vj$d$.
Comys Robyn Hode and presentith	ls.
[Expenses identical with last account.]	
So rest all things content	xj$l$. xv$s$.

New Wardens W. Bronch and Richard Sugar and receive xl$s$. save ij$d$. and a sengyll plake.[1]

PAGE 30.

A.D. mcccclxxxxi, i.e., Jan. 14, 1491-2 for 1490-1.

T. Paty and John a Dene are as before.
It. of the yfte of Syr John Comb a supplyse.

The Maidens, Elenor Bocklond and Margett Elme bring	xvj$s$. ij$d$.
E. Bockland receives	iiij$s$.
The hoggelers	iiij$s$. ix$d$.
R. att Wyll receives	ij$s$.
The Tokers	iiij$s$. ij$d$. ob.
E. Bole receives	xx$d$
The young men	iij$s$. viij$d$.
E. Wyndelsor receives	xx$d$
Croke money	iv$l$. iv$s$. xj$d$.

[1] *I.e.*, "a single plack;" or coin.

W. B. presents of the pascall	. . . .	vj*s*. x*d*.
Do. for St. Michael	. . . .	ij*s*.

[Expenses identical with the last, only W. Toyte now gets xvj*d*., and there is no organist paid.]

Remaining	ix*l*. v*s*. iiij*d*.
W. Bronch and Harry Mew are chosen wardens and receive	. . xl*s*.

PAGE 31.

A.D. mccccxxxxii, *i.e.*, Jan. 12, 1492–3 for 1491–2.

T. Paty and J. A. Dene as before.

The Maidens Johan Bronch and Johan Mew bring . . .	xviij*s*. iij*d*.
J. Mew receives	iiij*s*.
The hogglers	iiij*s*. iv*d*. ob.
R. at Wyll receives	ij*s*.
The Tokers	ij*s*. v*d*.
Ed. Bole receives	xx*d*.
The young men	v*s*. ij*d*.
Ed. Wynser receives	xx*d*.
Croke money	iij*l*. vij*s*. iv*d*. ob.
W. Bronch brings of the pascall	v*s*. viij*d*.
Do. of St. Michaell	v*s*. j*d*.

[Expenses as before, only now keeping the croke is omitted.]

Remaining	ix*l*. xv*s*. save j*d*.
W. Bronch and Richard att Wyll are chosen Wardens and receive . . .	xl*s*.

PAGE 32.

A.D. mccccxxxxiii, *i.e.*, Jan. 11, 1493–4 for 1492–3.

W. Bronch and Richard att Wyll Wardens.
T. Paty and J. A. Dene as before.

It. of the yfte of Johane Tropnell	ij*s*.
Do. Wyllyam Baker . . .	xvj*d*.
Do. of W. Chompyon ys prentyse .	xx*d*.
Do. Johane ap Rychard . . .	xvj*d*.
a gown of John Lovell	vij*s*. viij*d*.

A kerchew of Margery Phelpe and a ryng of sylver.
The same of Margett Apendylton.
A kerchew of Margett Davy ys mayde.

[The only other receipts mentioned are]:—

The hogglers	vj*s*. j*d*.	The young men .	v*s*.
Richard Vowles receives . . .	ij*s*.	E. Wynsor has . .	xx*d*.
The Tokers	iij*s*.	W. B. brings for the pascall	
E. Bole has	xx*d*.	Croke money . .	iiij*l*. xij*s*. vj*d*.

[This is crossed out.]

The Wardenys owyth to the chyrch for the rent thett browgtyn (Broughton) recevyd of W. Wynsor for the chefe[1] rent of my lady ys closis and the almyshowse .	iijs. iiijd.
Remaining	xijd.
The church owed to W. Champion	vjs. viijd.

PAGE 33.

𝕬. 𝕯. mcccclxxxxiiii. *i.e.*, Jan. 10, 1494–5 for 1493–4.

W. Bronch and Edward Bole, Wardens.
T. Paty and J. a Dene as before.

It. Annys Bygge	xijd.
It. Annys Weste	ijs.
It. Johane Harper, a harneyste gyrdell, with a blew corse.	
It. Johane More—a ryng of sylver.	
The hogglers bring	iiijs. vd.
Harry Mew receives . . .	. ijs.
The Tokers bring . . .	ijs. viijd.
E. Bole receives . . .	xxd. ob.
The young men.	
The Wardeyns presentith in for the pascall . . .	. viijs. jd. ob.
Croke money	. vl. vs. vjd.
The Maidens bring	. xxxvs. ivd.
Elsbete (Elisabeth) Joce and Jone Carter receive .	. xxvjs. vd.
Robyn Hode presents in	. xlvjs. viijd.
Paid to Harry Mew for keeping the Crok . . .	. ijs.
Washing and scouring and the clock as usual, and kepyng the cherch	. viijs.
For mending windows	viijs. xjd.
Remains	. vjl. xs.
W. Bronch and W. Carpynter (incoming Wardens) receive .	. xlvjs. viijd.

PAGE 34.

𝕬. 𝕯. mccccclxxxxv. *i.e.*, Jan. 16, 1495–6 for 1494–5.

[First time it is called "Croscombe."]
WILL. BRANCH, WILL. CARPUNTYR, WARDENS.

Itm. of the yefte of Richard Sugar	vjs. viijd.
Do. Isabelle Harrysonys Moder	. xijd.
Do. John Toyt	. viijd.
The hoggelers bring	. ivs. vijd. ob.
W. Branch takes	ijs. viijd.
The tokers bring	ijs. xjd.
E. Boll takes of the same	. xxd.
The yonge men bring	vjs. viijd.

[1] It appears that there was an endowment in land for the altar of the Blessed Virgin, subject to a chief rent (as were the almshouses) payable to the Lord of the Manor. In 1526–7 the lord distrained for this rent.

J. Cartar and J. Phyllyps takes	ijs.
The Mayduns bring	xxvs. iv*d*.
Delyveryd to W. Carpyntar for the maydyns lygth	iiijs.
Croke money	iiij*l*. xiiijs. j*d*.
It. resevyd of W. Carpyntar yn mony	xxxvijs. x*d*.
and in costys viijs. x*d*., the sum of all	xlvjs. viij*d*.
[No new items of expense and no organist.]	
Remains in stoke.	xj*l*. vs. xj*d*.
The same are to be wardens for the coming year and receive (*i.e.*, for a stock)	xls.
More to Harry Mew of the said sum to by ches[1] (to buy cheese)	vs. vj*d*. pay.

PAGE 35.

𝔄.𝔇. mcccclxxxxvi. *i.e.*, Jan. 7, 1496-7 for 1495-6.

Same Wardens.

Rec. of the yefte of Alsun Sugar a gyrdyle and a peyre of beds (beads) with ij ryngs and a crucyfyx.

Do. of Alsun Sowythmore a peyr of beds of jett with v gawds of sylver and a tuell of dyapper.

Do. of Isblle Rymon a gold ryng.

Do. of Jelyan Lovyn[2] of Ham a ryng of sylver and gylte.

Do. Alsun Sugar for her pytt[3]	vjs. viij*d*.
Do. Mr. John Mawdlyn for a grav	iijs. iiij*d*.
Do. Thomas Champyon of Schepton	xx*d*.
Do. Jelyan Bowly	xij*d*.
Do. of gaderyng the pascalls	vs. iiij*d*.
The hoggelers bring	iiijs. ix*d*.
Richard Vells takes	ijs. iiij*d*.
The tokers bring	iijs. ij*d*. ob.
E. Boll takes of the same	xx*d*.
The Mayduns bring	xxvijs. iv*d*.
The Croke money	iiij*l*. ijs. viij*d*.
Received of W. Carpyntar in money	xxxijs. ix*d*.
and in a bill for costs	vijs. iij*d*.
[Expenses as last year].	
Remains in stock	iij*l*. vijs.
Mem. that the parysch payde for ij coppus (Copes)	xij*l*. xs.

---

[1] Mew being keeper of the "Croke," the cheese was probably for the refreshment of the processioners who followed him.

[2] Julian Lovaine.

[3] Pit must mean a grave in the church. The repair of the pavement fell upon the wardens, who regularly charge 6s. 8*d*. for the privilege of burial. What is meant by the grave charged 3s. 4*d*. does not appear.

PAGE 36.

A.D. mcccclxxxvii, i.e., Jan. 13, 1497-8 for 1496-7.[1]

The same Wardens.

T. Paty, J. a Dene, Alsun Sugar, A. Southmore, J. Rymon, J. Lovyn, as before.

Itm. of the yefte of Isbella Hylee a peyr of bedds of corell with xvj gawds of sylver and ovyr gylte and a . . . gurdyll with boculle (buckle) and penant (pendant) of sylver and xix steds (studs) theryn.

Itm. of Master Richard Mawley and Alsun his wife a portoos[2] called a leger a grayll and presecioner and ij new corches (kerchiefs) and ther wedyng ryng[3] of gold to our lady.

The hoggelers bring . .	vjs. vd.
R. Wells takes of the same .	ijs. viijd.
The yong men bring . .	iijs. vd.
R. Jons and W. Hadle take .	ijs.
The mayduns bring . .	xiijs. jd.
W. Branch takes of the same	iiijs.
The tokers bring . . .	iijs. vijd. ob.
E. Bole receives of the same. .	xxd.
W. Branch brings for the pascall .	vs. iijd.
The Croke money . . .	iijl. xiijs.

PAGE 37.

[Costs as usual, but the following is a new expression.]

Paid to W. Toyt for tynnyng (tending) of the lygtht	xvjd.
Remains in the box clear	iiijl. xivs.
delivered to W. Branch (as incoming warden) . . .	xls.

PAGE 37.

A.D. mcccclxxxviii, i.e., Jan. 12, 1498-9 for 1497-8.

W. BRANCH AND JOHN DUNPAYN, WARDENS.

[All the early entries of the last repeated, with the addition to Isabella Hilles of "a hellyng (covering) of rede and yelowe."]

after R. Mawley and wife's gift.

---

[1] The numerals used for the headings of these accounts undergo an entire change this year. Thus the page (36) from which the above extracts are taken is superscribed—

"Ano. Dm. 1497."

The old notation, however, is retained in the *body* of the account ; *e.g.*, two lines below the above head ing :—"yn ye yr of our lord gode MCCCCLXXXXVII"

Roman letters for the headings are once more resumed in A.D. M.VC.XX (*i.e.* 1520), p. 67, until Ano. 1548, p. 110, when the Arabic figures are again employed to the end of 1558, then 1559 and 1560 are written in the Roman letters.

[2] Service books. See Glossary.

[3] Wedding rings were often given after the death of the wife. In this case both parties being alive, the ring was probably promised in reversion.

Itm. of the yeft¹ of my lady Mayowe a gold ryng to our lady, and a nobule for her pytt.
Do. of Yed (Edward) Vynsent a jetyn (of jet) beds and viij*d*.
Do. of Master Wasun a ryng of sylver gelte.
Do. of Alsun Martemar a ryng of sylver and gylt.

PAGE 38.
Do. of John Jons a newe and a lam (an ewe and a lamb).

The hoglars bring	vj*s*.
R. Volls receives of the same	ij*s*. viij*d*.
The young men bring	iij*s*. j*d*.
R. Jons and W. Browne receive of the same	ij*s*.
The maidens bring	xxij*s*. v*d*.
The tokers bring	ij*s*. xj*d*. ob.
E. Boll receives of the same	xx*d*.
W. Branch brings of the pascall	v*s*. ix*d*.
Expenses as in the last, including tynyng the light.	
The Croke money comes to	iv*l*. iv*s*. ij*d*.
Remains clear	vij*l*. xvij*s*. x*d*

W. Branch and Hew Morgan, the new Wardens, receive xl*s*.

PAGE 39.

𝔄.𝔇. mcccclxxxxix. *i.e.*, Jan. 13, 1499–1500 for 1498–9. { W. BRANCH. HEW MORGAN. }

[The early entries, as far as the Mawdley gift, the same as the last.]
Itm. of the yeft of the Vecor (Vicar) of Pylton xij*d*., viij*d*. to the bells and iiij*d*. to our lady.
Do. John Hache ij ryngs of sylver and ovyr gylt, and a therdyn cerchewe (threaden kerchief).

Do. of Jerman	iv*d*.

Do. of Alsun Prystan a ryng of sylver and a myllyde (enamelled).
Do. of W. Carpyntar 1 lb. of wax and xij*d*. in money.
Do. of John Champyon a ryng of sylver and ovyr gylte, and vj*s*. viij*d*. for his grave.
Do. of John Yng and Annys his wife and oyll fatt (oil-vat or vessel) of sylver.
Do. of my lady Mayow a gold ryng to our lady, and a nobule for her pytt.
Do. of Yed Vyncent a jettyn bedys and viij*d*.
Do. of Master Wassun a ryng of sylver and gylt.
Also A. Mortemer and J. Jons as in the last.

PAGE 40.

The hoglars bring vj*s*. j*d*., and take	ij*s*. viij*d*.
The maidens	xx*s*. iv*d*.
The young men v*s*. j*d*., and (take) ij*s*. The tokars iij*s*. and (take)	xx*d*.
The pascall brings vj*s*. St. Michael Crok	xviij*d*.

Expenses as usual.

---

¹ The ring and noble must have been a promise, repeated yearly at the audit. See following years.

Paid to W. Toyt for tynnyng of the lyght and the holy[1] lofe xvj*d*.
The Croke money . . . . iij*l*. xvj*s* vj*d*.
Itm. recevyd for vantage (*i.e.*, nett profit) of the crokbred[2] ij*s*. ij*d*.
   There remains clear . . . . x*l*.
Hugh Morgan and John Derrant, incoming wardens, receive xl*s*.

PAGE 41.

𝔄.𝔇. mccccc. *i.e.*, Jan. 16, S. Marcel, Bp. and M. 1500–1 for 1499–1500.

HUGH MORGAN, JOHN DURRANT, WARDENS.

Itm. of the gyffte of Isabel Toytt a ryng of sylver.
  „ of John Halse to owr lady xij*d*. and to the Roode xij*d*. and to the bellys viij*d*.
    and for his grave . . . . vj*s*. viij*d*.
  „ of the gyfte of Maister W. Champyun a mass boke of veln (vellum) lymmyde,[3]
    with claspys of sylver, and a pax of sylver and gylt and anamelled.
  „ of Thomas Costrell to owr lady . . . . . . xx*d*.
  „ of Maister John Mawdley, for his chyldys grave . . . iij*s*. iiij*d*.
Sum of the receipts in money x*s*. iiij*d*. and a ryng of sylver.
The pascall produces vij*s*. viij*d*. St. Michael's croke . . . . . xx*d*.
Hught Morgan maketh a cownt of xl*s*. recevyd in the yere past as it aperyth by a byll.
The hogglers bring iiij*s*. vj*d*., and H. Mew receives . . . . . ij*s*. viij*d*.
The Towkarys bring iiij*s*., and E. Boll receives . . . . . xx*d*.
The young men bring iiij*s*. iiij*d*. and J. Ing the younger receives . . . ij*s*.
Comyth in Robyn Hode and Lytyll John and presentyth in . . . xv*s*.
J. Dunpayn presents of the Croke moneye . . . . iij*l*. xj*s*. ix*d*.
  and ther off he ys delyvered to by chys with. . . . . vj*s*. viij*d*.
Paid to Alice Dunpayn for kepyng of the Croke . . . . ij*s*.
  „ W. Toyt for tyndyng of the lyght and the church loffe . . . xvj*d*.

PAGE 42.

Itm. comyth in Hewight Morghan and bryngeth in for rent of the church londe . v*s*. x*d*.
Remains in the box . . . . xij*l*. xvij*s*. viij*d*.

𝔄.𝔇. mcccccj. *i.e.*, Jan. 8, 1501–2 for 1500–1.

HUGHT COLYNS, JOHN DERRANT, WARDENS

First the Wardens present in for the yere past in primis a gold ryng of the gefte of
  Allson Mayner of Wells.
Itm. of the gift of John Dyer of Wyncauntun . . . . . . x*s*.

---

[1] The first mention of this general custom. The "panis benedictus" was baked in the Church-house, blessed by the priest, and sold to the people. "Holy Ale" was in some places treated in like manner.
[2] Was it so called from bearing the sign of the cross? and how differing from the holy loaf?
[3] Limned, *i.e.*, illuminated.

Itm. of the gift of Isbell Harryson ij ryngs of sylver and gylte.
„ „ of Master Thomas Morris of Septon a payr of beds of corell of xvij setyn [set] with xxj gawdes of sylver and gylte with gowld ryng and vrinakull.[1]
„ of Allsun Lyde a ryng of sylver and gylte.
„ of Master Hymmyford to the bell . . . . xij*d*.
„ of Anys Benat. . . . . vj*s*. viij*d*.
It. ij crowns of sylver and gylt to our lady and a nother to hyr sett [seat] ovyr the vaute [or vante], of the gyfte of J. Ing and his wyfe.
Itm. a manwell [manuel] of the gifte of W. Champyon.

PAGE 43.

The hogglers bring	iiij*s*. vj*d*.
R. Voll receives	ij*s*. viij*d*.
The tokers	iij*s*. iiij*d*.
E. Boll	. xx*d*.
The young men	v*s*. iiij*d*.
R. Bokland	. ij*s*.
The maydens	. xxj*s*.
Paid of the same for wax and making of the light .	viij*s*. viij*d*.
The wardens bring for the pascall	iiij*s*. iiij*d*.
„ „ S. Michael Croke	. xv*d*.

Washing, scouring, kepyng the Croke, as usual.
To W. Toyt for kepyng of ye lyzthe.
The sum of the Crokmony comyth to with the vantech of the bred . . . lij*s*.
There remains in the box clear . . . . x*l*. ij*s*. iiij*d*.
R. Costrell and John Derrant, incoming wardens, receive . . . . xl*s*.

PAGE 44.

(A.D.) mcccccii. *i.e.*, Jan. 14, 1502-3 for 1501-2.

The wardens present in
First a ring of silver and gilt the gift of J. Heyman.
„ of Margaret Cornyshe of Wells . . . . . . xij*d*.
„ of William Anys and his wife a ryng of sylver and . . . xvj*d*.
„ of R. Ellys of Pennarde . . . . vj*s*. vij*d*.
„ of Yedith (Edith) Bylstone, Anys Donny's sarvant . . . . xij*d*.
„ of Isabelle Wevar, servant to John Bokland a ryng of sylver and . . viij*d*.
„ of Margery Wynsor a payr of beds of corall with xvij gawds of sylver and gylt, and ij ryngs of sylver and gylt and vj*s*. viij*d*. in mony.
„ of John Honythorn a ryng of sylver and gylt and a synat (signet) of sylver and viij*d*. in mony.
„ of Anys Downe a gyrdyll with boculle and pennant of sylver and gylt, and v gyngylls [jingles] of sylver hangyn in the pennant, and viij steds of sylver and gylt in the core.[2]

---

[1] Qy. Vrinakutt, *i.e.*, vinaigrette.   [2] The inside? or the crop or knob which held the studs.

E

Item of Thomas Symes	iiij*d*.
„ of Alson Reve of Dynder	xii*d*.
Sum of resayt in money and gefts xviij*s*. and vij ryngs of sylver.	

PAGE 45.

The hoggelers bring	iiij*s*. ix*d*.
R. Woll receives	ij*s*. viij*d*.
The tokers bring	iij*s*.
R. Costrell receives of the same . . .	xx*d*.
The young men bring	xlj*d*.
R. Bockland of the same	ij*s*.
The maydyns bring	xvj*s*.
Jone Knap of the same	iiij*s*.
The Wardens for the pascall . .	iiij*s*.
„ for S. Michael's Croke .	xx*d*.
Comyth Robart[1] Hode and presentyth in .	xl*s*.
[Washing, scowring, &c., as usual.]	
This year W. Toyt for "tynning" the light .	xvj*d*.
The Croke money with the vanteg of the brede .	xlv*s*. j*d*.
Remains in the box clear	xvj*l*. xvij*s*. v*d*.
Delivered to the Wardens	xl*s*.

PAGE 46.

𝕬.𝕯. mcccccíií. *i.e.*, Jan. 13, 1503–4 for 1502–3.

W. BRANCH AND JOHN DYRANT, WARDENS.

The Wardens present first of the yeffte of W. Evans iiij*d*. to the bells for his fadyrs knyle.[2]

Of the yefte of Rd. Brasytar, hys wyvys wedyng ryng and viij*d*. in money.	
„ W. Wynsor	vj*s*. viij*d*.
The hogrars [*sic*] bring	v*s*.
R. Voll of the same receives	ij*s*. viij*d*.
The tokers bring	iij*s*. iiij*d*.
R. Costrell of the same receives . . .	xvj*d*.
The young men	v*s*.
Godeall of the same receives . . .	ij*s*.
The maydens	xviij*d*.
To Jone Bronch the hole ageyn.	
St. Michael's Croke	xij*d*.
[Keeping the Church, the Croke, washing, &c., as usual.]	
The Croke money with the vantage and all . . .	liiij*s*. x*d*.
Rests in Dunpayn ys hands for to by ches . .	vj*s*. viij*d*.
Rests in a stoke in the honds of W. Branch . .	xviij*s*. iiij*d*.
And more over in the box of refows[3] money resteth . .	xi*s*. iiij*d*.

    [1] Note the change of title. See A.D. 1505.   [2] A knell to be rung for his father.
                  [3] *I.e.*, refuse, or broken money.

PAGE 47.

𝕬.𝕯. mccccciv, *i.e.*, Jan. 12, 1504–5 for 1503–4.

W. BRANCH AND EDWARD WYNSOR, WARDENS.

First the wardens present of the qwest of John Bervu	x*s*.
„ „ of the quest of Elenor Portar and her wedyng ryng gylt and	xij*d*.
„ „ of the quest of Sevyn Bolloks wyfe of Dynder	iiij*d*.
Itm. that W. Branch hav resevyd of Roger Frawnceys for a ryng	xij*d*.
„ ij ryngs sowlde to Harry Harrysons, the prys	ij*s*.
„ John Jose a golde ryng, the prys x*s*. non solvyt.	
The hoglars bring	vj*s*. ij*d*.
R. Vole receives of the same	ij*s*. viij*d*.
The tokars bring	ij*s*. xj*d*.
R. Costrell	xiiij*d*.
The young men	v*s*.
Goodeall	ij*s*.
The maidens	xiij*s*.
No return.	
No S. Michael's Crok.	
The pascall	iij*s*. vj*d*.
Dunpayn presenteth in for ij tewells.	
[Expenses as usual.]	
The Croke money with the vantag of the brede xlij*s*. xj*d*. Presentyd in of the Kyng revyll [*i.e.*, the King's Revel]	xxiij*s*. x*d*. ob.
that restys yn Master Mawdley ys hondys.	
Restys in the honds of Dunpayn to by ches	vij*s*. vj*d*.

PAGE 48.

Rests in the box	iiij*l*. ij*s*. viij*d*.

of the wych is delyvered to W. Branch of the same xx*s*. and of the said xx*s*. ys paid to W. Branch for kepyng of the cherche.

Also ther ys in ryngs of sylver and gylt xix and v of golde.

𝕬.𝕯. mcccccv, Jan. 1505–6 for 1504–5. { W. BRANCH. E. WYNSOR.

First the wardens present of the yeft of Isbel Olyvar a tuell and	iiij*d*.
Next they present for the pascall	iiij*s*. ij*d*.
Itm. for a payr of beds that was sold of corell the wygte a nownce and dim [*i.e.*, 1½ ounce] and dim. qu. scant [*i.e.*, scarcely half a quarter]	v*s*.
„ for a ryng that Branch sold	xiiij*d*.
„ for ij gold rynges that John Jos bowte (bought)	xx*d*.
„ for a pys of tymber that the wardens sold	vj*d*.

PAGE 49.

The hoglars bring	iij*s*. ix*d*.
R. Wolls receives	ij*s*. viij*d*.

The tokars bring	ij*s*. x*d*.
R. Costrell receives	xiiij*d*.
The young men bring	iiij*s*. viij*d*.
Godall receives	ij*s*.
The Maydens bring	xvij*s*. v*d*.
[Expenses as usual, the clock, washing, scouring, keeping the Croke, the light, and the church]	xxij*s*.
The Croke money with the vantage.	xlij*s*. x*d*.
Presented in of the sport of Robart Hode and hys company	lij*s*. iiij*d*.
the wych resteth in the hands of W. Carter.	
in the hands of W. Dunpayn to by ches	vj*s*. viij*d*.

In the box vj*l*. ix*s*. of which xx*s*. is delivered to J. Phillips.
Also these are xviij silver rings and v of gold.

PAGE 50.

A.D. mcccccvi, *i.e.*, Jan. 1506–7 for 1505–6. { W. AND J. PHILLIPS.

First the Wardens present of the yefte of Alsun Abbat a payr of beds of jett with a ryng of sylver and xij*d*. in money.

„ of Anys Morgyn a ryng of sylver and gylt and .	xij*d*.
„ of Isbell Branch a ryng of sylver and gylt and .	xij*d*.
„ of a sarvant of Water Jons	xij*d*.
„ of W. Evan ys wyfe a ryng of sylver and gylt and a sett.	
They present for the pascall	iij*s*. ix*d*.
The hoglars bring .	iv*s*. vij*d*. ob.
R. Volls receives	ij*s*. viij*d*.
The tokars bring .	iij*s*. vj*d*.
R. Costrell receives	xiiij*d*.
The young men bring ij*s*., which rests in J. Edmund's hands.	
delivered of the same to J. Cute	ij*s*.
The maydins bring .	ix*s*. ij*d*.

PAGE 51.

[Expenses]	xv*s*. viij*d*.
Presented in[1] for the sporte of Robart Hode .	xliij*s*. iiij*d*.
(Crossed out.)	
Mem. that the Croke yeld this yere .	lij*s*. ij*d*. ob.
There rests in a stok of church money .	xxij*s*. ix*d*.
Wher of is delivered to W. Branch	xx*s*.
x rings of silver and gold remain.	
In the hands of Dunpayn for [to] by ches	vj*s*. viij*d*.

[1] Robin seems to have ceased coming in person.

Ⓐ.Ⓓ. mcccccvii, *i.e.*, Jan. 13, 1507–8 for 1506–7.

W. Branch and E. Bolle, Wardens.

First of the yefft of Jone King, a ryng of sylver and gylt.
" of the gyfft of John Howell a payr of beds of corell with xiij stons of [*i.e.*, set in] sylver.
" of Amys Donpayne a rynge of sylver and in mony . . . . . . iiij*d*.
" of R. Jones a rynge of sylver and gylt and . . . . . . xij*d*.
" of Margytt Gye a rynge of sylver and gylt and . . . . . . xij*d*.
" of Jone Calloe in money . . . . ij*s*.
" of Allse Costrell ryng of sylver and gylt and a twell [towell] of dyaper, with iij*d*. in mone.
" of Jone Roger a ryng of sylver and gylt and a certcher.

Page 52.
for the Pascall . . . . iiij*s*. viij*d*.
The hoglers bring . . . . iiij*s*. v*d*.
R. Voll receives of same . . . . ij*s*. viij*d*.
The tokers bring . . . . iij*s*. x*d*.
R. Costrell receives of same . . . . xiiij*d*.
The young men . . . . iiij*s*.
John Redmunys receives of same . . . . ij*s*.
The Maidens . . . . xiij*s*. j*d*. ob.
The wardens present for the sport of Robart Hode . . . ix*s*. viij*d*.
In the hands of Donpayn to by chese . . . . . vj*s*. viij*d*.
 In the box iij*l*., of which xx*s*. is delivered to the new wardens.
The Croke yielded . . . . xj*s*. ij*d*.
 Paid by W. Cartar of the sum above written . . . xxij*s*. viij*d*.

Page 53.
The hole sum . . . . xiij*l*.
Itm. John Carter Jorge maker, Vre massyn [Free mason] of Exeter that receyved off
 the parech of Croscomb the som of . . . . iiij*l*.
Itm. payd the fryst day of January to the same man . . . . iiij*l*.

Ⓐ.Ⓓ. mcccccviii, *i.e.*, Jan. 14, 1508–9 for 1507–8.

Water Johnys and Ed. Boll, Wardens.

First, a yeft of Johan Wylls a ryng of sylver and gyllte and . . . iiij*d*.
Itm. the Croke this yere . . . . xlix*s*. iiij*d*.
Mem. there are in the box vj rings of silver, and one of gold.
Itm. Commyng[1] in of the pascall taper . . . . . . iiij*s*. ij*d*.

[1] This new form of entry prevails henceforth, indicating that the contributors no longer appeared in person, but sent their "commyng in," *i.e.*, the income of their guild. This change matches with the addition of the Vestry, part of the Freemasons' work (see next year), which was probably used for audits instead of the Church. N.B.—The weavers' guild has dropped out, perhaps absorbed in a new one for the cultus of St. George.

Do. of the maydens . . . . xvs. vjd.
Do. of the hoglers . . . . . vs.
Do. of the towkers . . . iijs. iiijd.
Do. of the young men . . . iijs. viijd.
and no return to any of them.
[Expenses] . . . . . xxixs. iiijd.

PAGE 54.
In the hands of J. Dunpayn for to by chese . . . . . vjs. viijd.
In the box iijl. xiiijs. xd. of which xxxs. is delivered to the new wardens.

A.D. mcccccix, *i.e.*, Jan. 12, 1509–10 for 1508–9.

"the fyrste yere of Kyng Hary the VIIJ."

[The Regnal year is noted henceforth.]

JOHN MORS[1] AND EDWARD BOLLE, WARDENS.

The Croke money this year . . . . lixs. iiijd.
The wardens present the yefte of J. Cartar, Weke, a ryng sylver and gylt and iiijd. and a sett.
" of Alys Vaysse a rynge of sylver and a serppelys.
" of Isbell Broke a lawnde charche [a lawn kerchief] and . iiijd.
" of John Dyrrente . . . . xxd.
The comyng in of the pascall taper . . . . vjs. ijd.
" " maydens . . . . . xvjs.
" " hoglers . . . . . iiijs.
" " towkers . . . . iijs. iiijd.
" " the young men . . . . iijs. iiijd.
In the box vj rings of silver and one of gold.
[Usual expenses]. . . . . . xvjs.
The comyng in of Robyn Hode (John Honythorne) iijl.

PAGE 55.
Delivered to Jo. Paynter and Rd. Rowland . . . . . . ijs.
" Jo. Phelyppys . . . . ijs. viijd.
" Owyn Porter . . . . xiiijd.
In the hands of J. Carter xxiiijs. ijd.; of W. Carter xxvjs. viijd.; of J. Felippes and R. Crose liijs. iiijd.; in the box of the church . . . . lixs. viijd.
J. Donpayne to by chesse . . . . vjs. viijd.
Itm. the wardens Owyn Porter and Edward Bolle hath y payd owtte of the box of the cherch money xxxs. unto John Carter the Jorge maker at the settyng oppe of the Jorge [image of St. George].

---

[1] Mors = Morris.

PAGE 56.

A.D. mccccx, i.e., Jan. 11, 1510–11 for 1509–10.

The second yere of Kyng Harry the VIIJ.
BOLLE AND OWYN PORTER, WARDENS.

First the yefte of Master Water Bockelonde	xxd.
,, of Johan Jonys	viijd.
,, of Hew Colyng a meyser [maser, or mazer-bowl] of wode.	
,, of Margette Dyrrynte a autter [altar] cloth and a cotton[1] and a ryng of sylver.	
The comyng in of the pascall taper	vjs. iiijd.
,, ,, maydens	xvjs. xd.
,, ,, hoglers	iiijs. ijd. ob.
,, ,, towkers	iijs.
,, ,, young men	iiijs. vd.
The Croke box for this yere	iijl. vs. xjd.
Delivered to O. Porter for the towkers	xiiijd.
,, J. Felyppes for the hoglers	ijs. viijd.
,, W. Tore for the young men lygte	ijs.
[Usual expenses]	xvijs.
For kepyng of the vestrye[2] [a new entry]	iiijs.
Comyng in of Robyn Hode	iijl. vjs. viijd.
To J. Donpayne for by chesse	vjs. viijd.

PAGE 57.

Remain v rings of silver and one of gold, and money	iiijl. xs. vjd.

A.D. mccccxi, i.e., Jan. 17, 1511–12 for 1510–11.

ED. BOLLE AND RICHARD MOLDE, WARDENS.

First the yefte of Margett Lyde a ryng.	
,, of Felypp Leyws	iiijd.
,, of Alys Canning, Marsh, a brason pott.	
Comyng in of the pascall taper	vjs. vijd.
,, maydyns	xxs.
,, hoglers	iiijs. viijd.
,, towkers	ijs. xjd.
,, young men	vs. xd.
Itm. the Croke box	iijl. ixs. jd.
,, ,, Robyn Hode (J. Honythorn and J. Stevyn)	xxxvs. xd.
Delivered to J. Felyppes for the hoglers	ijs. viijd.
,, ,, for the young men	ijs.
To Harry Vorde	xiiijd.

---

[1] A curtain. [2] Newly erected in the S.W. angle of the Church; called also the Treasury.

PAGE 58.
[Expenses as usual] . . . . xix*s*.
In the box are v rings of silver and one of gold.
In money . . . . xiij*l*.
Also in the Church viij lb. of wax.
Edward Bolle and Richard Poclon [*i.e.*, Boclond] are chosen wardens.

A.D. mccccxii, *i.e.*, Jan. 15, 1512–13 for 1511–12.

EDWARD BOLLE AND RICHARD BOCKLOND, WARDENS.

First the yefte of John Yng a pype with wode.
    „   Margette Davy a ryng of sylver and gylte and a Rochate (Rochet).
    „   John Tayler's wyffe a ryng of sylver and gylte.
    „   a sthere [steer] of Richard Wasyn.
    „   of Water Vynsente for his father and mother . . . viij*d*.
The comyng in of the pascall taper . . . . vj*s*. iij*d*.
    „   „   maydens . . . . . . xviij*s*. vj*d*.

PAGE 59.
The comyng in of the hoglers . . . . iiij*s*. vij*d*.
    „   „   towkers . . . . ij*s*. ij*d*. ob.
    „   „   young men . . . . iiij*s*. v*d*.
    [The usual sums are delivered to each of the above.]
Itm. the coste of the Gorge, the holle sum of all the coste[1] . . . xxvij*l*. xj*s*. viij*d*.
The incrysse of Croke . . . . iij*l*. iiij*s*. iiij*d*.
[Expenses as usual.]
There remain v rings of silver and one of gold and in money . x*l*. iiij*s*. vj*d*.
There rest in the wardens hands . . . . . . xxiij*s*. iiij*d*.
The new Wardens are Ed. Bolle and W. Carter.
Mem. that the wardens hath delyvered unto Roger Morris, R. Costrell, a pype with wood and a mesure the pryse x*l*. that shall be ypayd at Cryste masse comyth twelmotte that shalbe in the yere of our Lord MVXV [1515.]

PAGE 60.

A.D. mccccxiii, *i.e.*, Jan. 20, 1513–14 for 1512–13.

THE WARDENS, ED. BOLL AND JOHN CARTER, THE ELDER, AND WILLIAM HIS SON.[2]

Do present for the lyyng of Wyllyam Carter and his wyff in the chyrche vj*s*. viiij*d*., and a ryng of sylver and gylt, and xij*d*. to the bells and cerchew [kerchief] to Saynt Marget.

---

[1] This large outlay, and employment of a skilled body of Freemasons from Exeter marks an addition to the Fabric. It consisted of a Chapel on the N.E., at the opening of which St. George's image was set up with light burning before it, and the Vestry or treasure-house on the S.W., with its two chambers, upper and lower, strongly barred for safe custody of the increasing store of valuables. In later accounts, 1516-17, St. George had a Box, a Collection, and an Ale, 1523-4. There was a guild organized to maintain these observances. See 1516-17.

[2] N.B.—A third warden to help the older one.

Itm. a ryng of gold of the yefte [of] Mastress Bassyng.
Itm. a ryng of fylver and gylt of the geft of Alson Jamys of the paryshe of Schepton.
Itm. of the geft of Amys Harrys . . . . xij*d*.
" " John Reve a whether schepp J. Jose hath paid . . . xij*d*.
" " John Abatt . . . . xx*d*.
" " my lady Schepton to the belles . . . . . viij*d*.
Received in by Sir Thomas for my lady Schepton berel [burial] . vj*s*. viij*d*.

PAGE 61.
[The pascall taper, the maidens, hogglers, tokers, the young men as usual.] Total xxvij*s*. v*d*.
The Croke box this year . . . . ij*s*. x*d*.
P. Thomas and J. Vord received of the stoke . . . . ij*s*. and j*s*. ij*d*.
There are ij gold and vj silver rings in stock.
The usual expenses come to . . . . xiij*s*. viij*d*.
Delyvered to J. Phyllip for the hoggler stoke . . . . ij*s*. viij*d*.
The remains for the Crok vj*s*. iiij*d*. and in the box . iij*l*. iij*s*. x*d*.

[The year 1514-15, *i.e.*, for 1513-14 is omitted.]

PAGE 62.
A.D. mcccccxv, *i.e.*, Jan. 13, 1515–16 for 1514–15.
EDW. BOOLE AND WILLIAM GOODALL, WARDENS.
Alys Downpayne has given a pair of ryngs of sylver gylt.
John Rede . . . . x*d*.
Isabell Boole a ryng of sylver gylt.
The maidens, young men, hoggelers, tokers, and pascall money . . . ij*l*. ij*s*. ix*d*.
J. Fyllypps hoggeler receives ij*s*. viij*d*., H. Harryson toker xiiij*d*., W. Jose ii*s*.
Ed. Boole made his acownt for the cherce lond, in the yere abowfe (above) said, for
 iij yere and halfe . . . . v*s*. x*d*.
Mem. the yere [of the lease] be kynnyth at our lady day in lent—after [*i.e.*, henceforth].
There are ij gold and viij silver rings.
Delyveryd to W. Payne vj*s*. viij*d*. for by chesse . . xvj*s*. iiij*d*.
Remains in the box . . . . v*l*.
The new wardens receive . . . . . xxviij*s*. x*d*.

PAGE 63.
A.D. mcccccxvi, *i.e.*, Jan. 13, 1516–17 for 1515–16.
ED. BOLL AND JOHN PHYLLYPS, WARDENS.
The wardens present of the gift of John Boklond . . . . . xij*d*.
" " Jon Brown a ryng of sylver and a frontlett.[1]
" " Hew Sherwell . . . . iiij*d*.
" " John Phyllyps of Schepton . . . . iiij*d*.

[1] At the marriage of Sir Gervase Clifton, A.D. 1530, amongst the "expenses of the apparel," is
"A frontlet of blue velvet, xvij*s*." Bailey, Annals of Nottinghamshire, Vol I, p. 380.

Itm. her comythe yn John Phyllyps and Wyliyam Payn an present for Sayntt Gorg ys lyght	xij*s*.
The maidens, young men, hoglers, tokers, and the pascale	xxxvij*s*. j*d*.
Delivered to J. Phyllyps for the hoggelers light	ij*s*. viij*d*.
Itm. paid chyrche costs drwwytt [draweth] to	xxxvj*s*. ij*d*. ob.
To Grayson and J. Vord for toker lyght	xiiij*d*.
The Croke hath yncressyd thys yere	iiij mark[1]
[Usual expenses].	xvj*s*
There are viij sylver and one gold ring.	
Reckenying for the Church land the whole year	xx*d*.
Rest in the box for the yere past	x*s*. ij*d*
To the Wardens	xx*s*.
Rest in the box of Saynt Jorys [George's] mony	xij*s*
Rest yn W. Payn hond for to by chesse	vj*s*. viij*d*
The key of the Crok box John Morrys hond.	

PAGE 64.

A.D. mccccxvii, *i.e.*, Jan. 17, 1517–18 for 1516–17.

ED. BOLL AND JOHN HORDAR, WARDENS.

Ed. Jenkyll, Corff [? Carver] presents a ring of sylver and ij ygylt.	
John l'lenty do.	
Harry Mew do.	iiij*d*.
John Hordar presents in for Sayn Jorys lyght	xvj*s*. viij*d*.
The maidens, hoglers, tokers, young men, and the pascall present in	xxvij*s*. viij*d*.
[Expenses.]	
Rings, x silver one gold.	
To J. Hordan and R. Male for the lyght	ij*s*.
To J. Phyllps for the hoglers lyght	ij*s*. viij*d*.
To Harryson for lyght	ij*s*.
To R. Brown for to by chesse	vj*s*. viij.
The Croke hath yncrest this yere	xxxxiiij*s*. ij*d*.
In the cherche box in mony	xxij*s*. iiij*d*.
Itm. there ys Sir Thomas Vox owt [oweth] for my lady Schepton	vj*s*. viij*d*.
In the box the whole sum of all mony	iiij*l*. xiv*s*. viij*d*.

PAGE 65.

A.D. mccccxviii, *i.e.*, Jan. 15, 1518–19 for 1517–18.

ED. BOLL AND MORGAN PHYLLVPS, WARDENS.

A. Wattys presents a ryng of Sylver and ygelt [gilt].	
W. Brane presents a Serplys and a iiij*d*. to the bell.	
The Croke hathe incressyd thys yere	xliij*s*. ij*d*.

---

[1] *I.e.*, ij*l*. xiij*s*. iiij*d*.

The hoglers, tokers, young men and maidens present . . . . xxix*s.* vj*d.*
[The usual sums are delivered out and paid away.]
Itm. therys ypott [put] yn to the box v nobylls and xxxx*d.*,[1] and ryngs of silver and gylt.

PAGE 66.

A.D. mccccxix. *i.e.*, Jan. 14, 1519–20 for 1518–19.

ED. BOLL AND RICHARD SEUGAR, WARDENS.

The gift of Alsun Whytyng of Pylton . . . . iiij*d.*
„ Phylyp Bys . . . . vj*s.* viij*d.*
„ Isbell Sadler . . . . ij*d.*
„ Anys Carter a ryng of sylver and . . . . . . vj*s.* viij*d.*
The hoglers, Tokers, young men, maidens, and pascall . . . . xxxviij*s.* vj*d.*
[The usual sums are delivered out and paid away.]

PAGE 67.

A.D. m.vc.xx. *i.e.*, Jan. 14, 1520–21 for 1519–20.

ED. BOLLE AND JOHN EDMONDS, WARDENS.

Anys Yng presents a boke, a chalys, a peer [pair] of vestements, at the parylle [apparel] of the awlter, also a rynge of golde.
Itm. Master John Edmonds a relyke of Synttc[2] Thomas of Canterbyrye.
W. Stevyns and Alys uxor ejus a ryng and . . . . viij*d.*
Alys Jarman a peer of bedys and a ryng.
Alys Mew a plat(er) and xij trenchers.[3]
Jone Haukor . . . . iiij*d.*
[The hoglers, towkers, young men, maidens, the pascall, and S. George's profits as usual.—The only change in the regular entries is instead of Croke—paid for kepyng of the tresur[4] house.]
The sum remaining in the box is . . . . vij*l.* xiij*s.* iiij*d.*
A gold ring is sold for . . . . . xiij*s.* iiij*d.*

PAGE 68.

A.D. m.vc.xxi. *i.e.*, Jan., 1521–2 for 1520–21.

ED. BOLLE AND JOHN HONYTHORNE, WARDENS.

Paid for the lyyng[5] of Whytte Wolle . . . . . . iij*s.* vj*d.*
„ „ of John Joysse in the Chyrche ij torchys and iiijlb. of brasse.

---

[1] *I.e.*, j*l.* xvj*s.* viij*d.*
[2] Probably obtained on pilgrimage. This was the year of the last Jubilee of the Martyr. What was done with the relic?
[3] Outfit for the Church house.
[4] The cross, with the other valuables, was now kept in the strong room at the S.W. angle of the Church.
[5] Were these cases of the corpse being laid out in the Church before burial, with lights burning?

PAGE 69.

[Among usual entries]

Ed. Wynsor geve unto the chorch ij yows [ewes] the prisse . . . iijs. iiijd.
Mem. that the sayd wardens had for to by wex iijs. iiijd. of the croke box.

PAGE 70.

A.D. m.vc.xxii, *i.e.*, Jan. 1522–3 for 1521–2.

ED. BOLLE AND RICHARD WAYSSE, WARDENS.

The gifts of—

Sir Stevin Edmonds iij bokys of Canan.[1]	Anys Taytte, a ryng of sylver.
Anys Hogys a ryng of sylver.	Elizabeth Shepperd do.
Thomas Chaunler of Hame . . iiijd.	Jone Bladon a charch and do.
Elynore Sowthmore a carcho [kerchief]	Maude Brasse do.
and . . . . . . iiijd.	Thomas Amerike . . iiijd.
W. Persse of Hame . . . . viijd.	Robard Heth . . . iiijd.
J. Horder . . . . . xd.	Robard Hopar of Wells . iiijd.
Jone, daughter of W. Towker . . viijd.	

A servant of J. Mors a carcho and peer of bedys.
R. Voll a platter, a poger,[2] and . . . . iiijd.
R. Chester . . . . xijd.
John Molde . . . . iiijd.

[The hoglers and outgoings as usual.]

[The entry "to by chesse" does not now occur, but the sum allowed for that purpose,
viz., vijs. viijd. does, though without description of its application.]

PAGE 72.

A.D. m.vc.xxiii, *i.e.*, Jan. 17, 1523–4 for 1522–3.

[Originally so written; but one of the units has been scratched out. The same
remark applies to the heading of the next year.]

ED. BOLLE AND RICHARD BROWNE, WARDENS.

Gifts. John Carnycke a massebocke.
,, Sir Umefry John son . . . . xijd.
,, Watt Vynsentte . . . . ijd.
,, Oleffe Lame a ryng of Sylver and gylte, and a peer of bedys of gette [jet] and
   a charcho.
,, Alys Sheppard a ryng of sylver and gylte.
,, Anys Brade of Comton Dondayne . . . . xvjd.

[The hoglers, young men, maidens, and Towkers as usual, expenditure ditto.]

The crysse of Syntte my helle [Michael] . . . . ijs.
Payd for the wesch [washing] of the hy aulter . . . . . iiijs. viijd.
The crysse of Syntte Gorgys alle [Ale] . . . . . xiijs. viijd.
   xv rings of silver, ij of gold.

---

[1] Probably three books of the Canon of the Mass for use at the Altar.
[2] Porringer.

PAGE 73.
In the hands of Ed. Wynsore iiij yousse [ewes].
Delivered to R. Brown to by chesse . . . . vjs. viijd.

PAGE 74.

𝔄.𝔇. m.vc.xxiiii. *i.e.*, Jan. 16, 1524–5 for 1523–4.
ED. BOLLE AND JOHN VORDE, WARDENS.

Gifts. Anis Josse, a ryng of Sylver.
xv silver and ij gold rings in the box.
[Receipts and payments mingled].
Rest in box . . . . iij*l*. xiij*s*. iiij*d*.
besides ryngs and vj ewes.

PAGE 76.
TERMS OF SHEEP-LEASE.

John Felyppes and Jone his wife vj yows [ewes], and iij ryngs of sylver. The whych you scheppes [ewe sheep] beth delyvered unto Hew Morganne for the space of vij yere, the said Hew for to pay by the yere the sum of ij*s*. for to pay hit at the Countt day. If so be as eny of thes scheppe doth dy or mynish, the said Hew pay for them xvj*d*. a pesse [apiece], the scheppe be of the age of iiij yere, all of one age, the said Hew for to delyver at the vij yere ende the scheppe or ells [else] . . . . viij*s*.

[All the usual entries of receipts and payments, except that there are no S. Michael or S. George receipts.]

Itm. ther rest in the hands of Ed. Wynsor, vj scheppe, the whych thay be yous [ewes] all, the sayd Edward for to pay for the same scheppe at all tymys vj*s*. viij*d*., or ells [else] the scheppe.

PAGE 78.

𝔄.𝔇. mccccxxv. *i.e.*, Jan. 21, 1525–6 for 1524–5.
ED. BOLLE AND JOHN FORDE, WARDENS.

Gifts.	Harry Cornysch of Wells	iiij*d*.
„	the wyfe of John Dylte of Wells	ij*d*.
„	the wyfe of Lewis Tayler a sylver ryng and a charcho, and a cotton [curtain] and bowese of wett [a bushel of wheat], and	iiij*d*.
„	the wyfe of Water Jonys a ryng of sylver and a carcho of lawne [lawn].	
„	the wyfe of W. Towker a charcho and	xvj*d*.
„	Johan Chanler of Hame	viij*d*.
„	Alys the wyfe of Feleppe Morgan a ryng of sylver and a charcho.	
„	Jone the wyfe of Robard Cosyn of Baltsborrew [Baltonsborough] .	iiij*d*.
„	Rychard Bolloke a peer of crewatt [cruets].	
„	John Jevans a platter and ij sowsers [saucers] and a peny.	

[The usual entries of hoglers, &c., but no S. George].

Hew Morgan pays rent for the vj sheep . . . . ij*s*.

PAGE 80.

A.D. mccccсxxvi. i.e., Jan. 19, 1526-7 for 1525-6.
ED. BOLLE AND JOHN KYNGDON, WARDENS.

Gifts.	Sir Jon Rodneye	iijs. iiijd
,,	Jone Parfytte of Doltyng	xxd
,,	Elizabeth Corage a ryng of sylver and gylte.	
,,	John Dylte a wytte of lydde [weight of lead] . . .	xxviij lb.
,,	W. Josse	iiijd.
,,	Robyn Hode[1]	iiijl. iiijd.
Itm.	payd to Rychard Brown for corpes[2]	xjd.

Item. ther was payde owtte of the chyrch box for all the parysch whane ther was a strayne[3] taken for the lorde . . . . xxs

[4]Hew Morgan to pay for the vj sheep ijs. a year for the space of vij years at the last year xvjd. for apes [apiece].

There rest in the hands of Ed. Wynsor for vj sheep . . vjs. viijd.

PAGE 82.

A.D. mccccсxxvii. i.e., Jan. 18, 1527-8 for 1526-7.
ED. BOLLE AND JOHN MORS, WARDENS.

Gifts.	Jone Sevons of Schepton Mallatte a ryng of golde.	
,,	Jone Shepperd of Stoke My hell [S. Michael, or Stoke Lane], a ryng of sylver.	
Itm.	Syntte Gorgys alle [Ale] the sum	xxxiijs. iiijd.
	The rent of vj sheep for ij years	iiijs.

Mem. that Owyn Porter hath ypayd unto John Broke for his warke and to John Coke for the mendyng of the horne[5] of the cherch, and to Gornay and to the wardens the sum [of] forti shelyng, and so[6] the parysch doth owe on to Chantre . . xls.

PAGE 84.

A.D. mccccсxxviii. i.e., Jan. 23, 1528-9 for 1527-8.
ED. BOLLE AND JOHN PELTON, WARDENS.

Gifts. John Sowthmore	viijd.
Richard Pers of Hame [Ham]	iiijd.
Alys Mew a rynge of silver.	
Ther was made of Syntte Gorgys alle [Ale] by John Pelton and Rychard Vaysee	lvijs. iiijd.
Received for a cotton [curtain] of Edw. Bolle	xijd.
,, from Edmonde Carter for beryng of mother[7]	vjs. viijd.

[The usual entries of hoglers, &c., and expenses.]

---

[1] The first time since 1510-11.   [2] Qy. Corporas.

[3] A distraint made by the Lord of the Manor for chief rent (see the year 1493-4), due for our Lady's closes and the almshouses.

[4] A summary of the terms given in full, 1524-5.

[5] Some jutting corner or pinnacle. The cost required a loan.

[6] I.e., the parish borrowed from the Feoffees of the Palton Chantry.

[7] The stated fee for burying in the Church, the wardens making good the pavement.

PAGE 86.

A.D. mccccxxix, i.e., Jan. 22, 1529–30 for 1528–9.[1]

ED. BOLLE AND WILLIAM MOLDE, WARDENS.

Gifts of John Bockelon	xij*d*.
Anys wife of J. Torne, a ryng of sylver and gylt	j*d*.
Rd. Brown son of R. Brown	iiij*d*.
Made of Seyntte Gorgis alle [Ale]	xxvj*s*. viij*d*.
Received from Ed. Bolle for the cris [increase] of the lon [land]	ij*s*. vj*d*.

[The usual entries of hoglers, &c., and sheep, and payments].

PAGE 88.

A.D. mccccxxx, i.e., Jan. 28, 1530–31 for 1529–30.[1]

ED. BOLLE AND RICHARD MOLDE, WARDENS.

Gifts of Sir Thomas Rogers of Wells, preste [priest]	xx*d*.
„ Rychard Goodall	xij*d*.
„ John and Elizabeth Morris	ij*s*.
„ the Lady Elizabeth a rynge of golde.	
„ Anys daughter of John Edmonds a platter and	iiij*d*.
„ the sayde Anys Edmonds a carcho or els [else]	viij*d*.
„ Allys Goodall, daughter of William	iiij*d*
„ Elyn Nicolas, a ryng of sylver.	
„ Alys wyfe of W. Molde, a rynge of sylver and a carcho of lawnde.	
„ W. Wooke	vj*d*.
„ Ed. Sewgar a bason, and	iiij*d*
„ Jone Carter a ryng of sylver.	
„ Master Moris Walker, perste [priest]	vj*d*
„ Ed. Campe	vj*d*.
„ Cryten Horsynton, a ryng of sylver.	
„ Isbell Carpyter, do.	
„ Thomas Jacobe	iiij*d*.
„ Dorothe Bellman, a ryng of sylver.	
„ John Porter	iiij*d*.
„ W. Lews	ij*d*.
Ed. Bolle received for fessel [vessel]	ij*d*.
Gift of Alys Blakedon, a ryng of silver.	
Made at Seyntt Gorgys alle	xiij*s*.

[The hoglers, &c., as usual.]

The Church Croke this year	xxxix*s*. x*d*.

[The usual entries of expenditure.]

---

[1] Regnal year given all through this period.

PAGE 91.

A.D. mccccxxxi, *i.e.*, Jan. 13, 1531-2 for 1530-1.[1]
ED. BOLLE AND OWYN POTTER, WARDENS.

Gifts.	Sir Nycolas Garlantte	xx*d*.
,,	Margaret Chester a ryng of Sylver, and a stone and . .	iiij*d*.
,,	L. Watts of Schepton	iiij*d*.
,,	Jone Tucker of Noney [Nunney]	iiij*d*.
	S. George ['s Ale]	xxvj*s*. viij*d*.

[The hoglers, &c., as usual, and the usual expenditure.]

PAGE 93.

A.D. mccccxxxii, *i.e.*, Jan. 11, 1532-3 for 1531-2.
ED. BOLLE AND WILLIAM WATTS, WARDENS.
GIFTS—

Em. feyse	iij*d*.	The Maydens incres	.	xvij*s*. iiij*d*.
John Meryfylde and Edeth . .	vj*d*.	The young men .	.	ij*s*. viij*d*.
John and Wyllyam Phelyps . .	iiij*d*.	The hogelers . .	.	iiij*s*.
St. George Croke Alle [Ale] .	xviij*s*. iiij*d*.	The towkers . .	.	xxj*d*.
The Pascall	iiij*s*. viij*d*.	The Croke box increse	.	xxx*s*.

[The keys of the box are in the hands of J. Delton, as usual not one of the Wardens.]
[The usual expenses.]

John Bolle for pewter vessells[2] debeth [debet, *i.e.*, oweth] . . . . . ix*d*.

Itm. Owyn Porter debeth onto the Chorch of Corscomb xl*s*., for to be ypaid in the space of iij yere that ther shollde be ypayd at the day of the countts nextte commyng by Owyn Porter . . . . xiij*s*. iiij*d*.

John Bolle debeth for the rent of the Chorch . . . . . . ij*s*. vj*d*.

PAGE 94.

mccccxxxiv, Lease of ten sheep: Jan., 1534-5 for 1533-4.

In the rayne of Kyng Hary the VIIJ the xxv yere, the xviij day of January, the Wardens of the parysch Chorch of Corscomb, Symon Brone and John Bolle other wys Mydel have I sette to farme unto Rychard Downe of Corscomb x scheppe for the tyme of vij yers, and the sayde Rychard for to pay by the yere for the rente of the x scheppe ij*s*. vj*d*. for to be ypayd at the day that the Chorch Wardens doth make ther countte at the parysch Chorch of Corscomb every yere for the tyme of vij yere for to pay ij*s*. vj*d*. by the yere and to have the vij yere paste, the said Rychard Downe for to delyver the sayd x scheppe so good as they ware or ells xiij*s*. iiij*d*. in good and lawfoll [money].

ther to consentteth Thomas Downe and Hary Jamys schomaker for to se the sayd payment welle and trewly payd in the payne. [under penalty.]

---

[1] Regnal year given all through this period.

[2] The vessels of the Church house are now let out on hire, as in other parishes. Hitherto the house has yielded nothing to the wardens.

PAGE 95.

𝔄.𝔇. mccccexxxiii. *i.e.*, Jan. 10, 1533–4 for 1532–3.

JOHN CARTER AND JOHN MYDEL, WARDENS.

By the byquest of John at Wylle of Dynder	iiij*d*.
the byquest of Thomas Carpynter	viij*d*.
the byquest of Wellcheen [Wilkin] Chester	iiij*d*.
and a ryng of sylver and gylte and a carcho.	
the byquest of Rychard Jonys	v*d*.
the byquest of Jone Bockelen of darke shelle[1] . . .	iij*s*. iiij*d*.
the ryng of Mr. Thos. Fy [Fitz] James	iiij*d*.
Itm. John Mydel hath delyvered for the pewter fessell . .	xj*d*.
[The pascall taper, the maidens, &c., the increase of St. George, &c., as usual. As also the usual sums returned to the maidens' light, hoglers' light, &c.]	
J. Mydel debeth for the rent of the Chyrch	viij*s*. vj*d*.
[The usual expenses, for keeping the clock, and washing, &c.]	
Th. Downe debeth on to the chyrch for lampe . . .	viij*s*.
Itm. ther ys payd to the Clarke for his wagys[2] . . .	vj*s*. viij*d*.
Money in the church box	xj*s*. viij*d*.
John Chester for a carcho (the whych ygeven by his wyfe Welcheen) debeth . .	ix*d*.

PAGE 97.

𝔄.𝔇. mccccexxxiv. *i.e.*, Jan. 9, 1534–5 for 1533–4.

JOHN MYDELL AND SIMON BROWNE,[3] WARDENS.

[They first present all the bequests.]	
the byquest of Rychard Crosse, a ryng of sylver and . .	viij*d*.
,, Amys Camell	iiij*d*.
J. Mydell hath delyvered for pewter vessell	xiij*d*.
[Receipts and expenditure under the usual heads.]	
The sum that cherch coste of Rep(rea)ssig [Reparation] . .	v*l*. xiiij*d*.
Tho. Downe debeth unto the chyrch for the rentte for the lamp [Mayow's endowment]	viij*s*.
R. Downe debeth for the rentte for x[4] shepe	ij*s*. vj*d*.

PAGE 99.

𝔄.𝔇. mccccexxxv. *i.e.*, Jan. 8, 1535–6, 1534–5.

EDMUND QUAR AND JOHN MYDDEL, WARDENS.

The byquest of Water Jonis	xij*d*
,, Edward Bolle	viij*d*.
,, John Pers of Hame	iiij*d*.
[Receipts for the Pascal, &c., as usual, and usual outlay.]	
J. Bolle paid for pewter vessels	xviij*d*.

[1] *I.e.*, Darshill or Dursill, in Shepton.   [2] A new entry.
[3] The wardens who leased the x sheep.   [4] None for the vi sheep.

Owyn Porter debeth	. . . . . .		xiij*s.* iiij*d.*
W. Payne „	. . . . . .		iij*s.* iiij*d.*
T. Downe „	at My helle Mass [Michaelmas] .		. viij*s.*
J. Moog „	. . . . . .		. iij*s.*
J. Bolle „	. . . .		ix*s.* vj*d.*
W. Frensch „	. .		. iij*s.*

PAGE 101.

𝔄.𝔇. mcccccxxxvi, *i.e.*, Jan. 13, 1536–7, 1535–6.

JOHN INGSTRE AND JOHN BOLLE, WARDENS.

The byquest of Isbel Molde a ryng of sylver and gylt.

[Receipts and expenses as usual.]

J. Bolle bryngeth for pewter vessels	. xiij*d.*
The sum of costys done by John Yngstre this yere . . .	. iij*l.* xj*s.* ob.
Received of J. Bolle for a ryng	. xviij*d.*

PAGE 102.

Received of J. Kyngdon for tymber	v*s.* iiij*d.*
Edmond Quar debeth for lyde [lead]	j cwt. j qr. xviij li[1]
The prisse of the C of lyde	iiij*s.* viij*d.*
There rests in the hands of Jelyan [Julian] Harys for to by chese for the Croke [*i.e.*, for the Procession][2]	iij*s.* iiij*d.*

[Various sums are owing as usual.]

PAGE 103.

𝔄.𝔇. mcccccxxxvii, *i.e.*, Jan. 19, 1537–8 for 1536–7.

JOHN STEVYNS OTHERWISE SADELER, AND JOHN MYDELL OTHERWISE JOHN BOLLE, WARDENS.

The bequest of Yede Suger, a ryng of sylver.

„	N. Goodall	iiij*d.*
„	Yede Robins of Wotton . . .	iiij*d.*
„	Margaret Mawdelyn of Wells . . .	iiij*d.*
„	Anys Towker, a towelle and a yow schepe.	

[Receipts and outlay under the usual heads.]

J. Mydell for pewter vessels	. viij*d.*
T. Downe debeth for the lampe (*i.e.*, Mayow's) dew at Michaelmas	. vij*s.*
There rests in the hands of J. Harys for to by chese for the Croke .	iij*s.* iiij*d.*

[Various sums are owing as usual.]

---

[1] These 143 lbs. of lead probably had been given to the wardens by mining parishioners, for lead ore was at that time found along the whole range of Mendip.

[2] This allowance is now reduced to half the ordinary payment for these occasions.

PAGE 105.

𝔄.𝔇. mcccccxxxviii, i.e., Jan. 11, 1538–9 for 1537–8.

THOMAS DOWNE AND JOHN MYDELL, WARDENS.

The bequest of John Hardwylle	iiij*d*.
,, John Paynter	iiij*d*.
The incres of the pewter vessels	vj*d*.
[The accounts this year are much less regular than hitherto.]	
The pascall taper iiij*s*. vij*d*. S. George's alle [ale]	xxvj*s*. viij*d*.
The maydens	iiij*s*.

PAGE 106.

Jelyan Harys is paid for washing and tynyng the light.

J. Laffe oweth for a yowe	xxij*d*.
John Ford oweth to the chirche for the rest of his[1] ale mony .	iiij*s*. viij*d*.
Received for the pascall at Easter	iiij*s*. vij*d*.
For rent from W. Sugar	iij*s*. iiij*d*.
,, J. Sadeler	vj*s*.
,, Mogg iij parts rent	iij*s*. ix*d*.
,, R. Phelyppes for the vantage of bredde .	xxij*d*.
,, Hill of Compton for rent . .	iiij*d*.
,, John Bysse	vij*s*. iiij*d*.
,, J. Edwards for last yere	ij*s*. iiij*d*.
,, T. Stevens for J. Edmonds rent this yere .	xx*d*
Received for a knylle [knell]	iiij*d*.
,, of Edyth Honythorne for a knylle and the pall[2]	vj*d*.
,, Margery Mether for our worst[3] pall . .	ij*d*.
More for lyme to John Medyll	j*d*.

PAGE 107.

[One page at least has been cut out with scissors.
There is the heading of an account 33 Hen. VIIJ, *i.e.*, Apr. 1541 to Apr. 1542.
Harry Mede and Richard Goodall, Wardens, crossed out.]

𝔄o. 𝔥en. viii. xxxvi°.[4]   JOHN CARTER AND JOHN STEVENS, WARDENS.

Receyvyd at our comyng in at the accompts day in money	xiiij*s*.
Payd to the obytt for all gode doers[5]	ij*s*. vj*d*.
,, for yoyle [oil]	iij*s*. viij*d*.
Paid for hewing timber to Broke	x*d*.

---

[1] John Ford had either given an ale, or had collected at an ale for the Church, and not paid the collection in full.

[2] First mention of a pall as a parish property.

[3] Worn, and therefore not a new possession.

[4] If dated from Jan. to Jan., as usual, this official year ran from Jan., 1545-6 to 1546-7. The King died Jan. 28, 1547-8.

[5] The parish benefactors, named in the Bede-roll.

Paid to Broke for makyng of the frame[1]	x*d*.
,, for belropys	.ij*s*. ix*d*.
,, for making of wax	ij*s*. iiij*d*.
,, for a tweyste and naylys and greffe[2]	iij*d*.
,, for greffe (?) thred and silke	iij*d*.
,, for caryng of the banor to Care [Cary]	iiij*d*. ob.
,, for mendyng of the cloke	.x*d*. ob
,, at vysytation[3] at Bruton	iiij*d*.
,, for caryng home of Tymber and Woode	xij*d*.

PAGE 108. MEM. [Interpolated to record Kingdon's debt from 1542.] That Edward Kyndon and John Stevyns be chosyn Wardens for the yere. Wheras delyvered them in hande xiij*s*. x*d*. in the yere of the rayne of Kyng Harri the VIIJ, xxxiiij.

Soe Edward Kyndon doth owe viij*s*. and xx*d*. for chese [chest].

This is of John Carter and John Stevyns yere.

Paid for makyng a wheel to the little bell	iij*s*. iiij*d*.
,, cutting trees and stopping of scherdys [gaps]	v*d*.
,, bokes for the prossyon[4]	xj*d*.
,, coppys [copes]	xxj*d*.
,, going to visitation	ij*s*.
,, pweyntyng[5] of the Chyrche	x*d*.
,, for lime	x*d*.
,, for oyl[6] and veyre and drynkyng and grese	xij*d*.
,, ffre sute and kyngs sylver[7]	xx*d*.
,, wax xvjlb. at v*d*. ob. the pound.	

PAGE 109.

A.D. m.vc.xlvii. *i.e.*, 1547–8 for 1546–7.[8]

JHAN BYSSE AND JOHN MYDEL, WARDENS.

The bequest of Rychard Bockland	vij*s*.	The Croke to eche [each of the Ales?]	
the pascall taper	iiij*s*.		xxxiij*s*. j*d*. ob.
the maydes ayll [Ale]	xxij*s*. vj*d*.	They levyeth for the fyne of John	
The Ale att Wytsontyde	xvij*s*. ij*d*.	Jeffrey	xij*d*.
		for John Kendon for hys fyne	ij*s*. iiij*d*.

[1] *I.e.*, a bell frame.
[2] Qy., "grease"? grease for the bell-wheels.
[3] First mention of a visitation. Previous wardens must have comprised it in their bill of costs.
[4] Procession, *i.e.*, the Litany, newly put forth in English.
[5] Painting; probably painting out something newly condemned.
[6] Oil, fire, and grease, *i.e.*, for a bonfire on Midsummer Eve.
[7] If this refers to the King's revel (hitherto a source of income) and not to a legal process, the suit must be a dress provided for the mock king, and the silver a tribute paid to him.
[8] Spoliation begins, and voluntary offerings die away.

Mem. Jhan Bysse doth . . . detter [debtor] before all the pareche for certen
plate sold hytt [or att] and awtrer [Altar] to the side of ys . . iiij*l.* vj*s.* iiij*d.*
Itm. John Jeffrey do owe of hys fyn . . . . vj*s.*
Thomas Stevyns do owe for iij parts of the year . . . . . ij*s.* vj*d.*
[Several other debts.]

PAGE 110.

Mem. that 38 Hen. VIIJ[1] Jhan Bysse and Jhan Phylepes were chosen Wardens.

A̅o. 1548, *i.e.*, 1548–9 for 1547–8.

[A list of nine men who owe sums from xx to iv shillings; for what is not stated; only]
T. Downe do owe for a ryng   vj*d.*

PAGE 111.

A.D. mcccccxlviii.[2]

The Church rents the first day of September.
[A list of nine names, each owing for five quarters' rent in sums from xv*s.* to v*d.*]

PAGE 112.

A̅o. 1550, *i.e.*, 1550–51 for 1549–50.

JOSEPH CARTER AND THOMAS FASY, WARDENS.

[The whole page is taken up with a list of sums owing to the parish, the following only specify for what the sums were due]:—

T. Downe for rings . . . . vj*d.*	the person for a blew cloth . . xij*d.*
T. Hyll for rent . . . . . v*d.*	T. Wills for a brouder [broidery] . vj*d.*
the person for xv lb. of wax . . iij*l.*	R. Fasy for a ber[4] . . . . xiij*d.*
the person for the perrafrase [Paraphrase][3] . . . . . v*s.* ij*d.*	E. Quar for a ber . . . . xix*d.*

---

[1] If in January, a few days before the King's death on the 28th.
[2] In this year Edward VI's Commissioners seized the Chantry endowments, *i.e.*, the lands and Chapel of East Horrington, and the Mayow lands and houses.—See Som. Record Soc., vol. ii.
[3] The Paraphrase of Erasmus on the Gospels and the Acts, first published in English in A.D. 1547, from the Translation by Nicholas Udal, a protégé of Queen Katherine Parr.—(Strype's Memorials, vol. ii., part i., p. 45.)
[4] *I.e.,* "bier," either for the use of one, or perhaps to purchase it.

PAGE 113.

A.D. "yn the ffyfe yere of our soffreyn lorde kyng Edward the Sext," Dec. 6, *i.e.*, 1551–2 for 1550–1.

Mem. that the parish of Corscomb hath chosen to be Wardens, John Goodall and John att Wyll, in the fyffe year of our sovereign lorde Kyng Edward VJ the vj day of December.

And John Enstryge and Rechard Felyps to have the over sight.

Mem. Wardens made "ther a cownt a newerds eve (New Year's Eve) 1552."

"The paryche ys depytte" . . . . iv*s*. vij*d*.

A.D. 1553, *i.e.*, 1552–3 for 1551–2.

The same Wardens. And John Myddyl and Richard Whats to help sell[1] the tymber and other things.

Mem. Jhan Goodall, Jhan Attwoll, hath mayd ther acownte to Jan. 1554, and they doth owe to the paroche . . . . xiiij*li*.

PAGE 114.

A.D. "yn the fryst [fyrst] yere of the rayne of oure most sovreyne lady the queen Mary," *i.e.*, 1553–4 for 1552–3.

RICHARD WATTS AND RICHARD DOWNE, WARDENS.

They have received[2] a sylver challys, and a cover.

Itm. a boxe of coper for the sacrament.
 ,, a blake palle of blake velvet and red.
 ,, a paule of blew damaske.
 ,, a paule of green silke.
 ,, a awter cloth of green and gold saten of bryges [Bruges] silke.
 ,, iij lynen awter clothes and a towell.
 ,, ij serples.

Itm. ij barres of yeron [iron] with a slege [a sledge-hammer] and a stone sawe.
 ,, j peke [pick] axe and a spade.
 ,, j wyte bason and a towell.
 ,, a streymer and a bayner logge.[3]
 ,, a kerchowe that did serve the canapy with torcells.[4]
 ,, a canapy to hange the sacrament over.

---

[1] Spoliation going on. Overseers appointed to watch the wardens.
[2] *I.e.*, recovered goods, hidden during Edward's reign. Mary's accession was July 6, 1553.
[3] A flag and banner "lug," *i.e.*, string.
[4] Tassels.

Itm. ij long towels for Ester.
„ a cope of blue vellat [velvet] and a westment of blew and red bryges [Bruges] saten, withall thyngs to hit belonging.
„ a crosse of coper, ij candeelstekes of laten.
„ ij boxes for mony bowned with yron [iron]

Itm. a grete cheste bownd with yron.
„ a pere of sensers [censers].
„ a bybell.
„ iij stoles.
„ iij famels.[1]
„ a tabell for the communyon.
„ a grete cheste in the vestre for copes.

PAGE 115.
Mem. they have receyvyd in redy mony . . . . xiiij/.
[Four debtors are to pay within a year. The names of xxiij men who are present when the above agreement is come to, are given.]

PAGE 116.

A.D. 1555, Jan. 12, *i.e.*, 1555–6 for 1554–5.
RICHARD WATTS AND RYCHARD DOWNE, WARDENS.
[No accounts.]

A.D. 1556, Jan. 18, *i.e.*, 1556–7 for 1555–6.
JOHN CLYVE AND JOHN BLAKMAN, WARDENS.
[Only two entries of receipts of xvj*s.* from two debtors.]

A.D. 1557, Jan. 9, *i.e.*, 1557–8 for 1556–7.
JOHN MYDDLE AND RYCHARD MOLDE, WARDENS.

The next Wardens are to be R. Mowlde and Joseph Cartter.
Received of John Godwyn of the bequest of Jone Buclond, Wydow . . iij*s.* iiij*d.*
Received more of the said J. Godwyn for the burial in the Church of the said Jone Buclond, and the wife of Joseph Carter her daughter . . . . xiij*s.* iiij*d.*
[Three debts are paid.]
Remayneth owing by John Goodall for the buryall of hys wyfe in the Churche . vj*s.* viij*d.*
[pp. 118, 119 of the accounts are blank.]

PAGE 120.

A.D. 1558, *i.e.*, 1558–9 for 1557–8.
JOHN COLYER AND NYCHOLAS WYLLS, WARDENS.

They present the geffte of Sir Smyth . . . . . . vj*d.*
„ „ James Carter . . . . . xij*d.*
Total receipts . . . . xxv*s.*

---

[1] "Famels," *i.e.*, "fanons," maniples.

PAGE 121.

Payments.

Payd for making of the pascall . . xxij*d*.	Payd for a tonge for the second bell . j*d*.
,, for francincense and pyns[1] . . ij*d*.	,, for mending a hole in the led . ij*d*.
,, for the maken clene of candel-sticks . . . . . . j*d*.	,, for carryage of a shete of led . iij*d*.
	,, to Vysytation . . . . ix*d*.
,, for weshyng a qayrt [? quarter] . vj*d*.	,, to makyng up of the byll . ij*d*.
,, att Brewton at Vysytation . xij*d*.	,, to a rope for the whyrelgok[2] iij*d*.
,, for the hyre of a horse . . iiij*d*.	,, for keepyng of the cloke . viij*s*.
,, for mending of the bere . . ij*d*.	,, for Washing . . . vj*d*.

PAGE 122.

𝔄.𝔇. m.vc.lix. *i.e.*, 1559–60 for 1558–59.

HARRY WYLLS AND RYCHARD BYSSE, WARDENS.

[No items. Due to Wardens] . . . . xj*s*. viij*d*.

𝔄.𝔇. m.vc.lx. *i.e.*, 1560–61 for 1559–60.

JOSEPH CARTER AND THOM MEAD, WARDENS.

Payd for Visitation	v*s*.
,, for bred and wyne from passyng Sonday[3] thys day .	ij*s*. iiij*d*.
,, for washing the whole year	xij*d*.
,, for mending of a serpless	iij*d*.
Tot.	xix*s*. xj*d*.

THE END.

[Several pages apparently lost.]

---

[1] Pines, either (a) pine boughs, used as well as juniper, for purifying the Church : or (b) for torches to be carried by the acolytes.
[2] Whirl-cock, whirligig.
[3] Passion Sunday.

Pilton:

Circumstances of the Place.

Glastonbury Abbey was the Lord of the Manor including Wootton (an acreage of 7,139 acres), and sole known Landowner. The Abbot kept the Manor-house close to the Church fit for his occasional residence. He had there a park, a vineyard, and a large demesne, on which stood and stands a noble barn.

The Church

Was dedicated to St. John the Baptist. Our Lady's Altar stood in the North Aisle. The women seem to have used that part as their special chapel and place of offering. There were two guilds, that of St. John the Baptist, and that of the Hogglers, who maintained a light at some altar unnamed. The Church-house, called St. Mary House, repaired in 3rd of Hen. VIII., and now standing, afforded ample room for all the brotherhood meetings and festivities. The Rectory, valued in 1537 at £24 6s. 3d. nett, was appropriated under a compact with the Abbey, the original patron, by Bishop Savaric, *circa* 1200, to the Precentorship of the Cathedral. The Precentor thenceforth nominated the Vicar to the Bishop for Institution. The Chapter, in lieu of the Archdeacon, gave induction, but the disciplinary authority of the Ordinary was vested in the Precentor.

The rectorial and vicarial houses with their tithe-barns must have formed part of the surroundings of the Church. The Vicar was bound to serve North Wootton Chapel.

Fiscal System.

Until the year 1530 a single Warden administered the parish funds. He alone was responsible to the visiting authority, and accounted to the parishioners, but under him there were—it would seem—no less than four pairs of Wardens, viz., Our Lady Wardens, those of S. John's Brotherhood, those of the High Light on the rood-loft, and those of the Key, Kye or Cows, the form of live-stock by which the rich pastures could best render their tribute to the Church. A Key-warden's Account will be seen on p. 64, but dateless. Each cow, it will be seen, had a surety, "borow" or "pledge" to certify her good treatment. A large proportion of parishioners was in these manifold ways engaged in the responsible service of the Church. Save only a few small gifts from the wealthy, the funds flowed from within, and always sufficed.

NORTH WOOTTON.

This Chapelry had its pair of Wardens, who were presumably answerable directly to the diocesan authority for the fabric and its offices. Besides a subsidy to the Easter light of Pilton, they paid 3s. 4d. per annum to the Mother Church, the usual form of recognizing a daughter's former dependence. In the Chapel there was a Light endowed with six acres of land yielding 10s. when confiscated to the King in 1548. [*See* Som. Rec. Soc., Vol. II.]

THE CHURCH-BOOKS.

Vol. I contains two leaves of parchment, the rest of paper. It is bound in parchment, measuring 11½-in by 7¾-in. It is made up of three pieces, the first enclosed in parchment with eight sheets within. Of the second and third no less than seven leaves are maimed or cut away.

Vols. II and III beginning in 1584, and 1626, ending 1641, do not fall within the present range of research.

The subjoined **Table of Contents** will show that the accounts are neither perfect nor continuous, nor arranged in time. The paging is that of the original MS.

	Date.	Page in MS.		Date.	Page in MS.
Inventory	1508	1–4	Competus of Wm. Woky,		
Competus of Wm. Knoll	1508	5–8	14 Hen. VII, A.D.	1498–9	27
,, Wm. Vowles	1509	9–11	,, Thos. Schetes,		
,, John Capell	1510	12–14	15 Hen. VII	1499–1500	29
,, Thomas Cawndeler	1507	15–16	,, John Canard	1514	32
,, John Browsse, of			,, Thos. Ede	1515	34–5
Compton	1511	17–19	,, John Wilkins	1516	36–7
,, John Browsse, of			,, Wm. Tokar	1517	39–40
Pilton[1]	1512	22	,, John Holder	15[18]	42–4
,, the Wardens of the			Note of Receipt by Mathew		
Key for 3 years dateless		24	Trym of the balance of his		
Inventory of "goods longyng to			predecessor, John Lane		
Wardyngs," xv of H. VII, *i.e.*, 1499–1500			Warden in 1519	1520	45
List of the Key Wardens, Townsend and Dore, May 1	1507	25	Competus of Will. Sargeant	1521	47–50
List of Debts owing to Church	1507		,, Will. Vowllys	1523	51–3
A remembrance (Inventory) of			,, Wm. Lamman	1525	55
ornaments Our Lady's		26	,, Rob. Herris and		
Wardens, xv of Hen. VII	1499–1500		Walter Bayle	1530	56
List of rings	1503		In 1522 Wm. Canard was Warden, in 1524 John Rogers, but their accounts have perished.		

---

[1] Succeeded by John Watts, whose account is lost.

[1]Inventorium omnium bonorum ecclesie parochialis Sti Johannis Baptiste de pulton factum p Willelm. Jones vicarium eiusdem ecclesie et pochianos tempore Willelmi Knoll gardiani vicesimo quinto die mensis Aprilis die Sti Marcii. Anno Dni millesimo quingentesimo septimo[2] et anno Henrici septimi vicesimo[3] [the year has been altered by a later reviser's hand to "xliiij[4] of Hen. VIII,"[5] and a note added. viz.] V nobiles ad Stum Jacobum.

Fyrste iij Crosses one of Copyr and gylte with Mary and John and a staffe of copyr and gylte.
Item ij other Crosses of tree and sylvered uppon.
Item a pyxte of sylver to bere yn the sacrament.
Item ij sylver candelstikes.
Item iij chalys one gylte weying . . . [blank].
Item one littel chalys half gylte weying . . .
Item one chalys parcell gylte, weying . . .
Item one stonding maser to serve for Brydes at theyr weddyng, weying . . .
Item one paxbrede of sylver parcell gylte of the gyfte of William Mowett and Alis is wiff weying . . .
Item Rynges sylver and gylte xxxiij and viij besyds our lady mantell and xiij in the mantell with saynte James schell of sylver and other broches.
Item ij Clappesys of silver that was uppon the ordinal.
Item a maser off the border sylver and gylte ye gyft of Walter Sargent.
Item for ij Rynges one ye bequeste of Anys Symond.
Item ffor a nother off the quest of Alyss of quortt.
. . . of ppull sylke harnes wt. sylver. vacat.[6]
. . . of . . . Capell of   Pennard by quest of William dere for x*s*.   vacat.
of . . . of . . Calowe ys biqueste of sylver and gylte. vacat.
              Itm. Ryngs iiij.
              Sma. of Ryngs, xxxiij xxx [erased].

ffyrste a hole sewte of Pleyne damaske of the biqueste of Walt. Wry wt. a cope of whyte and hanckyngs for the hyght aut [er].
Itm. a hole sewte of grene wt. a cope.

---

[1] The heading and the whole list has undergone at least two revisions and two checkings of the inventory.
[2] Altered to xxxix as if to make it 1539 Ap. 25, 1539 = 31 Hen. VIII.
[3] Altered to octavi followed by something illegible, probably at first scdō.   April 25, 1507 = 22 Hen. VII.
[4] Belongs probably to date as last altered, 1544.
[5] The King having died in his 38th regnal year, this was a scribe's error.
[6] *I.e.*, the article was dropped from the inventory.

Itm. a westement of grene wellwett of John Wry is biquest.
Itm. a westement of blewe damaske of Edm. Selepark biquest.
Itm. a westement of whyte wt. skalloppeys schells.
and ij Chesabylls of whyte and sylver of the biquest of panys.
Itm. a westement of . . . and grene of Ser Thomas Wade biquest.
Itm. a westement of whyte of doctor Sugar[1] biquest.
Itm. a westement of (whyte) for lent.
Itm. a westement of blacke.
Itm. a westement of flowerey saten of master Thomas Bolen[2] bequest.
Item a grene westemente of grene.
Item a worse westemente of grene.
Item a westement of grene of ser Johan Wullners biqueste.
Item a cope of redde wt. grene bawderyck.
Item a cope of grene.
Item a hangkyng of whyte damaske branched wt. flowres and ij Curtene of whyte Sarton of the gyfte of Agnes Rickeland and a hangkyng for the aut of whyte sylke sett wt. flowres browdered and a crucifixe in the mydde of the gyfte of my lorde Edmund (?) channl of Wells.
Item a cope of redde velvet IHS.
Item a peace of westement of redde welvet with bere.
Item on hanerykyng with ij curtens steyned of the gift of John W———
Item on hangyng for the high auter of saynte Johan Baptist and saynte Johan Evangelyste.
Item iij stenyed clothes at saynt Kateryn and saynt Nicholas auter.
Item a canype steyned to hold over the sacrament Corpus Christi ys day.
Item iij baner clothes of sylke steyned with our Lady and saynt Johan Baptist and the signes of the passyon.
Item ij other baner clothes of sylke of the gyfte of Alys Volks.
Item a mantell of purpull wellwent and parseled with black wellwent of John.
Item a mantell of blew wellwent for our lady at the Wante [font ?].
Item a palle, Item ij other baner clothes of cloth and ij other steyned clothes, one of saynt Katyn and others.

The bokes of ye Churche
- Fyrste a masse boke of master Thomas Bolen bequest.
- Item a masse boke prynted. Item ij baner clothes of ye pascion.
- Item ij old massebokes. Item a pillo of purpyll velvett.
- Item a grayle noted.
- Item a prosessionary covered with blacke
- Item iiij prosessionaries prynted.
- Item a quayer of the newe feste notyd
- Item a manuel boke. Item a manel boke prynted.
- Item an ordinall and a festivall.
- Item an old portuas and ij old antiphoners.
- Item . . of other olde bokes.
- Item and ij new bokes—a manuel boke
- Item a grett portuas of prynte.

[1] One of Bp. Beckington's executors. [2] Precentor, 1451-1471

Item iiij Serples.
Item auter clothes, iij of Johan Wardeford bequeste.
Item xxxij Kercheffes grete and smale for images.
Item a clothe for the sepulcre steyned.
Item steyned clothes for lent steyned wyth the signes of ye pascion.
Item a kerchoff of John Howder.
Item iiij Auter clothys and ij Kerchoffs.
Item vj erds of redde saye and vj of grene.
Item iij corporas casse of velvett.

Firste a grete brasse pott, of John Warde biqueste.
Item six other brasse pots and iiij pannys.
Item viij tabyll clothes.
Item j basen and j laver of laten.
Item a pollyse of iron and ij polys [pulleys] of brass nowe beying at Pyll.
Item a slegge to breke stones at the quarey.
Item a bollte of iron and grete crokes and a chayne of iron.
Item a payer of vestymenttes of whyt of the bequeste of Willyam Fowllys ye wyche is of whyt Damaske.
Item a payer ot Vestymentes of Rede Velvett of the bequeste of my lorde of Glastynbery.
Item xxj polle of puter vessell.
Item iij brochys and brondeyron.
Item iij sponys of silver of the gift of Wat. Sargent.
Item j spone . . . Johan Geteven.
Item j spone . . . Agnes.
Item an oyle vatte of sylver.
Item j lytell boxe of silver and gelt of master Chanter bequest, of doctor Pirsse[1] byquest.
Item vj spones of John Holder bequest.
And a maser with a bande of silver a pere of bedes of jete with xij gaudes of sylver.
Item a

[The next entries are scribblings on a page left blank between Warden Knoll's receipts and payments. The first entry states the number of Rings in stock in 1500. It recurs below. The numbers and dates are confused by repeated alterations, which mar the value of the record.]

The Some of Rynges in the ere of our Lord Gode mccccc [xxli, xli][2] and a crusifix.
Item [i]ij[2] Rynges.
Item the recept of Rynges yn my yere.
Firste receved of Issabel Hayne bequeste j rynge.
Item receved of Margarete Coke ys bequest ij rynges.
Item receved of Johan Calowe ys bequeste j rynge and saynt James schell.

---

[1] Dr. Pyers. Precentor, 1513-1535. [2] Evidently altered from time to time.

Item receved of Alys Trynme ys bequeste j rynge.
"   "   Margery Danyell   "   j rynge.
"   "   Alys Torner   "   j rynge.
"   "   Johan Barett   "   j rynge.
Item John Kanerde a cowe the geft of John Brok p'ci [price] the cow—xjs. viijd. the hyre xxd.
The summe of rynges in the ere of our Lord Gode mcccccxxxix, xxv and a crusifix.
Item a gerdyll with vj stodes of silver with a bokyll and a pendend of sylver of the geft of angnis [Agnes] Bokeland.
Itm one spruc.

Competus Willm. Knoll gardiani ecclesie pochialis Sti Johannis Baptiste die Sti Marcii die Mensis Aprilis Anno Dni millesimo quingentesimo octavo.

Fyrst Receved of Wm. Champyon for Thomas Chaundeler		vli. xs. viijd.
Item Receved of Willyam Townysende and John Dore for Key Whyt[1]		ixs. vd.
Item receved of Willyam Tucky		vjs. viijd.
Item receved of Estyr Ly3ght		xvjs.
" " Wotton for Estyr Ly3ght		vs.
" " Johan Brousse		vjs. viijd.
" " Willyam Mylleward		ijs.
" " Willyam Dore the elder		viijd.
" " John Wattes		vs.
" " Thomas Chaundelere		iijs. iiijd.
" " John Brousse of Compton		vjs.
" " John Elyns		iiijs. vjd.
" " Alys Tornere		iiijs. iiijd.
" " Walter Sergeant the elder		xiiijs.
" " Richart Sergeant		ijs. iiijd.
" " Richard Mylleward		vjd.
" " John Wrye		xxd.
" " Wyllyam Mere		xijd.
" " Margerete Wallter ys byqueste		xxd.
" " Ric. Mylleward ys biqueste		xijd.
" " Agnes Natteley ys biqueste		viijd.
" " John Smyth and Johan Canard our lady wardens		lvjs. ixd.
Item Receved of Wm. Dyke		iiijs. vjd.
" " for the Sepulture of John Dore		vjs. viijd.
" " of the biquest of John Man		xijd.
Item receved of the parish gathering for the coueryng of the rode lo3ffte		viijs. ijd.
Sm. xiijli. xiiijs. viijd.		

[1] Before the commutation of tithe, 1835, "Cow-white" was the customary term for the fixed payment, or modus, due to the Vicar in lieu of the tenth of milk. In this case the sum paid by the Cow-Wardens must have been the yield of the milk of their Herd. See their account, p. 64, to the Warden for the benefit of the Church.

Competus Willmi Knoll gardiani ecclesie pochialis Sti Johanis Baptiste de Pulton A° Dni millesimo quingentesimo octavo. Soluciones eiusdem Willam Knoll in singulis.

First payed and delivered to John Smy3th and John Canard our lady wardens	xxs.
Item payed to dd. [David] Jonys the peynter of the Rode lo3the the xijth of aprile	xxvjs. viijd.
Item to Wyllyam Ffeyzand sunt [servant] of the sayed dd. on saynt Marke ys day	xiijs. iiijd
Item payed on saynt Marke ys day to the vicar, the clerke, and the ringes for Dyryge of the Benefactours of the chyrche	viijd.
Item payed for di on [half one] qyer of papyr and di for the boke of a compt	iiijd.
Item for waxe and makyng of Trendell	ijs. iiijd.
Item for vij lbs. of waxe and makyng of the same waxe at Estyr	iijs. viijd. ob.
Item for skowryng of the Candillstykes	iiijd.
Item payed to John Foreste, smyth for yron werke for ye Rode lo3fte	ijs. vd.
Item payed to dd. Jonys peynter at divse tymes for hys coste	xd.
Item payed to hym that brow3th a brason pott fro Balysborowe	iijd.
Itm. for wex and of ij tapers agenst the dedicasyon	vijs. ob.
Itm. payed to the clerke of Saynt John ys fraternyte	xd.
Itm. payed to dd. Jonys peynter the day of the feste of Saynt Petyr and Paule	iijli. vjs. viijd.
Item for a lowans of badde grotes cryppe[1]	iijs. ijd.
Item Reckshokes and gret pynnys for the Auters	jd.
Item for Reparacyons of the Bawdryckes of the bellys	iiijd.
Item for the reparacyons of the Churchhey gates	iijd.
Item payed to the peynters	xiijs. iiijd.
Item payed to Edward Holdyn for the peynters tabyll	vs.
Item payed to the plumere	vjs. viijd.
Itm. for my labor on[e] day	iijd.
Item for the mowyng of the churche hey	iiijd.
Item payed to the peynters	xxvjs. viijd.
,, ,, ,,	xlviijs. jd.
Item payed to the clerke for his ernest peny	jd.
Item payed for the makyng of saynt Nicholas ys staffe	jd.
Item payed for the makyng of a tapere	jd.
. . . . makyng of ij tapers agenste the feste of the Nat. of Cryste	xd. ob.
Item payed for xij ellys of lenyn clothe for the Rode lo3fte	vijs. vijd.
Item for lynes and rynges for the sayed clothe	vijd.
Item for waschyng of the churche clothes	xvjd.
. wrytyng of myne a compte	viijd.

Sm. xiijli. iijs. vd. ob.
Reste to the churche clere   xvjs. viijd. ob.

---

[1] Used again in p. 60 = clipped coin.

Competus Willm Wowlys gardiani ecclesie pochialis sti Johannis Baptiste de Pullton in die Sti Marcii Evangeliste A° Dni millesimo quingentesimo nono et anno Henrici Octavi p'mo.

RECEPT.

Firste received of on Estir Day	. . . . . .	xvjs. jd.
Item R. of Willyam Knoll	. . . . . .	xvjs. viijd.
,, John Holler	. . . .	xxxs.
,, Herbert Kerver	. . . .	xs.
,, yong men lyght	. . . . . .	iiijs. vijd.
,, the bequestse of John Deran ys dowter	. . . .	xijd.
,, ,, Thomas Townisende	. . . .	vjd.
,, ,, John Rede	. . . . .	iiijd.
,, for a peyr of bedes of the biqueste of John Hollere ys wyff.		
Item of Wotton Estyre lyght.		
,, R. for a peyr of bedys geete	. . . . .	viijd.
,, R. of the biquest of Johan Denam	. . . .	xijd.
,, R. of Thomas Schepard	. . . . .	ixs. iij½d.
,, R. of John Brusse and John Ragg	. . .	vjs.
,, R. of Robert Kerver	. . . . . .	xxs.

DETT.

John Browsse and John Ragg	. . . . .	vjs.
Robert Kerver	. . . .	xxs.
Wm. Stewyns	. . . .	xxxs.
Item for viij yere j cowe	. . . . .	viijs.
. . . John Bigoy	. . . . . .	iijs. ivd.
Sum tot. recep	. . . . .	vjli. xjs. vijd. ob.

Solluciones ejusdem Willm Gardiani.

EXPENSE.

First payed for viij lbs. wax agenst Estir	. . . . .	iiijs.
Item the makyng	. . . .	ijd.
Item delyved to John Holler, our lady Warden	. . . .	xs.
Item for Dyryge Messe for ye benfactors on saynt Marke is day	. .	viijd.
Item for Waschyng or Whytyng of the church	. . . .	vijs.
Item for lyme and pargyttyng	. . . . . .	xviijd.
,, for a paylo	. . . .	iiijd.
Item payed to John Wardeford for pargyttyng of the tour and stoppynt of the skaffold holys	. . . .	iiijd.
Item for on yron for the ledde at saynt Mary housse xv li. di [15½ lb.]	.	xijd.
It. a putteful of erth	. . . .	iijd.
It. j lb. of waxe to renewe the p'ket' [pricket] agenst Wittsonday and the makyng		viijd.

Item for skowryng of the Candellstyckes	iiij*d*.
Item for mowyng of the chirchyard	iiij*d*.
„ wax for the trendell and makyng	ij*s*. vj*d*.
„ wax and makyng of ij tapers	ix*d*.
„ „ „ at ye Dedicacyon	xiiij*d*.
Item for ij newe bele ropys	xv*d*.
„ mendyng of Beer [bier]	ij*d*.
Item delivered to Robert Kerver	x*s*.
„ „ Willm. Sergeant and John Canard	xl*s*.
Item for wex and makyng of ij tapers agenst the Feste of the Nat. of Cryste	xiiij*d*.
Item lether and reparacyon of ye bawderickes	vj*d*.
Item for oyle for the bellys	ij*d*.
Item the plummer and sawder	viij*d*.
Item payed to proctour of saynt John is fraternite	x*d*.
Item payed to Thomas Man for a Riage [arrearage] of a compe of a more sum for saynt Mary house	vj*s*. viij*d*.
Item for waschyng of the churche clothes	xvj*d*.
Item for mendyng of the cope	ij*d*
Item for wrytyng and makyng of the boke of a compte	viij*d*.
Sm. iiij*li*. xiiij*s*. viij*d*.	
Reste to the church clere	xxxvj*s*. xj*d*. ob.

The Recept of John Capell.

Competus Johannis Capell XXV° die Mensis Aprilis Anno Dni millesimo quingentesimo decimo et Anno p'mo Henrici octavi.

Firste of Wyllyam Wowlys Warden next by for hym in money the daye of a compte	xxxvj*s*. xj*d*. ob.
Item receved of Estyr ly3ghte of Pyllton Estyr Day	xvj*s*. iiij*d*.
Item receved of the biqueste of John Brederyppe of Pylle	xij*d*.
Item receved of John Deverell and Wm. Rug, Wardens of Wotton	v*s*.
Item from Wyllyam Sergeant and John Canard saynt Mary Wardens	lv*s*. vj*d*.
Item for Issabell Man for hokelyng ly3ghte	ij*d*.
Item of John Forest for his mother bequest	xij*d*. and a ryng.
Item receved of Richard Merke ys bequest	xx vij lbs. of ledde.
Sm. v*li*. xvij*s*. ix*d*. ob.	

The costes of the same yere above rchersyd.

Fyrste payed to John Sergeant	vj*s*. viij*d*.
Item payed to Richard Shete	iiij*d*.
Item for viij lb. wexe agenst Estyr Day, the Paschall want [font] tap and ij tapers	iv*s*. viij*d*.
Item for dyryge messe for the benefactors on saynte Marke is day	viij*d*.
Item for a rope for the Trendell	ix*d*.
Item for a key for the cofyrs that Wm. Schepard gave	ij*d*.

Item for waxe and makyng of iiij tapers the dedicacyon day	ijs. iiijd. ob.
Item payed to the plumber, sawder, and his labour. .	ijs. vjd.
Item a laborer to serve hym	vjd.
Item for a plancke to rayse the ledde . . .	ijd
Item for skowryng of the Candellstyckes . . .	iiijd.
Item for iij newe belle ropys	xxjd.
Item for mowyng of the churcheyard . . .	iiijd.
Item payed to the pcto. [proctor] of saynt John ys fraternite	xd.
Item for a new lantern	vijd
Item for a locke for the towr door . . .	ijd.
Item for a newe spade and showell . . .	xijd.
Item for sope and waschyng of the Corporas . .	ijd.
Item for lynes for lente clothes	vjd.
Item for reparyng of beer	ijd.
Item for oylying of the bellys	ijd.
Item for reparying of the bawderyckes . . .	iiijd.
Item for iij lb. of wexe and makynge of iiij tapers agenst Nat. Di.	xxjd. ob.
Item for makyng of a newe gate yn the Churchyard, bordes, tymbir and ij lode stones	xxiijd. ob.
Item for settyng of free stones that John Wardeford gave . . .	jd.
Item for waschying of the churche clothes and ye kercheff of ye canepy . .	xvijd.
Item for wrytyng of the a compte	xijd.

Sm. xxxjs. iijd. ob.

Rest to the Church clere . . . . iijli. xvijs. ijd.

The Dettes that remayneth the said yere.

Fyrste Wyllyam stevyns for iij key . .	xxxs.
Item for the heyr of the key	viijd.
Item John Elyns for hokelyng a yere and a half.	
Item John Baron	iijs. iiijd.
Item the Vicar that Wyllyam Champyon for	xd.
Item Thomas Sergeant and John Paty wardens of the hyghe crosse lyght	iijs. iiijd.
Item Wyllyam Wowlys for hys ere for Wotton.	
The Rynges John Capel ys Dayer.[1]	

Sm. of all the rynges v., vij. [*i.e.*, 127.]

Item a rynge Johan Wardeford.
Md. that Tomas Sergeant oweth to ye cyrch . . . xiiijd.

---

[1] *I.e.*, Dairyman.

Competus Thomæ Cawndeler factus in die Sti Marcii XXV° die Mensis Aprilis Anno Dni millesimo quingentesimo septimo, et Anno Regni Regis Henrici septimi vicesimo secundo vel[1] 3°.

THE RECEPT.

Fyrste receved of Estyr lyghte Ester Day	xvj*s.* viij*d.*
Item receved of Wotton for Ester lyghte	v*s.*
Item for yong men lyght	iiij*s.* iiij*d.*
Item for one peyr of Bedys	viij*d.*
Item receved of Wyllyam Champyon	lix*s.* x*d.*
Item receved of our Lady wardens John Wylkyns and John Man	iij*li.* vj*s.* viij*d.*
Sm. tot Recepcois vij*li.* xiij*s.* ij*d.*	

IN ANNO REGNI REGIS xxiiij [later hand].

Item in rynges sylver and gylt xxvj.
   j wt. a crusifix.
Item on rynge.

Followeth the costes of the sayed Cawndeler churche-warden of Pulton the yei moneth and daye afore wrytte

Fyrst for making of Estur lyght	iiij*s.* xj*d.*
Item for saynt John is lyght	iij*s.* iij*d.*
Item for makyng of the lyght at the Nat. of Criste	xiiij*d.*
Item payed to saynt [John] ys fraternite	x*d.*
Item payed on saynt Marke ys day for dirige and messe for the benefactors of the Churche	vj*d.*
Item for waschyng of churche kercheffes	v*d.* ob.
Item for makyng of a newe gate agen churchchey	ij*s.* iiij*d.*
Item for mendyng of the howsyng over the crucifixe	viij*d.*
Item for mendyng of the ber and the skaffold	xx*d.*
Item for one lyne for the canapy and naylys	ij*d.*
Item payed to the plumer	xvj*d.*
Item for my labour with the plumer and the schaffold	vj*d.*
Item delivered to Wyllyam Townesende	x*s.*
Item to Richard Sergeant for pavyng of the tour	ij*s.* ij*d.*
Item for waschyng	xij*d.*
Item for makyng of the churchhey gate, nayles, and j barr	xiiij*d.*
Item for the yer of Ric. Sergeant for saynt John is fraternite	x*d.*
Item for mendyng of the baner clothe of our lady	iiij*d.*
Item for skowryng of the candelstyckes	iiij*d.*
Item for mowyng of the churchhey	ij*d.*
Item delivered to the Vicar and Wyllyam Vowlys yn crypped grotes	xj*s.*

[1] In spite of the endeavours of later hands to correct the original error, the true date of this Audit must remain unsettled. The XXIInd year of Hen. VII, ran from Aug. 22, 1506, to Aug. 21, 1507.

Item a lowans for Robert Herdewyke and William for they w^t hold Estyr lyghte	iiij*d*.
Item for blessyng of ij corporas and j auter clothe	ij*d*.
Item Wyllyam Mylleward w^t hold frome	ij*s*.
Item for the Ryngers on saynt Marke is day	ij*d*.

Sm. total xliij*s*.

Et sic remanet clere ecclesiæ . . . . v*li*. xvj*s*. ij*d*.

Competus Johannis Brousse gardiani ecclesie pochialis de Pullton, in die Sti Marci, Evangelist. A° Dni millesimo quingentesimo xj°.

Recept ejusdem gardiani.

Fyrst Receved on Estyr day for the hy crosse lyght	xv*s*. x*d*.
Item receved of the wardens of Wotton	iiij*s*. viij*d*.
Item receved of John Cabell of the Church stocke	iij*l*. xvj*s*. ij*d*.
Item receved of Thomas Sergeant and John Style lady wardens	xlvij*s*. iij*d*.
Item receved of John Broderyppe and Wyllyam dore our lady ly3gth	viij*s*. ij*d*.
Item receved of John More and William Wowlys	v*s*. j*d*.
. . receved of John Wardeforde ys bequest	viij*d*.
. . . . . . Johan Wardeforde ys	iiij*d*.
. . . . . . John Wry ys bequest	xiij*s*. iiij*d*
Sm. . . . . . viij*li*. xj*s*. v*d*. ob.	

Item the coste of the clocke this same yere content and payed and performed bi the vicar Wyllyam Jonys and the parishioners . . . . . iiij*li*. viij*s*. viij*d*. out of the warden ys a compte part.

The dettes [*i.e.*, Arrears due] belongyng to the Churche of Pullton over the a compte of the sayed John Brousse, of Compton, and be longyng to John Brousse over his a compte.

Wyllyam Stevyns for iij Key	xxx*s*.
Item for the hyr of the sayed Key	viij*s*.
Item John Elyns for hokelyng lyght his part with John Man.	
Item Thomas Sergeant and John Paty	iiij*s*. iiij*d*.
Item Robert Kerver	x*s*.
Item Johan Brousse	xviij*d*.

Item the hy crosse lyghte of Wotton, Thomas Grene and Thomas Cleament wardens.
Item of the l:y crosse lyghte part behynd in the yer of John Brousse of Compton.

The Costys of the sayed John Brousse.

Fyrste for Estyr ly3th	v*s*. vj*d*.
Item for the dyryge for the benefactours on saynt Marke ys day	viij*d*.
Item for mendyng of the clepers of the bellys	iiij*s*.
Item for mendyng of the shorpells [surplices]	iiij*d*.
Item for the skowryng of the Candellstyck	iiij*d*.

Item for makyng of the benche on the sou3th side of the chirche and stares [stairs] .	iiij*s*.
Item for ij tapers agenst trinyte tide	xx*d*.
. . . . the dedicacyon day	xx*d*.
Item payd to the clerke of saynt [John] ys fraternite	x*d*.
Item for mowyng of the churchyard	iiij*d*.
Item for casting of ij new smale bellys	ij*s*.
Item for ij tapers at ye feste of ye Nativite of Criste	xviij*d*.
Item for ij quarters of lyme	viij*d*.
Item for the new handyng of the bellys	ij*s*. vj*d*.
Item for makyng of the trendyll	ij*s*. x*d*.
Item for makyng of the bawdryckes and gressyng	vj*d*.
Item for waschyng of the chyrche ornaments	xvj*d*.
Item for the smyth for mendyng of the clocke .	iiij*d*.
Item for vyre and mendyng of the hamer	x*d*.
Item for the warnyng bell and iiij polysse	ij*s*. viij*d*.
Item for ij ropys for the grete peysse and the lytyll peysse[1]	xviij*d*.
Item for a peyc of . . . . . and iij bordes	xvj*d*.
Item for nayles and tockynge gyrdell	v*d*.
Item for a locke	iiij*d*.
Item for castyng of the peyses and makyng of the dore	vij*d*.
Item for John Browsse for vij days yn the chyrche worke and poyntyng of the logge .	ij*s*.
Item for Ric. Shete for Rydyng of the chyryard	iiij*d*.
Item for wrytyng of the boke a compte	viij*d*.
Sm. . . . . . . xlij*s*. vij*d*.	
Sic restat clere ecclesiæ de Pollton supra debita . . . . et remanet in manus John Browsse de Pullton gardiani.	vj*li*. ij*s*. iiij*d*.

Et supra competum predictum remanet ecclesie omnia debita ut supra, et de illis qui sunt a retro p. luminibus alte crucis annorum Johannis Brousse de Compton et Johannis Brousse de Pyllton.

Numerus annulorum v. viij. [*i.e.*, 108] præter annulum Johanne Brousse nuper defunctæ.

Item the increse of the churche Key of Pulton in the yere of Ric. Sergeand and

---

Numerus vaccarum et in quorum manibus sunt vaccæ et nomina de plegge vaccarum.

Johes Shepart of Compton receve plegge for a cowe for John Shepart of Benagre his son . . . . x*s*.

---

[1] Peysse = Clock Weight.

Item a boxe with a xj dedys wrytynge.
Item the encrese of rynges to the church in the yere of John Canard and John Sargeant . . . . xxvj.

Competus Johannis Brousse de Pullton gardiani ecclesie pochialis Sti Johannis Baptiste xiij die mensis Maie die Sti Marci Evang. anno Regni regis Henrici octavi tertio.

RECEPCIONES EJUSDEM JOHIS BROUSSE CUM DEBITIS.

Fyrste receved of John Brousse of Compton late warden	vj*li*. xl*d*.
Item rec. on Estyr Day in Pullton is Cherche for heyth crosse light . .	xv*s*. iiij*d*.
Item rec. of John Ede and John Burford our lady Wardens encresse . .	xlv*s*. viij*d*.
Item rec. of John Galantonn and Thomas Collys wardens of the cherche of Wotton	
	iiij*s*. viij*d*.
Item rec. of the bequeste of Johan Brousse of Pulltonn	. xviij*d*.
Sm. . . . . . . ix*li*. x*s*. vj*d*.	

The costys of the sayed John Brousse, Warden.

Fyrst payed for Estir lyght wex and makyng	iij*s*. v*d*.
Item for dyryge and masse on saynt Marke is day for the benefactours . .	. viij*d*.
Item for waschyng of the corporas and sope	. ij*d*.
Item for a bokyll for a bawderike	. ij*d*.
Item for ij newe bawdericks	. xiiij*d*.
Item for iiij tapyrs agenste the feste of saynt John Bapt^e	. xvij*d*.
Item paied to the proctor of saynt John Bapt^e fraternite	. x*d*.
Item paied to ye glasyere	. xvij*d*.
Item for wexe and makyng of iiij tapyrs agenste dedicacyon day . .	ij*s*. ij*d*.
Item paied to John Horsley parisch clerke for kepyng of the clocke . .	. xl*d*.
Item for skowryng of ye grete candellstick	iiij*d*.
Item for mowyng of ye chercheyard	iiij*d*.
Item for a new processionary printed	. xvj*d*.
Item in expensis to Wells to bey the boke	ij*d*.
Item for viij ells of lenyng cloth for a surpeles for the Vicar . .	. vj*s*.
Item for makyng of the surpeles	iij*s*. j*d*.
Item for v yards of lenyn clothe and makyng of a surpeles for ye clerke . .	. xx*d*.
Item for waxe and makyng of iiij tapyrs agenste the feste of the Nativite of Criste	. iij*s*. j*d*.
Item for gresyng of the bellys	j*d*.
Item for waschyng of the chyrche clothes	. xvj*d*.
Item for wrytyng of the a compte	. xij*d*.
Sm. . . . . . . xxxiij*s*. ij*d*.	

The costes of Saynte Mary house now Reparying.

Item paied to John Sergeant, John Brousse and William Knoll	xxs. iijd.
Item for lathe and nayle	. vjd.
Item for ij.c [= 200] lathes	. xxd.
Item for cariage of iij lode tymbyr	iijs. vd.
Item for stones and caryage	. xixd.
Item iij.c rede[1] [300 bundles of reed]	ijs. iiijd.
Item j.c rede of Margyry Wry	. xxijd.
Item iij.c rede of William Wowle	ijs. iijd.
Item ij.c rede of the Vicar	. xijd.
Item Philippe Gele for drawyng of lead	. vjd.
Item for helpe to sett the tymper	. xixd.
Item for castyng of the ledde	ijs. iijd.
Sm. . . . . . . xxxixs. iijd.	
Sm. tot. Reparacionis . . . iij*li*. xijs. iijd.	
Sm. tot. Recepcionis . . . ix*li*. xs. vjd.	
Alloc. [Allocatur, there is allowed] pro reparacionibus . . iij*li*. xijs. iijd.	
Sic remanet clare supra onera ecclie de Pullton	v*li*. vjs. viijd.
Præter debita quæ sequuntur singulis nominibus cum debitis.	
Willm Stevyns pro 3 bus waccis [vaccis]	. xxxs.
Item pro redditu illarum vaccarum	. viijs
Item John Elyns for hoggelyng lyght	. ijs.
Item Thomas Sergeant John Paty wardens of the hygh crosse lyght . .	. xiiijd.
Item John Pennard and John Donkurton	vs. ijd.
Item Thomas Grene of Wotton and Thomas Clement for hyghe crosse lyght.	
Item Christian Kelly the bequeste of Water Kelly her husbant for his sepullture	vjs. viijd.

Ric. Sergeant and Willyam Canard, Wardens of the churche Key, the a compte for iij yers.

Firste for the hyr of vj key ij ere . . .	xijs.
of this sm. provided a cowe more except vd. ob.	
Item for the iij yer the hire of the key	vjs.
over all charges remaneth to the chirche stocke . .	iiijs.

The names of them that hath the key to hyr wt. ther borows and plegge.
 Fyrste John Elyns j cowe.
 Item William Canard of Estn [*i.e.*, Eastern] Compton j cowe plegge John Canard.
 Item Johan Knoll a cowe plegge Johan pennard.
 Item John Dunkerton a cowe plegge Johan Baron.
 Item Johan Brousse of Pulton a cowe plegge Ric. Sergeant.
 Wyllyam Knoll a cowe plegge Wyllam Canard.
 Stephans Aylwarde for a cowe, plege Wylelm Aylwarde at Crosse.
 John Tounysende of Westcompton a cowe plege Edwarde Holdson.
 Itm. Rob. Stoke a cowe precio xiijs. iiijd. plege John Mog John Wardeford.

[1] Straw unthreshed and prepared by bleaching for the thatcher.

[A parchment leaf, the 2nd half of the Sheet wh. begins the Book.]

Anno Regni regis Henrici Sept. xv. [A.D. 1499.]

A remembrans off the chyrche gods longyng to the wardyngs,[1] fyrst a sewte of blew damaske branchyde of Wat. Frys byquest wt. a kope to the same.

secunde a sewte of grene wt. a kope too the same.

Itm. a blew westmente off Chris [*i.e.*, Christopher] Paddocke byqueste.

Md. of the Kye and the encresse the fyrste day of the moneth of may the yere of our Lord God mccccvij, Wyllyam Townsende and John Dere, Wardens.

Fyrste for vj Key ij yeres	xij*s.*
Alloc. for the makyng of the sepultur taper	ij*s.* ix*d.*
Rests clere to the chirche	ix*s.* v*d.*
Delyvered to William Knoll[2]. [See p. 54]	ix*s.* v*d.*
Remanet in the handes of John Baron	iij*s.* x*d.*

A remembrance of the chirche dettys the firste day of the moneth may, Aº Dni millesimo quingentesimo septimo.

Fyrste John Browse	vij*s.*	Item William Fenor	viij*d.*
Item William Tucky	vj*s.* viij*d.*	„ John Ewan	iiij*s.* vj*d.*
„ Alys Torner	iiij*s.* iiij*d.*	„ William Mylleward the yonger	ij*s.*
„ Johan Brousse	vj*s.* viij*d.*	„ William Dyke	vj*s.* vj*d.*
„ Walter Sergeant the yelder	xvj*s.*	„ Thomas Chaundeler	iij*s.* iiij*d.*
„ John Elyns	ij*s.* ix*d.*		
Sm. Tot.		iij*li.* v*d.*	
Item Willyam Stevyns			xxx*s.*

Anno Regis Henrycy the Sevynth, xv.

A remembrance for our ladys mantell wt other thynges longing to the same wardyns fyrst the mantell selfe off vellett.

Item yn the same mantell off rynges xiiij a flate ryge and square.

Item iij schellys of seynt Jame.

Item iij brochys off kyng henry and one lytyll broche.

Item a peyr of bedes off ambur wt gette gaydys.

Item a peyr of gette bedes off Margaret Martyn byquest.

yn the same bedes owte off the mantell.

Item one peyr off gette bedys off Jo. Smyth byquest.

Item another bedys off gette of Johan Hallere bequest.

---

[1] This very small stock must have belonged, not to the parish but to Our Lady's Wardens.

[2] To the High Warden for the High Light. In 1548, three cows, the remnant of this herd, were seized for the King on the ground of their being given for maintenance of the High Light in the Church. The hire, *i.e.*, rent paid by the dairyman for the cows' milk was 2*s.* per annum.

Item a peyr of bede of gette wt gawdes wt a buckell of silver.
Item a peyr of lanbur [amber] bedys off Margaret Spycer byquest to o^r lady yn the quer.
Item a kercow off alson borford byquest and a zetter.
Item a kercow and a quetyn [? cushion].

Md. the sum off ryngs yn the streng amowntthyth to lxxxviij [added afterwards] wt other yn the mantell, the nomber lxxxviij [with 3 more added in a later hand].
Item a kerchow to yor lady off goody sergentes by quest. ⎫ An° Dni
Item off Margaret Maners by quest a nother kerchow.   ⎬ M^{lo} v^c iij°.
Item iij mo off others by questes.   ⎭

Thys boke made xxviij day off Aprill in the xiiij yere of oure soverayne lord Kynge Henry the VIJth [*i.e.*, 1498-9] and ordayne(d) to the chyrche off Pylton for a remembrance of all such goodes as long therto and to make & tytyll atrew acownttys off all wardens ther withyn and all other things that encresse to the same.

To his acowntts cumythe Wyllm. Woky, off Ham, being wardyne yn xiij yere off Kyng Henry the VIJ, and by for the pryste maketh hys acowunte for the yere above rehersyd yn thys forme folowynge.

Fyrst resevyd off Water Sergeant the younger, wardyne next by fore hym yn money . . . . vij*li*. ij*s*. ob.
Allso leyd to the same reseyte to be levyd at thys hys acownttes ij detters.
Water sergente the elder . . . . v*s*.
Wyllyam Tutky . . . . vj*s*. viij*d*.
Item Rec. for Estyr ly3t off Pylton . . . . xvj*s*. iiij*d*.
  ,,   ,,   ,,   Wotton . . . . v*s*. ix*d*.
Item rec. for my lady Mayow of Croscombe off by queste . . . . xij*s*.
Item rec. off Wyllyam Dore off by quest a heffer, p'co . . . . v*s*. viij*d*.
Item rec. off old Brusse wyffe . . . . vj*s*. viij*d*.
Item rec. of the younger Knolle and Wyllyam Fowlys mane for young men ly3th iij*s*. v*d*.
Item rec. for scaffold tymber off . . . . xiij*d*.
Item rec. of Water Sergent younger for scaffold tymber . . . . iij*d*.
Item receved of hoglyng money of our lady wardens . . . . . vj*s*.
Item receved of rente for the lede . . . . xx*d*.
Item receved of our lady wardens . . . . iiij marks, iiij*s*.
Item receved of chyrche rente . . . . xviij*d*.

Sm. totalis Rec. xiiij*li*. xix*s*.

Md. for coste yn the same yere a bove rehersyd.

Fyrste for vij li waxe at Ester	iiij*s*. ob.
Item for derege one Seynt Markes Day	viij*d*.
Item for bell ropys	viij*d*.
Item for mendyng of a candellstycke to John Browse	v*d*.
Also for my lady Mayowsse derege	viij*d*.
Item payed to the payntters	viij*li*.
Item payd for ij quarters lyme to the northe wyndow yn oure laydys yele	viij*d*.
Item for one powne waxe	vij*d*.
Item for makyng off iij lb. waxe a geynst our dedicacyon day	j*d*. ob.
Item to the frary clarke	x*d*.
Item for makyng klene the bole of the crosse	iiij*d*.
Item for makyng the trendell and the makyng off iiij tapers with the waxe to the same	iiij*s*. xj*d*.
Item payd to John Wardeford for takyng downe off the nort wyndow yn our lady yele	xij*d*.
Item payd to Robert Carver for makyng off the Trayle under the rodelofte	iij*s*. vj*d*.
Item payd for drawyng off viij lode stonys to makyng off the chyrcheyerd walle	xvj*d*.
Item payd to Thomas Akort for caryeg of the same viij lode stonys	xvj*d*.
Item payd to John Sergent for takyng downe of the north wyndow yn our lady yele	xij*d*.
Item for remevying off the scaffold timber	x*d*.
Item for beryng away the rubbyll	ij*d*.
Item for strekyng the wyndows and wallys	iiij*d*.
Item for takyng downe the scaffold and for alle [ale]	j*d*.
Item for mendyng of a spade and a schowle	ij*d*.
Item for gresse to the bellys	j*d*.
Item for mowyng the chyrche yerd iij tymys	iiij*d*.
Item for wassyng the chyrche clothys	xiiij*d*.
Item for makyng of the chyrche yerd walle	iiij*s*. viij*d*.
Item for beryng owte off the snow and dryyng off banarse	iij*d*.

Md. that Thomas Schetes hate rec. yn hys yere of the wardynwycke yn the xiiij yer off Kyng Henry the VIIth.

Fyrst of Wyllyam Woky of Ham wardyn next by fore hym yn money	xxj*s*.
Item rec. off our lady wardyns	iiij marke, iiij*s*. vj*d*.
Item leyde to the same v*s*. whyche restyth yn Water Sergent hondes.	
Item vj*s*. and viij*d*. whych restyth yn Wylm Tuckes hondys.	
Item leyed to the same iiij*s*. vj*d*. whyche restythe yn Thomas A corte handys left off glasyng off the wyndow yn our ladys yele [*i.e.*, a balance left from the glazing].	
Item for Estyr lyȝth of Pylton	xvj*s*. x*d*.
. . . . Wutton	iiij*s*. iiij*d*.
Item off our lady wardynse	xl*s*.
Item off by queste of Isbell Tyrpyns	vj*d*.

Item to the bellys for Thomas Schet by quest . . . . iiij*d*.
Item v*s*. to the encresse off the hye crosselyȝth yt. restyth yn Stevens Haynes hande and Water Sergent the elder.
Item for the chyrche lede iiij*d*. off Tho. akort.

Sm. totalis recevyd vij*li*. xvj*s*. vj*d*.

MEM. For costes yn same yer. [No entries].

Memorandum that John Wattes yn hys yer of ye wardyn wyke yn ye yer off Kynge Henry ye VIIth hath ylde [yielded] up off y*e* yn cresse off y*e* chyrche of sentt John of Babtys.

Sm. totalys v*li*. xiij*s*. vj*d*.

Allsoo y*e* seyd John wattes hath resevyd of John[1] Browsse, of Pulton, viij merke.

Sm. totalis v*li*. vj*s*. viij*d*.

[Loose entries in later hands.]

Itm. Wylleam Sergentt owynge unto ye churche for yor lady lyȝt iiij*s*. and vj*d*.
Item of ye bequeste of Thomas Grene iij*s*. iiij*d*. restyng yn y*e* honnys of Wylleam Jonys.
Item John Gregory off Barow and Thomas Collys for ther [Wootton] yester lyȝt   iiij*s*. ij*d*.
Item Rychard Kynge and Wylliam Browsse beyng yownge men wardens howynge to the churche . . . . iij*s*. iiij*d*.
Wyllm Hobbys oweth to the churche . . . . . . xij*d*.

Competus Johanni [*sic*] Canarde Gardiani ecclie paroche Sti Johis Baptiste die Sti Marcii anno Dni m°ccccc°xib°.

Item recevyd of the Ester lyght	xvj*s*. viij*d*.
Item recevyd of Water Wekys for y*e* Estyr lyght . .	iiij*s*. iiij*d*.
Item recevyd of Willm Mylward	xxx*s*.
. . . Willm. Stevyns	xviij*s*. save ij*d*.
. . . John Paty for y*e* kepyng of ye hygth crosse lyght .	xxij*d*.
Item receved of Thomas Sargant hys fellowe . . .	xij*d*.
. . . Willm Wylcokes sone	ij*s*.
. . . of a pore man bequeste to ye bellys . .	iiij*d*.
. . . John Wattes	vj*s*. viij*d*.

Summa recepcionis iij*li*. ix*s*. viij*d*.

Md. that John Canard ys surty to ye chyrch for a brasyn morter the pryse of . vj*s*. viij*d*.
[The wyche nobyll ys caste yn ye cownte of the recepcois.]
Md. that Thomas Eed have recevyd of John Canarde the wolde warden vjxx*li*. *s*. viij*d*.
[*i.e.*, £6. 0*s*. 8*d*.]

---

[1] Warden in 1511–12: Watts served in 1512–13, probably.

Md. that of John Brousse ys detter unto yᵉ cyrche . . . . . . vjs. viijd.
Md. that John Canard yn hys yer the ere off yowr suffryn Kyng Harry yᵉ VIIJth hatth yelde uppe off ye yn cresse [revenue] off ye cherche of Saynt John off Bapptist iiij nobylls and hee ys dyschardgyd.

Competus Thomi Ede gardiani ecclie parochialis Sti Johis Baptiste dominica post festum Sti Marcii, A.D. m°ccccc°xb°.

Receptoes ejusdem Thomi Ede cum debitis.

Fyrste receved off John Canard off Pylton late warden	viijs. viijd. (xx)
Item R. on Estyr Day for the Ester lygth	xvjs. vd.
Item R. off yownglyng lygth	iijs. ixd.
Item R. off yower ladey wardyns	iiijs. xjd.
. . . . John Brusse at the Elme	vjs. viijd.
. . . . yowe of Wotton	iiijs. iiijd.
. . . . John Wyllcock for a ev [ewe] and lame	xxd.
. . . . John More off yᵉ questh off hys weyffe	xijd.
. . . . ye yownglying lygth	vs. ijd.
. . . . yᵉ cherche lands	xviijd.
. . . for yᵉ ledde haxyn [lead-ashes]	iiijs. iiijd.
Sm. vijli. xviijs. vjd.	

The coste of the sayed Thomas Ede, warden.

Fyrste payed for Ester lygth wex and makyng	iiijs. iiijd.
Item for dirige and Masse on saynt Marke day for benefactors	viijd.
Item for mendyng of ye cherche gate	ijd.
Item for makyng off a key to a lytyll cofer	ijd.
Item to makyng off yᵉ klypper to ye lytyll bell & schyttyng a erde [i.e., casting a mould]	jd. ob.
Item for ye beying iij bussells off axyn [ashes]	iiijd. ob.
Item for yᵉ rungyng of yᵉ cherche laddyr	iijd.
Item for yᵉ makyng of a bawderike to yᵉ lytyll belle	vjd.
Item for ye makyng off iiij tapyrs agenst seynt Johne Day	xvjd.
Item for ij lode of wode for ye plumer	iijs. iiijd.
Item for nayles for plumer to nayle yᵉ ledde	ijs. vjd.
Item for lathys and bowrde to make yᵉ gutter	vs. iiijd.
Item for heryng [hiring] off workmen abowth cherche workes	ijs. iiijd.
Item for to John Baron for yᵉ fetyng [fetching] off plumer stuffe att West Penard	vjd.
Item for fetyng off flakes [i.e., for the scaffolds] and hurdylls and rede and postes for yᵉ plumer	vjd.
Item for fechyng xv hundyr off ledde at Mendeypp	xijd.
Item for ye carryng of ye ledde axyn to Chewton	xvjd.

Item for yᵉ clarke for makyng clenne off ye cherch erd and kyppyng off yᵉ clocke	iijs. viijd.
Item paied to yᵉ plumer for sowdyr and ys labor	iij pounds.
Item paied to frayry clarke	xd.
Item paied for makyng off iiij tapyrres agenst Crystmas	viijd.
Item I bowth off Plumley of Septon iij hundyr ledde yᵉ prysse	xjs.
Item for yᵉ fetyng xij hundyr ledde att Mendyppe	xlviijs.
Item for yᵉ wessing off cherche clothes	ijs.
Item for mendyng and dresyng off iiij bells	iiijd.
Item for mendyng off bere	iijd.
Item for Thomas Edes ys labor the space off xviij days	iijs.
Item for Master Officiall [the Ordinary's judge] costes att yᵉ visitacion	xviijd.
Sm. vijli. xvjs.	

Md. that Thomas Ede hath made hys countes byfore yᵉ pars [parish] the laste daye off Aprille the here off yowʳ lorde mᵒccccᵒxbᵒ. yn yᵉ yere off yowr sufferen kyng Harri the VIIJ, and hatth elde [yielded] uppe to yᵉ cherche ijs. ijd., the wyche wasse bestowyde amongste yᵉ clerkes off yᵉ quere.

Competus Johan Wylkyns xxv die Mensis Aprilis et in anno Dni Milesiᵒ quingentesimo deciᵒ sexto.

Item R. off Estyrly3ght	xvjs. xd.
. . . . yᵉ youngling wardens	ijs. iiijd.
. . . . John Lane for a pere of bedys	xd.
Item R. off yᵉ zonysswyff [son's wife] for Kerchowys.	xviijd.
. . . off Thomas off oldett [old debt] .	xiiijd.
. . . John Pennard of Howlth	ijs. vjd.
. . . off John Dunkarton	ijs. vjd.
Item R. off Wyllyam Hobbys off dettes	xijd.
. . . Wyllyam Canard of Compton	iijs. viijd.
. . . John Knolle of Compton	iijs. iiijd.
. . . off Wardyns off Heycroslyth [High Cross Light]	vjs. viijd.
. . . off wardens of Wotton	iiijs.
. . . off yourʳ lady wardyns	viijxxxs. viijd.
Item R. off Fowlys for Elys	ijs. ijd.
. . . off yᵉ bequest of John Walter	xijs.
. . . . John Myllard	iiijd.
. . . . Thomas Myllard	iiijd.
. . . Thomas Ede and John Rogers of bequest	vjd.
. . Wyllyam Thownsyn and John Canard bequest	vjd.
. . Jane Coppe bequest	xvd.
. . John Canard bequest.	ijd.
. . off bequest John Vene	ijd.
. . . . Water Myllard	iiijd.

. . . off M. Kelle	. . . . . .	vjs. viijd.
. . . Wyllyam Brusse	. . . . . .	vjs. viijd.
. . . Wyllyam Canard for cherche lands	. . . .	. xviijd.
. . . off John Grygory off Barow	. . . . .	ijs. viijd.

The costes off the sayed John Wyllkyns, Wardens.

Fryst payed off Estyr ly3ght wax and makyng . .	vs. ixd.
Item for derige and masse on Saynt Markes daye .	. viijd.
Item ffor ij Newebellropes	. xvd.
Item receyved for y⁰ clarke att y⁰ counte . . .	. iiijd.
Item paied to John Pyper for hys labyr . . .	. viijd.
Item for makyng off iiij tapyrs agenst Vittsonday .	. iiijd.
Item ffor makyng off a new bere	. xijd.
Item ffor y⁰ clarke for kypyng y⁰ clocke	iijs. iiijd.
Item ffor y⁰ beying of a new bawdrycke	. viijd.
Item ffor making off y⁰ trendyll	. ijs. vjd.
Item for bawdryck for y⁰ medyll bell	. vjd.
Item for mendying off a happys [hasp]	. ijd.
Item ffor fraywry clarke	. xd.
Item ffor costogges [costs] att visitasion . . .	iijs. iiijd.
Item for makyng off iiij leyttes	iijs. ijd.
Item ffor setting and reparyng off lamps . . .	. xxd.
Item ffor mendying off y⁰ clocke	. ijs.
Item ffor coveryng off y⁰ Sayntes att lent . . .	iijd. ob.
Item ffor driying off y⁰ ornamentes off y⁰ cherche and clarkes labyr .	. ijd.
Item ffor mendying off y⁰ helyng off j⁰ . . . ? .	. ijd.
Item ffor wassing off y⁰ cherche clotthys . . .	. ijs.
Item ffor pekyng and dressyng of y⁰ belles . .	. iiijd.
Item ffor pekyng off y⁰ bawdrycke	. iiijd.
Item ffor mowyng and keyppyng of y⁰ chercheyd .	. iiijd.
Item ffor skowryng off y⁰ canstycke	. iiijd.
Item ffor y⁰ makyng off y⁰ pateyn and gyltyng . .	. xviijs.
Item ffor mendyng off y⁰ ffowth [foot] off y⁰ chalys .	vijs. vd.
Item ffor y⁰ laboryss and fetthing home . . .	. vjd.
Item ffor lettyng abowth y⁰ cherche workes y⁰ off xviij days . .	. iiijd.

Md. that John Wylkyns hath delyveryd unto Wyllyam Tocar, off Ham, vli. xls. vjd. in y⁰ here off kynge Harre VIIJth, and y⁰ here off yowr lorde godde m°ccccc°xbj°. and ys dyscharggyd a ffore the pars off hys here [year of office].

A remembrans off the cherchis dettes in the here off Wyllam Tocar cherchewardin and the ffrist dae off y⁰ munthe off May, A°. Dni. m ccccc xvjᵗᵒ.

John Grygory of Barow	. xxd.
Wyllam Sargant	iiijs. vjd.

Pilton Church-Wardens' Accounts.

Itm. the bequeste off John Syppard of Chewton	vjs. iiijd.
Itm. a rynge of syller and gyltt off the quest Annys Syppard wt. ij kerchows.	
Item the bequeste off Edytt Webb	xxd.
Item the queste off Wate Sladde sum tyme delyng yn Pulton . . .	xijd.

Competus Gyllelmi Tokar de Pulton Gardiani ecclie parochie Sti Johs Bapt xx sexto die Mensis Aprilis die post festum Sti Marci, Evang., A.D. m°cccc°xbij°.

Receptiones ejusdem Gilhelmi Tocar cum debitis.

Firste receved off John Wylkyns off Pulton late wardeyn . .	. vli. xls. vjd.
It. R. on Ester Day in Pulton is cherche ffor heyth crosse liyth	. . xvijs.
It. R. off our Lady wardyns lytys encresse	. xijs. iiijd.
. . . . . . ye young men iygthes	. vijs. vijd.
. . . . . . John Knoll off Wester Comton . . .	. iijs. iiijd.
. . . . . off ye Est. lygth off Wotton	. iiijs. jd.
. . . . . off yowr lady Wardeyns yn cresse off ther alle [Ale]	iijli. iijs. iiijd.
Item for ye salle off ij peyrs off Bedes	. . viijd.
Sm. . . . vijli. xiijs. xd.	

The coste off the seyde Wyllyam Tocar, Wardeyn.

Itm. ffor the coste of wexe and the makyng ffor the hole here	. xvijs. vijd.
Itm. ffor yo makyng off ye candellsticke	. vli. vs.
Itm. ffor ye makyng off a klypper	ijs. iiijd.
Itm. ffor ye mendyng off a bawddrire . .	. viijd.
Itm. ffor seynte Marke duryge	. viijd.
. . . . . ye Frarey clarke	. xd.
. . . . . clarke ffor ye kyppyng off ye clocke	iijs. iiijd.
Item for j tapeyr bey fore ye sepultar . . .	xxd. ob.
. . . . . ye visitacion	. iijs.
Item for ye [rough] castyng off ste John Chambeyrd .	. xxd.
Item ffor ye blessyng off ye leyttyl challs [chalice] .	. viijd.
Itm. ffor ye wessyng off ye cherche clothys . .	. ijd.
Itm. ffor skoweryng off ye grette candyllstyckes .	. iiijd.
Itm. ffor mowyng off ye chercheyerd . .	. iiijd.
Itm. ffor gressyng off ye bellys	. iiijd.
Itm. ffor off ij Rocchett and mendyng off iij obys [albs] .	. viijd.
Itm. ffor mendyng off ye grett paxkes [pax] . . .	jd.
Itm. ffor sonnynge [sun-drying] off ye ornamentes that longeth to the cherche .	. viijd.
Itm. that I wasse lett the space off iiij days goyng yn and yowte to Bruton ffor ye canstickes and also yn castyng a weye off ye snowe that wasse apon the ledde ande also yn goyng to Welles, to Glastonbery and to Bruton to have the challis y blessyd	. viijd.
Sm. . . . vjli. xvijs. iijd. ob°	

[A line interpolated here is omitted.]

Item Gardianus resepit a Johan Kolle	iijs. iiijd.
Item recepit a Wyllyam Sergant	iiijs.
. . . . Hollys.	
Item exposuit inter cantores [the singer's fee]	iijs.
Item Johs Browysse per precul	viijd.

Md. that Wyllyam Tocar yn hys here off wardeyn wycke yn the here off Kyng Harry the VIIJth hatth helyd [yielded] uppe the encresse off the cherche off saynt John off Bapptyst and ysse dischargeydde hy ffore the parish and John Holder off West Humle [? Holm] ys takyn yn to hys wardeynscheyppe to fulfyll hys Roume [room] the space off thewlmownthes.

Competus Johis Holder de Pulton gardiani ecclie poch Sti Johis Baptiste xxvj^{to} die Mensis Aprile die Sti Marci Evang., Anno regni regis Henrici octavi.

Receptioes ejusdem Johis Holder.

Frest reseyd yn the comtysday	iiijs.
Itm. reseved on Ester Day yn Pulton Scherche for the lyttes	xvjs. ijd.
Itm. reseyd off ower lady Wardens	ijli. xs. xd.
. . . . . Wyllyam Sergant	iiijs.
. . . . . Wyllyam Hobbes	xijd.
. . . . off Johis Browsse for a peyr of bedes	viijd.
. . reseyd off Johis Marke off ye bequeste off hys mother	iiijd.
Sm. . . . iijli. xvijs.	

The Costes off the sayd Johis Holder.

Fyerst payed ffor the Ester lytes wex and makyng	iiijs. iiijd.
Ite. ffor ye dirige and masse on Saynt Markes day	viijd.
Ite. that hee put ffowrthe a mongyst ye syngars.	iijs.
Ite. ffor ye mendyng off ye clocke	vs.
Ite. ffor ropes, locckes, neyles, gemmowys	xxd.
Ite. ffor the gressyng off the belles	iiijd.
Ite. ffor the makyng of the lytys agenst Wyssoner day	iijs. iiijd.
Ite. ffor ye carryge of stownys to make the Cherche valls [walls]	xijd.
Ite. delyverde unto the clarke at y^o fyrst comyng off ys ownants [earnest]	jd.
Ite. ffor a lyne ffor ye canapy	jd.
Ite. ffor a sowelle [shovel]	ijd.
Ite. ffor the makyng off ye leytte agenst yow^r dedicacyon day	ijs. iijd.
Ite. paye to ffrayery Clarke	ixd.
Ite. for ij bawdryckes	ijs.
Item for ye makyng off ye cherche wall	iiijs. vjd.
. . . ffor ix lode of stonys and ye carryge off them	ijs. viijd.
Item ffor ij belroppe the prysse	xvjd.

Pilton Church-Wardens' Accounts.

Item ffor yᵉ makyng off leytte agenst Crystenmasse	xix*d*. ob.
Item ffor yᵉ makyng off ij tapyrrs agenst Candylmasday	iiij*d*.
Item ffor the strekyng off yᵉ chercheerd	iiij*d*.
Item ffor the mowyng off yᵉ cherchyerd	iiij*d*.
Item ffor vj erds off clotth to make a syrplys	v*s*.
Item ffor yᵉ wessyng off yᵉ cherche clotthys	ij*s*.
Item ffor ij holes makyng under yᵉ canstyckes	ij*d*.
Item ffor yᵉ makyng off iiij tapyrrs affore Synt Jon	ij*d*.
Item ffor yᵉ mendyng off yᵉ glassyn wyndowys	ij*s*. vj*d*.
Item ffor yᵉ wex off yᵉ hey crosse lyttes borrydd off yᵉ wardes	xvij*d*. ob.
Item ffor yᵉ visitacyon un to yᵉ officiall	iiij*s*. viij*d*.
Item ffor a loke and gymowys [hinges] to yᵉ coffer yn yowʳ ladey yelde	v*d*.
Item ffor yᵉ gyfte unto yowʳ lady wardyns	xiiij*d*.
Item ffor yᵉ greye cottes	v*s*. iiij*d*.
Sm. total . . . viij*li*. j*d*.	
Sic remanet ecclie . . . xix*s*.	

Resayttes of Mathew Trym, of (from) John Lane.

Be yt knowyn to all the holle paryshe that I John Lane of Pyltun, chyrche wardene for on yere the yer of ower Lord A mccccc and xix hathe geffyn a trewe a comttes off all maner of resayttes bothe of mony and of all maner of ornamenttes of the chyrche and mor ovyr the sayde paryshe hathe alowyde me of the a for sayde for all maner of costes doone yn my yere mor ovyr I John Lane hathe lefte in the handdes of Mathewe Tryme styll remaynynge for hys yere . . xxxxxiiij*s*. x*d*.

Coste layde owt be Mathewe Trym.

In prs for Esterlyght	viij*s*.
Itm for yᵉ Trendell	iij*s*. x*d*.
Itm iij*li* waxe	ij*s*. viij*d*.
Itm ij belroppys	xviij*d*.
Itm to yᵉ ryngares and to yᵉ clarke	iiij*d*.
Itm to yᵉ preste	iiij*d*.
Itm to yᵉ frary clarke	x*d*. ob.
Itm for a rochet v yarddes	xx*d*.
Item for mendyng of yᵉ chales	iij*s*. iiij*d*.
Itm for makyng of yᵉ booke	iiij*d*.
Itm for ij bookes bowht be yᵉ prest	x*s*.

Compotus Willmi Sargeant gardiani ecclie Sci Johis baptiste in Pulton in die dnca asensionis Dni Anno Dni, m°ccccc°xxj°.

Redita bonorum ecclie de Pulton.

Itm rec. of Mathew Trym at the day of his a contes . . . . xxvjs. viijd.
Itm rec. of the hole paryshe for Ester ly3th . . . . . xvjs. xd.
Itm rec. of Thomas Browne for Ester ly3th . . . . . . iiijs. iiijd.
Itm rec. of John Layne vjd. Item rec. of John Layne . . . . . vijs.
. . . John Paty viijs. . . . John Coppe and Davy Dey owre lady wardons lvjs. Itm rec. of John Gregory of Barrow vjd. Item rec. of Mathew Trym in die omn. stor. [Omnium Sanctorum] xs. Item rec. of John Chandellar xxd. Itm. rec. of yᵉ be queste of Thomas Chandellar xijd. Itm. rec. of yᵉ be queste of Willm Volkes vjd. Itm rec. of yᵉ bequest of Davy Prichett . . . . . iiijd.
    Sm. total . . . . vjli. xiijs. iiijd.

Rynges.

Itm rec. of yᵉ be queste of Jone Wardforde . . . . j Rynge
Itm rec. . . . . . Alys Penard . . . . ij Rynges
. . . . Jone Wylcokes . . . j Rynge

The Costes of yᵉ sayd Willm.

Item payd for vjli. waxe ijs. price of every powne—xd. and so yᵉ hole sum ys—vs. Item payde for makyng—ijd. Item payd for makyn of ij tapers—ob. Item payd for a quarter of a li of wexe to make ij tapers to the hy aulter and for yᵉ makyn—iijd. ob. Item payd for iiijli. wexe to yᵉ trendell price yᵉ li.—xd. so yᵉ hole sumys, iijs. iiijd. Item payde for makyn—viijd. Itm payde for a li wexe to make ij tapars for yᵉ hy auter—xd. ob. Itm payd to Master Vycary for a li and a q. wexe xijd. ob. Itm payd for makyn of ij tapers to yᵉ hy auter—jd.

Of oyer [other] costage ydon.

Itm payde for sayng of dyrige to Sir Willm—iiijd. Itm payd to the parysche clarke—ijd. Itm payd to the ryngers—ijd. Itm payde for a letheryn baag to ber yᵉ keys—iiijd. Itm payde for mendyng of a sorplys and a rochet—vd. Itm payde for mowyn of yᵉ cherche-yerde—iiijd.
Itm payde for nalys and mendyn of yᵉ cherche gytes—ijd. Item payde to John Wylmat for brygyng of a leytter ffro hys master and for hys labor to Glastonbery to speke wᵗ my lorde [i.e., Abbot]—viijd. Item payde to Johan lanman for makyng of a canepy and for v tasselles and a laysse [lace]—xvjd. Item payde for mendyn of a surplys—iiijd. Item payde to coppe for wyre to yᵉ clocke—jd. Item payde for hangyn uppe of yᵉ leynt clothys—iiijd. Item payde for mendyn of yᵉ bawderikes to yᵉ belles—vjd. Item payde for thride to mende yᵉ vestmentes—ob. I payde for weschyn of yᵉ cherch clothys—ijs. Itm for myne expense to Exsetter to speke wᵗ yᵉ carvar—ijs. iiijd. Itm

payde for a yrynde bowe and hokes to hang a clothe be for owyr lady—j*d*. Item payde for Master docter Fythejamys [Fitzjames] dynner for kepyn of visitacyon, vj*s*. ij*d*. Item payde to John Morys for y*e* byll of seyntens [sentence]—ij*s*. iiij*d*. Item payde for drawyn and caryge of x lode stonys for the cherche walles—iiij*s*. iiij*d*. Item payde to John Sargeant for vj days warke—ij*s*. vj*d*. Item payde to John Dore for iij days and a half—xviij*d*. ob. Item for my labor iij days—vj*d*. Itm payde for grese for the belle—iiij*d*. Item for a sacke of lyme—iiij*d*. Itm for makyn of ij bolte of yryn to the crosse—j*d*. Item for keepyn of the guttris and makyn cleyne of the toure florys—ij*d*. Item for my labor to Wotton to sarche and know every man plase and cott[1]—ij*d*. Item payde for mendyn of the clocke—viij*d*. Itm payde to Walter Sergeant for mendyng of the cherche wall—x*d*. Item payde to John Dore for a days warke—v*d*. Itm payde to John Sergeant for a di days warke—ij*d*. ob. Item payde for lyme—viij*d*. Item for my labor on Fryday—ij*d*. Item payde to John Pleyter for mendyn of vestmentes and makyn of a canopy for ye sepulcor—xvj*d*. Itm payde for makyn of a rochett—j*d*. Item payde to Saynt Johis Clarke—x*d*.

    Sm. totalys de Costagio—xlij*s*. xxj*d*.
    Et sic dz.—iiij*li*. v*s*. iiij*d*.

Competus Willm Vowllys gardiani ecclie parochialis Sci Johis Baptiste de Pulton in prima dominica post festum Sci Marcij, A.D. m°ccccc°xxij°.

    Redita bonorum ecclie de pulton.

In primis recevyd of William Canerd the day of his a cowmt—viij*li*. xj*s*. ij*d*. Itm rec. for Estyr lyzght—xvj*s*. iiij*d*. Itm of Robert Browsse and William Scheppard owre lady wardyns—xxxij*s*. Itm rec. of John Stone of Wotton for Estyr lyzth—iiij*s*. viij*d*. Itm rec. of the bequest of John Schyppard—viij*d*. Itm rec. of y*e* be quest of Jylyen Canarde—iiij*d*. Itm rec. of y*e* be quest of Willm Melworde—iiij*d*. Itm rec. of Robert Harris for oure lady lyzth—xij*d*. Item rec. of Willm Canarde of Comton for the chorche rentt—ij*s*. Itm rec. of y*e* bequest of John Broderybe of Pyll—xx*d*.

    Sm. Tot. of my recete . . . . . xj*li*. ix*s*. x*d*.

    Rynge.

Itm. rec. of y*e* bequest of Alys Mylworde—j Rynge.
 . . . . Jelyen Canarde—j Rynge.

  The Costage Idon by Willm Vowllys, Warden of y*e* Cherche of Pulton.

Itm. payed for x*li*. and a half wex agenst Ester . . . . . . viij*s*. ob.
 . . . . . the makyng . . . . viij*d*.
 . . . . . wax and makyng of this same wex agenst the Nat. of saynt John Baptyst . . . . ij*s*. ix*d*.

[1] Some kind of census.

. payed for iij*li*., and a half of wex for the trendell . . . . . ijs. xjd.
Item payed for makyn vjd. Itm payd for a j*li*. and a half of wax for ij tapers to the hy Auter—xvd. Itm for makyn—jd.
   Sm. . . . . xvjs. ijd. ob.

Itm. payed on Saynt Marke is day to the Vicar, the Clerke and the ryngers for dyrige of the benefactors of the chirch . . . . viijd.
Itm. payed for movyng [mowing] of the chorche hey . . . . . iiijd
Itm. payed for skowryng of the iiij grett candellstyk . . . . . iiijd.
Itm. payed for the reparacyon of the bellys . . . . . . iiijd.
Itm. payed to the procter of saynt John ys fraternite . . . . xd.
Item payed for mendyng of the locke of the chorche dore . . . xd.
Item payed for a roope to the clocke . . . . vijd.
Item payed for a roope to trendell . . . . viijd.

Of other Costage Idon.

Itm. payed for a bell rope—viijd. Itm. payed for mendyng of the Chorche ledd—iiijd. Itm. payed for mendyng of thre pere of vestments and wessyng of the Chorch clothys—ijs. Itm. payed to the clarke ffor keppyng of the clocke—iijs. iiijd. Itm. payed to John Scharge and Richard Sargant for pargytyng of the towre and for lyme—xvs. vjd. Item for coveryng of sayntes at Leynt—iijd. Itm. payd to John Sargantt, Rich: Sargantt for nayelles and mendyng of the roffe in owre lady Elde [Aisle]—xijd. Itm. payed for mendyng of the chorche gate and for the cage of the bell—iiijd. Itm. payd for mendyng of the beste cope an the Palle—iiijd. Itm. payed to Jone lanmam for weschyng of v corpers—xd. Item payd for wrytyng of the boke of Compte—xijd.

Comput' Johis Lanma [n] gardiani ecclie parochialis Scti Johis Baptiste de Pulton dominica prima post festum Ascencionis Domini An^{no} Dni m̄dxxb.

In primis Rc. of John Roger the day of is a cote [Account] [No entries] . . vij*li*. vjs. vd.

Comput' Robti Harris & Walti Bayle gardianorum ecclie Sci Johis Baptiste de Pulton in prima dmca post octavam Pasche anno dni m°ccccc°xxx°.

Itm. recevyd of the chyrche	xls.
. . recevyd of the Ester ly3gt	xvjs. vijd.
Item recevyd for the lyche rest of Als [Alice] Vooles	vjs. viijd.
. . . . . of Ester ly3ht of Wooton . . .	vs viijd.
Itm. recevyd for a croke	ijd.
Itm. recevyd for a lyche of a rope . . .	ijd.
Itm. recevyd of the youngmen ly3ht . .	iijs. vjd.
Itm. recevyd of the gift of Als Vooles . .	ij ryngge.

. . . . . . gyff of Katerin Stevyns . . .	.	j ryngge.
. . . . for wex and hony	.	. vij$d$.
. . . . off the cherche	.	vj$s$. viij$d$.
. . . . . of Wyllim Brown	.	. xvij$d$.
Item recevyd of John Kene and John Prayter . . .	.	. xl$s$.
Item recevyd of the chyrch	.	. xl$s$.
. . . .	.	. xv$s$.

[4 leaves cut out.]

Yatton:

Notes illustrative of the MSS.

Manor. Added by Bishop Giso to the endowments of the See of Wells circ. 1066. Surrendered to the Crown by Bishop Barlow, 3 Edward VI, March 1st, 1549.

Valued at £20 in 1290; in 1537 at £62 2s. 7d. nett.

It did not embrace Claverham [Claram] manor, a lay fee held of the Honor of Gloucester by the De la Sores of Backwell, from whom the Rodneys inherited.

Acreage of the two Manors, 6,476.

The Parish. The whole rectorial tithe and glebe (stated in Domesday as one Hide), were appropriated to a prebend in Wells Cathedral, circa 1135, and the prebendary was invested with peculiar jurisdiction. A vicarial income was set apart. The Vicar was nominated by the prebendary to the Bishop for institution.

In 1327, the Bishop (see Reg. Drok., ap. Wells Registry), readjusted the Vicar's and Rector's incomes, after proof by inquest that whilst the one was worth 100 marks, the other was worth only twelve, with two chaplains to keep for service of two chapels.

The Chapels served by the Vicar were probably (1) that of St. James on the north-east of the church; and (2) a chapel in the churchyard, reported by the Chantry Commission in 1548 to be ruinous.

Two other chapels stood in the parish, both of them manorial, and not under the Vicar's charge. The one at Claverham Court was endowed with tithe, and presentative.[1] The other at Court de Wyke was probably maintained by the Lords of that Manor, *i.e.*, by the Newtons in the 15th and 16th centuries.

FISCAL SYSTEM FROM 1445 TO 1547.

The area of the parish was divided into three portions, the east and west, *i.e.*, Claverham and Cleve, being committed to two " Lightmen," sometimes called Wardens, who brought their gatherings, originally made for the support of lights in the Church, to the Wardens' audit. Central Yatton paid its offerings to the Wardens direct.

---

[1] The Wells Registers record the institution of no less than 11 rectors between 1420-1545, presented alternately by the Rodneys and the other representatives of the De la Sores. Sir Giles Capel presented in 1526, value in 1548 £2 8s. nett.

After the completion of the Church house, with its appliances for entertainment, the gatherings were made at the Ales, instead of from house to house, but the Lightmen of the east and of the west held their Ales separately.

These gatherings were the largest source of income.

Beside these, there was a yearly gathering[1] of 6s. 8d. for the font taper, and paschal taper, probably made at the Easter procession; and now and then special gatherings for foreseen outlays.

Arrears never occur. Gifts and bequests are recorded yearly, but there was no rating of property or gatherings in Church. These would have been counted "oblations" claimable by the Clergy.

In 1520 a fee of 6s. 8d. for inside burial begins; the Wardens taking the fee, and bearing the cost of replacing the pavement.

This parish had no landed endowment, and did not retain any live stock for income. It seems to have received no stated help from its great land-owner, the Bishop, or from its great tithe-owner, the prebendal rector.

The Newtons of Claverham Court are often recorded as benefactors, and probably joined the Church Ales with a full hand; but their burial aisle was repaired by the parish.

The widow, Isabel Lady Newton, was Warden in 1496.

Looking at the absence of gifts from the richer ones, the income raised by this population of peasants and yeoman, is most surprising.

There was always a balance handed over to the incoming Wardens, enough to meet their year's ordinary outlay.

But this wealth did not deaden zeal. The ritual aims were continually rising[2]; new objects of veneration, and new cults added[3]—the fabric was kept in the highest order, enlarged and adorned.[4]

The Churchyard was enlarged in 1485 at a cost of £3 6s. 8d., and in 1486 of £1 13s. 4d., for the consecration.

A noble Churchyard Cross was built in 1524, at a cost much exceeding £9, but not ascertainable from the brevity of the entries.

The Church house was thoroughly equipped for all its hospitable purposes. There was an organ and a clock. Minstrels were hired at Whitsuntide. The Organist, Clerk, and Sexton were salaried. The "Waking of the Sepulchre" from Good Friday to Easter morn by two paid men, was regularly observed. All vestments, and portable vessels, and even the stone altar slabs were carried to the Bishop for his blessing.

---

[1] Entered sometimes as for the font, sometimes for the paschal taper.

[2] Note the large sums spent on Vestments & Cope; *e.g.*, in 1481, £xxvj, in 1534, £xxx.

,, ,, ,, Service books, Manual, Mass-book, psalters, Processionals, 'portas,' gradual £v vjs. viijd. in 1460.

,, ,, ,, a ledger, £17 1s.

,, ,, ,, bells, 1451, £5, and often afterwards.

,, ,, ,, Processional Cross, 1499, £18.

[3] S.S. Katharine, Thomas, George, Nicolas, and Christopher, were added to the older cult of S. James, whose chapel on the north side of the Church was enlarged in 1451-2, and Ale instituted, and a stipend paid to the Chantry Priest.

[4] Specially note the Roodloft, with its Aler splendidly carved, gilt, and painted, and decked with over 80 images. The Carpenter's Account alone was £31.

The funds also were employed in upholding the Wardens in the enforcement of discipline.

The splendour of the Church was here, as elsewhere, a temptation to knavery. The endeavour to bring Davie Gibbes to punishment for stealing the Church goods in 1489 was very costly; so complicated as to baffle the modern reader, who can hardly understand how the numerous jurisdictions of the day required processes at Bristol, Ilchester, Wells.

Inter-parochial Ales.—This system was very complete. The Wardens attended these festivals at Ken, Kingston, Wrington, Congresbury, &c., with more or less regularity; making their contributions, commonly xij*d.*, in the name of the parish and at the cost of the parish, for in their persons the parish was deemed to be present. In return, the allied parishes attended the Yatton festivities, with " ale-scot " in hand.

Once, in 1537, an unusual charge of v*s.* is made for attending an Ale at Keynsham, far beyond the wonted girdle.

Civil charges.—The earliest charge for anything not ecclesiastical is in 1512–13, viz., 16*s.* 8*d.* to the " Constable and Tything man," repeated in 1513–14 at 11*s.* 8*d.*, but only once. It is unexplained, and probably may be found to be connected with one of the Commissions of Sewers, which had power to assess property for the maintenance of Seawalls, &c. Though the parish, as such, was not assessed, the landowners' and occupiers may have found a vote of vestry the easiest mode of discharging their burden.

In 1528 a sluice-gate is repaired, and later on the scouring of the "Yeo" is found a yearly charge.

No poor-relief occurs till 1549; then, a detached vote to 14 persons.

Buildings.—Around or near the Church stood the following :—

1. The Courthouse, no longer inhabited by the Bishops as Manorial lords, but by their Reeve; also used for the Manor courts.
2. The Rectory or Parsonage, in which the Bailiff, or lessee of rectorial tithes under the prebendal rector, lived.
3. The Vicarage, with perhaps a small house for the two chaplains.
    Each of these had Barns and Homesteads; required by No. 1 for the Lord's demesne lands, by Nos. 2 and 3 for collection of tithe in kind.
4. The Chapel, scheduled by Edward VI's Commissioners.
5. The Church-house.

Language of the Accounts.—From the beginning it is a medley of English and Latin, with no apparent rule. The Latin Heading was retained till 1481–2, probably from its being written by the Vicar presiding in Vestry, the remainder being left to the hired scribe, often specified in the payments to be the parish Clerk.

---

[1] In the 23rd of Hen. VIII, an Act was passed continuing the legislation of Hen. VI and VII, by which the Lord Chancellor could issue Commissions of Sewers, with power to survey and order needful works at the cost of landowners benefited, calling on the Sheriffs to aid in the levy. The Sheriff's collecting officers would be the hundred-constable, and his subordinate, the tything-man.

Church-Wardens Accounts.

[The earliest is a paper volume, 12 × 5 inches, containing 180 pages, and marked on the outside in a modern hand " A N° 1." The entries begin abruptly in the middle of an account of the year mccccxl, as it is conjectured, the earlier part having disappeared.]

PAGE 1.

A.D. m.cccc.xlv.   JOHN MOYE AND WM. REEVE, WARDENS.

Summa . . . £xvij xvjs. xjd.

Item y received of the bequest of Walter Modswyne and Egolyn his wife iij boshells of wete, the prysce of the iij boshells were ijs.
It. received of the bequest of Alis Ogyn a boshell of wete, the prisce vijd.
It. received of the bequest of R. Watts a boshell of wete, the prisce viijd.
It. received of William Hylle for plocks and sponys . . . . . . ixd.
It. received of John Goodknave for a bord . . . . jd.
It. received of the bequest of Robert Medwynter halfe a boshell of wete, prisce iiijd.
It. payd for ij pound wex to John Medwynter . . . .
It. received of the bequest of Jone Thurba [rne] . . . . . .
    Gefte money that was y geve to the settyng of the newe howes tymbyr [*i.e.*, the Church-house].

Isbell Browne . .	iiijd.
Isbell Wytyng .	jd.
Jone Kewe . .	jd.
Isbell Kewe . .	jd.
Edde Gamelyn .	jd.
John Brewer . .	jd.
John Roscheforth	jd.
Annys Bell	ijd.

[The only totals legible are,]
Remaines £xix xvijs. ijd.
Summa £xix iijs.
Summa totalis £viij vjs.
Receptiones £v xixs. vjd. . . Summa totalis £x xvs. vjd.

PAGE 2.

[Memoranda of divers dates and hands.]

Mem. Anno Domini mccclrvi. John Dole and Thomas,[1] Wardyns, hath received of John Avernaye and John Goodknave £x xvjs.
Mem. that Thomas Thurbarne and Thomas Knygth hath payd to John Bowton for mete and drynke abowgth the setthyng of the wyndowys vjd.

[1] This appears to have been Thomas Wale, p. 70 of the original account.

It. for ryses for the dawbes ij*d*.	
It. for the Cherch howse, of John Mariott	xvj*d*.
It. for the Cherch howse, of Thomas Clerke	xvj*d*.
It. of Symonde	xvj*d*
It. of R. Crew and John	xvj*d*.
for the hyr [hire] of chetill [kettle] of John Crose	iiij*d*.
for the hyr of the chetill of John Wild	iiij*d*.
that Thomas Thurbarne and Thomas Knygth, Wardynes, have payd for a cloth for the chalys	ij*d*.
. . . lampe oyl	iij*d*.
. . . hopyng [hoopyng]	ij*d*.

PAGE 3.

A.D. mccccxlvi. JOHN WYKE AND JOHN NEDE, WARDENS.

These ben the parcells that Jon Wyke and Jon Nede, cherchewardeynys of the parysche cherche of Yatton have resevyd and payde in there offyce beyng.

Inprimis, reseyvyd of Jon Moye and Welyam Reve, late cherchewardeynys	xlvj*s*. viij*d*.
It. reseyvyd for a cowe	iiij*s*.
It. reseyvyd of the queste of Roberd Reve	iij*s*. iiij*d*.
It. reseyvyd in mony to the Esterne tapyr	v*s*. vj*d*.
It. reseyvyd with owr taverne ale	lvj*s*. viij*d*.
It. reseyvyd of the bequeste of William Crosse	xx*d*.
It. reseyvyd for the heffer of Aneyse Hill	iij*s*.
It. reseyvyd of Jon Fischer and his felowes	l*s*.
It. reseyvyd of Wylyam Bonde	xxvij*s*. vj*d*.
It. reseyvyd for old potts	xvj*s*.
It. reseyvyd for ryndyn[1] of the oke	xiiij*d*.
Summa totalis receptionis £x xvj*s*. iiij*d*.	
It. reseyvyd for a basyn and a laver	vj*s*. viij*d*.
It. reseyvyd of Wylyam Colman	xxvij*s*. vj*d*.
Summa totalis receptionis £xij x*s*. vj*d*.	

[In a different hand and ink.]

It. that Wyliam Reynan howeth to the Church of Yatton a clere rekenyng	xx*s*.
It. John Averey outh to the same Church	xij*s*. xj*d*.
The seyde John Averey to the chapelle	vj*s*. viij*d*.

[Whether S. James', or the detached chapel, is doubtful, as in some other entries.]

PAGE 4. [Blank.]

---

[1] "Ryndyn," the plural of "rind," or bark.

PAGE 5.

Mem. de Solucionibus.

Inprimis payde for an oke at Brockle [Brockley]	vj*s*.
It. for the schaperyng[1] and the brynggng home and for the cariage of a weyne [wagon-load] of the seyde oke	iiij*s*. vj*d*.
It. for a bawdre [baldric] and a bokel	xxiij*d*.
It. for wex bowte agen Esterne	xl*d*.
It. for fettyng [fetching] home of iiij whelys	viij*d*.
It. for expenses upon ij tymes upon croyse[2]	iiij*d*.
It. for waschyng of clothys	ij*d*.
It. viij caryages [loads] was be hote [bought], of the wheche cam that daye but iiij. In expenses	xv*d*.
It. payd to Jon Hykkys and Jon Falew	xl*s*.
It. payd to Westbery	xviij*s*. viij*d*.
It. payd to Welyam Stonhowse for makyng of the dore in the vyse [winding staircase]	xl*d*.
It. for the stonys to the seyde dore	xviij*d*.
It. for the bryngng home of the seyde stonys	xij*d*.
It. for meltyng and makyng of the wex	ij*d*.
It. payd to Jon Sloo for gresyng of the bell	xx*d*.
It. for the chetyl and the keve [vat]	vj*d*.
It. for the brewerys here [brewers hire]	vj*d*.
It. for threshyng of wet[3] [wheat]	viij*d*.
It. for to [two] mennys labour to helpe brewe	x*d*.
It. payd for owr dyner for beryng up of benys [beans] whan we made clene the berne [barn]	iij*d*.
It. for ale to rese with,[4] and owr dyner	iij*d*.
It. for fellyng of an oke at Bacwell	
It. for markyng of the trendyl	x*s*. iiij*d*.
It. for colowrs to the trendyl	xx*d*.
It. for peyntyng of the trendyl	xij*d*.
Summa £iiij x*s*.	

PAGE 6.

It. for caryage of the bordys owte of the cherche yerde into the bushopys halle [at the manor-house]	ij*d*.
It. for makyng of the cherche dore keyge [keys]	vij*d*.
It. for gerdelys to the vestements	iij*d*.
It. for a corde to the canape [canopy]	ij*d*.
It. for hokys to the vyse dore	vj*d*.
It. payd to Westbery	xxj*s*.
It. payd for twests to the vyse dore	vj*d*.
It. payd for nayls to the same dore	iiij*d*.

[1] Shaping and dressing. [2] Cross, near Axbridge, or Cross, the carpenter.
[3] In the original, "Clet," a mis-spelling.
[4] To "raise" with; *i.e.*, to enable them to "bear up" or carry the loads of beans.

It. payd for a lok and a keye to the same dore.	iiij*d*
It. payd for makyng of the same dore	xij*d*.
It. payd for ferments[1] to the stepyl wyndowys bowte of Jon Smyth at the streme	vij*s*. x*d*.
It. payd to Jon Smyth of Comysbere [Congresbury] for makyng of al maner of eyreen [iron] werke for the bellys	viij*s*. viij*d*.
It. payd for bred and ale for to hange with the bellys, and fysche and flesche and chese and all thyngs cowntyd, summa	xiiij*s*. ij*d*.
It payd for ote mele	ij*d*.
It. payd to Jon Falew and to Jon Hykkys and to Jon Fyscher for here [their] compacion[2]	
It. payd for waxe agen crisemasse	xx*s*.
It. payd for roseyne	vj*d*.
It. payd for makyng of the waxe	iij*s*.
It. payd for the here [hire] of the rope and the caryage in and owte.	vj*s*. viij*d*.
It. payd for hors-mete to the wax-maker, and hys owne mete, and owr mete, whyl we made the sayd waxe.	xvij*d*.

PAGE 7.

It. payd for the new Crosse, and makyng of the canape, and the other crosse	xj*s*.
It. payd to the Veker for paper and makyng of the boke and wrytyng	xiiij*d*.
It. payd for talwe candel.	ij*d*.
It. payd to Wylyam Stonhowse for settyng in of to [two] femerell in the stepyl.	x*d*.
It. payd for washyng of surplyses and oder clothys agens Cristemasse	iij*d*.
It. payd for settyng of a brasen pelewe for worspryng	ij*d*.
It. payd to Jon Meke for ij horns	ij*d*.
It. payd for drynke when we boryn [bore] in the bordys	iiij*d*.
It. payd for drynge to Jon Smyth	ij*d*.
Summa totalis solutionum . . . £x xj*s*. j*d*.	

PAGE 8.

(A.D. mccccxlvi–vii.

Mem. quod Johannes Hullman et Willelmus Webbe custodes bonorum ecclesie de Yatton receperunt de Johanne Nede et Johanne Wyke . . . . xxxix*s*. v*d*.

Item	yreseived	of Jon Harte of Claverham	iij*s*. iiij*d*.
,,	,,	of dmn rec' byschype[3]	xiij*s*. iiij*d*.
,,	,,	of a man vor ryngyng ye bell	iiij*d*.
,,	,,	of Ester tapyr	vj*s*. viij*d*.
,,	,,	of . . . Karter	vj*s*. viij*d*.
,,	,	of the Wardeynys of the ale making at Whytteson day	£iiij xx*d*.
,,	,,	of the parasche to the [Easter] sepulcur, clare	xviij*s*. v*d*.
,,	,,	of John Rymer vor p[re] lubkys of the cherche	ij*d*.
,,	,,	of Lygtmen of Yatton, John Reyd and John	£iij vj*s*.

---

[1] Ferments = Ferramenta ; *i.e.*, iron work.   [2] In pity to them.
[3] *I.e.*, the Bishop's manorial Receiver or Steward.

Item yreseived of lygtte men of Cleve and of Claverham, William Watts and William Colynys			£iij vijs. vjd.
,, ,,	vor a gyrddvll that was for . . . Richard Byssechip,[1] Vyker of Yatton		xs.
,, ,,	of John Hurdewyche . . . the bygwyst of J. Ydward .		iijs. iiijd.
,, ,,	vor candyll of the [r]ell[2] ysowlle at divers tymys		vjd.
,, ,,	vor ryngyng of the bell of a munke of Staverdell		iiijd.
,, ,,	of William . . vor a rad . . .		
,, ,,	of Tybyt Scheryffe .		viijd.
,, ,,	vor a gowne, of the quyst of John Vyn		iijs. viijd.
,, ,,	vor a crokke, the quist of Robert Syms of Kenne		vs. xd.
,, ,,	of R. Gold and J. Vord vor wodde of the Chercheys[3]		xvjd.
It.	Receperunt modium frumenti de legatione Willelmi Attewyke, pretio		xd.

PAGE 9.

It. vor wodde of William at Wyke, and Robert Yogge and John Hyllman		viijd.
,, of Richard Benektun		xxjs. iijd.
,, of William Hyckys		xxd.
,, de Willelmo j bossall frumenti et j bossall ordii [hordei], the sum of ham [them]		xvijd.
,, vor a whyche		xijd.
,, of R. Thurberne vor iiij bussel ordii		ijs. iiijd.
,, of J. Meke vor a yhefyr [heifer]		iijs.
,, of R. Reve for a plock [block]		ijd.
,, of John Felpys		xiiijd.

Summa totalis receptionis £xviij iijs. xjd.

PAGE 10. [Blank.]

PAGE 11.

A.D. mccccxlvii–viii. JOHN HYLLMAN AND W. WEBBE, WARDENS.

Mem. quod Johannes Hyllman et W. Webbe expend.

It. y payde vor mette and dryncke vor iiij carige [loads] to the churche		vjd.
It. y payde to Hurneman vor ij takys[4]		vd.
,, ,, John Valoks and J. Hobkys vor mette and dryncke vor sowwyn [sawing] at Nayllese [Nailsea]		iijd.
,, ,, vor anoke [an oak] at Thurbbewyll		iiijs.
,, ,, to J. Valoke and J. Hobkys vor goyng thyddyr		vjd.
,, ,, vor ij bolts and a stapylle		vjd. ob.
,, ,, vor the cost of ij men goyng to Thurbbewyll		ijd.
,, ,, vor of the makyng of Ester tapyr		xxd.
,, ,, vor the beying [buying] of a loke		ixd.

[A few common entries about a few repairs.]

---

[1] R. Bishop was instituted 1440. How long he held office, unknown.
[2] "The reel ysold," the candle ends were thus turned to account.
[3] The Churchyard. Hey = enclosure.   [4] *See* Glossary.

It. y payde	vor the sepulcur kloth		xxixs. viijd.
,, ,,	vor ij candyll stykys		£ij
,, ,,	vor mat' ybowyete[1] to the weste dore		vjd.
,, ,,	vor iij men rydyng to Estun[2] to se the alle [alure], the cost of ham [them]		iijd.
,, ,,	to Crobbe and J. Hylman here [their] costys rydyng to Selwudde		viijd.
,, ,,	to W. Hurneman rydyng to Button [Bitton]		jd.
,, ,,	to John . . . vor vyllyng [felling] anoke		jd.
,, ,,	vor clothe y bowgte to the surplous		xiijs.
,, ,,	vor thredde to make the same		vd.
,, ,,	to W. Stubbe rydyng to Brystowe to see the tabylment[3]		iiijd.
,, ,,	at Cogybbyre [Congresbury] at Churche alle [Ale]		iiijd.
,, ,,	vor the mynd[4] of W. Bocktun		jd.

PAGE 12.

It. y payde	vor the mynd of W. Malsell		jd.
,, ,,	to J. Vysser beryng of a whele to Kynstun		jd.
,, ,,	in costes to rydyng [ridding] of the churche and vor dryng [drink] to the carpentorys to the settyng in of here [their] segys [seats]		iiijd.
,, ,,	vor ij puwns [pounds] of talowe to the carpenterys		ijd.
,, ,,	to John Valew and John Huckys		£iij vjs. viijd.
,, ,,	vor makyng of the surplys		vjs.
,, ,,	vor makyng of the rochette		ijd.
,, ,,	vor wex to the cherche		xiiijs. iiijd.
,, ,,	vor mete and drynke in makyng of the wex		viijd. ob.
,, ,,	vor the makyng of the pulpyt and ij awterys		iijs. iiijd.
,, ,,	vor lyme to the same y bowgt		vd.
,, ,,	vor bynnyng of a panna wyt yre[5]		xijd.
,, ,,	vor nayls y bowgt vor the segys		vjd.
,, ,,	vor strykyng of the churche		iijd.
,, ,,	to J. Parker vor goyng to Thurbbewyll to helpe hewwe the schudde[6]		iiijd.
,, ,,	to J. Slo vor kepyng of the bell		xxd.
,, ,,	to the writer of the bowke [the Account]		vjd.

Summa expensarum £ix xvjs. xd. ob.
Summa totalis solutionum £ix xvijs. ob.

Et remanebit in manibus Johannis Hylman et Willelmi Mydwynter erga proximum annum £viij vjs. xd. ob.

PAGE 13.   [Blank.]

---

[1] Matter or matters bought.

[2] Easton-in-Gordano, to see a model rood-loft with an Alure, before setting about their own, for which they were buying timber, in Selwood Forest.

[3] A carved or painted representation of a sacred subject.

[4] A commemoration of the departed, a month or a year after death. These two benefactors were commemorated for several years.

[5] *I.e.*, binding of a banner with iron.

[6] To hew the shroud *i.e.*, branches.

PAGE 14.

A.D. mccccxlvii–viii. J. HYLMAN AND W. MYDWYNTER, WARDENS.

J. Hylman and W. Mydwynter begin as above with £viij vjs. xd. ob.
Received of John Huredyche to chreche warkys [Church-works] . . . . viijd.
„ of the Ester tapyr . . . . vs. viijd.
„ vor a kowwe of Hurdewychys . . . . viijd.
„ of J. Horte of Claram [Claverham] vor a kowe of hys byquyst . . vjs. xd.
„ of the Wardeynys of John Hylman and William Mydwynter of makyng of
    Ale at Wyttesunday, to the cherche . . . . £iiij
„ of Alice Gowdman of the quist . . . . iijs. iiijd.
„ of John Rowlyng of quist . . . . xvjd.
„ vor ryngyng of the bell of the reseyver acorte day[1] . . . . viijd.
    [In another hand and language.]
Item recepimus de Edde Bustun nomine legationis . . . . . iijs. iiijd.
„ „ „ Johanna Wampervyle nomine legationis annulum et . . . xd.
„ de pro tabernâ Servicie[2] de collect. luminis de Yatton . . . £iij xvjs. viijd.
„ de pro tabernâ „ „ „ de Claverham . . . £ij xjs. viijd.
Item recepimus de Johanne Hykke . . . . vjs. viijd.
„ „ de J. Meke pro vitulo legato de J. Hurdewyche . . . . iiijs.
„ „ de Johanne Herte nomine legationis ij modios frumenti et ij modios
    ordii, pretio . . . . ijs. vjd.
„ „ de Jekyn att Wyke unum modium frumenti et alium modium ordei,
    pretio . . . . xvd.
„ „ de Johanne Avery de Huysch j modium frumenti et modium ordii
    nomine legationis, pretio . . . . xiiijd.
„ „ de J. Halle j modium frumenti nomine legationis, pretio . . xd.

PAGE 15.

Item recepimus de Johanne Knyght unam tunicam, pretio . . . . iiijs.
„ „ à W. W. Wever pro focis v de residuo lignorum dimissorum, pretio . xxd.
„ „ à R. Dornebarne pro ij bus tabulis vocatis "planks" . . . xijd.
„ „ à W. Mydwynter pro j tabula vocata "plank" . . . . iijd.
„ „ à R. Mei pro duobus lignis vocatis ij plocks [blocks] . . . ijd.
„ „ à J. Rynd pro ligno vocato a ploke . . . . . . ijd.
„ „ de Vicar, unam ollam eneam, pretio . . . . . . vs. xd.
„ „ pro olla Ricardi Wyllyngs . . . . vs.
„ „ pro modio frumenti nomine legationis à Johanna Knyght . . xd.
„ „ à Johanna Knyght certas partes, pret. . . . . . . vjd.
„ „ de legatione Johanne Garlonde in pecuniis . . . . . xijd.
    Summa remanens £xxj xs. viijd. ob.

PAGE 16.   EXPENSES.

It. ypayd vor weynscot [wainscot] . . . . vijs.
„ vor cariage of the same . . . . xiijd.

---

[1] On Manor Court day for the Bishop's receiver or steward.   [2] *I.e.*, cerevisie = Ale.

It. vor mendyng of awbys [albs]	vj*d*.
,, vor Ester tapyr and iiij precatys,[1] the makyng and costs	ij*s*.
,, to J. Valew vor makyng of werke of the cherche	vj*d*.
,, to ij men vor rydyng [ridding] of Syn Jameys schapell	iiij*d*.
,, vor anoke ybow3t of J. Hykks and the vyllyng[2] of the same	xiij*d*.
,, vor vyllyng of a chyde[3] at Herryherte	j*d*.
,, vor lamp oyle	iiij*d*.
,, vor warsyne [washing] of clothes to Alson Sawndes	iiij*d*.
,, vor mete and drynke vor trussyng of the bellys	ij*d*.
,, to John Blo vor kepyng of the bells	xx*d*.
,, to John Sty vor makyng of to [two] baner luggus[4]	iiij*d*.
,, to John Slyette vor makyng of ij banarys, and a clothe afore the tabylle, and mendyng of j awbe [alb]	xiiij*d*.
,, to J. Smythe vor makyng of a yryn croke and settyng	ij*d*.
,, vor ij days goyng to Cogysbyry to gete tymbyr vor the cherche, iiij men, the cost of ham [them]	ix*d*. ob.
,, vor the vyllyng of the same tymbyr	xiij*d*.
,, vor cottyng of the same tymbyr to v men in mete and dryng and hyre	ix*d*.
,, vor cariage of the same tymbyr in mete and dryng, in al costs	iij*s*. iiij*d*.

PAGE 17.

It. vor lyme to wassche the awterys	ij*d*.
,, vor the dyner of the man that come hydyr to se the playster of the stypyll	iij*d*.

[In another hand, with a mixture of Latin and English.]

Item solvimus pro confectione campane	vj*s*. viij*d*.
It. pro tabulis vocatis wenscote numero xxviij	xxiij*s*. iiij*d*.
,, in expensis in die emptionis tabularum[5] supradictarum	vj*d*.
,, pro caryage (vehitione) tabularum dict. de Brydstoll	xvij*d*.
,, pro vehitione tabularum à rypa Brydstoll usque portam de Radecleve	v*d*.
[Expenses in meat and drink at the same time]	iiij*d*.

[Hereafter the use of Latin only is resumed to the end of the Warden's period of office.]

Solvimus pro xliij modiis cementi vocati ' playster '	xxj*s*. vj*d*.
In esculentis et poculentis pro circa vehitiones de supradicta playster	xj*d*.
,, pro esculentis equorum eodem tempore	v*d*.
,, pro calciratione equorum eodem tempore	viij*d*.
,, pro conductione duorum operariorum	iiij*d*.
Solvimus operario de supradicto playster pro operibus manuum suarum	xx*d*.
,, pro ejusdem operarii esculentis	vj*d*.
,, pro duobus operariis et esculentis et poculentis eorundem	ij*s*.
,, Johanni Sloo pro duobus dictis circa opus supradictum	vj*d*.
,, pro anniversario Willelmi Bowdon	j*d*.
,, Johanni Crosse pro factura solarii[6] in parte solutionis	£v vj*s*. viij*d*.

---

[1] Prickets.   [2] Felling.   [3] *I.e.*, a shyde or shroud, the top and lop of a tree.
[4] Lugs, cords to keep the banner straight.   [5] Wainscoat boards.   [6] The Aler.

Solvimus Johanni Balwe et J. Hikke pro factura sedilium .	. .	£ij xviijs. viijd.
,, pro cera .	. . . . . .	xxixs. viijd.
,, pro rosen pro cera supradicta .	. . . .	iijs. ijd.
,, pro vehitione rosen et cere et aliis expensis	. . .	iiijd.
,, pro factura cere	. . . . .	xxd.
,, pro esculentis et poculentis circa facturam cere .	. .	xvjd.
,, pro lichline vel filo lichinis[1]	. . .	iiijd.
,, pro clavibus[2] sedilium .	. . . . .	viijd.
,, pro lotione vestimentorum ecclesie et surpiclis .	. .	ijd.
,, pro oleo lampadis	. . . . .	iiijd.
,, pro pastura unius vituli Willelmo Gene	. . .	vjd.
,, servicia[3] ecclesie de Congarisberi	. . . .	iiijd.
,, Johanni Balwe, Johanni Hylle, pro potatione, quum fecerunt finem de factura sedilium	. . . .	iiijd.
,, Ricardo Bowdon pro labore suo versus Worle pro cros	. .	ijd.
Summa expensarum . . £xiij xviijs. ixd. ob.		

PAGE 18.

Mem. quod remanebat in manibus custodum antiquorum, viz. Johannis Hylman et Willelmi Mydwynter, A.D.[4] m.ccccxlviii, in die Sancti Matthye Apostoli, omnibus computatis coram parochianis in ecclesia de Yatton £vij xs. viijd. que summa solvenda est novioribus custodibus, viz. : Willelmo Willyng et Thome Prewett.

PAGE 19.   [Blank.]

PAGE 20.

A.D. mccccxlviii. W. WYLLYNG AND T. PREWET, WARDENS.

These ben the parcelys that Vyl Wyllyng and Tom Prewet recevyd wyl they wer churche wardyns of Yatton yn the yer of our Lord mccccxlviii.

In primo for a taverne that ys ymade of ye Churche ale . . .		v marcs xjd.[5]
and the lightmen of Clyf and Clarham	. . .	iiij marcs[6]
,, for a payr of bedys of lambyr [amber]	. . .	. . vijd.
It. recepimus de J. Colman et W. Balwe custod :	. . .	v marcs iiijs.[7]
,, ,, de W. Stabbe pro salute animarum filiorum suorum	.	. . xijd.
,, ,, pro adimpletione rote[8] de certis personis	.	. . xvjd.
,, ,, pro candela de rota .	. . . .	. . ijd.
,, ,, de custodibus antiquis	. . . .	£vij xs. viijd.
,, pro antiquis tabulis quas vendimus Johanni Clerico	. .	. . xxd.
,, pro veste altaris solvendo Steby yn the merche [Marsh]	.	. . viijd.
,, de W. Stabbe de tabula	. . . . .	vjs. viijd.
,, pro candela paschali	. . . . .	vs. iijd.
[One or two more indistinct entries.]		
Summa receptarum . . £xviij iiijd.		

[1] Lamp-yarn.   [2] Qy. clavis, i.e., nails.   [3] = Cerevisia, the Church Ale.
[4] I.e., 1447, N.S. Feb. 24, 25th Hen. VI.   [5] £3 7s. 7d.   [6] £2 13s. 4d.
[7] £3 10s. 8d.   [8] The reel, or corona.

Mem. that ys y payd for the tabyl of the hye awter . . .	xj marcs x*s*.[1]
„ in costage of the same tabyl	xvij*d*.
„ for the bellys to Jon Slo	xx*d*.
„ for costage of to [two] wyng[s] of ray[2] selk for the hy auter	xvij*d*.
„ for a cloth of the tabyl ystenyd [stained] . . .	xx*d*.
„ for a clothe by for [before] the same auter . .	xx*d*.
„ for lyn cloth y bougt for the same cloths . .	x*d*.
„ for wyr and ryngs for the tabyl	xij*d*.
„ for four spykys	vij*d*.
„ for makyng of the sepulkyr tre . . .	xx*d*.
„ for waschyng of clothys	vj*d*.

PAGE 21.

„ for clensyng of ij candylstykky[s] of latyn and a sensa [censer] . .	iij*d*.
„ for Wyll Bonton ys mynde	j*d*.
„ for aschyd yfot at yde od [a shroud fetched at Yde wood] . . .	xvj*d*.
„ for wexe to the rele, and costage	v*s*. viij*d*.
„ for costage of the Ester tapyr	ij*s*. iij*d*.
„ for a rop for the sacryng bell	iiij*d*.
„ for scowryg of the grete semys	iiij*d*.
„ for the rodeloffte to Crosse [the Carpenter] . . .	viij marcs xiij*s*.[3]
„ for to sacryng bell	xiij*d*.
„ for a lege bell, and the mendyng of another . . .	ij*s*. ij*d*.
Summa . . £xv xij*s*. viij*d*.	

These accounts are presented, "coram parochianis," on Thursday before[4] S. Valentine's day, A.D., mccccxlix; and the balance of xlij*s*. xij*d*. is delivered to the new Wardens, John Cooke of Cleve, and John Hylman, junior, of Yatton.

PAGE 22.   A.D. mccccl.   J. HYLMAR AND J. COOKE.

EXPENSES.

In primis pro factura cere paschalis	iij*d*. ob.
„ pro lotione vestimentorum erga festum pasche . .	iiij*d*.
[Entries for wax, &c., as usual.]	
„ Johanni Crosse carpentario pro coopertione baptysterii [Font] .	xvj*s*.
„ pro glutuno et clavi eidem baptysterio . . .	vj*d*.
„ pro lotione vestimentorum	iiij*d*.
„ eidem Crosse sub nomine cure	j*d*.
„ pro cera empta baptysterio	ij*d*.
„ Johanni Crosse pro solario	xij*s*. iiij*d*.
„ for a lyne to the font	ij*d*.
„ schrydyng of treyes yn church hay . . .	j*d*.
„ pro vehitione unius querci de sylva . . .	viij*d*.

[1] £7 16*s*. 8*d*.   [2] *I.e.*, raye=striped.   [3] £5 19*s*. 8*d*.
[4] *I.e.*, before Feb. 14, A.D. 1448-9, for 1447-8, 27 Hen. VI.

for an yren tak to Spenser ys wene [wain]	ij*d*.
for the poley of yren to the fonte	xviij*d*.
for rede sylke to amende the cops [copes] herewith	ij*d*.
we delyvered to the clerke for quyste	iiij*d*.
for clapsyng [clasping] of ij boks	iij*d*.
for the auter clothe to the clerke	vij*s*.
for the rodeloffte to Crosse [the carpenter]	xl*s*.
for costage yn sekyng of a potte or a crokke	iiij*d*.
for wex and makyng of wex ayens Mydwynter, and other certeyn costs there upon	xvj*s*. viij*d*.
in the day of the capyter[1] for sewte of certyn personis	iiij*d*.

PAGE 23.

for a tapyr upon the northe auter	vj*d*.
payd to Crosse for the rodeloffte	vj*s*. viij*d*.
for seekyng of Crosse at Backwell	j*d*.
for a keye and nayl to the stypyll [steeple] dore	iij*d*.

[and a few small repairs.]

PAGE 24. [Blank.]

PAGE 25.

𝔄.𝔇. mccccli.

RECEIPTS BY J. HYLMAN AND J. COKE.

In primis	pro collectione cere paschalis recepimus	vj*s*.
,,	pro toga Johannis Parker	iij*s*. iiij*d*.
,,	pro taberna nostra in die Pentecoste	v marcs. v*s*. (²)
,,	de T. Hygans de pecuniis collectis tabule	x*s*. ij*d*.
,,	pro superiori parte unius quercus	viij*d*.
,,	de Th. Hygannys pro tabula	xij*d*.
,,	de Waltero Crosse et Edmundo Dole	xiij*s*. iiij*d*.
,,	de Vicario pro toga dornebarne [Thorbarne]	ij*s*.
,,	de Davy Cradock et Th. Kew lyghtemen	£iij
,,	de Waltero Crosse et Edmunde Dole	v nobil. iiij*s*. (³)
,,	pro olla enea de Vicario	xxij*d*.
,,	of the old wardens ad solvendum Crosse	vj*s*. viij*d*.
,,	of the old Wardens	vj*s*. viij*d*.

𝔄.𝔇., mccccli, on the Conversion of S. Paul the Wardens brought in the Accounts, and Thomas Hygams and William Watts were elected Wardens, receiving the balance £vj xix*s*. xj*d*.

---

[1] The R. Deanery Chapter was disciplinary, and was used for reporting offences to the Ordinary. In this case the cost of iiij*d*. shows that the Wardens did not go as far as Wells. *Vide* infra, 𝔄.𝔇. mcccclii., p. 94, from which it appears that going to Wells to a chapter cost ij*s*. iij*d*.

² £3 11*s*. 8*d*.   ³ £1 11*s*. 4*d*.

PAGE 26.

   Mem. de receptione custod. WILL. HYGHAM AND W. WATTS.

de Johanne Newton prolumine obitus filie sue pro eo quod expendidit de torticiis . xvj*d*.
Rec. de custodibus Hylman et Cooke . . . . £iiij x*s*.
 ,, de fonte taper . . . . v*s*. ix*d*.
 ,, de J. Goodman, lyghtman . . . . xxvj*s*. viij*d*.
 ,, de J. Maryotte ejus socius . . . . xvj*s*. viij*d*.
 ,, de domina p. de Wyke [Philippa Newton, The Lady of Court de Wyke] per manus J. Newton filii sui de legatione domini Ricardi Newton ad solvend. pro campana . . . . xx*s*.
 ,, de Johanne Hylman et Johanne Cooke . . . . . . xx*s*.
 ,, de Johanne Maryotte . . . . x*s*.
 ,, pro una olla enea vendita . . . . iij*s*.
 ,, de Weneman pro tabula . . . . xij*d*.
 ,, de Th. Sleche de Banwyle pro pulsatione [bell-ringing] . . . iiij*d*.
 ,, de W. Stable pro tabula . . . . vj*s*. iiij*d*.
 ,, pro taberna servicie in festo Pentecoste . . . . . . £iij
 ,, de custodibus luminis de Cleve et Claram, Knyght, et Hert, pro taberna propriorum[1] in festo Michaelis . . . . . £iij vj*s*. x*d*.
 ,, de Johanne Kynge de Cranemore, nomine legationis . . . vj*d*.
 ,, pro olla enea vendita Johanni Hykks . . . . . iiij*s*. vj*d*.
 ,, de legatione Johannis Wampervile . . . . ij*s*.

PAGE 27.   EXPENSES.

In primis for the auterclothys and the corporall and the clerke hys surplesse, and expenses yn beyng [buying] therof at the feyr [fair] . . . xiiij*s*. xj*d*.
Item for wax to the Vicary . . . . viiij*s*. viij*d*.
 ,, for yreworke for ij wyndowys to the smyth of Comysbery . . . iij*s*. ix*d*.
 ,, payede to Crosse for the aler [alure] . . . . . . xx*s*.
 ,, to Crosse ys chylde[2] yn reward . . . . xx*d*.
 ,, for caryage of the cabell and poley for the strekyng [striking] of the belle . viij*d*.
 ,, for wex to the fonte taper and costs ther to . . . . iij*d*.
 ,, for expenses in the day of the weyyng of the belle . . . xvj*d*.
 ,, for caryage of the belle to Redecleve . . . . . . v*s*.
 ,, for the furste payment for the belle at Brystowe to the bellman . £iiij iiij*s*.
 ,, for costs in strekyng the grete belle . . . . ij*s*
 ,, for expenses doo at Bristow yn tyme of the weyyng of the newe belle in makyng of our detys and oder expenses dyverse wyse . . ij*s*. vj*d*.
 ,, for custom [toll] for our wene to Bristowe warde comyng and goyng. . iiij*d*.
 ,, to the servant of Hew the bellman for clovys . . . . . j*d*.
 ,, for the takyng adowen of the old belle, and the hongyng up of the newe belle to the bellman . . . . iiij*s*. iiij*d*.
 ,, to Wyll Hurman for fettyng hume of the newe belle fro Radcleve . . v*s*.

---

[1] Of their own neighbours.   [2] A serving-lad.

for dyverse expenses yn mete and drynke yn the day of the caryage of the belle
homward . . . . iiij*s*. j*d*.
[other small items.]

PAGE 28.
for Crosse ys labour yn makyng of the lede for the holy water stone[1] . . . . ij*d*.
to the same Crosse for the Aler . . . . v*j*s. viij*d*.
to the belle yn the Wendisdaye of Wytsondaye tyme of our taverne we payede [the
money gathered at the Ale, and paid on spot] . . . . xl*s*.
to Crosse at anoder payment for the Aler . . . . . ij marcs iij*d*.[2]
for glewe to the Aler . . . . iiij*d*.
for the payntyng of the deske cloth . . . . xvj*d*.
  „ for the byndyng of the boks . . . . v*s*.

𝔄.𝔇. mccccłii.

On the Feast of S. Scholastica (Febr. x), the said Wardens made their account:
William at Wyke and John Valwe were chosen Wardens, and the balance of the
account is lviij*s*. x*d*.

PAGE 29.   𝔄.𝔇. mccccłi.

RECEIPTS.

FROM THE OLD WARDENS, W. HYGHAM AND W. WATTS.

In primis de legato Johannis Gybbis de Tykkenam [Tickenham] . . . . xij*d*.
Item de legato Th. Drewette, pro uno boviclo . . . . iij*s*. iiij*d*.
  „ de J. Dele et J. Crosse custodibus luminis de Yatton pro taberna ipsorum
                                                                                   iiij mark vj*s*. x*d*.[3]
  „ de legato Alicie Beny uxoris Johannis Webbe de Stoke . . . . xij*d*.
  „ de J. Wale de debito antiquo . . . . x*s*.
  „ pro ligniclis[4] de Vicario . . . . vj*d*.
  „ pro cera paschalis candele . . . . vj*s*. ix*d*.
  „ de legato R. Kyffte . . . . vj*s*. viij*d*.
  „ pro taberna J. Fischer et Philip Beny pro lumine de Clar et Cleve . xlvj*s*. x*d*.
  „ pro tabula de Johanne Salamon, juniore . . . . ij*d*.
  „ de eodem Johanne sub nomine legati pro pyxide . . . . . xij*d*.
  „ de eodem Johanne sub nomine legati ecclesie . . . . . . xij*d*.
  „ de W. Wyllyng ex debito antiquo . . . . vij*s*. j*d*
            Summa . . £xiij xix*s*. iiij*d*.

PAGE 30.   [Blank.]

---

[1] *I.e.*, Stoup.   [2] £1 6*s*. 11*d*.   [3] £3 0*s*. 2*d*.
[4] *I.e.*, small wood, probably shroudings of the Church-hay.

PAGE 31.   EXPENSES.

In primis	for wex boffte of the Vicar, xxj lb.	viijs. ixd.
,,	for wex boffte at Bristow, iiij lb.	xxd.
,,	to John Sloo, for his pension [stipend]	ijs.
,,	for takyng adown of the tymber of the Chapyll of Synt Jamys	vijd.
,,	for werkemanschyp of tymber to Synt Jamys ys chapylle	iijs. iiijd.
,,	for makyng of the walle to the same chapyl	ijs. jd.
,,	for the costage yn caryage abowte tyler and erthe and stone to the same chapyll	xiiijd.
,,	for latthenayles in numero M. pretio	xviijd.
,,	for tyle stone and the caryage of the same stone from Naylsey, and costs also to Hurman	ijs. iijd.
,,	for a precescionall boke to the cherche	xiiijs. viijd.
,,	for helyng [tiling] of Synt Jamys ys Chapell to R. Tyler of Backwyll	vs. vijd.
,,	for Ale gevyn to the parysch of Myll Blewett,[1] ys bayle yn rewarde	iiijd.
,,	for muse[2] gaderede [gathered] to Synt Jamys ys chapell	iijd.
,,	for costs doyn abowt the oke boffte from hyde wode	xxd.

PAGE 32.

yn costage to Well for sowte of [suit touching] the churche gods [goods] yn two tymes[3]	xviijd.
for makeng of the chyldren surpel [surplices]	xd.
yn costs for laboryng at Wells for Crosse	iiijd.
yn costs at Wells for the Chapter for the cherche ys neds at laste tymys[3]	ijs. iijd.
[Total expenses] £v xiijs. xjd.	

JOHN HYKKE and WALTER ROPER to be Wardens.

PAGE 33.

A.D. mcccclíiii.

RECEIPTS OF HYKKE AND ROPER.

de antiquis custodibus	£viij vs. vijd.
ex legato Roberti Ken	vjs. viijd.
pro vasto tortitorum [torches] obitus Roberti Ken	ijs. iijd.
de W. Durnebarne et Isabell Hurdewych protaberna ipsorum	£iij xxd.
[There is also the usual Pentecost Ale]	£iij vijd.
de W. Meye et R. Knyght de Claram [Claverham] pro taberna ipsorum pro lumine	xliijs. xd.
pro uno coopertorio de legato uxoris J. Hatte	vs.
pro vitulo de legato Steph. Colman	iiijs.
de legato W. Pyke de Ken	xvjd.

[1] *I.e.*, an Ale was given to the parish by one of the Blewett family, once seated at Hinton Bluet. His Bailiff in reward got a fee of iiijd.

[2] Moss was laid under the tiles, as felt is now, for a thickening.

[3] Understand some suit in the Consistorial Court of the Chapter of Wells touching the fabric or ornaments of the Church.

| PAGE 34. | [Blank.] |

PAGE 35.   EXPENSES.

pro consecratione campane, suffraganeo[1]	vj*s*.
pro manutergio paschali	iij*s*.
pro factura superpellicie	iij*d*.
pro terrubulo [thurible] et olei vase et canabo [canvas] et navi[2]	ix*s*. iiij*d*.
in expensis factis apud Wryngton in servisia ecclesie . .	viij*d*.
[a quantity of stone bought.]	
J. Crosse, Carpenter, and John Sutton are paid xx*s*. and xl*s*.	
[No other special entries.]	
Balance paid to incoming wardens	£x viij*s*. j*d*.

PAGE 36.   A.D. mcccclív.

W. BURNELL AND J. FYSCHER, WARDENS.
[Only one legacy.]

de vicario ex dono pro pavimento et solario	vj*s*. viij*d*.
pro tabula altaris	vij*s*. vj*d*.
de Philippa Newton pro vasto cere tortitorum in die sepulture filie sue, pro iiij lb.	xvj*d*.
pro taberna Thome Beny	v marcs iij*s*.
et R. Bowton juniore, custodi luminis de Yatton . . .	iiij marcs v*s*.
pro taberna J. Herte et J. Wyllyng custodibus luminis de Cleve et Clarum	
	iiij marcs iij*s*.[3]

PAGE 37.   EXPENSES.

In primis Johanni Crosse pro solario	. . . . .	xxvj*s*. viij*d*.
,,	for a lyne to the leynte clothe [Lent cloth] . .	ij*d*.
,,	for a glase to the lampe	j*d*.
,,	for a gurdell to the vestments	j*d*.
,,	for John Sloo ys salery	ij*s*.
,,	for expenses atte Cherche ale of Wryngton . . .	x*d*.
	[Many payments to Crosse.]	
,,	payede for divers colers to the Aler [Alure] . . .	vj*s*. vj*d*.
,,	costage yn settyng uppe of the Aler, the fyrste daye . .	ij*s*. vij*d*.
,,	payede an ernyste peny to the clerke	j*d*.
,,	yn laberyng yn costs to ryde to speke with the clerke atte Hunspylle .	iiij*d*.
,,	for colers late boffte at Bristow	ij*s*. j*d*.
,,	for the paynter ys hyre a wyke [week]	xx*d*.

[1] James, Bishop of Aghadoe, was at this time employed by Bishop Beckington.
[2] "Navis," generally "navicula," or boat; the vessel which is used to hold the incense before it is put with a spoon into the censer or thurible.
[3] £3 9*s*. 8*d*., £2 18*s*. 4*d*., and £2 16*s*. 4*d*.

for the same payenter ys bedde	ij*d*.
for yren worke for the syler [Cieler]	xx*d*.
for John Sotton ys labor in pavyng	xx*s*.
for bords from Sowtheampton	vj*s*. viij*d*.
for ij bords boffte at Brystow	iiij*s*. x*d*.

Page 38.

for caryage of the same borde by twyne[1] [South] Hampton and Chew	vj*s*. viij*d*.
for costs yn the bargan makyng	ij*d*.
for costs yn the caryage of the same borde betwyne Chew and home	x*d*.
for nayls boffte to the syler	j*d*.
for colers	xiij*s*. vj*d*.
for feschyng [fetching] of a stone from Chelvey to grynde colers therwith	j*d*.
for drawing of bords to schylyng [ceiling]	ij*s*. vj*d*.
to Crosse at a payment for the syler	xx*s*.
to Crosse at another tyme for the syler	xx*s*.
to J. Hykkes for trussyng of the [? s]hyde and the Crosse with the Maryes	iiij*d*.
for glovys[2] for dewtees to Crosse yn settyng uppe of the worke fesste of the syler	iiij*d*.
for one erneste peny to J. Smyth	j*d*.
for an ernyste to J. Hykkes in makyng of segs [seats]	j*d*.
to J. Sutton for pavyng, payed	xx*s*.
for wyndeyng oute of robell [rubble] at the awterys and oder thyngs	vj*d*.
for sawdyng [soldering] glew to crosse	iij*d*.
for a quarte of peyntyng oyle	v*d*.
for dyvers colers boffte [bought]	xxij*d*.
y payde to Crosse for the syler	vj*s*. viij*d*.
payede for golde to paynte the angell	vj*s*.
for mendyng of a keye to the vicedore	j*d*.
for yren to the rodeloffte, payde to J. Smyth	ij*s*. vj*d*.
Balance	xxx*s*. iij*d*.

The new Wardens are W. BREKEBEKE and THOMAS HARBELL.

Page 39.

De receptis pecuniis pro tabula altaris.

de Walt. Carter	vj*d*.	de J. Watts	iiij*d*.
,, T. Wyllyng	iiij*d*.	,, Stephano Coleman	xx*d*.
,, J. Bowden	iiij*d*.	,, W. Brekebeke	ij*s*.
,, T. Beny	xvj*d*.	,, J. Sloo	iiij*d*.
,, J. Scott	viij*d*.	Sa. vij*s*. vj*d*.	

---

[1] *I.e.*, between.
[2] Gloves as a complimentary fee to the Carpenter on completing his work for the ceiler's hands.

PAGE 40.

Summa solvendorum ex parte W. Wyllyng et Prewett . . . . . xxxvij*s.*
Mem. quod W. Wyllyng indebitus est ecclæ de Yatton à tempore quo erat custos
   eccl. sc. omnibus satisfactis satisfaciendis, et allocatis allocandis . . . vij*s.*
Et dicit quod solvit de summa dimissa a tempore suo J. Hylman et J. Coke success-
   oribus suis V nobiles per Wale et remiss. nobile de Welett istius debiti . . x*s.*
Remanet solvenda ex pte W. Wyllyng ecclæ . . . . vij*s.*
Solutum est J. Crosse pro solario diversis temporibus a diversis Custodibus, a tempore
   quo incepit opus suum in ecclesia de Yatton . . . . . £xviij xiij*s.*
Et sic remanet sibi [*sic*] solvendum . . . . £iij vj*s.* v*d.*

PAGE 41.

A.D. mccccl̃v, *i.e.*, 1455–6 for 1454–5.
W. BREKEBEKE, JUN., AND THOS. HARBELL.

Eighteen Bequests; some in money, some in kind, as a heifer, a sheep, a brass pot, &c.
Several gifts, *e.g.*:—

de dono Banvyle		vj*s.*
,, Canonici de Staverdale		iiij*s.*
,, J. Clerke quod Crede solvet		iij*d.*
,, W. Wever pro xij imaginibus		xij*s.*
,, Vicarii pro iij ,,		iij*s.*
,, W. Stabbe pro ij ,,		ij*s.*
,, T. Harbell pro ij ,,		ij*s.*
,, W. Brekebeke pro ij ,,		ij*s.*
,, J. Efle pro j ,,		xij*d.*
,, J. Pyke pro ij ,,		ij*s.*
,, R. Dornebarne pro ij ,,		ij*s.*
,, J. Hylman pro j ,,		xij*d.*
pro annulo aureo ex legato sororis J. Hylman		ij*s.* vj*d.*
pro taberna Roberti Yngram et W. Brekebeke custodum luminum de Yatton		£iij iiij*d.*
pro cera paschalis candele		v*s.* x*d.*
ex taberna Kysste et Brademerse		xlvj*s.* viij*d.*

Summa £xiiij xvij*s.* v*d.*

PAGE 42. [Blank.]

PAGE 43. EXPENSES.

a potell of paynters oyl	x*d.*
for vernaysche [varnish], a pound and a quarter	x*d.*
for glew and diverse colers for the loffte	iiij*s.* x*d.*
for chelke [chalk] and greye cayk [cake] and paper	j*d.*
for a buyschel of schyryds for make cole [charcoal]	iiij*d.*
Itm. for makyng and mendyng of glasse to the churche	

o

for a barre yn the cherche dore, and a crampe of yre [iron] in the sowthe syde of the soler   xij*d*.
for expenses at Crosse ys ale yn settyng uppe of the poste of the rode-lofte . . iij*d*.
Itm. ypayde to Crosse for hys labor yn the loffte . . . . . . x*js*.
Itm. for labour of ryngers and yevyrs [givers] of ale to [*i.e.*, at] Banvyle [Banwell].
for the chandeler yn the rodelofte, to Jenken Smyth of Comysbury . . . xiij*s*. iiij*d*.
for ale gevyn to Crosse yn certeyn tymis yn hys worke to make hym wel wellede [well-willed] . . . . ij*d*. ob.

PAGE 44.
for erneste peny to the ymage maker . . . . . j*d*.
to settyng up of the ymages . . . . iiij*d*.
for colde [charcoal] whyche J. Smythe made upon the yren werke . . . xviij*d*.
    [Many entries of large sums paid for the syler and for colours.]
for the ymages to the rodeloffte yn number lxix . . . . £iij x*s*. iiij*d*.
for fette a down a stone of the Spyre, the hyre and cost . . . . xviij*d*.
for makyng the wyndow yn the stepyll and the batylment . . . . iij*s*. iiij*d*.
for settyng up the yren worke to the syler . . . . . . v*d*.
for takeyng a don of the olde loffte and makyng of the trestell . . . . xij*d*.

PAGE 45.[1]
yn costys in ystyre [Easter] monday to tary at the Vycary ys hoce [house] for the preces [? priests] . . . . j*d*.
for j man to helpe to wymmynge [winnowing] the malte to [*i.e.*, at] the mylle . . ij*d*.

PAGE 46.   [Stone is bought at Dundry for the spire and steeple.]

PAGE 47.
to gaderyng of oyestere scellys [oyster shells] . . . . . j*d*. ob.
for takyng away of the corvyll [corbel] stonys of the Alere . . . xij*d*.
for mendyng of the wyndows and legynge of the dore above the stere [stair].
for the mynde of Wyllian Malsyll and Annese Harrys . . . ij*d*.
for the mynde of Wyllliam Bowton . . . . . . j*d*.

PAGE 48.
for makyng of the Threehewgll [threshold] to the porche . . . . ix*d*.
for the makyng of the hole above the stere . . . . . . xij*d*.
for cropys [cramps] to the tabyll [prob. Parapet] of the syde allee [aisle] . . ij*d*.
to Bole [Bull] of Axbridge . . . . lx*s*. xiij*s*. iiij*d*.

PAGE 49.
    [Eight small payments in Latin, and in a new hand.]
  [All the above pages from page 43 full of entries, but none at all unusual beside those noted.]

A.D. mccccłvi.   [Appears to be missing.]

---

[1] Page 45 of the original accounts begins here, and is entitled "Costagiys" [costages]. It is written in a new hand which lasts to near the end of page 48, and in very bad spelling, and in English.

PAGE 50.
𝔄.𝔇. mcccclvii, i.e., 1457–8 for 1456–7.
JOHN [HORTE] AND JOHN GOODMAN.

Receyvyd of Wyllyam Colinys and John [Stevyn the late Wardens] . . . . xj*d*.
[This page, 50, and page 51, have been left blank for the account of the Wardens Goodman.]

PAGE 52.   RECEIPTS.
of J. Godeman and J. Horte [successors to Colins and Stevyn] recevede for the
    pascall tapyr . . . . v*s*. ix*d*.
for [? from] the lytemen of Cleve, Recharde Hayman and John Coukar for the taveryn
    yrecevede . . . . iiij marke ij*s*. (¹)
for the lytemen of the northe syde, J. Pyke, and T. Avery, for a taveryn . . £iij xiiij*s*.
for the wardeyns of Yatton for a taverne ale, yn clere . . . . £iij x*s*. viij*d*.
of John Stevyn and Wyllyam Colyngs of the Recete of the rayer [rear] yere . . xj*d*.

PAGE 53.   EXPENSYS.
[Several purchases of colours at Bristol.]
to wrytyng of a boke to an ely [anneal] a syke man, to Thomas of Kyngnstun in all
    costys . . . . xviij*d*.
to the chorchemen for schryde wode yn the chorchehay . . . . . j*d*.
for clothe to make aubys [albs] to the chorche . . . . . . vj*s*.
for makyng faste of the emagys [images] at the hye Croce . . . xij*d*.
for the three "myndes," Malsell, Harris, and Bowton . . .

PAGE 54.
for wax ybowte to make the lyte to fore the crosse . . xxxiij*s*. iiij*d*.

PAGE 55.
MEM. The Wardynys of the Schorche of Yatton, Recharde Thorbarne and Ric.
    Knyhygt [Knight] recevede of the schorche godes in honde, £vij vj*d*.
[Receipts as usual.]

PAGE 56.   EXPENSES.
to J. Hyckys to make a Judas, and the font tapyr . viij*d*.
for xxvj cappys . . . . xiiij*d*.

PAGE 57.
for a corde to the canapy . . . . ij*d*. ob
[Much plumber's work in roof of porch.]

PAGE 58.
William Thorbarne and Davy Cradoke, the new Wardens, receive from R. Thorbarne
    and R. Knight the balance of . . . . £x xix*s*

PAGE 59.
[Detached entries belonging to Cradok and Thorbarne's year, but crossed out.]

£1 8*s*. 8*d*.

[The spire was still in hand; a regyl [rail?] was made about it, and much plumbing done; the surplus lead was sold to the Vicar.]

PAGE 60.   Nomina promitt. pro ymaginibus.   XV nomina.

MEM. that there ys payede to Crosse for the makyng and peyntyng of the Aler of the Chorche . . . . £xxxj ijs. xjd.

PAGE 61.

A.D. mccccllviii. *i.e.*, 1458–9 for 1457–8.

DAVY CRADDOKE AND WYLLYAM THORBARNE, SUCCESSORS TO R. THORBARNE AND R. KNIGHT.
Balance £x xixs.

RECEIPTS from ALES and BEQUESTS.

EXPENSES.

In lede at iiijs. viijd., the C. . . . . Summa £iiij xs. iiijd.
It. to make a regyll [? Rail] abowte the batylmente . . . . . xvd.
„ for a Plomer to hely the batylmente for the stypyle . . . . . vjs.
„ for Ire gare [Iron-gear] farmentes, hokys, and other thynges to the chorche euce [use], vj Skore li. [six score pounds of iron] at . . . . . xijd. a li.
„ for sande to ley the lede [for casting the lead] . . . . . . vd.
„ for makyng clene of Syn Jamys schapdell [chapel] . . . . . ijd.

PAGE 62.
„ for makyng iiij torches agenste candylmas . . . . ijs.
„ for byndyng of ij portoce bokys . . . . . iijs. iiijd.
„ for pavyng of the chorche, to W. Hyll . . . . . £iij

PAGE 63.

A.D. mccccllix. *i.e.*, 1459–60 for 1458–9.

WARDENS, THOMAS THOMAS AND WYLLYAM MAY.

RECEIPTS.

Balance from CRADOKE and THORBARNE £x xvijs. iijd., and xij ryngs.

EXPENSES.

It. for iiij bushels barleche [barley] of the queste of J. May   xxd.

PAGE 64.
It. to the carpynter for to cely [ceil] the Rodlofte (in erneste) . . . . jd.
„ for walsche [*i.e.*, foreign, probably Wainscot] bord and plankys . . . xxxiijs.
xxx zeme of bordys, xijd., the zeme, and iij zeme of plangys xijd. the zeme.
„ for lyme to pavy the chorch . . . . iijd.

PAGE 65.
It to a mendy a crosse of latyn . . . . . iiijd.
„ for pentyng [painting] the Rodlofte . . . . . £iij
„ for a croke to hang the Trendyll . . . . . vjd.

PAGE 66.

It. iiij*li.* wex to fulfyl the rele
„ for a staynede clothe to Syn Colas [S. Nicolas] auter . . . iiij*s.* ij*d.*
Total expenses . . . . £ix xij*s.*

SUPPLEMENTARY EXPENSES.

for Weeryner . . . . ij*s.* iiij*d.*
To Wylliam Hyll for ye batylmente of V panys [bays] . . . xxxv*s.*
To same Wyll, for ye playne worke at the weste zyn [west end] of y[e] cherche . xij*d.*
To same for makyng [good] ij brokyng panes . . . . . . x*s.*
For a newe pynnakyll . . . . xij*d.*
for the helyng of ij tomys [tombs] of Isbell Symnys and alys Fischer . . ij*d.*
for a carchawe [kerchief] to the chals [chalice] . . . . . ij*d.*
to the clerke for rep[er]yng [repairing] of and settyng on of a norfys[1] . ij*d.*

PAGE 67.

A.D. mccclx, *i.e.*, 1460–61 for 1459-60.

WARDENS, JOHN WYLLYNG AND W. AVERY.

receiving from Thomas and May . . . . . . Balance £ix xij*s.*

EXPENSES.

As for the grayell [grail] . . . . viij marcs[2]
for makyng of the stolys . . . . xiiij*d.*
for mendyng of the orgyns . . . . ij*d.*
for mendyng the hole in the cherche pavment in mendyng of the pylpyt . . v*d.*

PAGE 68.

Total . . . £ix xv*s.* x*d.*
Balance . . £xij xvj*s.*

PAGE 69.

Received for the quota [? quarter] . . . . v*s,* viij*d.*
„ for a coppe [cope] . . . . l*s.*
Total receipts [of John Bene and John Seffe, who present their accounts in the next
  page]. . . . . £xxij xij*s.*

PAGE 70.

A.D. mccclxi, *i.e.*, 1461–2 for 1360–61.

JOHN BENE[3] AND JOHN SEFFE, WARDENS.

receiving Balance from Wyllyng and Avery . . . . . £xij xvj*s.*

PAYMENTS.

for flakys [hurdles] to make scafote [scaffold] . . . . . . x*d.*
for a lampe of braste [brass] . . . . viij*d.*
for a clothe to the sepulkyr . . . . xxvj*s.* viij*d.*
for makyng of ij crosts [crosses ?] . . . . iij*s.*

[1] An orphrey.   [2] £5 6*s.* 8*d.*   [3] Called, in 1463, by his trade, Wever.

for ij scholys [shovels]	ijd.
for mendyng of abys [albs]	iiijd.
for frestonys	xviijs.
for bredd and ale and fysch to the caryng [carrying] of the stonys	iijs. xd.
[1]pro lapidibus	vjs. viijd.
pro ciphis	vijd. ob.
pro la panno benedicto	vjd. ob.
pro calcibus (et in expensis iiijd.)	xd.
pro emendatione pelvis sub lampade	ijd.
pro descisione arborum in cimiterio	ijd.
pro reparatione magnorum candelabrorum	iijs. iiijd.
pro tribulo [thuribulo] et patella ferrea	iiijd.
pro dealbatione ecclesie Willelmo Hill	xjs.
Item Willelmo Hill	xiijs. viijd.
pro una scala	viijd.
pro uno vase ad dealbandam ecclesiam	iiijd.
pro alio vase quod mutuati sumus vel conduximus à Joh. Pycke	iiijd.
pro disco stanneo ad reparationem candelabrorum	vjd.
pro calcibus	xiiijd.
pro expensis in adquisitione ipsorum	iiijd.
pro expensis in nundinis [Fair] S. Johannis, Bristollie	xijd.
ad turibulum novum argenteum et pyxidem	£iij
ad turibulum argenteum	xvjs. viijd.
pro capsulis ligneis pyxidis et turribuli	vjd.
pro una scapha [censer]	jd.
Item solvimus vicario	vjs. viijd.

[Several other entries, of stones, &c., and repairs of pinnacles.]

PAGE 71.

RECEPTA. [Four items; and also Eleven Payments belonging to Bene and Seffe. Then Four items of receipt belonging to their successors Brekebeke and Symmys, to whom they pay Balance] . . . . £iiij xivs.

A.D. mcccclxiii.

W. BREKBEKE, JUNIOR, AND RICHARD SYMMYS, *alias* HURDWYCH, WARDENS.

EXPENSES.

pro emendatione cerarum [locks] thesaurie [treasury, probably the parvise]	vijd.
pro virga ferrea, ad altum altare	jd. ob.
per Vicarium pro impetratione brevis circa [unfinished]	xxs.

PAGE 72.

RECEIPTS from the usual sources. Balance paid to Bene and Hillman   £viij xjd.

[1] Change of hand and language.

A.D. mcccclxiiii.

Th. Bene and William Hillman, Wardens.

Expenses.

Sacristario pro custodia campanarum . . .	iijs.
pro appositione cere ad hostium	jd.
pro clavis ad magnas ceras	ixd.
pro commutatione campane sacramentalis[1] . .	xvd.
pro commutatione phiolarum[1]	vd.
pro ij zonis vestimentorum	ijd.
pro emptura nove calicis	£v vjs. viijd.
[2]In costs to ryde to Woke [Wookey][3] to blesse the chals .	iijd. ob.

[Several repairs to the bells, and wax bought, as usual.]

Page 73.   Receipts.

In primis collegimus et recepimus pro cera paschali . . .	. vjs. jd.
pro superpelliciis antiquis venditis	. iiijd.

[From Bequests and Gifts in kind and money, and from Ales.]

It. Thomas [the Warden] dedit empture calicis . . .	. viijd.

Expenses [supplementary].

English {
for a case for the chals	. viijd.
for ye Plumer mendyng of the Sowthe Ele [Aisle][4] .	xjs. xd.
for ye molds makyng and costs	iijs. viijd.

Page 74.

A.D. mccccklxv.

J. Avery and J. Godknave, Wardens.

Receipts.

Balance from Bene and Hylman	£vij xiijs. iiijd.
received for torchys of my lady Nuton, bernyng at the [in]terment	xd.
,, of Jone Waltrys for candels to the trendel	jd.

[Fourteen contributions for candles,—a new item; nine bequests, three Ales.]

Page 75.   Expenses.

paid for the goggyn [gudgeon] of the grete bell	jd.
paid for chechyng[5] of too cruetts	vjd.
we paid at wakyng at sepulcure	ijd.
,, for fylling of a elme	ijd.
,, for frenge [fringe] to the curtens	xijd.
,, for rynghys [rings] to the curtens	ijd.

---

[1] Qy. whether exchanged for the new chalice.
[2] Bishop Bekynton's Manor-house.
[5] Mis-spelt for "fetching."
[3] Change to English.
[4] Also spelled Isle, Yle, Aisle, and Aile.

PAGE 76.
paid to schote the braste[1] . . . . ijs. viijd.
the costs to schote the same braste in mete and dryng . . . . jd. ob.
payd for coleryng and gyldyng . . . . iiiijd.

PAGE 77.

A.D. mccccxlvi.

J. DOLE AND T. WALL, WARDENS.
RECEIPTS.

Balance from Avery and Godknave . . . . . . £x xvjs.
From usual sources. Total . . . . . . £xxj ob.

PAGE 78.   [Blank.]

PAGE 79.   EXPENSES.

for makyng tymbyr,[2] and makyng of steches[3] . . . . . xxjd.
for ale to menne wakyng at the sepulcure . . . . . iiijd.
for a paks[4] . . . . xd.
for Annys Lancotynngs myne[5] . . . . jd.
for bred and ale to hyr myne . . . . ijd.
for the wyndow levys[6] . . . .
        Total expenses . . £iiij xijs. vjd. ob.

PAGE 80.

A.D. mccccxlvii.

T. KEWE AND JOHN HURT, WARDENS.
RECEIPTS.

Balance from Dole and Wale . . . . . . £xvj viijs. ijd.
of June Mey to the peyntyng of the Mary . . . . . ijd.
of June Kewe to the same . . . .
for a broken posenett [Pot] . . . . xvjd.

PAGE 81.   EXPENSES.
payd for angyng of wyndow-levys[6] in the treser-howse   vjd.
to make the scafote[7] to the peynter . . . .   iiijd.

PAGE 82.
to the peynter to peynt owre Lady . . . . . . £iiij
to J. Bowton to bryng home the auter clothe fro John Alangotyn . . iiijd.
to the peynter to peynt the Crystofer . . . . . . xxs.

[1] To cast the brass.   [2] Dressing the log.   [3] Stacks of small wood or bark.
[4] Pax.   [5] Mind.   [6] Folding shutters.   [7] Scaffold.

to R. Rowe to veche a capull[1] at Wrynton, and to lede hym home	ij*d*.
to gorney [Gurney's] son to lede home the capull	j*d*.
for a pyggs wote[2]	ij*d*.
Total, £ix xij*s*. ij*d*.	

PAGE 83.

[Three small items belonging to last account :—the rest blank.]

PAGE 84.

A.D. mcccclxviii.

J. KYNGE AND W. WHITYNG, WARDENS.

Balance from Kewe and Hort .	£xv viij*s*.
Receipts as usual. Total	£xxv xviij*s*. x*d*.

PAGE 85. EXPENSES.

[A bell is re-cast at Bristol.]

to the bellmanys man to wene[3] the bell	j*d*.
to help wyne[4] uppe the lytyll bell	j*d*.
payd to vetch the capull at Clevedon	ij*d*.

PAGE 86.

to J. Harnell for ij nygts wakyng the sepulcur .	ij*d*.
casting the bell alone cost	£iiij iij*s*. ix*d*.
for ij stavys to bere the cloth hover howr lord .	iij*d*.
for mendyng[5] iiij beryels in the chorche	xiiij*d*.
for a stafe, and to peynt the stavys .	iij*d*.
for peyntyng the crystofer	xxiij*s*. v*d*.

PAGE 87.

payd to John Kyng to lede the capul to Clevedon	j*d*.
Total, £ix xx*s*. iij*d*.	

PAGE 88.

A.D. mccccllxix.

T. AVERY AND J. TOWKER, WARDENS.

RECEIPTS.

Balance from Whyting and Kyng	£xv xviij*s*. vij*d*.
T. Kewe and J. Harte owyng to the parasche xx*s*. that they delyvered to the peynter with owte leve of the parasche .	
received of a chapman[6] to ston[7] in the porche .	ob.
„ of my lady Newton for bernyng of the torgs[8]	xij*d*.
„ of my mastras[9] for brenyng of the torges	xij*d*.

[1] A horse. [2] A pig's foot, a vessel for carrying coal or such like.
[3] Wene = either "win," *i.e.*, bring it home, or "wain." [4] Wind.
[5] The Wardens were liable for making good the pavement after interments, and on this ground took vj*s*. viij*d*. as a fee.
[6] A Pedlar allowed to sell his wares on some feast-day. [7] Stand, *i.e.*, with his wares.
[8] Torches. [9] Masters, the Newtons.

PAGE 89.   EXPENSES.
for ij regets,[1] and for threde therto . . . . vj*d*.
for a 3ete[2] . . . . iiij*s*.
for the caryng home of the same 3ete . . . . vj*d*.
to E. Gole to mend the bellyn[3] . . . . vj*d*.
for ij apryns[4] . . . . vj*d*.
for xiiij coppys[5] . . . . viij*d*.
for a corporas, and for makyng the panne to the censer . . . iij*d*. ob.

PAGE 90.
for iiij yerds of clothe to hang by fore the Mare [Mary] . . . . xxij*d*.
yn mete and dryngg to brek the wex, and mylte[6] hyt . . . . ij*d*.
payd for the enteryng at the corte to rere [? recover] the mony agenst J. Dole . . iij*d*.
to clerke to reppe[7] howte ye lynyng and settyng yn a [8]3e [or ye] in the vestments . . . . j*d*.

PAGE 91.   𝔄.𝔇. mccccℓxxx [by error for 1470.]
R. WYLLYNG AND R. BENE, WARDENS.
RECEIPTS.
including Balance £xxij ij*s*. v*d*. from Averaye and Towker . . £xxxj iij*s*. ij*d*.

PAGES 92, 93.   EXPENSES.
for reppyng[7] owte ye loke, and settyng yn a 3e of ye Treser-house dore . viij*d*.
for pavyng of Stabys beryell . . . . iiij*d*.
for sityng[5] of the Church Wardens . . . . iiij*d*.

PAGE 94.
𝔄.𝔇 mccccℓxx.   Feast of St. Matthew, Ap.
J. APPASSYE AND RICHARD WYLLYNG, PROCTURRS.
RECEIPTS.
Balance from Bene and Bowton . . . . £xxiiij x*s*. viij*d*.
of the bequest of the lady of Clevedon . . . . xij*d*.
[A most unusual number of bequests, 29 in all, both in kind and in money, but no gifts.]

PAGE 95.   EXPENSES.
in costs to ryde to Wells to speke with the recever, a ponne iij men . . ix*d*.
to the sextyn . . . . iij*s*.
in mete and dryngk a ponne vij men to chese[9] tymbyr. [repeated 1471.] vij*d*.
in do . . . . to bar yn ye tymbyr yn to Syn Jays[10] cherge . . ij*d*

---

[1] Rochets.   [2] Gate.   [3] Plural of bell.   [4] Aprons.   [5] A citation by the Ordinary.   [6] Melt.
[7] Ripping.   [8] A mark perhaps Y for Yatton, see next accounts.   [9] Choose.   [10] St. James'.

[Several entries about felling timber, quarrying stones, and "stabelyng"[1] of stones.]
PAGES 96, 97.
for amendyng of the vyne[2] in the rodelofte . . . j*d*

PAGE 98. **A.D. mccccLxxi.**

W. PREWETT AND J. KEWE, WARDENS.
RECEIPTS.

Balance from Appassy and Willyng . . . . . . £xxiij *x*s. xj*d*.
Bequest : viz., fro ij childryn . . . . xij*d*.
The Ales as usual.

PAGE 99.   EXPENSES.

to iij men to wake at the sepulcure . . . . iiij*d*.
to make a baner . . . . v*d*.
in mete and dryng upon men to speke to Fejamys[3] for the cherge howce[4] . . . v*d*.
for ij wey cole . . . . *x*s.
for makyng a kylle,[5] and ye lyme-berner . . . .
to bere hyt alonne[6] from the bote . . . . xiij*d*.
in cost in mete and dryng to carie home stonys and breyng[7] of the fundament . . *x*s. ij*d*.

PAGE 100.   [Much stone and lime bought, and lime burnt.]

to leying of the fundaments . . . . vj*s*. ij*d*.
for the weleberow . . . . xvij*d*.
for makyng a schorde[8] at the wyte croste[9] . . . . ij*d*.
for makyng of ye style yn ye Cherch hay wall[10] . . . . . . xxij*d*.

PAGE 101.   [Two oaks and some elm trees bought.]

for rydyng[11] of the new howse . . . . iiij*d*.
for makyng a cherche hay wall . . . . xij*d*.
for remeve[12] ij dores . . . . xij*d*.
to remeve the mantell broddyr[13] . . . . iiij*d*.
for wote mele[14] . . . . iiij*d*.

PAGE 102.
Have yn myne[15] that John Appassye and R. Wyllyng owyt to Will. Prewytt and John Kewe . . . . *x*s. x*d*.
and Jo. Bowton owyt to same men . . . . *x*s.

---

[1] The stone was quarried at Felton and Hendeley, brought home green, stacked—perhaps thatched—till seasoned enough for use in the building of the Church-house in 1471.
[2] The vine-pattern cornice.
[3] Fitz-james; probably of the family seated at Redlynch, near Bruton, the head of which became Chief-Justice, temp. H. VII-VIII.
[4] Church-house.   [5] Kiln.   [6] Along.   [7] Bringing.   [8] Shard, *i.e.*, a gap.
[9] The white Cross.   [10] Again, p. 101.   [11] Ridding.   [12] Removing.   [13] Broader.
[14] Oat-meal.   [15] Mind.

A.D. mccccbxxii.

J. THURBARN AND J. HYCKS, WARDENS.
RECEIPTS.

Balance from Prewet and Kewe	£xij vijs. ijd.
Total	£xxvj ixs. viijd.

PAGE 103.[1]

recevyd for the hyre of the chamber in the Cherche howse . xijd.

PAGE 104.[1]   EXPENSES.

for iiij hukmuckes[2] .	vjd.
for hopyng[3] .	iijd.
for mendyng of the chetyll and of the pannys .	iijd.
for makyng of a pygges fote .	iijd.
I payde at Wryngton at the Cherche Ale .	xijd.

PAGES 105, 106.   [Blank.]

PAGE 107.

A.D. mccccbxxii–iii.

J. THURBARN AND J. HYCKS, WARDENS.
RECEIPTS.

Balance from Prewett and Kewe	£xij vijs. ijd.
for candyls of the rele	jd.
and for chese that was yʒeve to the settyng up of yᵉ tymber .	vijd.

[Bequests and Ales as usual.]

PAGES 108-9.   [Nothing unusual in the payments.]

PAGE 110.

A.D. mccccbxxiii–iv.

W. STABBE AND J. HURDEWYCHE, PROCTYRYS.
RECEIPTS.

From the rather[4] Procturys Thorbarn and Hycks . . .	xvs.
from the Vikarye, for the new chamber . .	xd.
of J. Hurdewyche, for the hyre of the howse . .	xijd.
of W. Hoper, for the howse	xijd.
of W. Hyllman, for the Cherche howse . .	xijd.
of W. Hurdewyche for the howse . . .	xijd.

PAGE 111.

Total . . . . £xiij ixs. viijd.

---

[1] The date of these entries is doubtful, the sheet being misplaced.
[2] Something for wiping the feet. Cf. Jennings' Somt. Dialect.   [3] Hooping.
[4] Earlier, comparative of rathe = early.

PAGE 112.   Among the EXPENSES.

to Thomas Smythe for wrestys and hartys for yᵉ dorys . . . . . . xvj$d$.
for " motyng of the Asschys "[1] . . . . xx$d$.
for formes and Trestylls yn ye chamber . . . . ij$s$. viij$d$.
and for other small articles of furniture and plant, for entertainment in the Church house.
A well is lined with stone for the use of the house.

PAGE 113.
Total expenses   .   £vij ix$d$.

PAGE 114.   𝔄.𝔇. mcccclxxiv–v. Feb. vj.
W. BREDMERE AND R. WALE, WARDENS.

Balance from the " rather " Wardens[2] . . . . £vj vj$d$. and viij rings
Divers gifts to the Kyve,[3] and to the Church house.

PAGES 115–117.
[Bradmere and Wale's expenses, numerous, but usual, save continued outlay on the Church-house and its well. No balance struck.]

PAGE 118.   𝔄.𝔇. mcccclxxv. February viij.
J. MEY AND RIC. BRADMERE, WARDENS.
RECEIPTS.

Balance from Bradmere and Wale . . . . £vij xs. jd.
[Among these are six sums for the Church-house; but whether for hire of it, or as gifts is not stated.]

PAGE 119.   EXPENSES.
of Mey and Bradmere; no balance struck.

PAGE 120.   [No heading, date, or Warden's name.]
RECEIPTS.
[from bequests, chiefly for lime, and from gifts not summed up.]

PAGES 122–9.
Headed : " Expenses of the Cherche howse."
[carefully compiled from previous Wardens' accounts, filling 7¼ pages :—not summed up.]

PAGE 130.
[A memorandum of six persons from whom wax had been borrowed by the Wardens of 1476.]

---

[1] *I.e.*, grubbing up the Ash trees. " Moot " is in Somerset the part of the tree just above and below the ground-line.

[2] William " Brown " and J. Hurdewyche. " Brown " was probably the alternative name of W. Stabbe.

[3] Otherwise Kive or Keeve, a large brewing-tub.

PAGES 131-2.

A.D. mccccl×xvi–vii. January xxix.

W. Brekebeke (Cleve) and R. Gamelyn, Wardens.

the Successors of Mey and Bradmere, whose balance is specified, viz. . £xiij xijs. vd.

RECEIPTS.

[Six items for hirings of the Church-house of xvjd. each, and two for hire of the chetyll.[1]

The House and its utensils are a source of yearly revenue. Ales, bequests of money, corn, garments, rings, cattle, &c.]

PAGE 133. EXPENSES.

For iiij goote skynnys[2]	iijs. iiijd.
for mendyng of the organs for v wokes, labor, ijs. a woke	xs.
for hys table for ye sayd v wokes, and for hys bed, fyre, and candle	vs.
for verde grese[3] for torches	vd.

PAGE 134.

for the caryage of the Altar-table from Wellys[4] . . . . ijd.

PAGES 135-6.

A.D. m.cccc.l×xvii–viii. February vj.

J. Thurbarn and T. Knyght, Wardens.

RECEIPTS.

Balance from Brekebeke and Gamelyn . . . . . £xix xiijs. iijd.
[An unusual number of bequests: among them,]
Of the bequest of ye children of John Crosse . . . . xxd.

PAGE 137. EXPENSES.

to T. Hathwey for hopyng ye bokett and an yren chayne	iijs. vjd.
to W. Hoper for Trendellys	viijs.
for clensyng of ye hye chambyr	ijd.
for a markyng yere[5] [Iron] for vessells	ijd.

PAGE 138.

for Ryses for ye dawbes[6] betwene y^e to chambres . . . ijd.

---

[1] Kettle, i.e., caldron.   [2] Goat-skins for bellows.   [3] Verdigris.
[4] After the Bishop's benediction. It was a stone slab, portable on horseback.
[5] A brand for wood? or a punch for indenting metal?
[6] The partitions were of hurdlework and plaster, "wattle and dab." Ryse = a pliable branch

PAGE 139.   **A.D. m.cccc.lxxviii–ix.** Feb. xviij.

EDW. CRADOC AND JOHN CROSS, WARDENS.

RECEIPTS.

Balance from Thurbarne and Knyght xix*l*. xj*s*. viij*d*. besides xvj rings and the "harneyste gurdle."
seven hirings of the Church house at . . xvj*d*.
Total . . . . xxij*l*. x*s*. v*d*.

PAGE 140.   [Left blank. A list of names in later hand.]

PAGE 141.   EXPENSES.
payde for the mendyng the Rele and peyntyng of ye same . iij*s*. viij*d*.
„ for color for ye same Rele . . . . . . xxiij*d*.
„ for a dosen cuppys ayenst Whitsontide [ale] . . viij*d*.
PAGE 142.
paide for a pax brede . . vij*d*.

PAGE 143.   **A.D. m.cccc.lxxix.** March xv.

RIC. THURBARNE AND RIC. WORTHNELL, WARDENS.

RECEIPTS.

Balance from Cradock and Cros . . . . . . xxij*l*. x*s*. v*d*.
for makyng of Seynt Kateryn wex . . . . . . iiij*d*.
[Several bequests, and hirings of Church-house.]

PAGES 145–6.   EXPENSES.
[Many items for scaffolding.]
for spykes[1] for selyng the cherche . . . . iij*d*. ob.
to Sir Ed.[2] that lakkes of his wages . . . . iiij*s*. ij*d*.

PAGE 147.   **A.D. m.cccc.lxxx.** Feb. xv.

RICH. KEW AND JOHN WORTHNILL, WARDENS ELECT.

RECEIPTS.

Balance from Worthnell and Thurbarne . . . xxviij*l*. ij*s*. ix*d*.
a gurdle i solde to John Jagryn . . . . . xx*d*.

[1] Large nails.   [2] A chantry priest.

PAGE 148.   [Blank.]

PAGE 149.   EXPENSES.

In primis I paide to John Jagryn for the selyng of the Cherche . . . . vs.
I paide to J. Jagryn in part of payment for the closyng[1] of the arches . . xxvjs. viijd.
I paide for buckram, and for the fringe and the settyng over of the baner of Seynt Kateryn . . . . xijd.
I paid to Lyon for makyng of the peysys[2] of ledde upon the belowys . . . . xvjd.
I paide to Lyon for pleyng att the organe[3] . . . . . . xd.
I paide att Kyngeston att the Cherche ale . . . . . . xijd.
paide to Lyon for makyng of the drawgth of water at ye well[4] . . . xjs.
paide to Lyon for sowder.[5]

PAGE 150.
I paide for the changyng of the chalys . . . xvijs. vjd.
Item I paide for the change[6] of the chalys xv ryngs.
I paide for cariage of tymber fro Lyme Ryge[7] . . . .ijs. vjd.
I paide to John Jageryn for the closyng of the Arches . vjs. viijd.
„   for mendyng of the chetyl . . . . . iiijd.

PAGE 151.
I paide for the byndyng of the sawter[8] . . . . xvjd.
                [Half torn away.]
I paide to Julian Clerke for makyng of a Rochat . . . . . ijd.

PAGE 152. [Left blank.—In a later hand six names with sums of money against them, varying from xvjs. to iijs. Total iijl. vijs. xjd.]

PAGE 153-4. **A.D. m.cccc.lxxxi–ii. March vij.**
        W. BREKEBEKE, CARPENTER, AND JOHN CARTER, WARDENS.
                        RECEIPTS.
            Balance from Kew and Worthnell, £xxx xixs. iijd.
[The regular yearly entries of gifts in money, rings, collection for the Easter taper, bequests, hire of Churche-house and vessels; from the Wardens' Ale, and from the lightmen of Yatton, and those of Cleve and Claverham, £iiij xs., £iiij xs. viijd., and £iij iiijs., respectively. Total, £xij iiijs. viijd.]

PAGE 155.   EXPENSES.
for repayring of towr and ye pynnacles of ye cherche . . . . . xxiijs. iiijd.
for the blessyng of the Chalys . . . . ijd.
for mete and drynke at the hawsyng[9] of a pece of tymber into the steple . . . ix.
for repayring and poyntyng of the stepyll a noder tyme . . . . xs. and xvjs. viijd.
PAGE 156.
to John Brene, writer, in part of payment for the legger[10] the x day of June. £iij vjs. viijd.

---

[1] Parclosing? [2] Weights. [3] First time of this entry. [4] For making the pump draw.
[5] Solder.   [6] In exchange for. [7] I.e., Limebridge Wood near Tickenham.
[8] Psalter.   [9] Hoisting. [10] Ledger=the new bokes; infra.

for ij Amys, and strengs for same	x*s*.
I paide att Bristowe for a sewte of vestments and a cope . . . . . paide	£xxvj
in costs spende a bowgth the byyng of the same vestments	[no sum].
Item to John Brene for iiij quayres[1] of the new boke the xiij day of October .	xxvj*s*. viij*d*.
I paide to the Bushep ys man for halowyng of the new sute of vestements . .	vj*d*.

PAGE 157.

I paide for bords for the new cofyr	iiij*s*. v*d*.
for caryage of the same	iiij*d*.
for makyng of the Cofyr	ij*s*. viij*d*.
in costs a bowgth the byndyng of the cofyr	iiij*d*.
I paide to Rowland for bends and naylys for the cofyr	xj*s*. ij*d*.
for ij lokes for the cofyr	ij*s*. viij*d*.
I paide in costs to lett a rent to be paide to my Lorde[2] for the Cherche house .	ij*s*. iiij*d*.
I paide to T. Clerke for foldyng of the vestments[3]	iiij*d*.

PAGE 158.   [Blank, save a few memoranda.]

PAGE 159.   **A.D. m.cccc.lxxxii[iii]. Feb. xx.**

JO. MARYOTT AND JO. COLYNS, WARDENS.

RECEIPTS.

Balance from Brekebeke and Carter	£v x*s*. iiij*d*.
of the lygthmen of the West Syde,[4] Thomas Waren and J. Seffe . .	£v ij*s*. iiij*d*.
It. for candyll of the rele	ij*d*.
for brewyng in the Cherche howse vj persons at xvj*d*. and xij*d*.	

PAGE 160.

[This page having been left blank, has been used by the Wardens of A.D. 1486-7 for entering the Consecration Charges.]

MEM. The . . . day of Averyll **A.D. m.cccc.lxxxvi** that John Brekebeke and Lowys Watts hath ypayed for dyverse costs for hawluyng[5] of the Cherche erde.

In primis, payd to the Byschepe[6]	xxxiij*s*. iiij*d*.
It. payd to the coke	iiij*d*.
„ for horse mete	xij*d*.
„ for spysys	iiij*d*.
„ for ij ellys of cloth for My Lord's apryn	xviij*d*.
„ for a pygg and capone	xij*d*.
„ for iiij chykyn	v*d*.
„ for the brekefast of the Lords men	iiij*d*.

[1] *I.e.*, for writing four quires.
[2] Bishop, as Lord of the Manor. The fine of 2*s*. 4*d*. was paid in the Manor court for admission to the tenancy.
[3] An annual entry.   [4] *I.e.*, Claverham.   [5] Hallowing of the Church-yard.
[6] *I.e.*, Bp. Stillington's Suffragan, probably Bp. Cornish.

114   Patton Church-Wardens' Accounts.

It. payd for vele and lome¹		xx*d*.
,, for bred		viij*d*.
,, for rydyng to Wellys ij tymys		xij*d*.
,, for rydyng to Bristowe		xij*d*.
,, for settyng of the pypys, and cuttyng and other attendends		viij*d*.
,, for fewell		iiij*d*.
,, for dyverse vessels ybowgth to the balowyng of yᵉ Cherchyerd		ij*s*. viij*d*.
	Total² . . . xlvj*s*. vj*d*.	

PAGE 161.   EXPENSES.
                [viz., of Maryott and Colyns.]

paide for pauper
for the closynge³ betwyxte the chyrche and the chawnsell, and for mete and drynge,
    and naylys . . . . xx*d*.
we bowghte ayenste Whyttsontyde vj cuppys and iij bollys, price . . . v*d*.
for iij bord clothys⁴ to the Churche howse . . . . . . iiij*s*. vj*d*.

    PAGE 162.
to John a Brene for the boke⁵ yn partte of paymentte . . . . xxvj*s*. viij*d*.
to carrying the little bell to Bristowe and "whome ayene" . . . . xvij*d*.
for custom⁶ of the bell att Redclyff hyll, utwardys and whomwardys . . . vj*d*.
to the workmen at the castynge of the bell, off curtesy . . . . viij*d*.
    [This seems the equivalent of "rewards" often given above.]
to the scryvener at ij tymys for wrytyng of the new boke . . . xxxiij*s*. iiij*d*.
for caryage of hauser⁷ of lytyl bell and the pokysy . . . . . ij*d*.
Item we payde the olde freyr⁸ yat was cum fro maystyr newton to syng for the
    paryche . . . . viij*d*.

    PAGE 163.
to J. Bek to close the chancell . . . . ij*d*.

PAGE 164.   **A.D. m.cccc.lxxxiii[iv]. Feb. v.**
            WALTER MEEKE AND R. KNYGHT, WARDENS.
                        RECEIPTS.

Balance from Maryot and Colyns . . . . . £viij v*s*. x*d*.
                [from other sources, as usual.]

    PAGE 165.   EXPENSES.
To the boke-maker . . . . xx*s*.
Payde to Nycholas Ket, Scryvener, on Alhalow day in the presence of Syr Jhon
    Newton K[nt.] . . . . xl*s*.

---

¹ Veal and lamb.   ² See also Anno 1485, £iij vj*s*. viij*d*.
³ Parclose. N.B.—The Chancel-screen paid for by the Parish, as elsewhere, and not by the Rector.
⁴ Table-cloths.   ⁵ *I.e.*, writing.   ⁶ The city toll.   ⁷ Rope.
⁸ Friar. Probably the general anniversary of Benefactors.

Payde to the same Nicholas on Seint Thomas Eve before Cristemasse	xx*s*.
„ the Monday the xxiiij day of January then next followyng to the same Nicholas[1]	xxvj*s*. viij*d*.
„ for a paxe	vij*d*.

PAGE 166.

payd to the clerke, by the commandment of Master Newton . . xvj*s*. viij*d*.

PAGE 167. **A.D. m.cccc.lxxxiv[v]. Feb. xv.**

WILL. WEBBE OF CLEVE, AND JOHN COLLMAN OF HEWYSCH, WARDENS.

RECEIPTS.

Balance of Meke and Knyght . . . . £v ix*s*. xj*d*.
[Nothing unusual.] Total . . . £xix xxiij*s*.
[On this page there are several payments[2] to Ket "in the presence of Sir J. Newton"; all crossed out, being charged in previous account.]

PAGE 168.
for vij tavernys[3] made at the Churche howse . . . . . . ix*s*. iiij*d*.
[The other public taverns, as usual, produce several pounds.]

PAGE 169. EXPENSES.
Payd to Nicholas Scryvenyr, upon Synt Mathews day . . . . xlvj*s*. viij*d*.
to costs to rydy[4] for the Chals that waste ystole[5] . . . . . xij*d*.
payd to the Scryvener for the legerd . . . . xxj*s*.
payd to Nycholas Kette the xxix day of March . . . . . xlvj*s*. viij*d*.
payd to the Scryvener the xij day of March in the presence of Master Newton . iiij Marke.[6]
Total . . . . £xij xij*s*.

PAGES 171-2. **A.D. m.cccc.lxxxv[vi]. Jan. xx.**

J. BREKEBEKE AND LEWYS WATTS, WARDENS.

RECEIPTS.

Balance from Webbe and Colman . . . £vj ix*s*. xj*d*.
[As usual.]
of the bequest of ij chyldryn of T. Hyrbow . . . . . ij*s*.
of Annys Browne a gowne to ye reparation of Seynt James Chapell . ij*s*. viij*d*.

---

[1] Total paid to Ket, £11 14*s*. 4*d*.
[2] One of these reveals that the Scrivener's costly work was not a Service-book, but the Ledger. This book, prepared under the special care of Sir John Newton, must have been more than the Wardens' account-book, probably a Terrier recording the Deeds of Appropriation of the Rectory, the endowment of Vicarage, and establishment of the two manorial chapels and of that in the Churchyard.
[3] *I.e.*, private brewings, or entertainments for which the House was hired, at xvj*d*. each time.
[4] Riding.   [5] Stolen.   [6] £ij xiij*s*. iiij*d*.

[Owing to the probable loss of two leaves, the EXPENSES of this year, 1485-6, are missing, save those for Consecration, written on page 170. The RECEIPTS of 1486-7 are missing. Page 173 begins with the EXPENSES of Will. Stabbe and Thomas Colyns, Wardens of that year.]

PAGE 175. EXPENSES.

Payd for haluyng[1] the Cherche yerde[2] . . . . . £iij vjs. viijd.
„ to the bokebyner . . . . xxvjs. viijd.

PAGES 175-6.

A.D. m.cccc.lxxxvii–viii. Feb. xvj.

JOHN HYGGYN AND JOHN WATTS, WARDENS.

Balance from Stabbe and Colyns . . . . . . £x xvs.

RECEIPTS.—Nothing unusual.

PAGES 177-8. EXPENSES.—Nothing unusual.

PAGE 179.

A.D. m.cccc.lxxxviii[ix]. Feb. x.

JOHN LANG AND WILL.^{M.} FFYSCHER, WARDENS.

RECEIPTS.

Balance from Hyggyn and Watts . . . . . . £xvj iiijd.

PAGES 180-1. [Blank.]

PAGES 182-3. EXPENSES [of Lang and Fyscher.]

For a sommar, bowght of John Oter . . . . . . vijd.
For ledde for ye helyng of the Chyrche . . . . £v iijs. iijd.
To the lavender for wesschyng . . . . ijs.

PAGE 184.

A.D. m.cccc.lxxxix. Feb. xxij.

ROB. COLYNS AND THOMAS WAREN, WARDENS.

RECEIPTS.

Balance from Lang and Fysscher . . . . . £xvij iijs. xd.
  xxiij Ryngs in stock, besides gifts.
  of my Lady [Newton] of bequest of Maister Newton x marks.[3]
      Total . . £xxxvij xiijs. iiijd.

PAGE 185. EXPENSES.

For Tonne of Lyde[4] bowght at Beryngton[5] . . . £iiij xijs. viijd.
„ do.   do   and smaller quantities . . . . .
„ ij sakys of mese[6] . . . . iijd.

[1] Hallowing.   [2] The Suffragan's stated fee. Cf. *ante* p. 113.   [3] *I.e.*, £vj xiijs. iiijd.
[4] Lead.   [5] Burrington.   [6] Moss, for laying under lead on roof.

PAGE 186.

To plommer to wasche ye Axsyn[1]	vs.
for myltyng of ye ledde Axynne	ixs.
for waschyng ye ledde Axsyn	xd.
for takyng off and settyng on a cenne [sic] of yᵉ vestments	iiijd
Sma. £xxj vijs. vd.	

PAGE 187.

NOTE.—A ton of lead and xiijs. iiijd. [worth] of barryd[2] planks "remayneth in the sum of ye reseyts above, of Rob. Colens and Tho. Warryn."

PAGE 188.   [Torn ; very scant.]

A.D. m.cccc.lxxxx [xci]₊ Feb. viij.

THOS. DALE AND RIC. DYSMAN, WARDENS.

Balance from Colens and Waryn . . £xvj vs. ijd.

PAGE 189.   [Blank.]

RECEIPTS.—Nothing unusual.

PAGE 190.   EXPENSES.

For a dosyn of dhysters[3]	iiijd.
Payd for a copyll of cruetts, selver	xxxs.
for v score row[4] wex, vjs. and vijd. for a powne	£iij xxijd.

PAGE 191.

[Seven Receipts ; no date or Warden's name.]

PAGE 192.   EXPENSES.

For ij wey of cole carried by water from Ronam (Rownham-on-Avon) to Kingston, thence by land.	
for makyng of the sepulcure, and the cafe[5]	iijd.
for ridding and mending the Kyll[6]	vjd.
for CC yere[7]	xs.

PAGE 193.

for makyng of the pax	xs.
payd for Sint Sunday[8] [prob. for an Image]	xijs. ixd.

---

[1] Ashes, which seem always to have been worth washing and remelting.   [2] Bared = smoothed.
[3] Dusters.   [4] Rough.   [5] Cave.   [6] Kiln ; much lime being burnt.
[7] I.e., 2 cwt. of iron.   A Saint venerated in Cutcombe and other parishes of West Somerset. The real name is "sub-judice."

PAGES 194–5.   **A.D. m.cccc.lxxxi [ii].**

J. CRADÓKE AND W. HILMAN, WARDENS.[1]

RECEIPTS.

Balance from Dale and Dygheman . . . . £xix ixs. iijd
Item. the seid parties puttethe in knowleche to ye seid proctors, that folowyth, suche
 goodes as hereafter ys rehersed of the bequest of Julian Craddock.
In primis the apparell for the high Auter, viz., the ffront with the ij curteyns.[2]
a chalys . . . . prt. viij marke.
a peyre of vestments . . . . prt. iiij marke.
It. for a keverled,[3] of the bequest of W. Medwynter . . . . . ijs.
from Sir William for the Chamber . . . . viijd.
and for taverns of Ale . . . .

PAGE 196.   EXPENSES.
for chesyng[4] of the stonys to the masyner[5] . . . . . . vjd.
for dykyng of the fundament . . . . xviijd.
for xxviij weynys to cary home stonys and cole, in mete and drink . . vjs. viijd.

PAGE 197.
for xiiij lode of frestonys . . . . xxvs. viijd.
 [besides many other loads.]
for dykyng of stonys [? stacking them] . . . . xxd.
for poynting of spyre, of iij pynnaclys, and batylment of the tower . . vjs. viijd.
for the crane settyng uppe . . . . iijs. vjd.

PAGE 198.
paid to J. Bekke for steyyng[6] of the Chansell . . . . . iijd.
[Much freestone brought from Dundry.]

PAGE 199.
To cary owte the erthe owte of the cherche . . . . . . viijd.
for makyng of the Syntorne[7] . . . . ixd. ob.
 [Large building was going on, but no evidence, *where*. Unhappily, the account for
  1492–3 is missing.]

PAGE 200.   **A.D. m.cccc.lxxxiii[iv]. Feb. xx.**

RICH. THURBAN AND JOHN HERVOW, WARDENS.
RECEIPTS.

Balance from Colman and Roper, £xv viijd., ob., "of laful money of Engeland."
 For Pothynger and "sawser," and vjd.—bequest.

---

[1] The old Latin heading is now exchanged for English, taking the form of a Receipt of out-going Wardens' balance in cash, "in lawfull money of Engelonde."
[2] All crossed out.   [3] Coverlet.   [4] Choosing.   [5] Mason.   [6] Supporting.
[7] Centering.

PAGE 201.   EXPENSES.

payd for halfe C yere[1] and ij powne . . . . . . ijs. jd.
  „ for tymmer[2] to make ye yate[3] . . . . . xxs.
payd for a nowle[4] . . . . ijd.
              Much freestone hauled.

PAGE 202.

paid for xij seme of Walsche[5] bords . . . . . viijs.
payd to caram[6] to[7] the water . . . . . . iiijd.
payd to J. Lewys for the frette[8] . . . . . xijd.
for ij Tonne Ledde . . . . £viij xijd.

PAGE 203.

payd for half a C wex . . . . xxxijs. viijd.
[The making of the wax, rosin, and wick-yarn, are yearly entries, costing viij or ix shillings, besides meat and drink.]
payd to the clerke to voupp[9] the vestments . . . . . viijd.
payd for iij boschells of axyn[10] . . . . viijd.
[More freestone hauled and sorted by Fysscher, the skilled Mason; more moss, and Scaffold timber :—] .
Total Exp. . . . . £xviij vijd.

PAGE 204.   [Inventory of utensils :—]

This be perselles[11] that longyth[12] to the Cherche howse, the yere A.D. m.cccc.lxxxxii. delyveryd to the Wardens[13] that yere.

In primis a chetyll | It. kyve vate.[16]
It. ij grett crocks. | „ ij trowys.[17]
 „ ij lysse[14] crocks. | „ ix stonds.[18]
 „ iiij pannys. | „ ix barellys.
 „ a botum for a panne. | „ xxj trendyllys.[19]
 „ a brandyre[15]. | „ vj borde clothis.
 „ v tun vats. |

PAGE 205.

EXPENSES. [Only the last few items :—the rest missing.]
S^a Tot^s . . . . £xix vijs. ixd.
Balance . . . . £viij vs.

---

[1] Half a cwt. of iron.   [2] Timber.   [3] Gate.   [4] An awl.
[5] Welsh, i.e., foreign. Wainscot landed at the head of the tideway in the Yeo, and fetched from thence.
[6] Carry them.   [7] At.   [8] Freight.
[9] Fold up.   [10] Ashes.   [11] Parcels.   [12] Belongeth.
[13] I.e., the incoming Wardens.   [14] Lesser.
[15] Brand-iron for carrying the burning logs on the hearth, alias = andirons.
[16] See ante p. 36, note 3.   [17] Troughs, pronounced "trows," hodiè.
[18] Stands : called "standards," p. 210.   [19] Shallow tubs or vats.

PAGE 206.   **A.D. m.cccc.lxxxxiiii[v].** March v.

RICH. WAMPERFYLDE AND JOHN SEFFE, WARDENS.

Balance from Thurban and Hervow . . . . . . £viij vs.
RECEIPTS. Nothing unusual . . . . . . Total £xxiiij xvs.
EXPENSES [missing, all but the Total, viz.] . . . . £xj ixs.
Balance torn away.—

PAGE 207.   **A.D. m.cccc.lxxxxv.**

[Wamperfylde & Seffe served again as appears among their receipts, of which only 4
   remain, viz., a Pecas[1] and three Ales, and the Tot. . . . . £xx vs. ijd.

PAGE 208.   EXPENSES.
payd for a manuall[2] . . . . . xxiijs. iiijd.
 „ for papyr and russchys.[3]
 „ for frongkynsens[4] . . . . jd.
 „ for settyng uppe of yren gere before our Lady . . ixd.

PAGE 209.
payd for bords to syle[5] the chapyll . . . . . xxjs. viijd.
 „ for takyng downe ye crane . . . . . . xijd.
 „ for a pyggsfote to bare cols . . . . . . jd.
 „ for the closyng of the charnsell, to J. Austeyns . . . iijs. iiijd.
 „ for makyng of a nawter,[6] to Thomas Cotyng . . . vjs. viijd.
 „ for a stone to hele[7] the auter . . . . . . ijs.
Total Expenses . . . . £viij xiijs. ixd.
Remaynyng clyr to ye Chyrche . . . . . £xj xjs. iiijd.

PAGE 210.   **A.D. m.cccc.lxxxxvi[vii].** March xiv.

LADY NEWTON AND JOHN BULBEKE, WARDENS.

Mem. that my Lady, Dame Isabell Newton and John Bulbeke hath reseyvid of R.
   Wampfyld and J. Seffe . . . . . . £xj vs. iiijd.
Item. ix ryngs of sylver.
and the goods in ye Chyrche house. [List nearly the same as in p. 204.]

PAGE 211.   [Blank.]

PAGE 212.
Received of Saundyr Harrys for Seynt Kateryn light . . . iijs. vjd.

[1] Pick-axe.   [2] Manual.   [3] Rushes.   [4] Frankincense.   [5] Ceil.
[6] An altar.   [7] Cover.

PAGE 213.   [Blank.]

PAGE 214.   EXPENSES.

Payd for xiij yerdis of Iryshe clothe . . . . xviij*d*
  „ for herys for ij auters . . . . xvj*d*
  „ for ensens[1] . . . . ij*d.*

PAGE 215.

Payd for changyng of ij peyre of cruetts . . . . . . xij*d.*
  „ for the hangyngs of the hye auter, the utter[2] syde and the lynyng . xv*s.*
  „ for vj ells and a halfe of lynnyn for a surplesse . . . iij*s.* iiij*d.*
  „ for ij unces of selke, to frenge ye hangyng of ye auter . . ij*s.* viij*d.*

PAGE 216.

Payd for the changyng of iiij torchys agenst Crystymasse . . ix*s.*
            Total .   . £vij xj*s.* v*d.*

PAGES 217-18. **A.D. m.cccc.lxxxvii.** Feb. vj.
            JOHN THOMAS AND WILL. ROGERS, WARDENS.
                         RECEIPTS.

Balance from Dame Newton and Bulbeke . . . . £xxj xiij*s.* iij*a.*
For led aschys[3] . . . . x*s.*
Of ye parson of Kyngston for led . . . . . . ij*s.* viij*d.*
of Master Vycary[4] for a pane [pan] . . . . vij*s.*

   [Note in later hand.] Dame Isabell Newton dyed in the year 1458, which is 165 yeares agon to this present yeare 1663.—Nicholas Prater.

PAGE 219.   EXPENSES.

Payd for a proschensnall[5] . . . . ix*s.* iiij*d.*
  „ for new settynge of Oure Lady and the ly3ght . . . . iiij*d.*
  „ to Antony for dressyng of the yron, and a copys that beryth the ly3ght . iiij*d.*
  „ to Thos. Bene for a here to the hye auter . . . . . xx*d.*
  „ to Antony Smyth for makyng ij leggs to ye chetyll . . . . ij*s.*

PAGE 220.

Payd for mendyng of the hye booke[6] . . . . . . viij*s.*

PAGE 221.

Payd for castyng vij tonne of led . . . . . . xlvj*s.* viij*d.*
  „ for tonne and halfe of new led . . . £vj xj*s.*
  „ for makyng cofyr box and chyrch-hey yate key . . . xij*d.*

PAGE 222.

Payd for ij yrense[7] to hong ye curtense . . . . . iiij*d.*

---

[1] Incense.   [2] Outer.   [3] Ashes.   [4] The Vicar.   [5] Processional book.
[6] The Iligh Wardens Account book, *see inf.*, 1502.   [7] Irons.

PAGE 223. **A.D. m.cccc.lxxxviii[ix].** March i.

WM. WORNELL AND WM. BRADMERE, WARDENS.

RECEIPTS.

Balance from Rogers and Thomas	£xix ixs. vd.
For tyle of Seynt James Chappell	. . xxs.
Total . . £xxvij xiiijs. vijd.	

PAGE 224. [Blank.]

PAGE 225. EXPENSES. Nothing unusual.

PAGE 226.

Payd for mendyng y⁰ Rode-loft, and settyng of y⁰ crest of y⁰ hye awter	. iiijd.
„ for strekyng of the chyrch wythin and wythout . . .	ijs. iiijd.
„ to John Hyks for rent of the Chyrch Howse	. iiijd.
„ to R. Clerke for makyng of owre booke	. xijd.

PAGE 227.

Payd for halowyng of the chalyce	. xijd.
„ for iij men and iij horse to brynge y⁰ said chalyce to Wells	xd.
„ in costs for sekyng of the chyrch goods¹	vijs. viijd.
„ to John Payne and Thomas Wale for rydyng to Oxford²	. xxs.
„ for rydyng to Wells, for horse mete and man ys mete for W. Bradmere and y⁰ Smyth	iijs.
„ to Bowre of Banwell for beryng of y⁰ bill [Indictment] to Yelchester to y⁰ schesscheons³	iiijs. iiijd.
Total £viij ixs. xijd.	

PAGE 228. **A.D. m.cccc.lxxxix[md].** Feb. xvij.

W. KNYGHT AND J. TOKER, WARDENS.

RECEIPTS.

Balance from Wornell and Bradmere . .	. £x xjs. iijd.
Among the bequests 'a mete clothe,'⁴ and a ryng.	
It receyved of y⁰ gaderyng of y⁰ chalyce above y⁰ sum	. xiiijd.

PAGE 229.

Five Taverns of ale.

It. reseyved of R. Thurban for brewyng in y⁰ chorch chetyll⁵ . . . . iiijd

---

¹ Stolen by Davy Gybbes, *see* 1500. ² In search for the lost goods ? ³ Sessions.
⁴ Table-cloth.   ⁵ Kettle = caldron.

PAGE 230.   EXPENSES.

Costs of suit against D. Gibbes.
{ The sute of Davy Gybbys yᵉ fyrst day . . . . iiijs. viijd
It. the seyd D. Gybbys to yᵉ sute of yᵉ preve sesscheone¹ to yᵉ towne clerke . . . . vjs. viijd.
It. to hys ij servants . . . . viijd.
It. the Meyre ys sergents . . . . ijs. viijd.
It. in expenses and askyng of cownsell . . . . . . iijs. iiijd.
It. for yᵉ wrytyng of yᵉ oblygacyon and yᵉ endentyng² . . . . vjd.
It. the costs for owre cherche gode at Bristowe . . . . . xvjd.
It. payd to Master Rodney for yᵉ endyment³ of D. Gybbys . . . vd.
It. payd to Richard Clyfe when he rode . . . . . yᵉ cherche goode . vjs. viijd. }

It. payd for yᵉ halowyng of yᵉ chalys. . . . . viijd.
It. payd to W. Goffe for kepyng of yᵉ bells . . . . . . iijs.

PAGE 231.
*It. for yᵉ beryng of a letter to Master Malet . . . . . . xijd.
* ,, for yᵉ costs of scesscyonys yn Brystow aboute D. Gybbys . . . iijs. xjd.
,, for new Crosse . . . . £xviij
,, for a sencer of koper⁴ . . . . iijs. viijd.
* ,, delyveryd to T. Wale to bere a letter to Master Fyʒames⁵ . . . iijs. iiijd.
,, payd for yᵉ change of v score and xix lb. of torche wax . . . vijs. vjd.
* ,, payd for yᵉ makyng of yᵉ testymonyall to yᵉ notore⁶ for Davy Gybbys . xijd.
* ,, for costs att yᵉ same busyness . . . . vjd.

PAGE 232.
*It. for fachyng of Davie Gybbys fro Brystow to Yatton . . . . xxjs. xd.
*It. for yᵉ bryngyng fro Yatton to Wells . . . . ixs. vd.
*,, payd to yᵉ jugys⁷ att Wells for to make owre panell . . . . xxs.
*,, in costs yn mete and drynk, for horse mete, and manys mete . . . vijs. vijd.
MEM. Remaynys in ye hande of Jo. Holden xs. ffor yᵉ tymburs off Sentt Jamys Chapel, ye qwych ys uncountyd ffor off Wm. Knyght's deys.

PAGES 233–4.   **A.D. m.ccccc[i]. January xxij.**
W. AVEREY AND RICH. CREED, WARDENS.
RECEIPTS.
Balance from Knyght and Tucker . . . . . . £vj ijs. ixd.
[Nothing unusual.]
           Total . . £xvij xiijs. viijd.

PAGE 235.   [Blank.]

---

¹ Privy Sessions.   ² Indenting.   ³ Indictment.   ⁴ Censer of copper.
⁵ Fitz-james.   ⁶ *I.e.*, a notarial Act, recording the proceedings against D. G.
* All relate to this costly suit, in which it would seem 3 Lawyers, viz. : Rodney, Fitz-james, afterwards Chief Justice, and Malet were engaged. See also * in 1501.
⁷ *In re* D. Gybbys.

PAGE 236.   EXPENSES.

A new "Cofyr," with ij locks made . . . .
*to Averey for rydyng to Sesscheons . . . . . vs. vjd.

PAGE 237.
*for yᵉ sute of Davie Gybbys . . . . vijs. vjd.
to John Haryce for mendyng of yᵉ Lent clothe . . . . . iiijd.
to Antony[1] for schothyng[2] the clapyr[3] . . . . . . xiijd.
to T. Dale for leder[4] and thongs to make yᵉ bawdrys . . . . xd.

PAGE 238.
payd for[5] helyng of yᵉ maskoke[6] . . . . xvjd.

PAGE 239.   Ⓐ.Ⓓ. m.ccccc,[7] February iv.
              R. WYLLYNG AND J. KEW, WARDENS.
                         RECEIPTS.

Balance from Averey and Creed . . . . £xij xixs. iijd.
It. of Wyllyam Hylman, and of Syn Catyrne[8] men for wex . . . iiijs.
        Sumᵃ Receptionis,[9] pretii . . . £iiij xviijs.

PAGE 240.   [Blank.]

PAGE 241.   EXPENSES.

Payd to John Walle for Syn James Chapell . . . . xiijs. iiijd.
It. more to yᵉ seyd propters[10] with Nycholas Smalen ys mony . . xxs.
It. more to yᵉ seyd propters . . . . xxs.
             xx
It. payd for iiij lib. of wax . . . . xls.
„ payd for makyng of ij surpleyce to yᵉ bokbynder . . . . iijs.
„ payd to yᵉ seyd bokbynder for makyng of a nobe[11] . . . vjd.
„ payd for a bag to bere yᵉ keys in of yᵉ chyrch . . . . jd.

PAGE 242.
It. payd to Synt Jamys propters, to Thomas Dale and John Brokbek in yᵉ name of
    ye parysch . . . . £v vjs. viijd.
It. delyvered to seyd Jamys propters . . . . . . xxxiijs. iiijd.
It. delyvered to yᵉ seyd propters . . . . xs.
It. payd to yᵉ glasyer . . . . xs.

PAGE 243.
It. payd to Syr John for mendyng of yᵉ calyas [Chalice] . . . iiijd.
It. payd to Sent Jamys procterys . . . . . . £iij vjs. viijd.
It. remanet ecclesie ex claro . . . . £vj ixs. xjd.

    [1] The smith.   [2] I.e., casting.   [3] Clapper.   [4] Leather.
    [5] "Makyng," struck out?   [6] Mis-spelt for "mass boke."   [7] This ought to be MCCCCCI, for 1501-2.
    [8] S. Katharine.   [9] I.e., including stock.
    [10] I.e., proctors [wardens] of the Chapel.   [11] An alb.

A.D. m.ccccci. Feb. ix.

PAGES 244-5.

RICH. PYKE AND RICH. ALYN, WARDENS.

RECEIPTS.

Balance from Wyllyng and Kew . . . . . £vj ixs. xjd.
[Nothing unusual.]

PAGE 246. EXPENSES.

Payd to Thomas and John Brekbeke, propters of Seynt Jamys Chapell . xxs.

PAGE 247.
It. delyvered to Seynt Jamys propters . . . . vijs. viijd.
„ payd to Hew Smith for makyng of ij copy[s] to ye baner, loggs,[1] and a hoke, and settyng . . . . ijd.
„ delyveryd to Thomas Dale . . . . xvs.
It. „ to ye seyd Thomas . . . . xvjs. iiijd.
It. payd for a sakerynn bell . . . . xd.
„ for ye caryng of the krok[2] . . . . vjd.
„ delyveryd to Seynt Jamys propters to pay Water Krossman[3] . . . £iij
„ delyveryd to John Cradok and John Brekbeke, Seynt Jamys propters . . iijs. iiijd.

PAGE 248.
[Two memoranda of Wympeny's debt of a noble.]
payd for iij new herys to iij awters . . . . iijs.
payd for hawssyng[4] down of ye bell . . . . vjd.
„ for rydyng[5] of gotters of ye chyrch and ye gargells[6] . . . viijd.

PAGE 249.
a key is made for ye fyce door . . . . ijd.

A.D. m.ccccc.ii[iii]. Feb. xvj.

PAGE 250.

T. THURBAN AND R. WALE, WARDENS.

RECEIPTS.

Balance from Pyke and Alen . . . . . liijs. vd.

PAGE 251.
of ye gaderyng of ye bell money . . . . xxviijs. xjd.
of ye bequest of Syr Thomas, a crosbow, pretio . . . . . vjs.
Total . . £xviij ijs. vjd.

PAGE 252. EXPENSES.

For men and horse and oxsyn,[7] and for makyng of more wrytyng [a contract] at Brystow to ye castyng of ye bell . . . . . . xijs. iiijd.
also for bringing it home and hanging . . . .

---

[1] "Lugs," strings to keep the banner straight.   [2] Carrying of the Cross.
[3] Qy. the Maker of the Cross.   [4] Hoisting.   [5] Clearing.   [6] Gargoyles, or gurgoyles.
[7] Oxen.

PAGE 253.
mendyng ye West Window, costs . . . . . . xxijs. ijd.
[Coal hauled to the kiln, and much lime burnt.]

PAGE 254.
Payd to J. Horte for v daies laber for pargyng of ye Chyrch . . . . . xxd.
„ to Thos. Porker for kepyng[1] of ye lyme kyll for iiij wekes, bed and bord, and waggs . . . . xs. viijd.
„ delyveryd to J. Brekbeke to pay ye carpynter for Seynt Jamys Chapell . . vs.
payd for blessyng of ye vestment . . . . ixd.
payd in mete and drynk for bryngyng of Seynt Kateryne ['s Image] . . . . vd.
payd for half a bochell of salt to ye pargyng of ye Chapell " within and without "[2] . iijd.
payd for pargyng of ye chapell within and without . . . . . . vjs. viijd.
delyveryd to J. Brekbeke to pay ye carpynter for Seynt Jamys Chapell . . . vs.
payd for ij new pax . . . . vjd.
payd for ij new tokyng[3] gyrdylls . . . . ijd.
payd for ye mendyng of ye pynowne[4] wall of Seynt Jamys Chapell . . . xiiijd.
payd to ye plommer for leyng of ye leds to ye seyd chapell . . . . . iijs.
in costs in mete and drynk for ye halyng ope[5] of ye seyd led, and for ye leyyng . . xijd.

PAGE 255.
payd to ye Mason for ye makyng of Seynt Kateryne Awter . . . . . vjs.
payd for ye makyng of ye pynon of Synt Jamys Chapell, for ye row3ht[6] werke . . xijd.
payd for ye awter stone of Seynt Kateryne . . . . viijd.
payd for ye caryng of Seynt Jamys tabyll[7] stonys . . . . . . xijd.
payd in mete and drynk for iiij men Friday and Saterday for to ley ye seyd tabyll . xxd.
[Several more small items of expenditure on St. James' Chapel.]

PAGE 256.
payd to ye glasyer for mendyng of ij wyndowys to ye hye[8] book . . . iiijd.
It. payd for ye angell[9] that Seynt Kateryn stonds on . . . . . viijd.
payd for a box to put ye oblygacion in . . . . jd.
Total . . . . £ix xvjd.

---

[1] Watching the fires.

[2] It appears here and elsewhere that there was a large use of plaster and limewash [strekyng] on the outside as well as inside of the chapel, and of the church.

[3] Tucking.   [4] The gable end is still called the "pwining," *i.e.*, pointing end.

[5] Hauling up.   [6] Wrought.

[7] The parapet, or its cornice and coping. "Table" is much used by masons; *e.g.*, corbel-table, water-table.

[8] The high-book probably means this account now presented by the high wardens, so called in contrast to inferior wardens, such as those of St. James' Chapel.

[9] *I.e.*, carved corbel.

PAGE 257. **A.D. m.ccccc.iii[iiii]₊** March iv.
J. GORMAN AND J. CANYNGTON, WARDENS.
RECEIPTS.

Balance from Thurban and Wale . . . . xl*s*. vj*d*.
[Among the usual bequests are a few to St. James' Chapel from v*s*. to iij*s*.]
     Total . . . £vj xj*s*. iiij*d*.

PAGE 259. EXPENSES.
payd for ij clothys for ye chalyce . . . . . ij*d*.
„ for rydyng¹ of ye chapell.
„ for ye glasyng of ij wyndows in Seynt Jamys Chapell xx*s*.
The second bell was recast this year, and the year before.
The casting costs " ye halfe summe "² . . . . xxv*s*. iiij*d*.

PAGE 260.
payd for six skore pownds of wax for take such money as we toke in owre [?Ale] [*i.e.*,
 the wax sold for whatever the Ale might yield.] . . . . £iij.

PAGE 261.
For mendyng ye ij doors in S. Jamys Chapell . . . . . . vj*s*.
For hewyng of ye dornenys³ of ye seyd dor, and for a spade tre settyng . . . iiij*d*
For syting⁴ of Emot Thurban and Rych. Wamperfyld to ye Conystre⁵ for Claram
 Crosse . . . . ij*d*.

PAGE 262.

A.D. m.ccccc.iiii[v]₊ xixth of Fefrell.
JOHN OTOR AND RICH. MEY, WARDENS.
RECEIPTS.

Balance from Gorman and Canyngton . . . . . . £v. xvij*s*. ij*d*.
  [Nothing unusual.] Total . . . £xvij xviij*s*.

PAGE 263. [Blank.]

PAGE 264. EXPENSES. [as usual.]
    Total . . . £iiij viij*s*. ob.

PAGE 265.

A.D. m.ccccc.v[vi]₊ March xij for 1504–5.
JOHN CRADOK, AND NICHOLAS SMALCOM, WARDENS.
RECEIPTS.

Balance from Otor and Mey . . . . £xiij v*d*.
of ye bequest of John Edwards ij bushells of barly and for that⁶ I toke ij clepyd⁷ grotys
 on ye pryce of . . . . vj*d*.

---

¹ Clearing out, after completion. ² The other half in 1504-5. ³ Durns, or side-posts.
⁴ Citing. ⁵ Consistory. ⁶ *I.e.*, for the barley. ⁷ Clipped.

PAGE 266.　　　　　　　　　　　[Blank.]

PAGE 267.　　　　　　　　　EXPENSES.

Payd to Wylliam Krosse of old duty¹ of Seynt Jamys Chapell . . . . . x*s*.
Payd to yᵉ seyd Wylliam Krosse for makyng of yᵉ quere² and peyntyng of yᵉ selyng³
　of Seynt Jamys Chapell . . . . xxiiij*s*. j*d*.
Payd for tymber to make yᵉ quere in Seynt Jamys Chapell . . . . iij*s*. iiij*d*.
Payd for mendyng yᵉ organs . . . . xl*s*.
Payd at Gangarysbery⁴ to the schot⁵ on Wytwysday⁶ . .. . . . viij*d*.
Payd for festyvale⁷ . . . . xij*d*.

PAGES 269-70.

𝔄.𝔇. m.ccccc.vi[vii]. March xv.

W. WYLLYNG AND W. HORT, WARDENS.
RECEIPTS.

Balance from Cradok and Smalcom . . . . . . £xv v*s*. v*d*.
　　　　[Nothing unusual.] Total . . . £xxiij vij*s*. vij*d*.

PAGE 271.　　　　　　　　　EXPENSES.

For botomyng of yᵉ clensyng renge [sieve] . . . . . iiij*d*.

PAGE 272.

Payd⁸ in metall of yᵉ Church stufe⁹ to yᵉ bell of Seynt Jamys Chapell to yᵉ valor of
　weyӡht of xxxvij *li*.
Payd yᵉ overplus in money for yᵉ seyd bell and for stokkyng and hangyng　ix*s*.
In costs in mete and drynke for schrydyng¹⁰ of wood to oure Ale . . ij*d*.
Payd for a lok to yᵉ font . . . . iij*d*.
　　　　　　　　　Total . . . £vj viij*s*. iij*d*.

PAGE 273.

𝔄.𝔇. m.ccccc.vii[viii]. March vj.

J. MASKALL AND J. HYLMAN, WARDENS.
RECEIPTS.

Balance from Wyllyng and Hort　　　．　　　　　　．　£xiiij

PAGE 274.　　　　　　　　　[Blank.]

---

¹ Debt.
² Choir, *i.e.*, the east end of the chapel with its choir-like attributes of Altar, piscina, image, canopied ceiling, and perhaps reredos.
³ Probably the carved and painted ceiling over the altar.
⁴ Congresbury.　　⁵ Collection at a Scot-Ale.　　⁶ Tuesday in Whitsun-week.
⁷ Paid scot at a neighbouring ale.　　⁸ *I.e.*, contributed.　　⁹ Material in stock.
¹⁰ Shrouding, *i.e.*, lopping the heads of pollards.

PAGE 275.   EXPENSES.

Payd for a here to yᵉ hye awter . . . . xxij$d$.
Kreyskloth[1] and holland bought for bord clothes and surplices and rydyng to Wells to
    by yᵉ seid clothe . . . . vij$s$. xd.
Payd to yᵉ monke for caryng of yᵉ awter cloth to Wells for to be blessyd . . . vd.
for makyng of a newe ye to yᵉ iiij Bell-clapper, and for schotyng[2] of yᵉ schank . iij$s$. iiij$d$.
[The stock of trenchers, cups, and bowls, &c., for the Church-house is frequently
    replenished.]

PAGE 276.

Payd for a Masboke and a pye[3] . . . . xj$s$. vj$d$.
Payd for mendyng yᵉ red vestment, and yᵉ blak cope, and for dyeng of yᵉ old red
    vestment . . . . xl$s$.
Payd to Dan. Wyllyam, mownke[4] to his wages[5] . . . . . . ·ij$d$. vs.
   „ to J. Avery of Kyngeston for scheryng strayes[6] of yᵉ church hefer . . . iiij$d$.

PAGE 277.

Payd for a new offray.[7]
Balance . . .   £xxij xj$s$. xj$d$.

PAGES 278-9.   **A.D. m.ccccc.viii[ix]. Fefrell xix.**

J. HARRYCE AND T. HORYN, WARDENS.
                       RECEIPTS.

Balance from Hyllman and Maskall . . . . £xxij xj$s$. xj$d$.
Many bequests :—nothing unusual. Total . . £xxxv xviij$s$. ob.

PAGE 280.   EXPENSES.

Payd for makyng and settyng of vij mynells[8] to yᵉ sowth wyndow, and a west
    wyndow . . . . xviij$s$. vj$d$.
    [Freestone is bought for the window, and over iv Tons of Lead.]

PAGE 281.

Payd for pavyng of Harye Organs pytt[9] . . . . iiij$d$.
   „ for a cofyr for yᵉ torchys . .
   „ for a thrawll [the drawing gear] of yren to yᵉ well . . . . . iiij$s$.

PAGE 282.

Payd for yᵉ tylyng of yᵉ parsonage[10] . . . . ij$d$.

---

[1] "Crass" cloth, a coarse kind of towelling used for surplices.
[2] Casting.   [3] Ritual directory.   [4] Monk.
[5] *I.e.*, for celebrating on some set days. In 1510 we find Sir Richard Yorke engaged as Chapel-priest at fixed wages, xxvij$s$. iiij$d$. the quarter.
[6] The "strays" were probably fines incurred by a heifer impounded by Avery as hayward of Kingston. "Scheryng" may perhaps=sharing.
[7] Orphrey.   [8] Mullions.   [9] The organist's grave.
[10] The rectorial house belonging to the prebendal Rector. How were the Wardens concerned ?

PAGE 283.
Payd for xiiij yerds of lynyn to make yᵉ Lent clothe . . . . . iiijs. viijd.
It. for staynyng of yᵉ seyd Lent clothe . . . . vjs. viijd.
It. payd for ix yerds of bokeram for yᵉ Rod¹ clothe . . . . . iijs.
It. for steynyng of yᵉ seyd clothe . . . . xiijs. iiijd.
It. for x yerds of webb to fastyn yᵉ rynggs of yᵉ clothys . . . . vd.
Payd to yᵉ Mason for makyng of yᵉ mynells to yᵉ wyndow . . . xs.
PAGE 284.
It. to varmynge² of yᵉ churche well . . . . vjd.
   Total Expenses . . £xx xvjs. vjd.
   Balance . . . . £xv xviijd.

PAGE 285. **A.D. m.ccccc.ix[x]. March xxiv.**
J. AVERY AND W. HEYMAN, WARDENS.
RECEIPTS.
Balance from Harryce and Horyn . . . . £xv xviijd.
[All as usual, comprising the annual receipt for the Easter taper, vjs. :—also bequests, articles sold, a few sums of money, taverns of Ale, and rents for brewing in the Church-house. The following entry is new]:—
Receyvd of Saynt Jamys Ale . . . . iij Mark iiijs.³
[The other similar receipts this year are from the Ale at Whitsuntide, and from the light-men of Yatton.]
PAGE 287.   EXPENSES.
Payd to Syr Rychard Yorke,⁴ Chapell priest for yᵉ fyrst quarter wages . xxviijs. iiijd.
Payd for treyn⁵ platters and bollys⁶ . . . . vijd.
Payd to S. Hoper for mendyng yᵉ Church vessell[s] . . . . . xvjd.
 „ to W. Hort, Mason, for poyntyng of yᵉ spyre, and makyng of yᵉ tower to yᵉ chapell . . . . ls.
  [Stones and lime, sand and sawyng dust are bought for the work.]
PAGE 288.
payd for a lyne and a swystyng gyrdyll . . . . iiijd
payd for a bagg of leder⁷ to kepe yᵉ fyce door keyes . . . . iijd
payd to yᵉ hoper for hopyng of yᵉ kyve . . . . jd.
payd for ij tokyng⁸ gyrdylls . . . . jd.
payd for ij new apryns . . . . vjd.
 „ for wesyng⁹ of yᵉ tabernacyll . . . . xjd.
PAGE 289.
Payd for mendyng yᵉ tynnell pott . . . . jd.
   Total . . £xvij ixs.
   Balance . . £viij xvs.

¹ Rood. ² Forming. ³ £ij xvijs. vjd.
⁴ R. Y. was instituted Rector of Backwell in February this year. ⁵ Wooden. ⁶ Bowls.
⁷ Leather. ⁸ Tucking. ⁹ Washing.

PAGE 290.
    DETERRS TO Yᵉ CHURCH OF YATTON . . xxvijs. xjd.
Eight names with sums of money against each from viijs. iiijd. to iijs., and of two more who owe xxiijs. iiijd.

PAGE 292.
Thys detts folowyng of yᵉ Church-money to John Haryes and Thomas Horyn [Wardens, 1508–9]. The List partly the same as last.

PAGE 293.
Thys detts byhynd of Chyrch-money to J. Cradock and Nicholas Smalcom, Wardens, for ye year, A.D., m.ccccc.b, with dates at whych they are to be payd. Nine men owe xxxvijs.
   [The list is crossed out as if the debts had been paid.]
A similar list of "detts byhynd" due to W. Wyllyng and W. Hort, who were Wardens for the year, A.D. m.ccccc.bi.
   [Some pages seem to be missing here.]

PAGE 294.   [Loose and dateless.]
  [List of 16 bequests, to Church and chapel; the rest of the leaf scribbled over.]

PAGES 295-6-7.   [Blank.]

PAGES 298-9.
A.D. m.ccccc.x–xi. March xxviij.
JOHN WARE AND JOHN TORE, WARDENS "NEWE CHOSYN."
RECEIPTS.
Balance paid in parte from Avery and Heyman . . . . £viij
    Total . . £xxj xiijs.

PAGES 300-1-2.   EXPENSES.
For yᵉ canybe[1] . . . . iiijs.
With the parysh at Ken . . . . vijd.
To Syr Rich Yorke . . . . . . xxiijs. iiijd.
    Total . . £xiiij xiijs. iiijd.
So restyth yn yᵉ wolde Wardens, J. Tore and J. Ware . . xxxvjs. viijd.

PAGES 303-4. ### A.D. m.ccccc.xi [xii]. Febr. x.
JAMES COLEMAN AND R. SESSE, WARDENS.
RECEIPTS.
Balance from Tore and Ware . . . . . £xiiij xiijs. iiijd.
Of John Gurman for yᵉ Church harnes[2] . . . . xxijs.
Wolde[3] detts . . . . xxvjs. vijd.
   Total £xxv vs.

[1] Canopy. [2] Gear. [3] Old.

PAGE 305.   EXPENSES.
Paide for mendyng the best tenekles[1] . . . . . . iiij*d*.
  „   for a puone[2] stryng . . . . j*d*.
PAGE 306.
Paide at Ken[3] with ye Parysche . . . . viij*d*.
  „   to mend ye steyre in ye Churche howse . . . . . vj*d*.
  „   for ij processeners . . . . ij*s*. ij*d*.
  „   for mendyng of ye hye Crosse . . . . xij*d*.
  „   to John Wakelyn for peyntyng and gyldyng of ye churche . . £xij xvj*s*. viij*d*.
  „   to R. Wyllyng ye refe[4] for churche howse . . . . . iiij*s*.
PAGES 307–8.
Paide for floryssyng wax . . . . xij*d*.
  „   for colaryng[5] of ij surplesse . . . . . . xiiij*d*.
  „   for cloth to ye same surplesse . . . . . . ij*d*.

PAGES 309–10.   **A.D. m.ccccc.xii [xiii]** Febr. xiv.
T. AVEREY AND W. MEY, WARDENS.
RECEIPTS.

Balance from Sesse and Coleman . . . £vij xiij*s*. iiij*d*.
A pynnaculle of ye best crosse.[6]
Receyvyd of ye rele [still a usual entry] . . . j*d*.
PAGE 311.
of J. Bek for his taverne of Ale at Hoc-day[7] . . xxxvj*s*. viij*d*.
              Total £xviij xv*s*.

PAGE 312.   EXPENSES.
Payd for gyldyng to John Wakelyn . . . . . . xxvj*s*. viij*d*.
It. to ye same for gyldyng . . . . xxvj*s*. viij*d*.
It. to ye same J. Wakelyn . . . . . xx*s*. and vj*s*. viij*d*.
PAGE 313.
Payd for x yardys of cloth and a halfe to make tabul clothys to ye church house   iij*s*. xj*d*.
  „   for ij flowrs[8] to ye Rode lofte . . . . iiij*d*.
  „   to N. Smalcum for ij flaks[9] to ye church . . . . . ij*d*.
  „   for cloth to ye hye beme, xxx ellis, ye price viij*d*. a nelle . . . xxx*s*.
  „   for wyrs to ye hye beme . . . . xvj*d*.
PAGE 314.
Payd more expenses in making ye said cloth, and rings for it.
  „   for schewyng of John Tors howse to John Penny . . . iiij*d*.
  „   at Combyrsbere[10] with ye parysch . . . . . . vj*d*.

---

[1] Tunicles.   [2] Pound of string.   [3] At the Church-Ale given there.
[4] Reeve, or Bailiff of the manor.   [5] Collaring.
[6] Henceforth handed on as an heir-loom, until sold in 1549.   [7] First mention of Hock-day.
[8] Floors.   [9] Hurdles.   [10] Congresbury Ale.

Payd to J. Wakelyn for gyldyng . . . . xxs.
„ to yᵉ seyde John for yᵉ dext¹ cloth . . . . . . ijs.
„ to yᵉ constabul² and yᵉ tethyng³ man for yᵉ parysch . . . xvjs. iiijd.

PAGE 315.
Payd yn expences for hevyng⁴ up yᵉ cloth afore yᵉ rod lofte . . . . iijd
„ for yᵉ canebe . . . . vs. xd.
„ for Wassyng yᵉ hye auter . . . . ijs. viijd.
„ to J. Wakelyn for gyldyng . . . . vjs. viijd.
„ to W. Hathewey for yre⁵ to yᵉ hye beme . . . . . vs.
„ for mendyng yᵉ best sewe⁶ . . . . xxd.

PAGE 316.
Payd in expenses when we made yᵉ hye lygth . . xxd.

Total £xiiij xvs.

PAGES 317-18.   [a torn leaf.]

PAGE 319. **A.D. m.ccccc.xiiij[xiiij]. March xij.**

MATHEW TORE AND T. PASCALLE, WARDENS.

RECEIPTS.

Balance from Averey and Mey, xliijs. in part of £iiij vijd.

PAGE 320.
Receyvyd a pynnaculle of yᵉ best crosse.

Total £xiiij iiijs.

PAGE 321.   EXPENSES.

Payd for yᵉ doyng of yᵉ durre⁷ . . . . iiijd.
„ for gyldyng to J. Wakelyn . . . . . . xlvjs. viijd.
„ for tockyng gyrdylls . . . . jd.
„ to yᵉ constabulle and yᵉ tethyngman, for yᵉ parysch . . xjs. viijd.

PAGES 322-3-4.
Payd to W. Hort for makyng a nette and for tenys [tins], and a lyne to yᵉ chaunsell. iiijd.

Summa £ix ijs.

„ for trene⁸ platters.
„ for crest cloth to make aprons to the church house . . . viijd.

---

¹ Desk.
² The first draft on the Church funds made by any Civil officers. It was the forerunner of a great change. *See* charge repeated 1514.
³ Tithing.   ⁴ Heaving.
⁵ The iron and wire gear now attached to the high beam, probably that of the Nave-roof, would seem to be for the double purpose of hanging a lamp so as to cast light upon the rood, and also for veiling the rood in Lent.
⁶ Suit.   ⁷ Door.   ⁸ Wooden.

PAGES 325-6. **A.D. m.ccccc.xiiii[v].** Feb. xvij.

J. BENE AND W. HYCKS, WARDENS.

RECEIPTS.

Balance from Tore and Pascall	£v xxij*d*.

Sums of money, bequests, &c., as usual.

Total £vj ix*s*.

PAGES 327-8. EXPENSES.

For a schote to ye Welle	vj*d*.
For a schote to ye wenche[1]	iiij*d*.
Payd to R. Kew for iij days warke to mend ye segesse[2] yn ye chyrch .	xij*d*.
„ to J. Avery for blake londe[3]	x*s*.
„ to J. Wakelyn for glasyng	ixxx*s*.[4]

PAGE 329.

Payd to J. Wakelyn	x*s*.
It. to ye seyd John Wakelyn	vj*s*. viij*d*.
„ to iij dayes warke to J. Wakelyn for plummyng . . .	ij*s*.
„ to ye seyd John for halfe days warke	iiij*d*.

PAGE 330.

It. to John Wakelyn for gyldyng Seynt Thomas and ye rele .	x*s*.

[Some smaller sums to J. W.]

PAGES 331-2.

It to Nicholas Smalcum for cariying home ye rele and Seynt Thomas	x*d*.
„ to John Harrys to fylle ye rele[5]	vj*d*.

PAGE 333. **A.D. m.ccccc.xv[vi].** Feb. vij.

WYLLYAM MERYOT AND THOMAS WARR, WARDENS.

RECEIPTS.

Balance from Bene and Hycks .	£vj ix*s*. vij*d*.

[Nothing unusual.]

Total £xv xvj*s*. vj*d*.

PAGE 334.

receyvyd an auter clothe of Rychard Webbe.

„ for Water Knyth lying yn y^e Church[6]	vj*s*. viij*d*.

PAGE 335. EXPENSES.

Payd to Thomas Avery for settyng up Seynt Thomas and pavyng y^e Church, and whyte lymyng	xij*d*

[1] Winch.   [2] Seats.   [3] Black lawn to veil the Rood in Lent.
[4] = 29th, the unit prefixed deducts from the later figures. *See* below in 1519, ixx = 19.
[5] Viz., with candles.
[6] First use of this phrase, which perhaps embraces the laying of the body in the Church before burial, as well as a grave beneath the pavement.

Payd to yᵉ chanon¹ for mend . . . yᵉ vestments	. .	xij*d*.
Payd for mendyng a croke² to a tynkar . . .	. .	x*d*.
Payd for xj ells of lynen to make ij albys and ij amys	. .	v*s*.

PAGES 336–7.

Payd for a schepe skyn to cover yᵉ boke . . .	.	ij*d*.
,, for mendyng yᵉ tabullment and Seynt Keteryne . .		iij*s*. v*d*.
Total . . . £iiij viij*s*.		

PAGE 339.   **A.D. m.ccccc.xvi[viij]. Feb. xviij.**

J. HANNAM AND SAUNDER HARRIS, WARDENS.

RECEIPTS.

Balance from Meryot and Warre . . . . . . £xj viij*s*.

PAGE 340.

[Nothing unusual.]   Total .   .   £xxv xj*d*.

PAGE 341.   EXPENSES.

Payd for yᵉ composition	vj*d*.
,, at Ken for yᵉ parysch	vj*d*.
,, for hopyng a trendelle of yᵉ churche	iij*d*.
,, for x yerds of crest clothe to make ij mete clothes to yᵉ churche howse .	ij*s*. vj*d*.
,, for a preket to set afore Seynt Kateryn	iiij*d*.

PAGES 343–4.

Payd to yᵉ chappell prist³ . . . . . . xij*d*.

Total .   £xxiij vij*s*.

PAGE 346.   [Blank.]

A.D. m.ccccc.xvii[viij].

T. KNYGHT AND J. FYSSAR, WARDENS.

RECEIPTS.

Balance from Hannam and Harris . . . . . . £xx vij*s*. xj*d*.

[Nothing unusual.]   Total .   .   £xxiiij xvij*s*.

PAGE 348.   EXPENSES.

Payd to Wyllyam Carpenter for goyng up to yᵉ rele, and for yᵉ mendyng .   v*d*.

PAGE 349.

Payd for a streymer and a baner	xxxiij*s*. iiij*d*.
,, for huckmocks	vj*d*.
,, for reban⁴ to mend yᵉ best sewte and yᵉ second kope . .	xvj*d*.
,, to Syr Rychard⁵	xij*s*. viij*d*.

---

¹ Probably an Augustinian Canon of the neighbouring House of Worspring.   ² Crock.
³ Priest, ?whether of the detached chapel or of St. James's.   ⁴ Ribband, ribbon.
⁵ *I.e.*, Sir Richard Yorke.

PAGE 350.

Payd for mendyng yᵉ segs in yᵉ churche howse	x*d*.
„ for a chalesse that was new cast	xviij*s*.
„ for mendyng anoder chalis	iiij*s*.
„ for blessyng yᵉ seid chalis	ij*s*.

PAGE 351.

Payd to yᵉ plummpe¹ maker	vj*s*.
„ for drawyng up yᵉ plumpe to yᵉ welle	j*d*.
„ to yᵉ chapell prist Syr Wyllyam	xxviij*s*. iiij*d*.
Total . . £ix xvj*s*. iiij*d*.	

PAGE 352.   [Blank.]

PAGES 353–4.

𝕬.𝕯. m.ccccc.xviii[ix].

W. KYNG AND R. WORNELLE, WARDENS.
RECEIPTS.

Balance from Knyght and Fysser	£xxiij xviij*d*.

[Nothing unusual.]

PAGE 355.   EXPENSES.

Payd for a purne² stryng	j*d*.
„ for ij casis for ij chalis	xiiij*d*.
„ for hangyng up yᵉ lampe in yᵉ chanselle	vj*d*.
„ for a lyne to yᵉ lampe	ij*d*.
„ for leying stones in yᵉ new chapelle	j*d*.

PAGE 356.

Payd for yᵉ sexton³	xviij*d*.
„ for iiij and 4 pownds of wax agenest crystymas⁴	xlv*s*.

PAGES 357–8.

Payd to yᵉ tynkar for mendyng yᵉ halywater stocke	xij*d*.

PAGE 359.

𝕬.𝕯. m.ccccc.xix[xx].

J. THURBAN AND W. HORDE, WARDENS.
RECEIPTS.

Balance from Kyng and Wornelle	£xxxiij iij*s*.
Reseyvyd of John Avery for his wyfes lyyng in yᵉ churche	vj*s*. viij*d*.
„ of William Hayman	xiij*s*. iiij*d*.
„ of John Cradock	vj*s*. viij*d*.
„ of John Mascall and John Hyllman	vj. viij*d*.
„ ij ryngs with a pere⁵ knyfes.	

¹ Pump.   ² Apron.   ³ A usual entry for some ears.   ⁴ A yearly entry.   ⁵ Pair.

PAGE 360.
[Taverns and legacies as usual, and then]
Resevyd of Rychard Legette for candyls of yᵉ rele . . . . jd.
Resevyd of yᵉ rele of T. Hurne . . . . ijd.
   „   of John . . . for yᵉ rele . . . . . jd.
   „   of Isabelle Tynkar for candylls of yᵉ rele . . . jd.

PAGE 361.   EXPENSES [nothing unusual].

PAGE 362.
Payd to a vestment-maker to make a vestment of yᵉ olde cope .   vs. iiijd.
   „   for a reband[1] to yᵉ seid vestment . . . . . . jd.

PAGE 363.
Payd to Syr Davy . . . . xxvjs. viijd.
   „   to Syr John . . . . vjs. viijd.
   „   for steynyng and gyldyng of yᵉ Crosse . . iijs. iiijd.
   „   for rydyng to Wells for yᵉ visitation[2] . . . viijd.
   „   expenses for rydyng to Dondre[3] . . . viijd.
   „   to Syr John for his wages . . . xxs. viijd.

PAGE 364.
Payd yn yernes[4] to yᵉ steyner . . . . . jd.
                Total . . £x iiijs.

PAGES 365-6-7.   **A.D. m.ccccc.xx[xxi].**

W. TAYLER AND ROBERT THURBAN, WARDENS.

RECEIPTS.

Balance from J. Thurban and W. Horde . . . . . £xxxviij iiijs.
[The receipts include several small bequests to the chapel, and one bequest of John
   Toore for "lyeng" in the church] . . . . . . vjs. viijd.
             Total . . £xlix xixs. vjd.

PAGE 368.   [Blank.]

PAGES 369-70.
Dettys to yᵉ Church, the which that the Wardens[5] be not charged.
J. Cadocke for his wyfys lynge in the Church . . . . vjs. viijd.
J. Thurban for his moder lynge in the Church . . . . vjs. viijd.
Matthew Toore for his sisters lynge in yᵉ church . . . vjs. viijd.
Three sureties delivered to John Wakelyn . . . xxvjs. viijd.
Three other men owe, each . . . . vjs. viijd.

  [1] Ribbon.   [2] First time of this entry.   [3] Dundry.   [4] Earnest.
  [5] Probably Tayler and Thurban; no date.

PAGE 371. EXPENSES.

Payd to W. Hatheway for settyng up yᵉ canebe . . xx*d*.
„ for x pownds wax to make yᵉ rele . . . vij*s*. xj*d*.
„ for makyng yᵉ seyde rele . . . . . iij*d*.

PAGE 372.
Payd for a cheyne to yᵉ canebe . . . . j*d*.
Nearly ij Tons of lead are bought at per ton . £iij x*s*.
Three tymes rydyng to Mendip . . . . . viij*d*.
Payd for castyng of vj ton of ledde . . V nobulls viij*d*. (¹)

PAGE 373.
Payd for beryng of yᵉ seyd olde ledde fro yᵉ chapelle to yᵉ parsonage ;
To Thomas Prewett yᵉ bocher² . . . . } ij*d*.
„ for beryng of yᵉ seyd ledde, to Thomas Prewett, John Berner, and Thomas Warre ix*d*.
„ for mete and drynke to makyng yᵉ molde³ to cast yᵉ seid ledde . . . vij*d*.
„ to yᵉ heyward of Comysbury for a cooppe wod, and for yᵉ cariage . . . xx*d*.

PAGE 374.
Payd for iij wekys and more to Thurban and Tayler⁴ for to yntende⁵ yᵉ seid
plommer . . . . ij*s*. vij*d*.
„ for halowyng a pere of vestments . . . . xij*d*.
„ at Bristow for bakarrs londs⁶ . . . . xij*d*.

PAGE 375.
Payd for iiij torchesse . . . . . . xiij*s*. v*d*.

Total . . £xvj xiijs. iiij*d*.

PAGE 376.   Ⓐ.Ⓓ m.ccccc.xxi[ii].

J. AVEREY AND W. FLICHE, WARDENS.

RECEIPTS. [A very short list.]

Balance from Tayler and Thurban . . . . . £xxxiij iiij*s*.
Total . . . . £xlv vij*s*.

PAGE 377. EXPENSES.
Payd for wakyng yᵉ sepulcre⁷ . . ob.
„ for schreds to bynd yᵉ lyme⁸ . ij*d*.

PAGE 378.
Payd to a mynnystrelle⁹ . . . . xij*d*.
„ to Syr John Masday . . . xx*s*. x*d*.
„ for ij ymnalls . . . . ij*s*. x*d*.
„ for wrytyng yᵉ boke at Stoke and at home . . iij*s*. iiij*d*.
„ to yᵉ clarke of Axbrige for peyntyng of yᵉ seid cloth . . xxvj*s*. viij*d*.

¹ *I.e.*, £liij vij*s*. iiij*d*.   ² Butcher.   ³ Mould.   ⁴ Wardens.   ⁵ Oversee.
⁶ Baker's lands ; where ?   ⁷ The Sepulchre has not been mentioned since 1507-8.
⁸ Cow-hair is now used by plasterers in like way.   ⁹ First entry.

PAGE 380.
In expenses for dyking yᵉ new yew[1] . . . . xxiijs. iiijd.
     Total . . . £xxxv xixs. xjd.
    THE CHAPELLE DETT.
  [The list comprises bequests of money and kind.]
Alys Wake for lyyng yn yᵉ chapelle . . . . vs.
John Cannyngton . . . . vs.
The hole sum of this boke to yᵉ Chapelle . . . . . xliijs. xd.

PAGES 381–2.
[An undated sheet entitled "Bequests gevyn to yᵉ parysch of Yatton by [= in] Wm. Wornell and Wm. Bradmere ys dayis" [1498], followed by bequests in Knight and Tucker's days [1499] and loose memoranda. The bequests amount to many pounds.]

    END OF VOLUME I.

    VOL. II.[2]

A paper book, 15 × 5in., bound in a vellum page of M.S. Office-book.

PAGES 1, 2, 3. 𝔄.𝔇. m.ccccc.xxiii[iiii].

  T. HYLMAN AND ROBERT THURBAN, WARDENS.
   RECEIPTS. [of the usual type.]
Balance from Avery and Fliche . . . . £xxxv xixs. xjd.
   Total . . . £lj xixs.

PAGE 4.   [Blank.]

PAGES 5, 6, 7.   EXPENSES.
For a pype[3] for yᵉ second belle rope to renne[4] yn . . . . . . iiijd.
to Keytyngalle for workyng yᵉ chirche werk . . . . . £iij vjs. viijd.
 [The pump still called a "plumpe." Much stone hauled from Felton.]

PAGES 8, 9.
Payd to yᵉ clerke of Axbrige for peyntyng yᵉ won[5] part of yᵉ cloth . . xxvjs. viijd.
Payd to yᵉ seid Massynnys[6] . . . . xls. xd.
 „ for settyng up of yᵉ old fynyalls . . . . xiijs. iiijd.

---

[1] The amount of the charge looks like the repair of the yeo, *i.e.*, main-drain; or of a yere = sluice.

[2] N.B. In this Vol. the date at which the accounts are made up is never stated. It is probable, however, that, as in other accounts, it is before March 25th. A figure is therefore added within brackets to represent the year according to our reckoning.

[3] Tube to protect floor against friction. [4] Run. [5] One. [6] Masons.

PAGE 10.   [Blank.]

PAGE 11.   **A.D. m.ccccc.xxiiii[v].**
              W. KYNG, CALLED BONNEWY, AND R. WEBBE, WARDENS.
PAGE 12.   RECEIPTS.
Balance from Hylman and Thurban   .   .   .   .   .   £xxxvij vjs. viijd.
[The three Ales yield the large sum of £xiij, and, with many bequests, and Balance,
   swell the Total Receipts to £xlxxxxj xjs.]

PAGES 13, 14, 15.   EXPENSES.
For a trawle to plumpe .   .   .   .   iijd.
for an apurne[1] to ye church   .   .   .   .   iijd.
for settyng up ye tabylment   .   .   .   .   ijd.
for stones for ye crosse .   .   .   .   xxvjs. viijd.
for vj waynes of stone fro Felton, and vj moe to Wm. Hort fre mason .   xxvjs. viijd.
for mendyng ye chaunsell .   .   .   .   viijs. viijd.

PAGES 16, 17.
for yryn barre for Westwyndo in ye towre .   .   .   .   .   .   ijs.
for do. do. to ye newe warke   .   .   .   .   xiiijd.
More waynes of stone from Felton.
for mendyng ye Constyke[2] in ye chaunsell   .   .   .   .   .   xiiijd.
to Wm. Hort fre mason .   .   .   .   xxs.
in expenses at Wells when we went to gefe an answere to Master Beckham[3] for ye
   parysch.

PAGE 18.   [Blank.]

PAGES 19, 20.
Dettes to ye church, ye which ye Wardens be not charged with.
[Items similar in character; many the same as in last list.]

PAGES 21-2-3-4.   **A.D. m.ccccc.xxv[vi].**
                   R. MAY AND JOHN VIGOUR, WARDENS.
                              RECEIPTS.
   Balance from Webbe and Bonnewy   .   .   .   .   .   £xxxiij viijs.
                 Several for lying in the Church.
of John Hort for a stone for his sister   .   .   .   .   .   .   iijs.
[The Ale days are specified as St. James' Day, Hock Day, and Whitsuntide.]
                       Total . . . £xix xs.

   [1] Apron.   [2] Candlestick.
   [3] Canon of Wells, holding the Visitation Court of the Prebendal Peculiar.

Patton Church-Wardens' Accounts.

PAGE 25.   EXPENSES.

For makyng a shote[1] and for hewing of ij shydes[2], and for warke on y⁰ chaunselle   ijs. iiijd.
for a carnocke[3] of lyme, and bryngyng home . . . . ixs.

PAGE 26.
for many loads of Felton stone . . . . ?
for ryddyng y⁰ ground to y⁰ Crosse, and shrydyng y⁰ trees . xvjd.

PAGE 28.
payd for stone to y⁰ hede of y⁰ Crosse   iijs. vjd.
,,   for bryngyng it home[4] . .   xs. iiijd.
,,   in expenses for rydyng to Bath   . xijd.

PAGE 29.
for sawyng y⁰ burdestocke[5] to y⁰ church . . . . ijs. vd.
for thungs and for a lace to y⁰ canebe . . . . jd. ob.
to J. Hort y⁰ fre Mason for rydyng to Bath to se y⁰ stonys [besides 3 payments of xiijs. and xxs. and liijs.] . . . . vjd.

PAGES 30-1.
         [Several entries of expenses for scaffolding.]
for settyng uppe of y⁰ schaffoold and of y⁰ crosse hed . . . ijs. viijd.
for settyng uppe y⁰ seid tymber and for thacking y⁰ crosse . . iijs. vjd.
for repyng of y⁰ rede[6] and for bryngyng home . . . . . iiijd.
to halfe an hundred of brymbylls[7] . . . . ijd.
to y⁰ gyltar . . . . xxs.
            Total . . . £xvj xixs. vijd.

PAGES 33-4-5.   𝔄.𝔇. m.ccccc.xxvi[vii].
        ROBERT THURBAN AND JOHN STRETYNG, WARDENS.
                   RECEIPTS.
    Balance from May and Vigour . . . .   £xxxiij xvjs.
For Wold⁰ dett . . . . vs. viijd.
For ryngyng Syr Wyllyams modor[9] kncle . . . . . . xxd.
          Total . . . £xxxxxj xvjs.
The receipts from the Ales this year are (as of old) from the "Lightmen of the East and West parts." The truth probably is that the Lightmen did their collecting work, whilst the people were assembled at the Ale in the Church house.]

PAGE 36.   [Blank.]

---

[1] Casting metal in a mould.   [2] Shroud-wood for fuel.
[3] Curnock. A measure of 4 bushels (Wright's Prov. Dict.)   [4] The finest Bath stone was used for the carving.
[5] Boardstock, *i.e.*, a trunk fit for sawing into plank ; board is still pronounced "boord."
[6] For thatching the Cross against frost, whilst the stone was green.   [7] Brambles for same purpose.
[8] Old.   [9] Mother's.

Page 37.

1 {
- Payd to yᵉ organ maker . . . . £xij
- ,, for makyng a fote[2] to yᵉ organs . . . . iiijs.
- ,, in expenses for yᵉ organ maker and for his company that gefe attendance with hym . . . . viijs.
- ,, for makyng priketts agenest Alhalowday . . . . . . ijd.
- ,, to yᵉ organ pleyer . . . . xxjd.

Page 38. Expenses. [Sundry repairs to pump, &c.]

For schotyng yᵉ draw3te[3] of yᵉ plumpe . . . . . . iiijd.

Page 39.

for a dext clothe of iij yerds . . . . xiiijd.
to Thomas Nefelle, gylder . . . . £iij

Page 40.

for ij awterclothes, won of diaper and another of bocaram, ye price . vjs. vjd.
for a manuall . . . . ijs. iiijd.

Page 41.

for ij awter clothes of vj yerds and a halfe, yᵉ price a yerd . ijs. vd. ob.
for halowyng of iiij awter clothys . . . . viijd.

Page 42.

for schotyng a broche[4] in yᵉ Church howse . . . . . ob.

Total . . . £ix xviijs. xjd.

Pages 43–4. (A.D. m.ccccc.xxvii[viii].

T. Kew and W. Wamperfylde, Wardens.

Receipts.

Balance from Stretyng and Thurban . . £xliij xvjs. vd.
Nothing unusual.

Total . . . £xxix xvijs. ixd.

Page 45. Expenses.

- Payd to yᵉ organ maker at Brystow . . . . xls.
- ,, at Bristow with yᵉ parich makyng yᵉ bargain . . . . . xxd.
- ,, for mendyng yᵉ bonds of yᵉ surplesse and yᵉ rochetts . . . ijd.

Page 46.

- Payd for makyng a myster[5] to yⁿ Church howse . . . . . iiijs. iiijd.
- ,, for a peer of gemows[6] to yᵉ seid myster . . . . . . xiijd.
- ,, for a locke, ij ryngs to yᵉ seid myster . . . . . . vd.
- ,, for ij dosyn and a halfe drynkyng bowls, and a dosyn and a halfe of mete dysses, and iiij dosyn trenchers and a ladylle . . . . xvjd.

---

[1] These items have been scratched out. No date. [2] A pedal? [3] Casting the drawing-rod of pump. [4] A spit. [5] Unexplained. [6] Pair of hinges.

[Much stone for the west window of the Church.]

Payd to John Wakelyn for glasyng . . . . vj*s.*

PAGE 47.

Payd for sprangs to church lader . . . . . . ij*d.*
" for makyng a yeere¹ to y*e* Church howse cowle . . j*d.* ob.
" to John Wakelyn for glasyng² . . . . . . £iij
" for iij boks³ to y*e* church . . . . . xlvj*s.* viij*d.*
" for mendyng of y*e* pyx of y*e* hye awter . . . . iiij*d.*
" to y*e* organ maker at Bristow . . . . xx*s.*
" in expenses for bryngyng home y*e* organs, and to y*e* seyd Halyar⁴ of Brystow vij*s.* ob.
" for mendyng y*e* hedde of y*e* West Wyndow . . . . iiij*s.*

PAGE 48.

Payd to y*e* organ maker . . . . £xij
Payd in expense for y*e* organ maker, and for hys compane that gefe attendance with
    hym to helpe hym . . . . viij*s.* viij*d.*
" to y*e* organ maker when that he was last payd of hys pay, for a reward⁵ . . xvij*d.*
" for makyng priketts agenest Alhalowday . . . . . . ij*d.*
" to y*e* organ pleyer . . . . xxj*d.*

PAGE 49.

Payd to John Felyps for pleying on y*e* organs . . . . viij*d.*
Payd for iij sacryng bells clepers . . . . j*d.*

[Waking the Sepulchre has disappeared.]

PAGE 50.   [Blank.]

PAGE 51.   **A.D. m.ccccc.xxviii[ix].**

J. CRADDOCK AND W. KYNG, WARDENS.

PAGE 52.   RECEIPTS.

Balance from Kew and Wamperfylde . . . . . . £xxix xvij*s.*
Resevyd of Matthew Toore for iij qurarters of saten of Bryge⁶ . . . . xij*d.*
" of my lade⁷ Rodne for lone of y*e* vestments . . . . . . ij*s.*

PAGES 53–4.

xxx gifts, very small, towards buying lime; the largest from Isabell Hort "for a
    carnocke lyme" . . . . viij*d.*

                        Total . . £xxviij xviij*d.*

PAGES 55–6.   [Blank.]

---

¹ Ear?   ² Too costly for plain glass.   ³ Books.   ⁴ Haulier.
⁵ A gratuity. Such "rewards" are common in the accounts.   ⁶ Bruges.
⁷ Lady Elizabeth Chaworth, widow of Sir W. Rodney, was living in the Rodney Manor-House of Backwell. She died 1537, after founding a chantry in Backwell Church.

PAGE 57.   EXPENSES.

Payd for a peynted clothe to yᵉ hye awter   .   iijs. iiijd.

PAGE 58.

Payd to R. Porcar for brannyng¹ lyme .   .   .   .   .   .   iiijs. iijd.
    [There are other like payments to him, and for coals.]

PAGES 59-60.
        [The spire is repaired and pointed :—three items.]
             [Coal hauled from Nailsea.]

PAGE 62.

Payd for wax, xx li. agenyst Saynt James Day².   .   ixs. vijd.
  „   to a mynstrelle for pleyng at .   .   .   .   . xijd.
  „   for hewyng a clavey³ to Church howse .   .   . iijd.

PAGES 63-4.

Payd for yᵉ iryn gere to yᵉ gownte⁴ dorre at Wemeram [Wimberham on the Yeo] . xvjd.
  „   to ij men for stoppyng yᵉ sayd water   .   .   .   . xvjd.

PAGES 65-67.   **A.D. m.ccccc.xxix[x].**

            WATER WILLIAMS AND J. WEBBE, WARDENS.
                         RECEIPTS.

Balance from Kyng and Cradock .   .   .   .   £xxviij xiijd.
            [Nothing unusual.]   Total   . £xxvj xjs.

PAGES 68-9.   EXPENSES.

Payd to yᵉ gyldar for yᵉ tabylment .   .   .   . xls.
  „   to yᵉ belle maker .   .   .   . £xix vjd.
[with many items for carrying the old bell into Bristol, and bringing back and hanging the new one.]

PAGE 70.

Payd for gyltyng of Saynt James   xiijs. vd.
  „   for gyltyng of owre Lady   . vjs.

PAGE 71.

Payd for xxviij piownde wexe, wyche made yᵉ torchys and yᵉ tapyrs, yᵉ wyche shall
    brene⁵ when yᵉ corse shall be presente .   .   .   . xviijs. viijd.
  „   for xiiij pownde of wekezerne⁶ .   .   .   . iijs. vjd.
  „   for makyng of yᵉ seyd torchys, and for expenses of yᵉ makyng of yᵉ seyd
      torchys .   .   .   . ijs.

¹ Burning.   ² Hitherto limited to Christmas and Easter.
³ Mantel-piece. Presumably so called as the place where the keys (claves) were hung.
⁴ Drain. The bursting of this sluice in the sea bank was a peril to the whole level, and therefore repaired by Church funds, without pressure from authority.
⁵ Burn.   ⁶ Wick-yarn.

PAGE 72.

Payd for framyng of yᵉ seegys¹ in yᵉ church, for makyng ij doerys² in yᵉ towre, and all yᵉ levys³ of yᵉ wyndowes in yᵉ Church-howse, with hookys, twystys, and haspys . . . . xxiijs. iiijd.
„ for yᵉ sege in yᵉ chaunsell to R. Kew for hys hondewerke, and for a bord to J. Harriis . . . . ijs.
„ for yᵉ koverynd⁴ of yᵉ ovyn . . . . xxd.

Total £xiiij vijs.

PAGES 73-4-5-6. **A.D. m.ccccc.xxx[i].**

MATTHEW TOORE AND W. ROME, WARDENS.
RECEIPTS.

Balance from Willyams and Webbe . . . . £xxxiij xjs. xd.
[Several old debts recovered, and three fees at vjs. viijd. "for lying in the church."]

Total £xlj ijs.

PAGE 77.   EXPENSES.

Payd for a horse⁵ locke to yᵉ cherche yatte . . . . . . viijd.
„ for makyng yᵉ tabernacle of Saynt Thomas . . . . . xxs.
„ for bryngyng home yᵉ same seid tabernacull to yᵉ carver . . . . xvjd.
„ to Thomas Partrych for makyng ij coppsys⁶, and an hapse to yᵉ cherche yatt iijd. ob.
„ for an ocke⁷ . . . . xxijd.
„ to Jo. Whyte yᵉ Belmaker . . . . xlixs. vjd.

PAGE 78.

Payd to J. Partrych for a bronde-yryn, and for naylys . . . . ijs. iijd.
„ for wadlyng⁸ yᵉ cherche howse . . . . viijd.

PAGES 79-80.

Payd to a mynstrell at Wytsonday . . . . . . ijs. viijd.

Total £x iijs. iijd.

PAGE 81. **A.D. m.ccccc.xxxi[ii].**

J. WALE AND T. TAYLER, WARDENS.
RECEIPTS.

Balance from Toore and Rome . . . . £xlj ijs. iijd.
[After xiij items of receipt the account ends, but it is resumed with formal heading and I.H.S. on page 83, beginning with the xiij items. Two pages have been cut out.]

of Master Capel for a reward⁹ to yᵉ Churche . . . . . . xxd.
of a bequest of Syr Davy . . . . iijs. iiijd.

¹ Seats.   ² Doors.   ³ Shutters.   ⁴ Covering.   ⁵ ⁶ Unexplained.   ⁷ Oak.
⁸ Wattling.   ⁹ Gratuity.

U

PAGES 84-5-6.
[The three Ales are still very fruitful, yielding £xvij viijs. iiijd.]

PAGE 87.   EXPENSES.
to ye Bellator[1] of Brystow at makyng ye bargain . . iiijs.
payd for ij kynterkynnys to ye cherche howse . . . viijd.

PAGE 88.
payd for rydyng to Bristow on ye Ascencione day . ijd.

PAGES 89-90.
payd for ij salt celars and a dosyn dysses with a dosyn of trenchers . . . vd.
" for iij huckemocks to ye cherch . . . . . . vjd.
[A large number of entries again this year about the casting of a bell at Bristol.]

PAGE 91.
for makyng wax ageynst Saynt James day[2] . ijd.

PAGES 92-3-4.
for reparations on ye chapell of my Lady Newtons . . . . vijs. xjd.
to a Mynstrell . . . . xiijs. iiijd.
                Total   .   £xj xvs.

PAGE 95.   **A.D. m.ccccc.xxxii[iii].**

J. BEKE AND J. VIGOR, WARDENS.
                RECEIPTS.
        Balance from Wale and Tayler . . £xlvij
                [Nothing unusual.]
                Total   . . . £xlviij xvijs.

PAGE 97.   EXPENSES.
Payd to R. Kew for crossebarrs and rounds for ye peyse[3].
This yere Robert and John Grenefylde is paid for pointing and other work on the
    Church . . . . £viij vjs. vd.

PAGES 98-9.
Payd to J. Rylbere for stonys to ye Chapell wyndow. . . . . vjs. viijd.
 " to R. Grenefylde for takyng downe an elder tre out of a pype abooffe in ye towre iiijs.
 " for mendyng of a gargyne[4] hede . . . . xxd.
 " to a mynstrele at Wytsontyde . . . . vjs.
 " for assyon cuppys[5] . . . . iiijd.

PAGE 100.
[The great bell re-cast at Bristow, and rehung.]

[1] Bell-rounder.   [2] A regular entry.   [3] Clock-weight.   [4] Gurgoyle
[5] Ashen cups.

PAGE 101.
payd for xxviij yards of Irys[1] cloth for a hussyllyng[2] cloth the price . . vs. ijd.
„ for mendyng a sylver canstyke[3] . . . . xvjd.
„ for vj yards of lasyng to mend old vestments . . . . . vd.

PAGE 102.
payd to R. Grenefelde for poyntyng a tornelle[4] of ye cherche . . . ijs. viijd.
„ for mendyng ye surplesse collars, and for a new amysse . . . . xijd.
„ to J. Meryfeld for makyng a croke to ye Sacrament over ye hye auter . . jd.
     Total . . £xvj vjs. xd.

PAGES 103–4.   [Blank.]

[After a page cut out, p. 105 shows a Heading for 1533–4 crossed out. pp. 106-7-8 contain expenses, probably of Cooke and Payne, but crossed out, with "verte" in the margin.]
     Total . . £liij viijs.
[Some of the items on pp. 107–8, which are not found in the audited account, are given here.]

PAGE 107.
for makyng of halfe a dosyn of towells of ye olde hoselyng[5] cloth . iiijd.
to ye gyltdar[6] [twice the same] . . . . xiijs. iiijd.

PAGE 108.
for halfe a dosyn heryng barells   iijs.

PAGES 109–10. **A.D. m.ccccc.xxxiiii[iiii].**
EDWARD COOKE AND WATER PAYN, WARDENS.
     RECEIPTS.
Balance from Beke and Vigor . . . . £xlviij xvijs.
    [Nothing unusual.]
    Total . . £liij xs.

PAGE 111.   EXPENSES.
Payd to Thomas Jeferes, bellatur[7] of Bristow in part   xlixs. vjd.

PAGE 112.
Payd to ye gyltdar . .   xiijs. iiijd.
„ to Syr John Batell .   . xxxvs.

---

[1] Irish.
[2] Houselling cloth spread over the rails during the Communion of the faithful. Appointed in the Coronation Services of the Georges. Still used in some Churches in the Diocese of Winchester, at St. Mary's, Oxford &c.
[3] Candlestick.   [4] Turret.   [5] Gilder.   [6] Bell-founder.

PAGE 113.
Payd for a serche[1] to y e cherche howse . . viij*d*.
  ,, to a Mynstrell . . . viij*s*. iiij*d*.

PAGE 116.
Payd for a ryng and stapull to y e font . . . . . . j*d*. ob.
  ,, for a hole peesse[2] to make fronts to y e syde auters . . xix*s*. viij*d*.
  ,, in yerneste[3] for a cope . . . . iiij*d*.
     Total . . £xv x*s*. vij*d*.

PAGE 117.   [Blank.]

PAGES 118–119.

J.Ḣ.S.   A.D.   m.ccccc.xxxiv[v].

J. ERLE AND J. BENE, WARDENS.
     RECEIPTS.

Balance from Cooke and Payne   .   £liij x*s*.

PAGE 120.
[Besides usual gifts, are vj*s*. for "an ocke," ij*s*. for "y e croppe of an ocke."]
of John Wassborowe for lygthmanshepe[4] . . . . vj*s*. viij*d*.
    Total . . £xxiij xiiij*s*.

PAGE 121.   EXPENSES.
Payd for mendyng y e vyce durre locke in y e towre . . . . vij*d*.
  ,, for makyng yryn pynnys for y e foore locks in y e medyll flore . j*d*.
  ,, to T. Organs wyfe for makyng a canebe to y e hye awter . vj*d*.
  ,, for mendyng a coveryng to y e font . . . . . xij*d*.

PAGE 122.
Payd for a hole sewte of vestments with a Coope . . . . . . £xxx
  ,, at Thomas Prewetts with y e parysch of Comysbure[5] and Yatton for brynggyng
 ther sewte of vestments, in expenses . . . . ij*s*. x*d*.
  ,, to T. Tucker of Comysbure for beryng y e sayd vestments home . . . j*d*.
  ,, to J. Meryfeld for scowryng of canstyks, and mendyng y e canebe, and for iij
 new cheynys, and mendyng a quart, and for crooks to y e awter clothes, and
 mendyng a frunt over y e hye awter . . . . ij*s*. x*d*.
  ,, to Terre Lucocke for makyng y e fronts of y e new awter clothes and a cooshen . viij*d*.

PAGE 123.
Payd to J. Jeferes of Brystow, y e bellatur[6] . xlix*s*. vj*d*.

---

[1] Survey?   [2] Whole piece.   [3] Earnest.
[4] Not a private gift, but to be added to his collection as Lightman.
[5] The parish of Congresbury seems to have bought a suit likewise, and to have greeted the arrival of the two suits at a joint Church Ale, given by T. Prewett.
[6] Most of these items are repeated, pp. 137–8. There are no yearly entries of payments to an organist besides those noted.

Payd to yᵉ organ maker	xiijs. iiijd.
,, at yᵉ tewnyng of yᵉ sayd organs, in expenses for Peter and Thomas in wyne .	ijd
,, for forks, forlocks, pynnes to yᵉ bales [bellows]	
,, for mendyng iij sacryng bellys, and yᵉ Church chetyll	xijd.
,, at Keynsam to yᵉ sumnar¹	jd.

PAGE 124.

Payd at Brystow to yᵉ browdurar²	£vj
,, for a crosse at Saynt James tyde	lvjs. viijd.
,, to yᵉ bale³ of Wellys for ookys⁴ in Kyngs wood	xliijs. vijd.
,, in expenses for yᵉ chosyng of yᵉ Woke⁵	iiijd.
,, for wax at Mychalmas, for xxvj pownds, at vjd. a pownde . .	xijs.
,, to Syr Rychard, prist⁶	vs.

[Not totalled.]

PAGES 128-9-30.   **A.D. m.ccccc.xxxv[vi].**

T. WYLKYS AND CALYX SPREDE, WARDENS.

RECEIPTS.

Balance from Erle and Bene   .   .   £xxiij xiiijs.

[Nothing unusual.]

PAGE 131.   EXPENSES.

Payd for mendyng yᵉ best canstyke and scowryng a sensar . . .	xviijd.

PAGE 132.

Payd for makyng iiij rochetts	xvjd.
,, to yᵉ Carpynter four sums besides earnest: to carver . . .	xxs.

PAGE 133.

Payd at Banwell for halowyng yᵉ sewte of vestments . . .	viijd.
,, with yᵉ parysch at Comesbure upon Wyttewysday⁷ . . .	xxd.
,, for makyng ij new awter clothes	iiijd.

PAGE 134.

Payd for xvj eils of cloth for yᵉ hole sewte vestments . . .	xs. viijd.
,, for makyng iij albys, iij amys, for yᵉ sewte	xd.
,, in expenses at yᵉ makyng of yᵉ sege in yᵉ church, for iiij dayes warke	viijd.

PAGE 135.

Payd for ij ells of dyaper for ij awter clothes	xs. viijd.
,, iij ernest pense, won to Osburne and another to Sperark yᵉ carver, and Grenefyld	iijd.
.Total . . £xj xvs.	

¹ Summoner, or Apparitor, of Visitation Court.   ² Embroiderer   ³ Bailiff.   ⁴ Oaks.
⁵ Oak.   ⁶ Priest.   ⁷ Whit-tuesday.

PAGE 136. [Blank.]

[After one page cut out, pages 137–8 contain sundry payments of A.D. 1534–5 to be found on pages 123–4.]

PAGE 139.

J.H.S. A.D. m.ccccc.xxxvi[vii].

J. CRADOCKE AND J. COLMAN, WARDENS.

Balance from Wylkyns and Sprede . £xxix ij*d*.

RECEIPTS.

Resevyd of Isabell Avery a pelow and auter cloth.
„ of John Avery a bequest of . . . . . vj*s*. viij*d*.
„ for a bequest of Master Perceval[1] . . . . . v*s*.
[with many more.]
Total . . £xij ij*s*. vj*d*.

PAGE 143. EXPENSES.

Payd for makyng a sege, and for makyng a dext . . . . iiij*s*. iiij*d*.
[The timber bought above is now sawn and brought home.]

PAGE 144.
Payd to Thomas Carpynter for a settyng up ye pascall . ij*d*.
„ „ „ laying up the tymber[2] . .
„ to a carver . . . . xlvj*s*.

PAGE 145.
Payd to ij mynstrell . . . . vj*s*.
„ to Syr Robert for makyng an auter cloth . . xx*d*.
„ for makyng ij clappsys[3] to ye Coope . . . vij*d*.
„ for withdrawyng ye constre[4] cowrte . . . . iij*d*.
„ for ye mendyng a coppys of a coffur in ye chaunsell sett . ij*d*.

PAGE 146.
Payd for drawyng of strake[5] schyd to ye sayd pytte . . . v*d*.
„ for makyng of hawfe[6] ye pytte . . . . . vj*d*.
„ to Wm. Sensam in ernes for makyng a clock and chyme . j*d*.

---

[1] A family seated at Tickenham Court.   [2] For seasoning.   [3] Clasps.
[4] *See* above, A.D. 1503; suit instituted in the Consistory Court, and now withdrawn.   [5] ?
[6] ? A hovel-shed run up to cover the saw-pit.

PAGES 147–8.   **Ⱥ.Ð m.ccccc.xxxvii[viii].**

J. HANNAM AND J. SMYTH, WARDENS.
Balance from Cradocke and Colman . . £xxix vjs.

Stock transferred to yᵉ New Wardens.

Pinnacle of best cross.¹	Twenty-five Rings.
Silver studs of girdle.	Two kerchiefs.
Two girdles—harnessed.	Pillow and altar cloth.

RECEIPTS.

of Master Choward,² yᵉ ornaments of yᵉ Church at Backwell . iijs. iiijd.
                Total   .   .   £xliij xiijs.

PAGE 149.   EXPENSES.

Payd to Syr Harry . . . . xiijs. iiijd.
  „ to Syr John Batell . . . . vijs.
  „ for mendyng yᵉ font and a chalys . . . . . iiijs.
  „ for yᵉ parysche at Comesbure . . . . . xxd.
  „   „   at Ken . . . . xvjd.

PAGE 150.

Payd to yᵉ gyltar . . . . xxs.
  „ to yᵉ Mynstrells . . . . xs. jd.
  „ to yᵉ gyltar . . . . xliijs. iiijd.
  „ to yᵉ buckebynddar . . . . . . xxiijs. iiijd.
  „ more to yᵉ buckebynddar . . . . . xvs.
  „ for yᵉ furst buke to yᵉ sayd buckebynddar . . vjd.
  „ in expenses with yᵉ parysch at Keynsam³ . . vs.
  „ to yᵉ buckebynddar for another bargayn . . xxvjs. ixd.
  „ to T. Stone for makyng yryn gere to Saynt John . vjd.
  „ in expenses for makyng a scaffold to Saynt John⁴ . ijd.
  „ to yᵉ gyltar . . . . xvijs.

PAGE 151.

Payd for a locke and a key to yᵉ font . . . . iiijd.
  „ for a shyde⁵ to yᵉ pytt to saw a pece of tymber apon . ijs. jd.
  „ for fyllyng⁶ yᵉ sayd shyde, and for bryngyng to yᵉ pytt . viijd.
  „ for sawyng of yᵉ sayd tymber for yᵉ clocke howse . vs. iiijd.
  „ for beryng in yᵉ sayd tymber into yᵉ chapell . . xijd.

---

¹ Went on till 1546, then sold.
² The executor, probably of Lady Elizabeth Chaworth, widow of Sir Walter Rodney. She borrowed vestments in 1528-9, for which it would seem compensation was paid. She died 1537, June 3rd. See her monument at Backwell.
³ A visitation or an Ale?   ⁴ Viz., on the Roodloft.   ⁵ Shroud, or branch, for the saw-pit.
⁶ Felling.

PAGE 152.
Payd to yᵉ peynter for yᵉ last bargayn makyng . . . . . xxvjs. viijd.
„ to yᵉ buckebyndar . . . . vjs. viijd.
„ for settyng yᵉ plate afore Saynt Jorge[1] . . . . . . ixd.
„ to Thomas Bredmere for yᵉ sexteneshepe[2] for yᵉ halfe yere : . xviijd.
Total . . £xviiij xs.

PAGES 153-4.   ['Torn away.']

PAGES 155-6-7. **A.D. m.ccccc.xxxviii[ix].**
T. GYLLYNG AND J. SOMERSETT, WARDENS.
RECEIPTS.
Balance from Hannam and Smythe . . . . . . £xxv vjs.
[Nothing unusual, but a] bequest from a poore woman . . . iiijd.
Total . . . £xxxviij viijs.

PAGE 158.
Detts to yᵉ Church wyche we be not chargyd wt. [9 names.]
Detts owyd for berying in yᵉ Church. [18 names; some crossed out as having payd after.]

PAGE 159.   EXPENSES.
Payd to yᵉ clocke howse makyng in yᵉ Church . . . xiijs. iiijd.
„ to yᵉ bede man for makyng a dycke in yᵉ parsonage . . viijd.

PAGE 160.
Payd for Lyme at Chewton . . . . iijs. iiijd.
„ for fetchyng Osburne . . . . . iiijd.
„ in expenses on Schere Thurssday[3] . . . iiijd.

PAGE 161.
Payd for hewyng a tre for yᵉ clocke howse   ijs.
„ to Osburne[4] . . . . .   £iij

PAGE 162.
Payd for a by byll[5] . . . .   ixs. vjd.
„ for yᵉ Mynstrells . . .   . xs.
„ for mendyng of a chales . .   . ijs.
„ to yᵉ buckebyndar . .   xxvjs. iiijd.
„ to William Sensam for yᵉ clocke   . xxs.

PAGE 163.
Payd for ij hundryth of bords to make yᵉ Church coffur . iiijs. viijd.

PAGE 164.
Payd to Syr Harry for a bucke[6] . . . . . . viijd.
Balance . . £xx xs. ob.

[1] A new entry.   [2] Sextonship.   [3] Maundy Thursday.
[4] The maker of the Clock-house.   [5] Bible.   [6] Book.

Yatton Church-Wardens' Accounts.   153

PAGE 165.　　　　　　　[Blank.]

PAGES 166-7-8.　　　A.D. m.ccccc.xxxix[xl].
　　　　　　T. MYDWYNTER AND J. HYLMAN, WARDENS.[1]
　　　　　　　　　　RECEIPTS.
of Humfrey Lett, Clarke of ye sayd parysch　.　.　.　.　ijs. iiij*d*.
for candels of ye rele from J. Avery .　.　.　.　.　.　j*d*.
　　　　　　　　Total　.　.　.　£xxxv xviij*s*.

PAGE 169.　　　　　　　EXPENSES.
[Three loads of timber hauled, a stair in the Church-house and a window added.]
PAGE 170.
Payd to Syr Robert Cocke for mendyng and peyntyng the cloth of ye sepulcre[2] and y^e
　　roode　.　.　.　.　.　.　.　.　.　.　.　ij*s*. v*d*.
　„　for takyng down of ye clocke howse[3]　.　.　.　.　.　.　xij*d*.
PAGE 171.
Payd to a pryste of Brys . . . for comyng to Yatton　.　.　.　viij*d*. (⁴)
　„　for mendyng ye patent[5] of the chalesse　.　.　.　.　.　.　xvj*d*.
　„　in expenses at John Wyld for the cownt makyng of mastres Mydwynter and
　　　Hylman.[6]
　„　for an ell of cloth to make iiij corporas　.　　　　　　　　　xv*d*.
　„　for a locke to ye font　.　.　.　.　.　　　　　　　　iiij*d*.
　„　for ij yards of here cloth for an awter　.　　　　　　　　　xv*d*.
　„　for vestments in part payment　.　.　　　　　　　　　£vj

PAGE 172.
Payd to J. Meryfyld for makyng a cheyne to ye bybyll　.　.　.　.　viij*d*.
　„　stoppyng of the holes under ye clocke howse .　.　.　.　.　ij*d*.
　„　in part for ye clocke　.　.　.　.　.　.　.　.　xxxiij*s*. iiij*d*.
　„　to . . . and to ye seid Clockmaker .　.　.　.　.　.　xx*s*.
　„　to Thomas Carpynter for a hole wekes worke and hys man Nycholas　.　vj*s*. vj*d*.
　„　to Nycholas for ij days worke more　.　.　.　.　.　.　xiiij*d*.
　„	for mendyng ij lokkys on ye regester coffer　.　.　.　.　.　ix*d*.

PAGE 173.
Payd for makyng clene ye lampe in ye chaunsell　.　　　　　　　j*d*.
　„	for bryngyng home ye clocke .　.	.	.	.	.	ij*s*. viij*d*.
　„	do.　do.　do.　ye frame of ye clocke　.　.	.	.	vj*d*.
　„	to J. Tayler for rydyng to Wells　.　.	.	.	.	xx*d*.
　„	in expenses when we fett[7] ye crosse from Brystow　.	.	.	v*d*.
　　　　　　　　Total　.　.　.　£xv x*s*.

[1] Thos. Brodmere is surety for payment of xl*s*. not paid by the late Wardens with the rest of the balance £xx x*s*.
[2] Not mentioned for many years.　　[3] *I.e.*, the old one.　　[4] Torn.
[5] Paten, first time it is mentioned.　　[6] *I.e.*, the defaulting Wardens.　　[7] Fetched.

END OF VOLUME II.

VOL III.

[A paper book, 13 × 8 inches, also, like the last, bound in pages of MS. Service Book.]

PAGE 1.

𝔄.𝔇. m.ccccc.xxx₊ by error for m.ccccc.xxxx[i].

W. TUCKER AND R. HORT, WARDENS.

Balance from Mydwynter and Hylman £xx ijs. ixd.
God be praysed in all his workes.

RECEIPTS [as usual].

PAGE 2.   EXPENSES.

Payd to J. Stretyng for goyng to Uphill when yᵉ goods of yᵉ Chyrche was gone . ijd.
  ,, to Wardens of Congsbury for[1] yᵉ Chyrche chetyll . . . . . viijd.
  ,, to sawyng yᵉ quyrbys to yᵉ Furnes[2] of Chyrche howse . . . . vjd.

PAGE 3.

Payd for iij awter clothes halowyng . . . . xijd.
  ,, for ij mynstrells . . . . vjs. ixd.
  ,, to William. . . . . . . for hys with iiij other menys[3] expenses when yᵉ chyrche was robbed . . . . vs. iijd.

PAGE 4.   [several entries of expenses in seeking the goods.]

Payd for makyng a byll of indytement at Wellys sessyns . . . . viijd.
                     Total . . . £xj xvs. xd.

PAGES 5, 6.   𝔄.𝔇. m.ccccc.xxxxi[ii].

J. ERLE AND J. STAPERCHYLDE, WARDENS.

Balance from Tucker and Horte £xxij xiijs.

Wherof they toke thys dett followyng as mony £v iijs.[4] and at yᵉ accompte [were?] dyschargyd yᵉ same £v iijs., and yᵉ same prout[5] in yᵉ dett-boke.

[RECEIPTS unfinished. Nothing unusual.]

PAGE 7.   EXPENSES.

Payd goyng to Ilchester sessyons for yᵉ Chyrche goods . . . . viijs. vjd. ob.
  ,, for iij stavys to bere yᵉ pawle[6] cloth . . . . iiijd.
  ,, to W. Rome and Edward Avere for leyng a tumbe in yᵉ chyrche, with other reparations . . . . xijd.

PAGE 8.

Payd to Syr John Frenshman for mendyng yᵉ sayd surplesse and rochettes . . xijd.

---

[1] I.e., for the hire of.   [2] Much outlay on Furnace.   [3] Men's.   [4] Details omitted.
[5] Qy., put out.   [6] Pall; a new entry.

Payd to yᵉ Clarke for keepyng yᵉ clocke	iiijs.
„ to yᵉ mynstrells at Wytsonday	vjs. viijd.

PAGE 9.

Payd for makyng yᵉ wax at Seynt James tyde and at halowntyde . .	jd.
„ for iiij score pownds of wax ageynst Crystymas . .	xxxviijs. viijd.
„ for ye parysch at Kenston	xvd.
Total . . £viij xviijd.	
So remayneth clere and al dyschargyd	£xxij xixs. vijd.

PAGE 10. [Blank.]

PAGE 11. [Begins with]

EXPENSES [of Wardens unnamed; Heading and Receipts being lost].

For a pece of brode yncull[1] for gyrdyllys	vd.
for xvij sheets of dubbell plate	vs. iiijd.
for ij hundryth and an halfe and iij powndes yryn to make a beme a fore the hye awter, yᵉ price	xvs. vjd.
to Smyth for makyng yᵉ sayd beme	xs.
to a smyth of Brystow for makyng a beme afore the hye awter, in part of payment	xvjs. viijd.
for caryng home of yᵉ sayd beme	ijs. iiijd.
to W. Rome for settyng in the foresayd beme in yᵉ chaunsell afore yᵉ hye awter, and for mendyng yᵉ wall[2] in yᵉ chyrch	viijd.

PAGES 12, 13. [several more entries upon the same work.]

to a gylter of Brystow for gyltyng yᵉ kyngs armys	xiijs. viijd.
for yᵉ parysch at Kynston Seymer	xvjd.
for ij banners	xxjs. xd.
to John Lynch, Mynstrell	vs.
Total . . . £xiiij xvjs. vd.	

PAGE 15. **A.D. m.cccc.xxxxii[iii].**

J. IRYSCH AND T. PARTRYCH, WARDENS.

Balance from Cradocke and Meryfield £xxiij ijs., of yᵉ wych ys xiiijs. of brokyng money, dandepratts[3] and Irys grots.

RECEIPTS.

Resevyd for yᵉ Chapell bocke . . liiijs. vd.[4]
Total . . £xli xs.

---

[1] A kind of broad linen tape: bleached yarn.   [2] *I.e.*, at the beam ends.

[3] A small coin, not in lawful currency. (Halliwell.)

[4] A special subscription for outlay on the Chapel of St. James, or on its Services, growing in costliness. Burials are now allowed in it, at a fee of vs.

PAGE 17.   EXPENSES.

For mendyng of ye organs	xxvjs. viijd.
For a pawle[1] cloth	xiijs. iiijd.
Payd to ye commysnarrs[2]	vjs. viijd.
„ to C. Tanner for vij dayes warke makyng clene the rode lofte, and the glasyn wyndows	iijs. jd.

PAGE 18.

Payd for the Kyngs subsyde[3]	xiijs. iiijd.
„ to a vestment maker for makyng of a chesypull of an old cope	ijs. vjd.
„ for lynyn cloth to ye chesypull, and threde	iiijd. ob.
„ to the Chapell prist[4]	£vij
Alowed to John Irys and Thomas Partrych for the brokyn sylver	vs. viijd.

Total . . . £xxij vs. iijd.

PAGE 19.

Mem. that the Churchwardens hath bowyth of Thomas Brodmere iij acres of ereabull ground for the dett of xls. to the Church of Yatton for the space of foure jeres commyng next. Also yeffe, the sayd Thomas do paye at the day of the accounse next, xs., then he to have the ground that yere folowyng, yeffe not, the Church to take the prophete of the same sayde ground for the space of iiij yeres tyll the money be payd, that ys to say, iij acres above mere[5], ereabull ground.

Item[6], resevyd be John Stretyng and Wylliam Kew[7], xs. for the furst yere.

In lyke manner they have bow3th all Thomas Prewetts ground in Claram for iij yeres, and yeffe he bryng not in hys xs. a yere duryng ye space of iij counte dayes, then ye chyrch to take ye profett of ye sayde grounds for so moche as hyt comyth to.

Also moreover they have bow3th of Richard Heyman iij acres of Medow in lange-mede for ij yeres, except he pay the next comt day vjs. viijd., and so that tyme twelve monyth vjs. viijd. more, or ells the Chyrche to take ye profett of ye sayd ground duryng the yeres for so moche.

Item,[8] resevyd of R. Heyman be the honds of J. Stretyng and W. Kew . . . vjs. viijd. for ye furst year.

---

[1] Pall.   [2] Commissioners; a new entry.   [3] New entry.

[4] Priest. Probably entrusted to him for outlay on the Chapel. His own salary was not above xxxs. One ton, ten cwt. of lead are bought this year. In 1543-4 two sums, £v vs., and xxs., are paid to him besides his wages.

[5] "Above mere": a description of their whereabouts in the common field, which was divided by grass strips called "meres."

[6] In a later hand.   [7] Wardens in 1543-4.   [8] Later hand.

PAGES 21, 22.
J.H.S.   A.D. m.ccccc.xxxxiii[iv].
JOHN STRETYNG AND WILLIAM KEW, WARDENS.

Balance from Irys and Partrych . . . . £xix vs. ijd.

[Note added at the next audit, to the effect that only £xv being transferred in cash to Wardens Stretyng and Kew, the parishioners deem it due to make allowance in case of certain debts (specified) not being paid.]

RECEIPTS.

[Nothing unusual]. Total. . £xxx ijs. vjd.

PAGE 23.   EXPENSES.

Payd to the prist for hys wages	xvs.
„ to ye sayd prist	xxs.
„ to a browderer for makyng a pere of vestments, and for a pelow .	vs.
„ for whyte fusteen,[1] and for canvase to ye sayd pelowe . . .	viijd.
„ for xxx powndes of wax	xvs. xd.
„ to the prist	£v vs.
„ to iij mynstrells	xiijs. viijd.
„ for mowyng the yew[2]	iijs. iiijd.
„ for naylys at Danys yere[3]	iijd.

PAGE 26.

Payd for v score powndes of wax and rosen .	xljs. viijd.
„ for ij bokes for owr professyon[4] . . .	viijd.
„ for makyng of ij corporas . . .	xd.
„ for rydyng to Pennysford . . .	vjd.
„ to the Kyngs collectors	viijs.
„ for makyng a byll of the subsyde . .	xvjd.
„ for makyng a byll of the corne[5] . . .	ijd.
Total . . . £xvij viijs.	

PAGE 25.
J.H.S.   A.D. m.ccccc.xxxxiiii[v].
J. COLMAN AND THOMAS DUN, WARDENS.

RECEIPTS.

Balance from Stretyng and Kewe . . . . £xiij xiiijs.

[One bequest, three Ales, no lyings in Church, and no rents from the Church House.]

Resevyd from Thomas Don for a surplesse	xvjd.
„ for the font taper	vjs.
„ by the same Wardens for the Kyngs bere this present yere . .	xxxiijs. iiijd.
Total . . £xxvij viijs. vjd.	

---

[1] Fustian.   [2] The banks of the Yeo, or main drain.   [3] Sluice.

[4] A new entry. Qy., was this "The Institution of a Christian Man," issued in 1537, or "A Necessary Doctrine and Erudition for any Christian Man," published this year 1543, and known as "The King's Book."

[5] Corn grown on the mortgaged lands.

PAGE 27.   EXPENSES.

Payd to Syr John Danell in ernes	j*d*.
,, to y*e* sayd Syr John	x*s*.
,, to y*e* plummer for castyng of a peysse[1] and ij clothes[2] of led . .	vj*d*.
,, to John Vigour, constabull, for y*e* whyte cootes	£iij

PAGE 28.

Payd to Syr Danyell	xv*s*.
,, to y*e* sayd Syr John	x*s*.
,, to y*e* same Syr John Danyell for the subside makyng . .	viij*d*.
,, to y*e* same for makyng a byll of the subside	viij*d*.
,, to Syr Jo. Danell for hys wages[3]	xxv*s*.
,, for rydyng to Charleton at y*e* vysytation	viij*d*.
,, for mendyng a pax	j*d*.
,, to Syr John Danell	xiij*s*. iiij*d*.
Total . . £xviij xij*s*. ix*d*.	

PAGES 29, 30–1.
A supplementary account of "chargys of y*e* Kyngs bere."
[Showing the unprecedented scale of the Revel.] . . . £iij viij*s*. viij*d*.
              Grand Total of the year . . £xxij xvij*d*.

PAGE 33.   **A.D. m.ccccc.xxxxvi[vii].**[4]
                W. KNYGHT AND W. HARRYS, WARDENS.
                            RECEIPTS.

Balance from Dun and Coleman	£v vij*s*.
of John Irysse for that Robart Fesse was suspectyd for the suretyshepe of John Wakelyn, wych was delyveryd to Matthew Toore	vj*s*. viij*d*.
of Wyllyam Tyrry for his mothers lyeng in y*e* Chyrch . . .	vj*s*. viij*d*.
of W. Dale for his mothers lyeng in the chapell	iij*s*. iiij*d*.
of Jone Beme for her husbands lyeng in church	vj*s*. viij*d*.
of the bequest of Thomas Tayler	xx*d*.
of hys sayd bequest lykewyse to the chapell	xx*d*.
of Thomas Dun and John Colman[5] more, for that John Irys payd Syr John Danyell when he made defawte in service of Yatton and went to Comesbury at John Iryse desyr	iiij*s*. viij*d*.
of Thomas Wale for hys Whytmothers[6] lyeng in the church . .	vj*s*. viij*d*.
for our taverne Ale at Whytsondey	£iiij xiiij*s*. iiij*d*.
for the font taper	vj*s*.
for vij owncys and an halfe of ryngs, with ij gyrdylls, and a pynnacull of the beste crosse[7]	xxx*s*.

---

[1] Weight.   [2] Sheets.   [3] Was he the Chapel Priest?
[4] The missing year 1545-6 has been cut out between pp. 28–29.
[5] Late Wardens.   [6] Godmother?   [7] These long-standing heirlooms at last sold.

of parker for brewyng in the church howse	xij*d*.
for wax of the reele.	ix*d*.
of J. Beks for brewyng in the church howse	xij*d*.
of John Rome for brewyng[1]	xij*d*.
of Thomas Knyth and Robert Syms ly3thinen of ye wester part	£iij x*s*.
of J. Hylman and J. Tayler lythinen of ye ester part	£vj x*s*.
Summa receptus . . £xx xix*s*. ij*d*.	

PAGE 35. EXPENSES.

Payd for a skene of sylke to mend the second cope	ij*d*.
„ for iij yards of sylke of ij peny brede[2] to mend ye second cope	vj*d*.
„ to the subsyde	iiij*s*.
„ to Syr J. Danyell for hys wages	vj*s*. viij*d*.
„ to the same	x*s*.
„ for the sayd sowdears	xv*s*.
„ for reparation of the clocke all the yere	xij*d*.
[cost of wax this year]	xx*s*. vij*d*.
„ in expenses for goyng to ye Kyngs vysytors	iiij*d*.
„ to Syr Cristover of Kynston at ye vysytation for makyng a byll	ij*d*.

PAGE 36.

Payd for a locke and key to the font	v*d*.
„ for a showle to make graves in the church hey	ij*d*.
„ for whyte ynchull[3] to make amyss	j*d*.
„ to R. Wylimet, mynstrell, at Wyttsontyde	vj*s*. viij*d*.
„ for wax for Crystymas	xxv*s*.

PAGES 37–8.

Payd to J. Meryfeld for mendyng the wold crosse	iij*d*.
„ to Jone Beme for mendyng an awter cloth	ij*d*.
[Allowance for sundry bad debts.]	
Total . . . . . £xij ij*s*.	

PAGES 39, 40.

J.H.S.   A.D.   m.ccccc.xxxxvii[viii].

J. HANNAM AND ALEXANDER HARRYS, WARDENS.

RECEIPTS.

Balance from Knyght and Harrys	£viij xv*s*. ix*d*.
Our taverne Ale at Wysontyde	£v xx*d*.
of the west part M. Irys and J. Stretyng the elder for ye taverne at Hocday	£v xij*d*.
of J. Gernesse and John . . for ther taverne Ale at Mydsomer	lvij*s*. iiij*d*.
Total . . . . . £xxiiij ij*s*.	

PAGE 41. EXPENSES.

Payd for settyng furthe sowders[4]	xij*s*.
„ for settyng furthe sowdears	xxx*s*. ix*d*. ob.

[1] In the Church-house.   [2] Breadth.   [3] See p. 155, note 1.   [4] Soldiers.

Payd for the Omelys and the injuncsions	ijs.
„ in expenses for fechyng the sayd books	iiijd.
[other expenses, wax, minstrells, subsidy, visitation, scouring the Yeo, and repairs as usual].	
Payd at Bedmynster at the Kyngs vysytation .	iiijd.

PAGE 42.

Payd in expenses at yᵉ takyng down of the seyd images and the yryn in the church .	vd.
„ to W. Sensam and J. Stretyng for takyng down the same sayd iryne and images	xijd.
„ expenses at Chew at yᵉ vysytation, and for a byll makyng	vjd.
Total . . . . £vj xviijs.	

PAGES 43-4.   **A.D. m.ccccc.xxxxviii[ix].**

T. HOBBYS AND JOHN TAYLER, WARDENS.

RECEIPTS.

Balance from Hannam and Harrys . . . £xvij iijs. vijd.	
[accruing chiefly from sales of material no longer needed.]	
[The Lily pots had probably stood on the roodloft by the side of the Magdalen. Thomas Wale had probably bought articles which the Wardens did not like to specify. The Ales and other sources of voluntary revenue were dried up.]	
[One bequest of a bushel of wheat, several sums for iron sold.]	
of C. Predy for ij lyly potts with pewter	ijs.
of Thomas Wale	£iiij
[No ales or other usual receipts.]	
Total . . . £xxiiij ixs. ob.	

Thys yere the sylver crosse of owr church was sold by Master Kenne and xx of yᵉ honest of yᵉ parych of Yatton, and by there lyke assent the money of the sayd crosse was bestowyd by yᵉ hands of Wyllyam Cradock and Wyllyam Croke upon yᵉ makyng of a sirten sklusse¹ or yere agenste the rage of yᵉ salte water, callyd Danys yere, set and beyng yn West Wemerham, the wych yere then beyng ruynus and yn dekay, and the seyd perysheonars beyng chargyd with the makyng thereoff by the commyssyonars sewards² upon yᵉ paye³ of £x to be made by yᵉ seyd perysshonars by a day serteyne, by yᵉ same commyssyonars prefyyyd⁴ as yn yᵉ commyssyonars boks or decrees more playnly may apere.

PAGE 45.   EXPENSES.⁵

Payd for takyng down our Lady in yᵉ chaunsell	iiijd.
„ for makyng and settyng in an yryn in yᵉ pulpytt	viijd.
„ to the clarke for makyng the church buke, and for makyng up the vestments of the church	ijs.

¹ A certain Sluice.   ² Commissioners of Sewers.   ³ Pain.   ⁴ Prefixed or provided.

⁵ Great changes; *e.g.*, no outlay on wax, or lamps, or vestments; but the first item of poor relief, 14 men appears.

Payd to yᵉ poore men of yᵉ parysch, xiiij names, each receiving . . xijd.

PAGE 46.

Payd to Syr Nicholas Poore for caryeng out of yᵉ commyssyon . . . . iiijd.
„ for makyng a byll to yᵉ kyngs commyssyoners at Bedmynster . . . . viijd.
„ to W. Sensam and John Maryfyld for takyng down the clothes on[1] the Chapell . . . . iiijs. viijd.
„ for rydyng to Wells afore the Kyngs visitarrs . . . . . iijs. ixd.
„ for a bucke callyd paraphrasus and Erasmus . . . . . xjs. iiijd.
„ for a bybull of the largyst volume . . . . xjs.
„ for yᵉ sowders[2] at Banwell at yᵉ muster . . . . . xjs. iiijd.
„ to yᵉ peynter of Brystow[3] in part of peyment . . . . xjs.

PAGES 47–8.

more to yᵉ seyd peynter . . . . xijs. viijd. and xliijs.
„ to Syr Nicholas Poore for wrytyng yᵉ masse in Englych . . . . viijd.
„ payd to yᵉ peynter . . . . £v

      Total . . . £xv xviijs. xd.
      Balance . . £viij xjs. ijd.

PAGE 49.   [Note in an early hand.]

"An yll dede done. Here was a yere cutt out, Wyllyam Dale, junior, and Thomas Durban beyng wardens, as apereth by this booke."

PAGE 53.

[Pages 48–53 are blank, except the above note and apparently some pages have been torn out.]

A.D. m.ccccc.xxxix.

THOS. SMYTH AND WALTER LUKYN, WARDENS.

PAGE 105.   RECEIPTS.

Balance from Hobbys and Tayler . . . . . . £viij xjs. ijd.
From yᵉ clarke of Henbere for gylt of Images . . . . . xijd.
For a stone in yᵉ Chaunsell . . . . iiijd.
From W. Cradocke, for hys wyfe lying yn the Churche . . . vjs. viijd.
For our Taverne[4] of Ale . . . . ls.
Of Rich. Stallard for Sett[5] . . . . vjs. viijd.

      Total . . . . £xij xxijd.

PAGES 106–7.   EXPENSES.

At Axbrydge afore ye Kyngs Vysytars . . . . . . viijs. viijd.
For makyng yᵉ Font taper . . . . jd.

---

[1] Or "over."   [2] Soldiers.   [3] *I.e.*, for painting out proscribed things. The large sum below of £v looks like the substitution of Texts.
[4] Only one.   [5] *I.e.*, a single sitting, rented.

For rydyng to Wells for yͤ Chapell[1]	ijs.
„ mendyng a rochett	jd.
, caryng boke to Wells[2]	iiijs.
„ makyng of byll at Wells	iijs. iiijd.
To Syr John Smyth for yͤ injunctions	iiijd.
„ sayd Syr John for makyng a byll	ijd.
„ makyng a byll at Bedmynster	iiijd.
„ a tabull-bord	iijs. iiijd.
in expenses at Axbryge for yͤ Churche goods	xd.
for dressyng yͤ Auters,[3] and caryeng out of yͤ churche	vijs. xd.
for a byll to yͤ subsyde	iiijd.
to W. Croke for hys reward and paynys abowte yͤ makyng of yͤ newe yere,[4] as hit was agred at yͤ last acownt	vs.
Total . . . xlijs. iijd.	
Balance . . . . £vij vjs. iiijd.	

Page 54.

A.D. m.ccccc.li[ii].

J. LOVELL AND J. WYLLYNG, WARDENS.

The Wardens received from the old wardens, Dale and Durban, 1550-1, a balance of	£vij vjs. iiijd.
Whereof there most be allowyd for yͤ fall of yͤ money[5] in yͤ same year .	£iij vjs. iiijd.
And so remaineth clear	£iiij

PAGE 55. RECEIPTS.[6]

of J. Smythe for iiij platters of wood	ijd.
of Jordan for a scheste[7]	xvjd.
of M. Irysche for stonnes, yͤ which laye behynde yͤ tombe . .	xvjd.
of Gellys[8] Jordan for yͤ churche howsce and yeres rentt . .	vjs. viijd.
Summa	£iiij ixs. vjd.
Summa totalis of Reseptts[9] commythe unto yͤ sum . .	£vij xvs. xd.

PAGE 56. EXPENSES.

Payd for foldyng the vestements	xijd.
„ for mendyng ij pere of westements and yͤ surpelascy . .	xijd.

[1] Edward VI's Chantry Commissioners report that the inhabitants of Yatton made suit to buy the Chapel [of Clareham] to make therewith a "slluse" against the rage of the sea, for the safeguard of the country. The suit was in vain. The endowment lands yielding xlviijs. viijd. per ann. net, are scheduled in the report as annexed to the Crown. The Incumbent was a scholar of 18, and therefore unable to do duty. His predecessor is described as a "Scholar" also. The Chapel had probably been closed for some time [see Vol II, Som. Rec. Soc., pp. 88, 269]; the benefice treated as a sinecure.

[2] Visitation, prob. [3] Altars. [4] Sluice. [5] I.e., fall in the value of the currency.
[6] All items transcribed. [7] Chest. [8] Giles.
[9] I.e., reckoning them at the old value of the currency.

[A leaf lost, and with it the end of the 1551-2 account, and the receipts of 1552-3, Wale and Tayler.]

PAGE 57. [Headed.]
Payd by me Thomas Wale.
to T. Carpyter for makyng ye tabull in ye chansell . . . . . iijs. iiijd.
for leggs to the tabull . . . . viijd.
unto John Dale for makyng ye Inventorie when whe aperyd before ye Kyng Commissiners . . . . vjd.
unto Syr John for facchynng[1] the precepte . . . . . . ijd.

PAGE 59.[2]
for a boke for the Communion . . . . . iiijs. iiijd.

Total . . . . xxxvijs.

PAGE 61. **A.D. m.ccccc.liii[iiii]. Feb. x.**

W. ROKE AND EDMOND CADMAN, WARDENS.
[No accounts in this page.]

PAGE 63. RECEIPTS.[3]
of J. Let for ye cuttyng of ye sege endes[4] . . . . ijd.
of J. Let for the wood . . . . xiiijd.
of Syr John Smythe, parson of Weston, for an old pott . . . ijs. iiijd.
of hym for an old tryndell . . . . vjd.
the last day of May of John Meryfeld for ij hundreth weight of brasse of olde candelsticks . . . . xxxijs.
of Giles Jardyn for ye church howse . . . . vjs. viijd.

Total . . . £ix xiijs.
Jesus give us grace.

PAGE 65. EXPENSES.
Payd unto Thomas Brodmere for keepyng of ye bells ye x daye of Februarii . . xijd.
„ for bred and wyne from Alhowmas to crestymas, to Syr John Smyth . . iijs.
„ for bred and wyne the fryst Sonday in lentt . . . . . . iiijd.
„ for wyne ye ij Sondaye in lentt . . . . vjd.
„ for pavyng ye place where ye table standythe . . . . . . viijd.
„ to Jhon Owyns and Jhon Cooke cotthyng[5] of ye Seyggs, and makyng of ye same and the forms . . . . ijs. viijd.
„ for ye matt for ye tabull . . . . xjd.
„ for wyne in ye weke unto Syr Jhon . . . . jd.
„ for wyne in ye weke unto Syr Jhon . . . . jd.

---

[1] Fetching. [2] Headed "payd by me Willm. Taylor." [3] Items all given.
[4] Does this mean that the carving of some seat-ends was sold? N.B. Income wholly from sales, save rent of Church-house, now let as a dwelling.
[5] Cutting.

Payd a pan' the Sonday for wyne	. iiij*d*.
„ unto Jhon Lett for ye fryngge abowthe ye tabull	. iiij*d*.
„ for ye Church howse rent	. iiij*d*.

PAGE 67.

Payd for dressheng ye powdere unto a bowderer²	. vj*d*.
„ for wyne aster³	v*s*. iiij*d*.
„ unto Thomas Hariss all ye Lent and yens⁴ Ester for ye communion breyde at ye same tyme	. iiij*d*.
„ to T. Harris for bred for ye communion after to Midsomer . . .	iij*d*. ob.
„ for wyne for ye communion to ye xiij day of June	. viij*d*.
„ for wyne for ye communion to ye viij day of Julye	. viij*d*.
„ to ye ryngers at ye proclamation of our soverayn lady quene Marie . .	. v*d*.
„ the xxix day of Julye for wyne for ye communion	. vj*d*.
„ for communion bred betwext Mydsomer and holy Rode day . .	. ix*d*.
„ for candles at Chrysmas	. iij*d*.
„ for lyght a visityng⁵	. j*d*.
Total . . . £xlviij*s*. v*d*.	

THE POYNTYNG OF THE SPYRE.

The tablyng v*s*., and for naylys	. viij*d*.
„ expense in settyng up ye tablyng	. vj*d*.
„ for makyng of ye cradle	. viij*d*.
[and some small items.]	

PAGES 70, 71.   [Blank.]

PAGE 72.

THE BUYLDYNG OF THE AULTER.

It. to ye masons	. viij*s*.
„ to ye other ij worke men	. ij*s*.
„ for lyme	. xij*d*.
„ to Thomas Clarke	. vj*d*.
„ in expenses	. x*d*.
Summa . . . xij*s*. iiij*d*.	

PAGES 73–4.

A.D. m.ccccc.liiii[v]. Januarie xvij.

J. AVERY AND T. GAY, WARDENS.

RECEIPTS.

Balance from Roke and Cadman . . . . viij*s*. x*d*.

Item receaved of Rychard Stallard x*s*. upon condition that yf ye parysh do not stand to there promyse he wyll pay ye other x*s*.

¹ Upon.   ² Dressing the border, to an embroiderer.   ³ Easter.   ⁴ Against.
⁵ Candle carried in visitation of sick.

Item of Geyles Jurdayne in earnest for yᵉ church howse . . . . . . jd.
„ of yᵉ bells for Syr Roberts brother . . . . iiijd.
„ of Rychard Rome and Wyllyam Bell beyng ly3th men of yᵉ eyst partte . . xxs.
„ of Rychard Rome and Wyllyam Bell beyng ly3th men of yᵉ eyst partte . xxiiijs. viijd.
„ of Jhon Hortte and Mathu Irys ly3th men of yᵉ weste partte . . . . xls.
„ of Jhon Cradocke of Cleve for leying hys wyffe in yᵉ churche . . . vjs. viijd.
„ of Thomas Warre of cleve in full payment of all ys detts unto yᵉ church . xiijs. iiijd.
„ of Thomas Dorre and Jhon Kormer of cleve . . . . . . vijs. xjd.
„ of Mathew Ireyshe and Jhon Hortte in full payment of there yere . £v xs. iiijd.
    Summa totalis . . . £xij iijs. iiijd.

PAGE 75.   EXPENSES.
For makyng of a byll owt of yᵉ gatheryng booke, of the names of them that were
  unpayed . . . . ijd.
for a quere of paper . . . . iiijd.
to Thomas Lett for foldyng yᵉ vestments . . . . xd. ob.
to T. Brodmere for kepyng the bells . . . . iijs.
for a processyonal . . . . ijs. vjd.
for makyng of yᵉ sepulcre . . . . viijd. ob.
for iij Banner luggs . . . . vjd.
for wax makyng agaynst Ester . . . . vijs. viijd.
for a missall . . . . xvjs.
for a manwell . . . . vjs. viijd.
in expenses sekyng yᵉ seid books . . . . vijd.
for a sacryn bell . . . . iiijd.
for an olle fatte and an olle boxke¹ . . . . vjd.
for a cytte,² and yᵉ makyng of a post . . . . iijs. vd.
for yᵉ fychiynge³ up of yᵉ fre stonne, and settynge of the poste, to T. Meke, and in
  expenses . . . . vijd.
for dekynge⁴ wythoutt yᵉ new yere,⁵ to Hurdyche and Tedboll with theyr felous . vijs.

PAGE 76.
for a holle⁶ portas . . . . xxs.
for a censer and a paxys⁷ .
for yᵉ hoppyng⁸ to Mathew . . . for yᵉ church vessels . . . . ijs. viijd.
for bollys, cuppys, and platters, trenchers . . . . xijd.
to Rychard Partryge for naylys and yᵉ makynge of yᵉ yron that ys sette ower yᵉ auter xd.
for naylys for yᵉ wells⁹ . . . . viijd.
for expensys at yᵉ makyng of yᵉ wellys . . . . ijs. viijd.
for yᵉ nette clothe ower yᵉ pyxe . . . . xviijd.
for a new corporas clothe . . . . xxiijd.
for a key for yᵉ cheste . . . . viijd.

PAGE 77.
for iiij hundrye tylle fette at Naysey,¹⁰ to R. Freman . . . . . iijs. iiijd.

¹ An oil vat and an oil box.   ³ Seat.   ⁵ Fetching.   ⁶ Dyking.   ⁸ Sluice.
⁶. Whole.   ⁷ Pax.   ⁸ Hooping.   ⁹ Wheels.   ¹⁰ 400 tiles fetched at Nailsea.

[other expenses about this and lime.]

to Lache the tyler for yᵉ hellynge¹ of yᵉ church, and hellynge of the owen .	vjs. xd.
to Jhon Brofort for yᵉ fetthyng of rafters and tymber to yᵉ sterrs² . . .	
to T. Broudmore for mendyng of a Bradere³	xd.
to J. Lette for kepyng of yᵉ cloke	iiijs.
to W. Knyghte rent for yᵉ Church howse	iiijd.
demyssyons⁴ of the cortte	iijd.

PAGE 78.

unto Syr Jhon Smyth for thei men . . . . the whych dyd the pennans⁵ unto offial⁶ for a letter, yᵉ whych was ryd⁷ in yᵉ Church	ijd.
the demyssyons⁸ of yᵉ corte for yᵉ men that where putt in there	iijd.
for a punde of candells agens Crestemas	iijd.
for franckenserse	jd.
for tassells for yᵉ pyxk	ijd.
for makyng yᵉ boke unto Syr Jhon Smyth	ijs.
to T. Lette for foldynge the festements	ijs.

Sumina Totalis . . . £viij vijs. iiijd. ob.

So remaneth of thys account £iij xvs. xjd. ob., and allso yᵉ somme xxvjs. ixd., that whe hath gederyd of serten of yᵉ paryshe, the whych were to paye in a boke⁹ made by yᵉ assent of yᵉ a fore sayd paryshe. So yᵉ somme total that remaneth to yᵉ new wardens £v ijs. viijd. ob.

PAGES 79, 80.   [Lists of names.]

PAGE 81.   𝔄.𝔇. m.ccccc.lv[vi]. January xxij.

T. KNYGHT AND T. ROMME, WARDENS.

RECEIPTS.

Balance from Avery and Gaye	£v ijs. viijd.

[Some arrears paid; one for lying in the chapel; two sums paid for burying in the Church.]

of the font taper	vs. iiijd.
of Jhon Brodfortt for a peyse of a haffe,¹⁰ and for ther over plus for mendyng of the Church howse dore of ther kycchyng¹¹	viijd.
the lythemen of yᵉ wester syde	£viij vijs. iiijd.
the lythemen of yᵉ ester syde	£v xjd.

Total . . £xx vs.

PAGE 82.   EXPENSES.

Payd unto Wyllyam Taylor that he payd for the crosse	xxs.
,, Wyllyam Dale ,, ,, ,, ...	xxs.

¹ Tiling.   ² Stairs.   "Repairs to the Church-house stairs" is a common entry.   ³ Brand-iron.
⁴ Demissions, *i.e.*, relaxation of sentence in spiritual court.   ⁵ Penance.   ⁶ The official.
⁷ Read.
⁸ By charging these costs to yᵉ parish, it is plain that the Wardens made presentment of the offenders.
⁹ The Rate-book, as yet voluntary, is now first seen.   ¹⁰ ?   ¹¹ Kitchen.

Payd unto John Hanna that he payd for the crosse . . . . . xxs.
„ for a porse[1] to put y[e] keyes in . . . . ijd.
„ for mendyng of y[e] fayle[2] . . . . jd.
„ a lyne for y[e] vayle . . . . iijd.
„ for iij cloths' staffyng[3] y[e] which y[e] Scryptours where wrytten in and upon . vjd.
„ for ij proclamations concernyng the oon for reconciliation of y[e] people, y[e] other
   for y[e] bulls of y[e] pope of Rome, y[e] wych was reade in cena domini[4] . . vjd.
„ for ix poundes of wax and a quarter agenste Ester . . . . . ixs. iijd.
„ for iij yards of lynen cloth y[e] same tyme for y[e] Rode . . . . . ijs.
„ for lyme and charyche[5] unto J. Brodmore for y[e] Church of Yatton . . . ijs.
„ for wassyng of y[e] churche pollyng . . . . xd.

PAGE 83.
Payd for y[e] Rode clothe, the parysse for peinthyng . . . . . vs.
„ for halfe a ponde of frenkensesse . . . . vd.
„ for y[e] clarks waggs[6] . . . . ijs.
„ for walls[7] for y[e] Rode clothe . . . . ijd.
„ for y[e] lokyng[8] of y[e] boke at visitation . . . . . . iijd.
„ for mendyng y[e] kechyng dore of y[e] church howse . . . . . iiijd.
„ to W. Daye, senior, for y[e] pyxe and palle cloth for y[e] same xxs. viijd.
„ unto Mathew Ireyshe for the Crosse . . . . xxs.
„ expenses at y[e] counttes day[9] . . . .
   [Mowing the yeo is an annual Entry.]

PAGE 84.
Payd for going unto Wells garing[10] the boks, expenses . . . . . ijd.
„ for chandells goyng a Wysythyng,[11] unto Syr John Smythe . . iijd.
„ expenses for y[e] fatchyng y[e] paynted cloth at Brystow . . . xijd.
„ for payntyng of y[e] clothe of y[n] hye autour . . . . . viijd.
„ for wax unto Syr John Smythe for goyng a visityng . . . . . jd.
„ unto Syr John Smythe and y[e] towe[12] churchewardens for over lowkyng up y[e]
   Church boks, expenses at owre brekefaste at y[e] same tyme . . . viijd.
„ unto Wyllyam Cradocke for the Crosse . . . . . . xxs.
„ unto Menstrells at Wyttsondaye . . . . vs.
„ unto Syr John Smythe for makyng y[e] boke[13] . . . . . ijs.
„ unto Henry Wornall for y[e] Crosse . . . . xxs.
   [And many repairs to bells, &c.]
   Total . . £xij ixs. ixd.

---

[1] Purse. [2] Veil. [3] ?? both words obscure. [4] On Maundy Thursday.
[5] Carriage. [6] Wages. [7] Qy., nails? [8] Inspection. [9] Audit-day.
[10] Carrying. [11] Candles used in going to visit the sick. [12] Two. [13] I.e., this account.

A.D. m.ccccc.lvi[vii].

T. WORNELL AND T. WARRE, WARDENS.

PAGES 85–6.

Balance from Knyght and Rome . £vij xvjs.

RECEIPTS.

for thei fontte tapur . . . . vs. iiijd.
of Jhon Stabulchylde bequest . . . . vjs. viijd.
[No more entries; the page which was left blank for them has been partly cut off.]

[Between pp. 86–7, a page has been cut out.]

PAGE 87.   EXPENSES [belonging to A.D. mcccclbi–bii].

Payd for glassyng of ye Churche, to Averie of Brystow . . . . xxxjs. viijd.
„ at ye visitation of ye Archbysshoppe of Canturburie at Penford . . . vijs. xd.
„ for candells for goyng a visityng . . . . jd.

PAGE 88.

Payd for bred and wyne at Myssommor,[1] ij quarts of claret wyne, and a quarter againe
   of sacke . . . . iiijs. xjd.
„ for candells at myssumor to Syr John Smyth . . . . . . jd.
„ unto Syr John Smyth for candells goyng a visithyng before My3gheallmass . jd.
„ for a pound of candells for the rengars[2] . . . . iiijd.
„ at Bedmastur[3] at ye visitation, expenses . . . . xxd.

PAGE 89.

Payd for makyng of thei tabernaculle . . . . . . xxvjs. viijd.
„ for thei loeke and the gemmulls[4] . . . . xijd.
„ for ole[5] for thei lampe . . . . xjd.
„ for thei lampe . . . . iiijd.
„ for wyre for thei lamp . . . . jd.
„ for candells upon Crestemas daye . . . . iiijd.
„ owr expenses for goyng unto Banwell unto my Lorde bysshoppe to axe his
   counsell for thei tabernacull . . . . ixd.
„ for candells for goyng a visityng . . . . jd.
„ for mendyng and mowyng of the yowe[6] from Chramore gowtte unto the yer
   be . . . ? . . . . xijd.
   Total . . . £vij xvs. xjd.

---

[1] Midsummer.   [2] Ringers.   [3] Bedminster.   [4] Hinges.   [5] Oil.   [6] Yeo.

PAGE 91.   **A.D. m.ccccc.lvii.** Feb. xviij.

J. HORT AND J. STRETCHYNG, WARDENS.

RECEIPTS.

Balance from Wornall and Warre	£xij xiijs. xjd.	
Receved of Robert Wyllatt of money that he gave to owre chorche whan hys wyfe wos I buryed[1]	iijs. iiijd.	
„ of money that we gathered for the vawnte tabor[2]	iijs. iiijd.	
„ of Wylliam Crocke for tabors[3] whan hys wyfe wos I byryed	iiijd.	
„ made of a taverne	£iij	
Summa	£xvj xjd.	

PAGE 92.   EXPENSES.

Payd for the demission of the Cortte at Bedmaster	ijd.
„ at the visitation at Bedmyster	xiijd.
„ for the Rode makyng	xiijs. iiijd.
„ for sprycks and nayls and the settyng up of the same	xijd.

PAGE 93.

expenses for casting the little bell	
[4]Payd to Thomas Carpenter for makyng of the middle flore	xiijs. iiijd.
„ to Thomas Lett[5]	xijd.
„ to Isbell Taylor for the kepyng of Thomas Lett	iiijd.
„ to Jone Brodford for stryckyng of the church	ijd.
„ to John Hatheway for makyng clene of the tresore howse	iijd.
„ to the Mynstrell	vjs. viijd.
„ to Edmont Badmans buoye for wachynge of the oxen the nyght before they went to Brystowe	jd.
„ to owre dynner at W. Tyrryes att the mendyng of the myddle flore[6]	xvd.
„ to Thomas Lett for to helpe hym when he was up walkyng	jd.

PAGE 94.

Payd to Thomas Lett of that whyche the parysshe dyd award hym	xs.
„ to Syr Tomas for makyng the bocke to gather[7] to sette for the sodwdyars[8]	vjd.
„ to Thomas Erle for wrytyng of the mowster[9] byll	iiijd
Total	£x ob.

---

[1] Buried; the I representing the Anglo-Saxon prefix of the participle past.   [2] Font taper.
[3] Tapers.
[4] A Scrivener's hand here begins, marred with flourishes: but henceforth the year's accounts are balanced in due form, and with the formula, "all things charged and discharged."
[5] The Clerk, now disabled.   [6] Opened for lifting the bell to the cage in Belfry.
[7] A collecting list.   [8] A special collection for their equipment.   [9] Muster.

A.D. 1558 ye xxvj daye of February [1558–9.]

MATHEW IRYSCHE AND W. HURDWYCHE, WARDENS.

RECEIPTS.

Balance from J. Hort and J. Stretchyng	£vj xjd.
of Wyllyam Worthe for the lyche-reste[1] of Jone his wyf	vjs. viijd.
of John Cradocke for the lyche-reste of John Cradocke his father	vjs. viijd.
of John Hort for the lyche-reste of Alice his wyf	vjs. viijd.
for the lyche-reste of Wyllyam Cradocke	vjs. viijd.
of the lyghte men of the west parte	£vij xiijs. iiijd.
of the lyghte men of the est parte	£iij iijs. xd.

[No bequests, or gifts, or Wardens' Ale.]

PAGE 97. EXPENSES.

l'ayde for the mendyng the blewe cope and ij surplessis	viijd.
„ to W. Knyghts wyfe for healynge of Thomas Letts legge, whiche was dewe to be payde by J. Hort and J. Streathyng	
„ to J. Brodmore for wasshyng the Roodelofte in our yere	xvjd.
„ towards Averye for rearyng of a tombstone	iijd.
„ to J. Hatheway for v keyes and a hapse and naylis to sett the locke one	ijs.
„ for a locke for the vyce dore	iijd.
„ for makyng the subsidye byll	vjd.
„ at the vysytation for the continewance of Marye[2] and John	iiijd.
„ for mendyng the chetyll and the holye water pott	xijd.

PAGE 98.

Payde for whyt ynkle for ye booke	ob.
„ to the organ maker	xxs.
„ for Dychinge—the parishe woorke in ye Yo[3]	xvjd. and xijd.
„ for doynge ye Lordes[4] woorke ye Yo	vs.
„ to T. Lette for foldynge the vestments for iij quarters of a yere	xxiijd.
„ for v yards of dowlas to make a surples for the clarke	iiijs. ijd.
„ for candells at All Halomtyde and Crystmas	iiijd.
„ for a booke of the prossessyon[5] in English	ijd.
„ for makyng of ij muster bylls	xijd.

---

[1] This new phrase seems the equivalent of the older one "lying in the Church," *i.e.*, the privilege of burial under the pavement. *See* Glossary.

[2] Queen Mary died Nov. 17, 1558. The restored images of the Roodloft were again threatened, but a year's respite was obtained. *See* 1559–60.

[3] Yeo. [4] Lord of the Manor. [5] Litany.

𝔄.𝔇. 1559, the 23 of February.

PAGE 99.

JOHN WAULE AND R. SYMES, WARDENS.

Balance from Irysche and Hurdwyche . £xj ixs. iijd.
Debts due to yᵉ Churche.
Four lyche-restes at . . . . vjs. viijd. each.
[No Receipts.]

PAGE 100.   EXPENSES.

Payde for iij yards of dowlas, and iij yards of canvas, for to make ij cotes of fence[1]
                                                                        iiijs. vjd.
„ for makyng the same ij cotes . . . . viijs.
„ for candells to go a vysytynge . . . . jd.
„ for half a pound of frankencence . . . . jd. ob.
„ for a pounde of threde to make the cotes above wrytten . . . . xxd.
„ that there ys uppon the inventory of the churche goodys iij tabul clothys of the which one was occupyed to put in the forsayd cotes.
„ for vij pounds of wexe . . . . vjs. jd.
„ for mendyng a tombe and certain other places in the Church . . . iiijd.
„ to the mynstrell . . . . xs.
„ for bowles and dyshes . . . . ijs. ijd.
„ for ij salters[2] . . . . iijs. iiijd.
„ to Morris Dall, at the request of John Sannom and other of the paryssioners in his syckness. . . . . xijd.
„ for takyng downe the Roode . . . . vd.
„ in expenses at the plucking down of the Images . . . . . vjd.
„ for foldyng the vestments . . . . ijs.
„ for makyng a dore to the newe yere[3] . . . . vs. viijd.

PAGE 101.

Payde for the boke of common prayer . . . . vs.
„ for the tabull and the formes for the Communion . . . . . vjs.
„ expenses at Recly[4] at the vysytation . . . . iijs. viijd.
„ for makyng of our byll[5] there . . . . xxd.
„ for makyng the inventory of the church goods and for other charges at the delyvery of the same at Brystow[6] . . . . vs.
„ at Brystow[6] at the vysytation . . . . viijd.
„ for a bocke of the injuccions[7] . . . . iiijd.
„ for drawyng the koppye of the bryfes[8] of the stattutes . . . xijd.
„ for mendyng the tabul cloth in the church, and a surples . . . iiijd.
Total . . . . £vj xxijs. ijd.

---

[1]   [2] Psalters in English.   [3] Sluice.   [4] Redcliffe.   [5] I.e., of presentments
[6] I.e., at St. Mary's, Redcliffe, then within the diocese, and giving name to the Deanery.
[7] Injunctions.   [8] Abridgements probably of the Elizabethan Acts A°. I°.

PAGE 102.

A.D. 1560, the v daye of February.

T. MORE AND J. WARRE, WARDENS.

Balance from Waule and Symes . . . . £xiij xijs. xd.

RECEIPTS.

Five entries of lyche-restes at	vjs. viijd. each
for plate being sold by consent of the wardens. . . .	£xij xijs.
of the lyght men of the west part	£iiij vs. xjd.
„ „ „ east part	. lviijs. jd. ob.
Allowed to Warden for the fall of money	. xiiijs.
Total	. £xj xiiijs.

Byt remembred that thys yere was solde the sylver crosse, the accompte whereof remayneth in the hands of Thomas Wall and William Smethes.

PAGE 103.   EXPENSES.

Payd to the clarke for kepyng the booke	ijs.
„ to the same clarke for foldynge the vestments .	ijs.
„ for bred and wyne at Ester	xijs.
„ to the clarke for his wagis at our Ladye daye .	vjs. viijd
„ for takyng downe the alter . . .	ijs.
„ for a tabull cloth of vj yards	. ijs. ijd.

PAGE 104.

Payde for timber for the vawte of the church	xiiijs. iiijd.
„ for our expenses for mete and drynke, and for basting the ryng in whyt . .	vijs.
„ to Clevedon for makyng the ryng and the flowre, and other his workmanshepe	xxxiijs. iiijd.
Be it remembered that we provided to pay the clarke his part wagis, and to pay John Meryfelde for scowrynge the harnes, xijs. viijd., and before the day came, the moneye fell, be meanes whereof we loste	iijs. iiijd.
Payd for trimming and gresing the bells at Alhalontyde	iijd.
„ for fynyshyng the dore at the newe yere,[1] with all other charges therto belongynge	xjs.
„ for a glasse bottell to kepe wyne for the communion	vjs. vjd.

Page 111.   [Debts to the Church. No date.]

---

[1] Sluice.

Tintinhull:

Notes illustrative of MSS.

━━━━━━━━━━━━━━━━

The Manor, with Advowson of rectory, was vested in the adjoining Priory (Cluniac) of Montacute. The parish, probably co-terminous with the manor contains 1,828 acres.

The Manor house of the Prior stood on the south side of Churchyard. He was probably the sole landowner.

The Benefice remained a rectory till 1520, when it was appropriated to Montacute Priory, charged with £10 for the Vicar's sustenance. The whole tithe valued at £18 nett, was thereby vested in the Priory, and was secularised at the dissolution in 1539.

The Church, whilst unchanged in ground plan, was being continually improved. The accounts record the addition of a rood-loft and rood, built on the breastwork of a previous stone screen, the rebuilding of the south Porch with stone roof, the raising of the tower with turret-staircase; the enlargement of the west window, the addition of carved-oak benches, and the building of a "stonyn door," *i.e.*, a door-case of stone in the west wall of Churchyard. The bells too were recast in 1539. All these changes were effected by the bounty of the people, unaided by any large gifts either from without or from their own landlord. There were several low altars, one dedicated to St. Nicolas.

Fiscal System.

Two wardens were chosen yearly, either on Easter day, Palm Sunday, the Annunciation, or St. Margaret's, *i.e.*, the Dedication day, thus varying the length of the official year. Yearly accounts were as a rule rendered, even when the wardens were re-elected, which was not uncommon.

The funds accrued from (1) The Bakehouse (Pistrina); (2) The Brewhouse (Brasina); (3) (at later date) the Church house (Pandoxatorium); (4) Some strips of land in the moor, sometimes cultivated for grain, sometimes let for leaze; (5) live stock, *e.g.*, horned cattle, and bees; (6) Gifts, bequests, and special gatherings.

Of these sources, the Church-house, when completed in 1497, was the most fruitful. It combined the manifold purposes of entertainment, baking, malting, brewing. The Holy Loaf was baked there, the Holy Ale brewed there. There the parishioners were welcomed on certain Holy days after Divine Service, for some common amusements, during which their ale scot was levied. The allied parishes of Stoke, Montacute, and Chilthorne, sent their offerings in aid. The baking and brewing tackle were also let out for private hire, and a room or two sometimes let to tenants. The old bakehouse, when superseded, yielded a cottage rent.

The Lady-chapel and its special services were maintained by the Brotherhood of St. Mary, who also contributed sometimes to the Warden's funds, see 1437-8. In 1444-5 their steward bought 100 lbs. of lead from the Wardens.

The Hogglers were associated under a steward (procurator) to maintain a light.

The Warden's attendances at Visitations of Archdeacon, Bishop and Archbishop are unfailingly recorded, with the charge for the bearing of the banners into Ilchester. It seems to have been an honoured occasion, the officers marching with banners before them.

The Account Books.

The following extracts are made from the first of two volumes of Church-Wardens' accounts, which were bound and so preserved by Mr. T. Napper in 1723, and are now in the keeping of J. Penny, Esq., Tintinhull.

A few of the earlier pages have been transcribed verbatim, with the view of showing in what manner the accounts were kept. After this, entries which recur annually or very frequently, are omitted as a rule; but occasionally they are inserted, or a note is added, to show that they are still going on. Also when any new item of receipt or expenditure appears, it is noticed.

The greater number of the entries refer only to small necessary repairs, or to annual expenses for the bells, the purchase of small quantities of wood or stone, &c. Items of this kind are omitted; the object of these extracts being to exhibit such original entries as will enable a student to work out a good idea of the general life of a country parish until about the year 1560.

They are written in Latin up to a later date than usual in country parishes, but the scribes claimed the utmost freedom in dealing with tenses and cases.

Wardens' Accounts.

Page 29.

11–12 H. VI. [*i.e.*, A.D. 1433–4.]

Computus Willelmi Strecche et Johannis Aste, custodes bonorum ecclesie de Tyntenhull, a festo Pasche anno regis Henrici VJ^{ti} XJ^{mo} usque eundem festum anno ejusdem regis XIJ^{mo}

Idem receperunt de arreragiis computi precedentis . . .	ijs. viijd.
It. de collectione sacre ceree	iijs. vd.
It. de incremento unius brasine facte per Willelmum strecche .	vjs. viijd.
Summa . . .	xijs. ixd.

E quibus in expensis.

In primis ad faciendum sacre ceree	iijs. xd.
Item pro visitatione	vjd.
It. ad ligandum unum ordinale	xd.
It. pro lavatione velaminum	jd.
It. pro oleo	jd.
It. pro una cordula	vjd.
It. pro uno pyxide latino [latten] ad ponendum Corpus Christi . . .	xs. or xd.
It. solut. Johanni Capellano ad celebrandum pro animabus ceteri [*sic*] hominum[1]	viijd.
Summa omnium expensarum	xvjs. vijd.
Et sic excedit plus quam recepit	iijs. ixd.

A.D. 1434–5. 13–14 Hen. VI. a festo Pasche Anno regis H. VI^{ti} XIIJ^{o} usque eundem festum Anno ejusdem regis XIIIJ^{o}.

William Strecche and John Ansteys, Wardens.

Idem receperunt de collectione sacre ceree	iijs. iijd.
It. ex dono Willelmi Morys	xxs.
It. de incremento unius brasine facte per W. Strecche . .	vjs. viijd.
It. pro candelis venditis	iijd.
Summa . . . £iij ijs. xd.	ijd.

In Expensis.

Ad fac sacre ceree	iijs. iiijd.
It. pro lavatione velaminum, et ad faciendum tapyr et trendel .	iiijd.

---

[1] This entry, very varied in form, runs through the whole book. It is for the great Dirige or Anniversary in commemoration of all the benefactors of the Church [see A°. 1443] who were entered on the bede-roll. "Ceteri" seems to be meant for "diversorum."

It. solut. pro iij ropys ad campanas	xv*d*.
It. pro correo ad campanas	ij*d*.
It. pro oleo pro clocke	j*d*.
It. ad emendandum unum sorplys	j*d*.
It. Thome Capellano pro dimidio anno ad celebrandum	xij*s*. iiij*d*.
It. ad faciendum librum computi	iiij*d*.
It. de arreragiis computi precedentis que parochiani fuerunt in debito custodorum [*sic*] pro anno predicto	iij*s*. ix*d*.
Summa . . ix*s*. viij*d*.	
Et debent de claro omnia sibi Allocat.	xx*s*. vj*d*.

A.D. 1435–6. 14–15th H. VI. [From Easter to Easter.]

W. Strecche and John Ansteys, Wardens.

Inde receperunt de arreragiis computi precedentis	xxvj*s*.
Idem de Isabella Houchyn	xiij*s*. iiij*d*.
It. de legatione uxoris Johannis Broune	iiij*d*.
It. de candelis venditis de Trendale	j*d*. ob.
It. de Willelmo Strecche vj bussellos brasie frumenti pretii	vj*s*.
Page 30.	
It. de Johanne Aste pro j quatero brasie avenarum	ij*s*.
It. de Roberto Aste pro vj bussellis brasie avenarum	xviij*d*.
It. de Thoma Cole pro ij bussellis	vj*d*.
It. de Thoma Cole pro vj bussellis	xviij*d*.
It. de Johanne Trent pro iiij bussellis	xij*d*.
[Eight more similar entries.]	
It. pro quinque pecke de uxoribus datis, pretii	x*d*.
It. de Thoma capellano	xij*d*.
It. de venditione unius bovis	xij*d*.
It. de collectione sacre ceree	iij*s*. v*d*. ob.
Summa cum arreragiis computi precedentis	£iij ij*s*. x*d*.

In Expensis.

Ad faciendum sacre ceree et trendale	iij*s*. viij*d*.
It. pro lavatione velaminum et factura trendel et tapir	iiij*d*.
It. pro oleo pro clocke	j*d*.
It. pro uno skyppe [beehive]	iiij*d*.
It. pro uno lente clothe	xiiij*s*. ij*d*.
It. pro uno tapyr	xvj*d*.
It. in expensis apud Wellys	viij*d*.

It. solut. Johanni Davy ad faciendum muros circa cimiterium	xx*d*.
It solut. plomario	vj*d*.
Summa . . xxiiij*s*. iij*d*.	
Et debet	xviij*s*. x*d*.

A.D. 1436-7. 14-15th H. VI.
W. Strecche and John Ansteys, Wardens.

It. Ex legatione Thome Broune	xxij*d*.
It. Ex legatione Thome Broune iiij busselles frumenti	iij*s*. iiij*d*.
It. de Johanne et aliis de Mertock pro transgressione facta tenentibus Tyntenhull in le mersh	iij*s*. iiij*d*.
It. pro uno bove tradito Johanni Helyer	ij*s*. vj*d*.
It. pro uno [sic] vacc tradito Johanni Smyth de Ashe eodem modo . . .	ij*s*.
It. pro j vacc tradita J. Wylle eodem modo	xx*d*.

In Expensis.

It. pro lavatione mapparum.	
It. pro messore unius dimidii acri frumenti	vj*d*.
It. Thome capellano	viij*d*.
It. pro cloutyng lether pro iij ropys	xix*d*.
It. pro grece pro campanis	j*d*.
It. pro hamynge [hemming] pro auter clothys.	
It. J. Davy ad faciendum communem furnum	xxvj*s*. viij*d*.
It. diversis hominibus pro prandio	ij*s*. x*d*. ob.
It. pro visitatione	iij*d*.
It. pro uno capone	iij*d*.
It. pro labore de chalys, unde respecc [?]	iiij*d*.
It. ad scribendum computum	j*d*.
Summa expensarum . . . xlj*s*. vj*d*. ob.	
Et debetur . . . xix*s*. iiij*d*. ob.	

Page 31.

A.D. 1437-8. 15-16 H. VI.
W. Streche and John Trentte, Wardens.

It. de tota parochia pro una cruce et calice de novo emptis, ut patet per parcellam Ecclesie in custod. custodum	xxxvj*s*. x*d*.
It. de incremento unius brasine [a church-ale] facte pro S. Margareta . .	vij*s*. viij*d*.
It. de incremento unius brasine cervisie facte pro S. Margareta per custodes predictos in anno proxime precedente tunc non computato . . .	viij*s*.
It. de ligatione Johannis Aste pro domus pistrine faciendo et reparando hoc anno	xxxiiij*s*. iij*d*.
It. de ligatione Henrici Morys	v*s*.

It. de ligatione nuper uxoris Johannis Warwyke hoc anno . . . . . vjs.
It. de j vacca locata Johanni Smyth hoc anno . . . . ijs.
It. de j pelle proveniente dicte vacce mo [rientis] hoc anno . . . . . xijd.
It. de incremento domus pistrine hoc anno per appraiam [obscure] custodum . xvijs. vjd.
It. de Willelmo Panday de bonis S. Marie hoc anno . . . . vjs. viijd.
It. de candelis de le trendell hoc anno venditis diversis personis . . . . vd.
    Summa . . . £vj xjs. ixd.

In Expensis.

It. pro uno calice de novo empte per sacramentum computantum . . . . xxxs.
It. pro una cruce de copre et aurata hoc anno per sacramentum dictorum computantum xxjs.
It. pro emendandis iiij baudreyes campanarum . . . . . . iijs. iiijd.

Page 32.

It. mulieri locata pro lavatione vestimentorum altaris et pro les kecheves [kerchiefs]
 imagorum hoc anno . . . . vjd.
It. pro smygma et brymston emptis ad idem . . . . ijd.
It. domino Thome Brytell capellano ecclesie ibidem pro diversis obitibus . . . xijd.
It. pro vij lb. cere emptis pro uno cereo voc holy taper et le trendell hoc anno, una
 cum factura ejusdem . . . . iijs. ijd. ob.
It. in expensis apud Yvelcestre die visitationis archidiaconi . . . . vd.
It. pro domo pistrine hoc anno de novo facte, ut in arte carpentarii ex conventione cum
 eo facta in grosso preter mensam suam . . . . viijs.
It. solut. pro una mensa . . . . xijd.
It. in diversis victualibus emptis pro hominibus venientibus cum eorum plaustris pro
 dicto mearemio cariando . . . . iijd.
It. pro mearemio supradicto empto ad idem . . . . xijd.
It. pro emendatione fenestre veteris domus pistrine ex opposito le spere . . . vjd.
It. solut. uno homini pro dicto spere cum virgis vrydendis et desuper daubandis . iiijd.
It. uno homini locato pro le stubel vocato helmebought falcando hoc pro dicta domo
 pistrine cooperienda . . . . ijd.
It. in dicto stramine empto . . . . iiijd.
It. pro lapidibus emptis apud Stenteyate pro via in villa emendanda in diversis locis
 ubi indigebit . . . . iijs. vd.
It. pro emendendis le pykeys hoc anno . . . . iiijd.
It. in spire metendis ad idem . . . . vj. ob.
It. uno homini pro dicta domo watillando per unum diem . . . . . vd.
It. solut. domino Priori pro annuo redditu dicte domus pistrine . . . vijd.
It. pro ij bobus emptis pro stauro ecclesie hoc anno, j pro xs. et alio pro ixs. xd. . ixs. xd.
Et nota quod custodes debent de arreragiis xxxvijs. et unum bovem pretii xs.
    Summa . . . £v ixs. iijd.

PAGE 33.

A.D. 1438–9. From Easter 16 H. VI., to Easter 17 H. VI., and from that date to S. Mary Magdalene's Day, *i.e.*, for five quarters and more.

JOHN TRENTE AND W. STRECCHE, WARDENS.

It. de redditu communis pistrine tradite Stephano Baker ad terminum trium annorum
vj*s*. viij*d*.
[Receipts from the pistrina, from three legacies in money, and one of a green gown, from an Ale, and from the sale of an ox and a calf. A cow remains in stock and let to J. Somerton.]

IN EXPENSIS.

It. in una vacca cum uno vitulo emptis hoc anno	xiij*s*.
It. pro ix bussellis frumenti emptis ad valenc : ecclesie	ix*s*.
It. in j hostio pro domo pistrine cum j pare de dornes [durns]	iij*s*. iiij*d*.
It. in virgis emptis pro le Watilyng pistrine	j*d*.
It. pro j parcella de segg empt. pro coopertura pistrine simul cum le thetcchyng ad thascam	ij*s*. vj*d*.
It. pro j ulmo prosternanda pro le Gakehouse [Privy] facienda	j*d*.
It. in j trendale lignale empto de novo	ij*s*. ix*d*. ob.
It. in iiij lb. cere emptis pro dicto trendale faciendo et le pascal taper	ij*d*.
It. in emendatione oriscopii ville	v*d*.
It. capellano pro certis memorationibus in ecclesia	xij*d*.

PAGE 34.

A.D. 1439–40. H. VII., 17th–18th. St. Mary Magd. to same feast.

JOHN TRENTE AND W. STRECCHE, WARDENS.

[Receipts include the usual Ale, the rent of the cow, a gift of iij*s*. iiij*d*. from J. Aught, and Bakehouse rent.]

IN EXPENSIS.

It. pro vij lb. cere pro le pascal taper, et aliis cerulis ecclesie ad sepulcrum et alibi	iiij*s*. vj*d*.
It. in factura j pascal taper cum aliis cerulis	ij*d*.
It. pro una corda empta ad le trendel	iij*d*.
It. pro certis memorationibus Rectori[1] ecclesie	xij*d*.

[1] Hitherto a Chaplain has been paid for this Anniversary Mass.

It. domino Priori de redditu domus pistrine . . . . . . xiij*d*.
It. pro j scala xiij rongarum¹ empta pro le belfray . . . . . xx*d*.
It. J. Stephano Baker pro custodia oriscopii in ecclesia . . . . iij*s*. iiij*d*.

PAGE 35. **A.D. 1440–1. 18–19 H. VI.**

JOHN STACEY AND ROBERT ASTE, WARDENS.

RECEPT. BONOR.

It. de totis parochianis ibidem pro quatuor cereis prout plenius patet per parcellam remanentem in custodia custodum predictorum . . . . . xxxviij*s*. j*d*.

IN EXPENSIS.

It. pro xlvij libris cere emptis pro quatuor torticiis cereis de novo factis, prout patet xxix*s*. iij*d*.
It. pro xliij libris de rosyn emptis pro eisdem torticiis . . . . . iiij*s*.
It. pro iiij rones [runs] de matchyerne pro eisdem . . . . . . xv*d*.
It. Willelmo Roule locato per iij dies ad facturam dictorum torticiorum . . . ij*s*.
It. in diversis victualibus emptis pro predicto Willelmo, et custodibus tempore facture eorundem . . . . xx*d*.
It. in unguento pro manibus suis . . . . ij*d*.
It. pro vj libris, uno quartero, cere emptis pro le pascal taper et le trendell . iij*s*. ix*d*.
It. in factura et non plus . . . . ij*d*. ob.

PAGE 36.
It. Thome Somerton pro j formula et j lebitina² [basin] ab eo emptis . . . xiij*d*.
It. Johanni Bokebynder de Mertock de j missale et j portifurio de novo ligando et cooperiendo et certos defectus in eisdem libris emendendo ex conventione . xj*s*.

PAGE 37. **A.D. 1441–2. Hen. VI., 19th–20th.**

J. STACY AND R. ASTE, WARDENS.

[S. Mary Magdalene's Day is the day of account as usual.]

De vj*s*. viij*d*. receptis de legatione Johannis Hody militis . . . . vj*s*. viij*d*.
Et de j tauro coloris rubii pretii vj*s*. viij*d*. recepto ex dono Johannis Aste . . vj*s*. viij*d*.
Et de segitibus venditis in le more hoc anno ex assensu domini et tenentum suorum, viz., ad sustentationem ecclesie ibidem . . . . x*s*.
[The brasina revenue is obliterated "quia non brasina hoc anno."]
Et de locatione j vacce sic locate Johanni Devenysh . . . . ij*s*.
Et de pretio unius vacce in custodia eorundem procuratorum . . . x*s*.

IN EXPENSIS.

It. pro viij tabulis ligneis vocatis Weynescote borde pro australi hostio ecclesie de novo facte, pro tabula xiiij*d*. . . . . ix*s*. iiij*d*.
It. in cxx de five stroke nayles emptis ad idem . . . . v*s*.

---

¹ There was no stone staircase to the Tower until 1516, when the present one was built, and the Tower raised.

² Probably a diminutive formed from lebes, a kettle or caldron.

It. in iij twystys ferreis emptis ad idem . . . . iiijs. viijd.
It. Thome de Somerton carpentario conducto ad faciendum de novo dictum hostium
    ad thascam . . . . vjs. viijd.
It. in uno annulo ferreo cum le bose [boss] ferreo ad claudendum dictum hostium . xviijd.
It. in excambio ij cruettys hoc anno cambitis . . . . ijd.

PAGE 38.

ⓐ.ⓓ. 1442–3. Hen. VI., 20th–21st.

J. STACY AND R. ASTE, WARDENS.

[The receipts are a legacy of a sheep, ijs. from an Ale, and xiijs. iiijd. from Bakehouse,
the rent of the cow, and the sale of a bull, and of a pound of wax.]
In expensis pro visitatione Archiepiscopi Cantuariensis . . . . iijd.

PAGE 39.

ⓐ.ⓓ. 1443–4. Hen. VI., 21–22.

J. STACY AND R. ASTE, CHURCHWARDENS.

IN RECEPT.

It. de incremento velleris j Multonis [sheep] . . . iiijd.

IN EXPENSIS.

It. de una sera ad hostium ecclesie . . . . vs.
It. pro una memoratione animarum omnium benefactorum ecclesie ibidem de-
    functorum que teneri debeant annuatim per custodes ecclesie ibidem qui pro
    tempore fuerint . . . . viijd.
In expensis procuratorum existentium apud Yevelchester ad visitationem episcopi[1] . xijd.

PAGE 40.

ⓐ.ⓓ. 1444–5. Hen. VI., 22–23.

J. STACY AND R. ASTE, CHURCHWARDENS.

It. pro 100 libris veteris plumbi ecclesie venditis hoc anno procuratori fraternitatis
    sancte Marie de Tyntynhull . . . . vjs. viijd.
It. de una zona de viride serico et argentata pretii xs. per estimationem, que data est
    ad ecclesiam hoc anno per Johannem Aste.
It. de incremento de les hogeler ys lyght de Johanne Warwyke nuper uno procuratorum
    inde ijs.
It. de ixs. receptis de quatuor quarteriis et dim. fabarum hoc anno legatis ad ecclesiam
    per Isabellam[2] Bondwyrth et de quatuor buss. frumenti nichill hic, quia liberati
    fuerint pro pane ad communem brasinam venditam ut ad commodum ecclesie
    que remanet in manibus Johannis Trente, J. Stiby, T. Bole, et Roberti Aste.

[1] Bp. Beckington's primary visitation.
[2] Her gift of wheat was handed to the four Managers of the brewhouse to serve for an Ale. Its money value is therefore not stated.

IN EXPENSIS.

[Reaping, carrying home and threshing corn and beans from the Moor[1].]
It. pro una libra cere pro le trendell renovand. quia igne combustum fuit . . vj*d*.
It. pro una trabe ferri vocate Balaunce de novo empte . . . . ij*s*. vj*d*.

PAGE 41. **A.D.** 1446–7.

J. STACY AND ROBERT AUGHT, WARDENS.

It. in meremio empto ad stansile cimiterii ibidem faciendum . . . . xvj*d*.
It. in uno muro lapideo in occidentali parte ecclesie ibidem emendendo . ij*s*. ij*d*.
It. pro xlvij libris plumbi emptis pro wights[2] ville faciendo . . . ij*s*. iiij*d*.
It. pro locatione j domus brasine pro brasina cervisie intus facienda . . . vij*d*.

PAGE 42. 24–25 H. VI. **A.D.** 1446–7.

J. STACE AND R. AUGHT, WARDENS.

[The date from S. Mary Magdalene is altered this year to S. Margaret, and the time comprised in this account extends to Easter following.]

It. receperunt de una zona harnesiata cum Argento data ecclesie per Isabellam Aught et vendita Willelmo Garde hoc anno . . . . ix*s*. vij*d*.
It. de olla enea recepta de dono R. Corler hoc anno.

IN EXPENSIS.

It. pro una corda empta pro le lente clothe suspendendo . . . . . j*d*.
[The stock this year is one bull in the hands of J. Waryng, one cow in the hands of W. Prewers, four pounds of wool in those of J. Staci, and one brass pot measuring one lagena.]

PAGE 43. 25–26 H. VI. **A.D.** 1447–8.

W. Goleight, et T. Wilmett, custodes bonorum et catallorum ecclesie S. Margarete virginis.
It. de incremento unius brasine cerevisie facte ad usum S. Margarete ultra omnes custus [costs] hoc anno . . . . xij*s*. ij*d*.
It. de incremento unius brasine cerevisie facte circa festum App. Philippi et Jacobi ultra omnes custus hoc anno . . . . xiij*s*. iiij*d*.
It. de iiij libris lane grosse et fractt . . . . x*d*.
It. de j olla enea continente j lagenam et ponderante xviij lb. vendita . . . iij*s*.
[The rent of the cow is cancelled, "quia sterilis fuit hoc anno."]

---

[1] N.B.—Details of the harvesting of the parish grain crops on the Moor allotment, which was cultivated by the Wardens.

[2] Does not this mean weights, *i.e.*, standard weights kept at the common bakehouse for the use of the Village?

IN EXPENSIS.

It. pro ligatione et emendatione missalis ecclesie . . . . vij*d*.
It. pro emendatione ij chisipulorum ecclesie . . . . xvj*d*.
It. pro emend. ij aubis, et le perell [apparel] ij chisipularum, cum j dexte clothe, et j baner . . . . x*d*.
It. pro j corda empta ad le peyse oriscopii . . . . xvj*d*.
[The cemetery wall opposite the Manor-court is repaired.]
It. in uno libro processionali empto hoc anno . . . . . . iij*s*. viij*d*.
It. in panno lyneo empto pro aubis emendandis . . . . . . xj*d*.
It. domino Priori pro capitali rentale communis furni ibidem hoc anno . . . xiij*d*.
It. pro emendendo j cliper [clapper of bell] ecclesie . . . . xviij*d*.
It. pro ij plaustratis librarum petrarum ad communem furnum ville emendendum ibidem xviij*d*.
It. in uno lathamo. . . ad faciendum le mouthe et le foreborde pistrine, cum exaltatione eorundem . . . . v*d*.
It. in expensis ejusdem lathami et aliorum auxiliantium lathamum ad idem opus . x*d*.

PAGE 44.

It. in expensis apud Hamedun pro le fleure furni ibidem faciendum cum stipendio lathami, usque et in cibis et potibus emptis ad dictum lathamum . . . viij*d*.
It. in uno coopertore locato per ij dies et dein per diem iiij*d*., et in suo serviente locato x*d*.
It. in perlionebus [purlins] emptis ad idem opus . . . . ij*d*.
It. in falcatione j acre stipuli ad idem opus . . . . iiij*d*.
It. pro una tabula de alabastro empta ad summum altare ecclesie ibidem . . xxvj*s*. viij*d*.
It. ad ij tabula de alabastro empta per parochianos . . . . . . x*s*.
It. in expensis Regis[1] de Montagu apud Tyntenhull existentis tempore estivali . . iij*d*.

PAGE 45.
26–27 H. VI. ⓐ.Ⅾ. 1448–9.
W. GOLYGHT AND JOHN BROUN, WARDENS.

[A cow is sold for] . . . . vj*s*.
It. de denariis provenientibus de venditione unius tauri sic venditi diversis parochianis ibidem hoc anno ultra xij*d*. solutis ecclesie ad tabellam alabastriam per manus Roberti Sherene ut fatetur per parochianos predictos . . . . . . v*s*.
[J. Aught gives a red cow ad usum ecclesie, which is let for] . . . . xij*d*.

PAGE 46.   IN EXPENSIS.

It. pro lotricibus lavantibus linthiamina ecclesie nil capientibus preter expensas suas . viij*d*.
It. in carnifice loci ad necandum et distribuendum taurum supra venditum . . iij*d*.
It. in thumatione cum incenso . . . . j*d*.
It. ad emendandum lignum de trendale . . . . ij*d*.
It. ad faciendum de novo unum wherlegage positum ad scansile in orientali parte cimiterii pro animalibus extra cimiterium custodiendis . . . . iiij*d*.
It. solut. eidem Thome pro una libitina lignea ab eo empta hoc anno . . . viij*d*.

---
[1] A play-king enacted by Montacute people at Tintinhull. Each season seems to have had its mock monarch. At Croscombe he reigned in winter; at Bath in autumn; here in summer.

It. cuidam fabro de Kyngesbury locato ad emendandum unum kanillum oriscopii
    ferreum portantem le sayllor (?) . . . . iiij*d*.
It. pro ij acris prati in chestremede emptis pro domo pistrine communis cooperienda . viij*d*.
It. pro dicto prato falcando . . . . xij*d*.
It. rectori loci pro certis animis precandis per annum . . . . . xij*d*.

PAGE 47.   27–28 H. VI.   (A.D.)   1449–50.

W. GOLYHT AND J. BROWN, WARDENS.

[No brewery revenue this year.]
Et de iiij*s*. x*d*., receptis in allocatione unius xvme domini regis fisci villat. hoc anno
    allocat. ultra ij*d*., solitos clerico collectori regis.[1]
[Receipts this year only the rent of the pistrina and of the cow.]

PAGE 48.   28–29 H. VI.   (A.D.)   1450–1.

W. GOLYGHT AND JOHN BROUNE, WARDENS.

RECEPT.

De legatione Isabelle . . . hoc anno . . . . . iiij*d*.
It. de legatione Bartholomei fratris de Yevelchestre . . . iij*s*. iiij*d*.

[Expenses as usual.]

PAGE 49.   29–30 H. VI.   (A.D.)   1451–2.

W. GOLIGHT AND J. BROWN, WARDENS.

[The term of Account is still S. Margaret's Day.]

It. pro uno veteri hostio ecclesie vendito . . . . viij*d*.
It. pro duabus tabulis ligneis sic venditis . . . . iiij*d*.
It. pro uno trunco ligneo vendito . . . . ij*d*.
It. pro uno ligno quercino vendito . . . . v*d*.
It. pro ij lignis quercinis vocatis liernes de veteri rodelofte . . . xviij*d*.
It. pro vj gistis [joists] ligneis venditis . . . . iiij*d*.
It. de Waltero Sille, Johanne Sille, Thoma Bowryng, Johanne Fribbe, et Johanne Exale
    de incremento unius ludi vocati Christmasse play . . . vj*s*. viij*d*.
It. de Roberto Aught de dono patri sui . . . . . . viij*s*. iiij*d*.
Et de dono suo proprio . . . . vj*s*. viij*d*.
Et de dono patris ejusdem defuncti . . . . vj*s*. viij*d*.
Et de dono suo proprio . . . . vj*s*. viij*d*.
[Interlineations here make it uncertain if there is a repetition of the same entries].

---

[1] Were Churchwardens allowed a percentage on the allocation of the 15th?

It. de ijs. vjd. receptis de Johanne Gille, collectore quarte partis unius xvme domini regis hoc anno ut de denariis per prefatum dominum regem allocat. de antiquo po . . . (?)

PAGE 50.

Solut. Thome Dayfote carpentario locato ad faciendum le Rodelofte ut in Meremiis ligneis ex conventione . . . . xls.
It. Johanni Brayne de Stoke pro Meremiis vocatis waynscote pro dicto Rodelofte faciendo ab eo emptis in grosso . . . . vjs. viijd.
It. Johanni Stibi pro liberis petris pro dicto Rodelofte ab eo emptis . . . . xijd.
It. diversis hominibus locatis ad deponendum le Old Rodclofte · . . . . xviijd.
It. servienti Johannis Davy pro muro petrino in parte boreali de la Rodelofte emendando, cum ijd. solutis pro prandio suo . . . . vd
It. Henrico Mason de Odecumbe, et Thome Bouryng locatis ad emendandum defectus muri petrini ex utraque parte ecclesie, videl. ad implendum foramina ubi vetus Rodelofte, prius fuit, ad thascam . . . . vijd.
It. Johanni Broun uno homini locato ad adjuvandum dictum servientem Johannis Davy . . . . iiijd.
It. in expensis diversorum hominum adquirentum ij plaustratas Meremii a Montagu usque Tyntenhull . . . . viijd.
It. in clavis et ceteris ferramentis ad dictum Rodelofte emptis hoc anno . . viijd.
It. Johanni Brayne, cum serviente suo, locatis per unum diem ad bordandam et emendandam clausuram pone crucem, videl. inter naveu ecclesie et cancellam . xd.
It. Willelmo Perys locato ad faciendum de novo xl Judaces ligneas ad pertandum luminaria stantia coram alta cruce ad thascam . . . . . . xd.
It. in Meremio empto ad idem . . . . jd.
It. Willelmo Golyght locato per unum diem coadjuvante T. Dayfote ad levandum solarium subtus le Rodelofte ad thascam . . . . iiijd
It. Johanni Hare locato ad progettandum [pargetting] et dealbandum muros petrinos turris campanarum in grosso ad thascam . . . . xd.
It. cuidam homini vocato alabastre-man in arameanda et conventione unius tabelli alabastri . . . . jd.
  [The usual annual expenses, including those at visitation here follow.]
  Total . . . lxvijs. ijd.
Of which the cost of the Rodelofte is . . . . . . £ij ijs.

PAGE 51.

30–31 H. VI. A.D. 1452–3.

W. GOLYGHT AND J. BROUN, WARDENS.

[No revenue from brewing.]

A cow is sold for . . . . vijs.
A brass pot weighing xiiij lbs. is left by will.
Segetes in marisco vendite hoc anno nil hic, quia pecunia nondum soluta fuit.

PAGE 52. IN EXPENSIS.

It. mulieribus lavantes [sic], necessaria ecclesie non capientes preter expensas . . viij*d*.
It. pro uno veteri superpellicio hoc anno empto apud Montagu . . . . . xviij*d*.
It. pro eodem superpellicio emendando et lavando hoc anno . . . . . ij*d*.
It. solut. clerico facienti nunc computum ac pro computis quatuor ceterorum annorum proxime precedentum . . . . xx*d*.
It. Willelmo Passelow et aliis scribendis parcellam computi predicti ad vices . . iij*d*.
E quibus pecuniis allocatur de xxxvij*s*. iij*d*. solutis ad tabellam alabastriam nuper emptam ut fatetur per parochianos.
It. de vj*s*. viij*d*. solutis pro predicta tabella alabastria per manus Roberti Aught unde dicti custodes onerantur supra in arreragiis . . . ut fatetur super computum per parochianos predictos.

PAGE 53.

De incremento xx*s*. brasine cervisie ad festum nativitatis Domini nil eo quod singuli denarii predicti receptus fuerunt per alios parochianos et per manus eorundem soluti cuidam alabastreman pro tabella alabastrina ab eo empta sic quod nullo modo denarii ad manus custodum onerari deberent. Exonerantur per parochian causa predicta.
It. de xx*s*. de incremento alterius brasine cervisie anno predicto erga festum S. Margarete nil respondent causa predicta.
It. de xx*s*. provenientibus de ij plumbis pandoxaterii venditis nuper provenientibus de legatione Roberti Giles et Matilde uxoris sue nil respondent causa predicta.

[First use of the word pandoxaterium.]

Remanent adhuc solvendum.

Set tamen memorandum est de diversis denariis extra computum predicti custodis computantis in manibus diversis existentibus que fuerunt deo et ecclesie S. Margarete de Tyntenhill debitæ, viz., x*s*. remanent solvend, in manibus cujusdam Johannis Rede de Lange Sutton que debentur ecclesie predicte pro segitibus vocatis leverys de marisco nuper sibi venditis.

PAGE 54.

31–32 H. VI. Ⓐ.Ⓓ. 1453–4.
J. STACY AND W. SHODES, WARDENS.

Et de xx*s*. of the brasina of S. Margaret's Day of the preceding year, de dono parochianorum per supervisum Margarete Stacy et Isabelle Wilmot ultra . . ix*s*. j*d*.
Solut. pro uno superpellicio ad usum ecclesie de novo empto.

PAGE 55. IN EXPENSIS.

It. pro falcatione unius acre stipuli de dono Johannis Stacy pro reparatione communis pistrine . . . . iiij*d*.
It j coopertore pro thatchante.
It. pro ij plaustratis petrarum emptis pro le causey ex opposito domum communis pistrine emendando . . . . iij*d*.
It. pro ij ferreis vangalibus [spades] una cum uno ligno vangalis ad staurum ecclesie emptis . . . . ix*d*.

PAGE 56.   32–33 H. VI. (A.D.) 1454–5.
WILLIAM SHODES AND WALTER GILLE, WARDENS.
[Among the] Expenses.
Et in brimstone empto pro le flammeolis [veils] in ecclesia lavandis . . ob.
Et in Wexinge, j dipote cum j poyntell ad eandem emptam . . j*d*. ob

PAGE 58.   33–34 H. VI. (A.D.) 1455–6.
WALTER AND JOHN GILLE.

PAGE 59.   34–35 H. VI. (A.D.) 1456–7.
WALTER AND JOHN GILLE.
[Only the usual entries.]

PAGE 60.
Solut. uni homini ligatori conducto pro duobus septimanis pro libris ligandis capienti
   pro una septimana, ij*s*. iiij*d*. . . . . vj*s*. viij*d*.
It. eidem ligatori pro libris ecclesie ligandis per iiij dies capienti per diem vj*d*. ob. ij*s*. ij*d*.
It. eidem pro clapsys dictorum librorum . . . . vj*d*
It. pro co-operatione unius libri ecclesie . . . . iiij*d*.
It. pro tribus pellibus bidentum emptis pro aliis libris ecclesie cooperiendis . . viij*d*.
It. in una pelle de doeskyne pro eisdem libris . . . . vj*d*.
It. in quatuor pellibus pergamenis pro eisdem libris . . . . . . viij*d*.
It. in coreo de lether (?) . . . . iiij*d*. ob.
It. in gluwe ad idem opus . . . . ij*d*.
It. in filis emptis pro dictis libris suendis . . . . iiij*d*.
It. in coreo equino ad idem . . . . ij*d*. ob.
It. in gume pro eisdem libris . . . . j*d*.
It. Johanni Rede de Upton pro clogill empto in mora de Tyntenhull . . . x*s*.
Et remanet in custodia unus annulus argenteus deauratus [gilt].

PAGE 61.   35–36 H. VI. (A.D.) 1457–8.
WALTER GYLLE AND JOHN GYLLE, WARDENS.
[Nothing unusual in the receipts].
IN EXPENSIS.
It. rectori pro communi anniversario tenendo . . . . xij*d*.
It. pro fronkyncense seu thure . . . . j*d*.
It. in vij staples ferri de novo emptis pro baculis vexilli, cum uno crampo ferri empto
   pro ostio ecclesie . . . . viij*d*.

It. in uno antiphonali de novo ligato . . . . vj*d*.
[Two acres of straw and five bundles of spars (plionum) are bought from W. Montacute for thatching] . . . . xvj*d*.

PAGE 62.
It. pro portatione vexilli usque Yvelchester anno elapso et anno instanti . . . iiij*d*.
Ex dono rectoris ecclesie, iij quarteria avene et ij busselli frumenti.

PAGE 63.   36–37 H. VI. A.D. 1458–9.
ROBERT AUGHT AND WILLIAM WARFULL, WARDENS.
IN EXPENSIS.

It. pro emendatione de ponte juxta cimiterium . . . ij*d*.
It. aquebajulo ecclesie pro portatione vexilli usque Yvelchester ij*d*.
[First mention of the aquebajulus.]
It. in uno hyve empto pro apibus . . . . iij*d*.ob.
It. pro le pascal tapyr . . . . iij*s*. iiij*d*.
In expensis factis apud[1] Yelchester per parochianos de concordatione inter ipsos et dicti rectoris . . . . iij*s*. viij*d*.

PAGE 64.   37–38 H. VI. A.D. 1459–60.
BONA ECCLÆ. Note of goods remaining in hands of W. and J. Gylle, Wardens, 1457–8, viz., A ring, oatmalt, wheat-malt, and a sheep, and bees.
ROBERT BENET ET W. BOLE, PROCURATORES ECCLESIE.
RECEIPTS.

Bakehouse let to William Newman and J. Bremylcombe for the year . . . x*s*.
It. pro uno bidenti ex dono Johannis Weryn sic vendito . . . . . x*d*.
It. pro j brasina ejus ecclesie vendita in festo Inventionis S. Crucis in anno precedente . . . . xij*d*.
[and again this year, same day] . . . . ij*s*. iiij*d*.
It. brasina in festo S. Margarete . . . . vj*s*. viij*d*.
It. pro redditu unius camere communis pistrine a festo S. Michaelis usque ad festum S. Margarete . . . . vj*d*.

PAGE 65.   IN EXPENSIS.

It. in lotura flameoli et factura le pryket ut in potibus . . . . . ij*d*.
It. uno peynter pro peyntyng de la Rodelofte ut in parte pecunie sue . xiij*s*. iiij*d*.
It. in ridatione unius gutteri circa covam pistrine [vault of oven]. . . . iiij*d*.
It. in fodatione unius fossati pertinentis dicte pistrine apud moram . . . j*d*.
It. in una petra separali [detached, single] empta apud Hamden ad obstipandum os pistrine . . . . j*s*. ij*d*.

[1] Probably settled at the Visitation Court by Arbitration. The cause is not revealed.

[The capa and vestimenta are mended, and rebyn [ribbon] bought for them, as also bockeram, [blue] and white thread, thread de abisso [= bysso, flax], and linen de Crescloth.] . . . . ijs. vjd.
It. in smigmate et sulfur pro lotura pannorum lineorum.
It. in iiij saccis calcis uste pro fenestris . . . . ijs. jd.
It. in stipendio W. Warfull ad jactandam tabulam . . . . . . jd.
It. ad portandam calcem a Crukern usque Tyntenhull . . . . . ijd.
It. aquebajulo ecclesie ad portandum vexillum ecclesie ad Yelchester ad festum Pentecost. . . . . ijd.

PAGE 66.

38–39 H. VI. A.D. 1460–1.

ROBERT BENET AND W. BOLE, WARDENS.

RECEIPTS.

It. pro clogill vendito Johanni Rede ut de antiquo debitur . . . vijs. viijd.
It. pro parvis lapidibus fractis de remanent. fenestr. ecclesie sic venditis . . vijd.
It. pro quatuor annulis argenteis ex legatione . . . . ijs.
PAGE 67.
It. pro uno latice stangni de stauro sic vendito . xjd.

EXPENS.

In stangno empto pro fenestris ecclesie . . iijd. ob.
Pro cera pro cereo benedicto . . . . xxijd. ob.

PAGE 68.

1–2 Ed. IV. A.D. 1461–2.

J. BOLE AND J. CRYBBE, WARDENS.

[In this year £1 2s. 4d. was lent to six people in sums from 6s. 8d. downwards.]

PAGE 69.

A.D. 1462–3. 2–3 Ed. IV.

J. BOLE AND J. CRYBBE, WARDENS.

Solut. aquebajulo pro portatione vexilli in processione apud Yvelchester . . . ijd.
Allowed to J. Bole the sum which he had laid out for the painting of the Rood-loft . . . . xxd.

PAGE 70.
PAGE 71.

3–4 Ed. IV. (A.D.) 1463–4.

T. Wylmot and T. Predyll, Wardens.

Solut. uno homini locato ad deponendum vitrum de fenestra ecclesie ad finem occidentalem . . . . vj*s.*

PAGE 72.

4–5 Ed. IV. (A.D.) 1464–5.

J. Prydell and John Carsloo, Wardens.

Ex legatione Agnete Bretyll data ecclesie pro adorand.[1] in ecclesia eadem per annum . . . . vj*s.* viij*d.*

PAGE 73.

In expensis clerici ecclesie et unius hominis secum pro portatione vexillorum ad Yvelchester . . . . ij*d.* ob.
In emendatione unius candelabri auricalci [brass] fracti . . . . . ij*d.*
[For plumber's work] . . . . £j. js. xj*d.*

PAGE 74.

5–6 Ed. IV. (A.D.) 1465–6.

T. Stacy and Peter Bretell, Wardens.

[Michaelmas to Michaelmas.]

Ex legatione Johannis Trent, viz., pro j lodice [coverlet] de fustian, et j linchiamine, j manutergio sic vendito . . . . ix*s.*
De relevio [nett benefit] panis benedicti hoc anno . . . . . v*s.* x*d.*
Et receperunt de candelis pertinentibus dicto pani benedicto hoc anno [old candles sold to swell this item] . . . . iiij*d.*
Et de Willelmo Warefull et Johanne Trent de hogelers light hoc anno . . xxij*d.*

In Expensis.

It. in uno Pax empta ad usum ecclesie . . . . iiij*d.*
It. in queratione [the carriage] unius paris vestiment. a Wells usque Tyntenhull . ij*s.* v*d.*
It. pro uno trendell de novo empto . . . . vj*s.* iiij*d.*

---

[1] To be prayed for.

6–7 Ed. IV. A.D. 1466–7.

PAGE 75.

P. BRETELL AND J. AUGHT, WARDENS.

PAGE 76.   IN EXPENSIS.

It. in duobus zonis emptis pro capellano	j*d.*
It. pro factura et emendatione de les pryketts in ecclesia ardentibus per annum	j*d.*
It. in emendatione unius cere cum una clave ad idem empta . . .	ij*d.*
It. pro scrinio¹ in ecclesia et clavis emptis ad idem	v*d.*

PAGE 77.

7–9 Ed. IV A.D. 1468–70. [From S. Margaret's Day to the Conversion of S. Paul.] [*I.e.*, July 22, 1467, to Jan. 25, 1469.]

J. BROUN AND WALTER GYLLE, WARDENS.

RECEIPTS.

Pro j ulmo sic vendit	ij*s.* viij*d.*
It. pro meremio de ponte juxta stansile cimiterii hoc anno vendito . . .	ij*d.*
It. pro shrudatione unius ulmi in cimiterio	xij*d.*
It. pro brasina	xxvj*s.* viij*d.*
It. pro pane benedicto	v*s.*

PAGE 78.   IN EXPENSIS.

It. in j plaustrata petrarum ad communem furnum	
It. in j plaustrata petrarum querente apud Hamdon ad pontem juxta cimiterium	viij*d.*
It. in iiij lb. cere pro les trendel bis de novo factis.	
[The clerk (aquebajulus) carries the banner to Ilchester at Pentecost.]	
It. pro emendatione unius citule [bucket] pro aqua benedicta portanda.	
It. pro uno panno lineo empto ad pendendum ante altam crucem in ecclesia .	ij*s.* vj*d.*

PAGE 79.

9th–10th Ed. IV. From Conversion of S. Paul, Jan. 25, 1469, to Sunday before SS. Simon and Jude, Oct. 1470, 1 year 3 quarters.

J. BROUN AND WALTER GYLLE, WARDENS.

One brasina produces v*s.*, and the pistrina xxix*s.* iiij*d.*
One toga ex legatione is sold for viij*s.*
The vexillum is carried to Ilchester "per tempus computi."

---

¹ The word means both screen and desk.

PAGE 80.   IN EXPENSIS.

It. in una ropa empta pro canapy . . . . j*d*.
It. in uno cophino empto pro pane benedicto portando . . . . . iiij*d*.
[The Loaf, like the Holy Water, was carried to certain houses by the Aquæ-bajulus.]
In stauro vendito super computum. Pro uno annulo argenteo . . . . ix*d*.
Et pro alio annulo argenteo cum uno numerali vendito . . . . . xij*d*.
Et pro una patella enea de stauro vendita . . . . ij*s*.

PAGE 81.

11–13th Ed. IV. Two years from F. of SS. Simon and Jude, 1471–3.

JOHN TRENT AND R. STACY, WARDENS.

[Entries few and customary. The distractions of the Kingdom are probably reflected in the broken periods of the wardenships.]

PAGE 83.

13–16 Ed. IV. 🅐.🅓. 1473–6.

TRENT AND STACY [serving again for 3 years.]

Receipts for two years for the panis benedictus . . . . xij*s*.

IN EXPENSIS.

It. pro superpellicio pro sacerdote . . . . . ix*s*. viij*d*.
It.   „   „   pro clerico . . . . . ij*s*. iiij*d*.
It. cera pro cereo de fonte . . . . . ij*s*. viij*d*.
It. pro cera for the trendell . . . . . . xviij*d*.
It. pro factura de le bemme crucis [the high cross beam]'. ij*s*. vij*d*.

PAGE 84.

MEM. 16 Ed. IV. Joh. Bul and Thos. Prydell began to be Proctors at M'mas till M'mas next, succeeding Trent and Stacy.

Expenses, xij*s*. iij*d*. Balance handed over, £iij xix*s*.

PAGE 84.

17 Ed. IV. 🅐.🅓. 1477–8.

JOHN BOWL AND THOMAS PYCHER, WARDENS.

[The first account in English.]

For mawing and carrying home of strawe for the bakehouse.
It. for the bedrowyll to the brest [priest] at iiij tymys . . . xij*d*.
It. for the rope of the canapie . . . . j*d*.
It. to the clerk for bearing of the banner to Ylchester . . . ij*d*. ob.

It. for ij putts of stone to the church cawse [causey] . .	viij*d*.
It. for wyntering and summering of the . . . chyrche cowe	iij*s*.
It. for keepyng of a calfe fro mydwynter to after Easter . .	vj*d*.

PAGE 85.   RECEIPTS.

For Ayll [ale] ad fest. S. Margaret . . .	iiij*s*. vj*d*.
It. for the chyrche loffe [loaf] . . .	. v*s*.
It. for the owyn [oven let for private bakings] .	. viij*s*.

18–19 Ed. IV. A.D. 1479–80. S^t. Marg^t. to S^t. Marg^t.

THOMAS STACY AND JOHN BOWELL, WARDENS.

Balance	£iiij v*s*.
Receipts. See Items below	xl*s*. viij*d*.
Expenses. „ „	xxiij*s*. vij*d*. ob.
Balance . . . . £v. ij*s*.	

RECEIPTS.

De redditu communis pistrine.

It. for a cowe off J. Stacy	. viij*s*.
It. for the same J. Stacy	vj*s*. viij*d*.
It. for the wyffe of Peter Prettyll for agoyn [a gown]. . .	. v*s*.
It. for a croke of W. Undyrway	. iij*s*.
It. for the holy loffe	. v*s*. x*d*.
It. for sellyng of wax of the tryndyll	. iij*d*.
It. for ayll that was sold att the feste of Sanctt Margarett . .	iiij*s*. vj*d*.

IN EXPENSIS.

It. for deryge and masses for the fonders	. xviij*d*.
It sowder and led for ye blomere [plumber's] labour .	.

PAGE 86.

Ed. IV. 19. S^t. Marg^t. to Ed. IV. 22nd. Palm Sunday.

RECEIPTS.

It. pro taberna serevicie . . .	xj*s*. ij*d*.

EXPENSES.

It. carpentario pro reparatione ecclesie et domus servicie . . .	ix*s*. xj*d*.
It. W. Newman pro reparatione domus communis servicie . .	vj*s*. iiij*d*.

PAGE 87.
It. pro thressyng of whete . . . . iiij*d*.

PAGE 88. [detached scribblings.]

PAGE 89.   22 Ed. IV. A.D. 1482–3.
W. Aste and J. Bolle, Wardens.
Expenses.

Pro celatione Alti crucis . . . . xxiiij*s*.
et pro facture le mortyse ad deponendum lignum intus . . . . ij*d*.
[for the erection of the upright beam of the Crucifix.]

PAGE 90.   Richard III. A.D. 1483–4.
R. Prydyll and J. Carslow, Wardens.
Expenses.

Pro Taratantaryatione unius ligni pro pistrino . . vj*d*.
It. pro capistro ad portandum canipem Alti Altaris . j*d*.

Receipts.

Joan Trynt dedit ecclesie . . . . xij*d*.
It. pro pane benedicto . . . . . vs. x*d*.

PAGE 91.   [The scribe is quite confused about his date.]
Robt. Benet [al Smyth, p. 90] and W. Laurance, Wardens, succeeding
Carslow and Prydel.
Expenses.

It. pro scriptione[1] Visitationis beate Marie et beate Anne . . vj*s*.

PAGE 92.   [No date.]
R. Stacy and R. Bawnton, Wardens.

They receive of Smyth and Laurance . £vj vj*s*. viij*d*.
It. quinque annulos et unam zonam argenteam.
It. de Willelmo Merche in Coker ad orandum . . vj*s*. viij*d*.
It. de Roberto Pridyll ad orandum . . . . xij*d*.
It. pro uno thuriferario . . . . . . xvj*d*.
It. de Willelmo Aste unam vaccam.
It. de redditu pistrino . . . . xj*s*. iiij*d*.
It. pro prest unum? vj*s*. viij*d*. ad parochiam.
[Stacy and J. Trynte chosen Wardens, but their Account has been cut out.]

[1] Probably both picture and text touching the Visitation.

PAGE 93.   **A.D. mcccc.**   [No other date.]

J. BOLLE AND J. TREYNTE, WARDENS, after Stacy and Trynte. The only receipts this year are from the two taverns, the bakehouse, and the cow.

EXPENSES.

It. pro una mappa empta ad altum altare.	ixs. iiijd.
It. allowyde J. Treynte pro taberna.	iiijs. vijd.

PAGE 94.   **mcccc.**

T. STACY AND T. HOPKYNS, WARDENS, after Bolle and Trynte.

It. pro trigintalibus [anniversary] tenentibus per annum	xijd.

PAGE 95.   **mcccc.**

T. STACY AND PERRYS [PETER] BYRKYLL, WARDENS, after Stacy and Hopkyns.

EXPENSES.

It. pro le wyllyng [levelling] of the walete	iiijd.

PAGE 96.   [No date.]

J. BOLLIS AND W. LAURANCE, WARDENS, after Stacy and Byrkyll.

It. pro pane benedicto	vs. ixd.

EXPENSES.

It. pro le sylyng ecclesie .	ijs. ixd.
It. pro pictura alti crucis .	vjs. vijd.
It. pro pictatione alti crucis et pro cilatione supra	£iiij xld.
It. pro pictatione unius mappe	ijs. iiijd.
It. pro factura le cylyng .	xvs.

RECEIPTS.

It. pro una taberna servicie vendita in festo SS. Philip et Jacobi	xs.
It. pro domo pistrinarii .	xjs. iiijd.
It. pro pane benedicto .	vs. ixd.

PAGES 98–9.

12 H. VII.   **A.D.**   1496–7.

T. STACY AND T. HOPKYNS, WARDENS.

RECEIPTS.

It. pro vj bras. pandox. [private brewings in Church-house]	ijs.
It. pro patella enea apud domum pandoxeterii .	xd.

EXPENSES.

It. pro emendatione j shete dicti pandoxeterii .	iijd.
It. pro cccc arundineti pro emendatione dicti pandoxeterii	ixs. iiijd.

PAGES 100, 101.   [Blank.]

13 H. VII. ❡.𝔇. 1497–8.
T. Stacy and R. Stacy, Wardens.
Receipts.

Et de brasina ... in domo pandoxeterii, viz., W. Newman viij*d*., R. Bole viij*d*., R. Browne viij*d*., J. Rychards viij*d*., W. Predel viij*d*., hoc anno . . . iij*s*. iiij*d*.

PAGE 103.   EXPENSES.

It. in dabero, wallero, et frethero la sperys [dauber, waller, wreather of the spars] emend. dicte domus . . . . iiij*s*. viij*d*.
It. empt. j sakeryng bell . . . . ij*d*.
It. in emendatione unius domus vocate la olde bakehouse . . . . xiiij*s*. iij*d*.

PAGE 1.
[Owing to misbinding the next account is found at the beginning of the book. Pages 104 *et seq*., originally left blank, have been scribbled on later.]

14 Hen. VII. 1498–9.
Rob. Bole and Jo. Trent, after Stacy and Stacy.
Receipts.

3 Ales and 8 private brewings.
Panis ecclesiasticus, twice.   12 rings, gold and silver.

PAGE 2.   EXPENSES. [Customary ones.]
In stipendio Rob. Browne et jaole ? iiij*d*. . . . [Not balanced.]

15 Hen. VII. ❡.𝔇. 1499–1500.
Same Wardens.
Receipts.

De redditu domus pistrina . . . . . xj*s*. iij*d*.
 "   "   " voc. olde Bakehowse . . . . iij*s*.
 "   " ecclesiæ voc. Morelese ij ann. . . . xviij*d*.

Expenses.

customary, except escura [scouring] fossati et frething sepes [making hedges] apud old bakehowse . . . . ij*d*.

PAGE 5.   15–16 H. VII. (A.D.) 1500–1.
R. BOLE AND J. TRENT, WARDENS.

PAGE 6.   16–17 H. VII.
J. TRENT AND T. BROWNE, WARDENS.
RECEIPTS.
It. de incremento panis benedicti distrient [*sic*] per totam parochiam
[An inventory of Church goods and vestments in store.]

PAGE 7.   17–18 H. VII. (A.D.) 1501–2.
T. BROWNE AND W. NEWMAN, WARDENS.
EXPENSES.

It. for a quit rent for the church house	ij*d*. ob.
It. for cloth for ij awter clothys paynted by J. Stacy and J. Trent	xix*d*.
It. for cloth bowght for iij corpores	x*d*.
It. for a bottel for too ffett [fetch] wyne for the hye awter . .	viij*d*.
It. allowyd to W. Rychards for bakyng for the church . .	vj*d*.

PAGE 8.
Et notandum est quod preter summas predictas debentur ecclesie tres summa
  pecuniarum perquisitarum de incremento trium brasinarum de communi dono
  parachianorum, quarum prima vendita est per manus Johannis Trent et Stacy,
  et adduxerunt de incremento . . . . xxxvj*s*. viij*d*.
Secunda per manus W. Prydell et J. Bawnton et adduxerunt de incremento . xiiij*s*. x*d*.
Tertia per manus Thome Stacy et T. Hopkyns et adduxerunt de incremento . xj*s*. iiij*d*.

18–19 H. VII. (A.D.) 1503–4.
T. BROWN AND J. BAMPTON, WARDENS.
RECEIPTS.

It. de pastura pertinente domui pandoxaterii	ix*d*.
It. de W. Prydell pro una brasina brasiata in domo pandoxaterii hoc anno	viij*d*.

PAGE 9.   EXPENSES.

It. clerico ecclesie pro monstratione vexille apud Yevelchester ex consuetudine	ij*d*. ob.
It. in expensis apud Kyngesbury[1] pro consecratione ij corperalium hoc anno .	iiij*d*.
It. in denariis ballivo domini pro r[edditu] domus pistrine	xij*d*.

[1] The nearest Episcopal Manor. Bishop King was probably in residence there.

It. in denariis ballivo predicto pro r[edditu] domus pandoxaterii . . . . xij*d*.
[Among the stock.] una toga ex dono Alicie Stacy et unum linthiamen pro imagine beate Marie Virginis ex dono dicte Alicie.

PAGE 10.   ## Hen. VII. 19–20. 1503–4.
JOHN BAMPTON AND JOHN BREMELCOMBE, WARDENS.

PAGE 11.   ## Hen. VII. 20–21. 1504–5.
WILLIAM PREDYLL AND JOHN BREMILCOMBE, WARDENS.

Hen. VII. 21–2. 1505–6.
WILLIAM PREDYLL AND THOS. JENTTYLL, WARDENS.

PAGES 12–13.   ## Hen. VII. 22–3. 1506–7.
THOS. HOPKYNS AND T. JENTTYLL, WARDENS.
EXPENSES.

It. paid for iij awter clothys . . . . viij*d*.
It. for makyng and gyltyng of a chalyce with costs made in the puttyng owt of the said warke, ponderat. xxj unc. et dim. . . . . xlvij*s*. vj*d*.
[A standing crop given by T. Predyll; charge for harvesting 18*d*.]

PAGE 14.   ## 23–24 H. VII. 𝔸.𝔻. 1507–8.
T. HOPKYNS AND J. HOREWOODE, WARDENS.
RECEIPTS.

Pro una vacca vendita donata per Elizabeta Prydell . . . x*s*.
It. de legato W. Borow . . . . xij*d*.

EXPENSES.
For a new dext (desk) for the quere . . . . ij*s*
It. for costs done att the halowynge of the bellys and of the High Awter . . vij*s*. x*d*.
It. for adraw3tt maade for the sakerment with a coffer for the seide draw3tt, and fore the oyle vaatt . . . . ij*s*.
It. for yryn warke for the closure of the same and off the vautte . . . xx*d*.
It. for a roller to bere the [?] ewell at the Hyge Awter and for a cover to the vautte . xviij*d*.
It. for makynge of a frenge with bottyns [buttons] and tassels to a kerchew to hang over the sakerment . . . . ij*s*. viij*d*.

It. for mendyng of a sakeryng bell . . . . ob.
It. for mendyng of the vessells at the all [ale] house . vj*d*.
PAGE 15.
It. for mendyng of the arche at the chawncell door.
Et remanet de stauro antiquo ecclesie in manibus custodum de novo electorum.
[INVENTORY].
In primis, ij crewetts off sylver.
It. one gurdell with bokell and pendent of silver.
It. a peyre off beeds
It. one rynge ex dono Elizabet Prydell.
It. iiij*d*. [*i.e.*, a groat].
It. one pane [pan] appreciat. ad vs. viij*d*. ex dono Anisie Booles.
It. una vacca ex dono ejusdem Anisie.

PAGE 16.   A.D. 1510–11.   [2 Hen. VIII.]
J. HOREWODE AND W. SMI3TH, WARDENS.
Among the receipts.
It. for ij leggs[1] in the more . . . ix*d*.
EXPENSES.
It. for stuffe for mendyng off the mace [*i.e.*, mass] book, for wrytyng off the Kalender
    in the same . . . . iiij*s*.
It. in partte of payment for howsing of owr lady . . . . . iij*s*. iiij*d*.
To the Skynner of Kyngesbury ffor v queyres off velume p'c x*d*. . . . iiij*s*. ij*d*.
To Nowbyll ffor xvij queyres at x*d*.
To Cockes of Baltsborow ffor v queyres att xj*d*.
It. for v queyres for a greyyll . . . . v*s*. vij*d*.
It. for pryckyng, wrytyng and lymynyng [illuminating] of ye v queyres vj*s*. viij*d*.
It. for vj querys of velum at x*d*.
[See also Ao. 1511–1512.] For Velum for ye portuas and a greyyll . . xxij*s*. iiij*d*.
For pryckyng, wrytyng, and lymenyng of vj queyres . . . . . viij*s*. viij*d*.

PAGE 18.   A.D. [2]1511–2.
WILL. SMY3TH AND JAMES STACY, WARDENS, after Horewode and Smyth.
[Nothing unusual.]

PAGE 19.   A.D. [2]1511–2.
JAMES STACY, AND JOHN SMY3TH, WARDENS, after Smyth and Stacy.
Expenses. To carpenter for sawyng of tymber for seettys [seats] for ye churche and
    for cuttyng and framyng partt of ye same . . . . xxxiij*s*. iiij*d*.

[1] Allotments, shapen like a leg and foot, *i.e.*, one strip at right angles to the other, are still called "legs." These same pieces in later accounts, being let for leasing, are called leazes, leeses, &c.

[2] One of these dates must be wrong. Owing to the official year now beginning on Passion Sunday which might be before or after Lady Day, then the first day of the civil year, there was ample room for error.

PAGE 20.   **A.D.** 1512–3.   4 Hen. VIII.
J. SMYTH AND W. WHELER, WARDENS.
RECEIPTS.

[An Ale as usual on SS. Philips and James and S. Margaret's Day.]
It. off Robine Hoods All [Ale] only this once . . . . xjs.
It. a Jacobo Stacy per manus rectoris · . . . . . . viijs. xjd.
It. a Johanne Trentt for the oolde seets of the church . . . vs. iiijd.

EXPENSES.

It. carpentario for makyng of the segs [seats] . . vjd. viijd.
It. carpentario pro eodem opere . . . . . xls.

PAGE 26.   **A.D.** 1518–9.
W. PRYDELL AND J. HOPKYNS,[1] WARDENS.
[From Passion Sunday to Passion Sunday.]
RECEIPTS.

It. ex legatione Johannis Stacy . . . . xvjs.
It. ab executoribus ejusdem pro loco sepulture ejus in ecclesia [earliest entry] . vjs. viijd.

PAGE 27.

[Some details of repairs to the churchyard wall on the east side and a stonyn[2] door.]
It. paid for viij loode of stone from the hyle . . . . . . xvjd.
It. paid for ij loode from the castell [*i.e.*, ruins of Montacute Castle]. . . . xijd.

PAGE 28.

[A note that 3 leggs in the moor are allotted to the bakehouse and 3 to the brewhouse].

From **A.D.** 1519–1532.
[Very little change in the entries.]

---

[1] The addition to the Tower belongs to this Wardenship.
[2] A doorcase, still standing in the west wall of churchyard, but unused.

22–23 H. VIII. Lady Day, A.D. 1531 to Lady Day, 1532.

J. PRYDELL AND R. BROUN, WARDENS.

Special contributions to building the Church-house.
De Thoma priore Montis acuti ac rectore ibidem . . . . . . xxs.
De W. Newman vjs. vij*d*.; De J. Underway, iijs. iiij*d*.; De W. Bolerde, iijs. iiij*d*.; De T. Prydell, iijs. iiij*d*.; De J. Dollynge iijs. ii*j*d.; De J. Prydell, xx*d*.; De J. Bampton, xx*d*.; De W.Wheler, xij*d*.; De J. Rychard, ijs. iiij*d*.; De W. Smyth, xx*d*.; De W. Gyll, xij*d*.; De S. Towker, xij*d*.; De J. Burne, xij*d*.; De R. Broun, xij*d*.; Summa, lijs. iiij*d*.; [Payments for stone and labour follow. Total £iiij vijs. vj*d*.]

PAGE 21.

A.D. 1513–4.

W. WHELER AND JOHN STACY, WARDENS.

RECEIPTS.

It. de Thoma Tokar pro redditu domus sue .	. xv*d*.
It. a diversis pro brewing at the All [Ale] howse	ijs. vj*d*.

EXPENSES.

It. laid owt at the Churche alle at Montague for the deffawtt of apparance of owr neybars	. xx*d*.
It. for pavyng of the churche . . .	. xviij*d*.
It. for blessyng of a pair of vestments	. ij*d*.
It. for ij peire of crewetts .	. xx*d*.

PAGE 22.

A.D. 1514–15.

JOH. STACEY AND JOH. PYCHER, WARDENS.

[From Passion Sunday to ye same day.]

W. Wheler de industria sua obtulit pro pictura Altaris ex parte australi	. xs. j*d*.
W. Ootts obtulit ad idem opus	. xs. j*d*.

PAGE 23.   **A.D.** 1515–6.   7 Hen. VIII.
J. PYCHER AND J. TOKAR, WARDENS.
RECEIPTS.

It. de pecuniis collectis in vigilia Epiphanie . . . . . . ijs. iiijd.

EXPENSES.

It. payd to the paynter at one tyme (fil cum syr[1]) . . . xvjs. ixd.
It. eidem similr. . . . . xxiiijs. ixd.
It. for payntyng of the kynggs crowne[2] . . . . . ijd.
It. for honggyng of the clothys at the low awters . . . . . vjd.
It. for clarifyyng of olde wexe—and for takyng of ye tapers to for the crosse . iijd.

PAGE 24.   **A.D.** 1516–7.
J. TOKAR AND W. OOTTS, WARDENS.
EXPENSES.

It. apud Stooke, Montegow, and Chilthorn, at their churche ayles . . vjd.
It. for clothe to mend the low awter clothys . . . . . . ixd.
It. dat. in regardo pictori for Seynt Nicholas awter . . . . iijs. iiijd.
It. for clothe of heere [hair] for the low awters . . . . . . ijs. ijd.

[On a half page, sewn in, is a rough statement of the "makyng off West wyndow yn the towre," for raising the tower and adding a turret staircase. The rector received £3 13s. 4d. from Warden Hopkyns, and with other aids completed the work. The masons' wages, paid weekly whilst working on le Sterr=£10 10s.]

PAGE 25.   **A.D.** 1517–8.
W. OOTTS AND W. PRYDELL, WARDENS.
[The copes are repaired and new coloured.]

PAGE 116.

23–24 H. VIII. Lady Day, 1532, to Lady Day, 1533.

J. HOPKYNS AND J. DOLLYNG, WARDENS.

[Among the revenue items are rents "veteris pandoxaterii," and "pandoxaterii," *i.e.*, the new Church-house with its bakehouse and brewhouse.]

[1] ? The son with the sire.   [2] On one of the pictures or images.

PAGES 117-120.

From Lady Day, 24th Hen. VIII, to Lady Day, 25th Hen. VIII.
THOMAS AND JOHN PRYDELL, WARDENS.

Lady Day, 25th Hen. VIII, to Lady Day, 26th Hen. VIII.
THOMAS PRYDELL AND JOHN BAMPTON, WARDENS.

[On a fly leaf, pinned to p. 119, are two supplements to this account, containing the following Bill of particulars transcribed in full.]

SUMPTUS T. PRYDELL.

Item for ij loade off store stonys	ij$s$. iiij$d$.
„ the helyng stonys fett [fetched] at Hardyngton for the porch	vs. iiij$d$.
„ making of the bartin wall	vs. viij$d$.
, costyge [costs, costagia] at Visitation	. xx$d$.
„ borde naylys	. ij$d$.
., beryng of y^e banner	. ij$d$. ob.
„ frankynsens	ob
., ye paschall taper	ij$s$. iiij$d$.
„ one bawdry	xiiij$d$.
	xviij$s$. xj$d$.

SUMPTUS J. BAWNTON.

Item payd to plumr. for mendyng lede of Chyrche . .	. vj$s$.
„ helyer for y^e coveryng of y^e porche	. vs.
„ for lyme	. ix$d$.
„ Bell ropys	. iij$s$.
.. wex for y^e trendyll	vj$d$. ob.
„ sope	iij$d$. ob.
,. lathys to cover y^e porche	. xd.
„ lathys nayls	. vd.
	xvij$s$. xj$d$.

Summa hujus billæ . . . xxxiij$s$. xd.

PAGE 121.

28-29 H. VIII. A.D. 1537-8.
P. TOUKER AND R. BROWNE, WARDENS.

RECEIPTS.

It. de redditu unius pistrine hoc anno	xj$s$. iiij$d$.
It. de redditu unius cottagii dimissi A. Domytt	. xv$d$.
It. de redditu unius camere in domo pistrine dimisse Agnete Cocke . .	. viij$d$.

[Next Wardens, R. and W. Gelle. Accounts missing.]

PAGE 125.

29–30 H. VIII. A.D. 1538–9.

J. BURFORDE AND T. PRYDELL, WARDENS, after Touker and Brown.

RECEIPTS.

It. receperunt de incremento panis benedicti hoc anno ex antiqua consuetudine . . . iiij*s*. iij*d*.
It. de domino[1] Episcopo Solubrensi ad sustentationem unius paris vestimentorum empt. . . . . xiij*s*. iiij*d*

PAGE 126.   EXPENSES.

It. carpentario ad faciendum finem operis domus ecclesie, viz., silarium ibidem . xj*s*. iiij*d*

PAGE 129.

30–31 H. VIII.

J. BURFORD AND T. PRYDELL, WARDENS.

[Besides the usual Ales.]

It. de venditione unius cerevicie in quarta septimana Quadragesime ut per sacramentum dictorum computantum . . . . xiij*s*. iiij*d*.
[List of 39 Subscribers ad sustentationem campanarum empt. hoc anno.]
[Next 20*s*., by John Hopkyns, senior, and the rest range from 13*s*. 4*d*. and 6*s*. 8*d*. to 4*d*.]
It. cvij lib. [of bell metal] de parochianis de Clowesworth hoc anno (eis ?) venditis
  [*i.e.*, old bells sold to Closworth] . . . . . . £vij *vs*. iiij*d*.
        Summa . . . £xv ix*s*. v*d*.

PAGE 130.   EXPENSES.

It. pro le cage campanarum de novo plena solutione . . . . lxviij*s*. iiij*d*.
It. Roberto Cuffe de Yelchester pro duobus campanis ab ipso emptis hoc anno . £xx.

PAGE 132.

31–32 H. VIII. A.D. 1540–1.

J. PRYDELL AND W. GYLL, WARDENS, after Burford and Prydell.

De festo Annunciat.

RECEIPTS.

De dono Thome Solubriensis Episcopi in augmentationem camp. hoc anno   vj*s*. viij*d*.
It. de Johanne pro occupatione domus ecclesie hoc anno . . . . . xij*d*.
It. de J. Broke   Ditto   Ditto . . . . . . xij*a*.
It. de J. Cuffe   Ditto   le Bruerne hoc anno . . . . . viij*d*.

[1] Thomas Chard, Prior of Montacute, Rector of Tintinhull, by the Act of Appropriation in 1521. He had been consecrated in 1508 for Suffragan Service by a title "in partibus."

PAGE 133.   EXPENSES.

Jo. Apsey, carpentario, tam ad deponendum iiij campanas quam ad levandum, necnon pro laboribus super ad emendandum campanas in clastico hoc anno.

It. Johanni Belluter[1] pro factura quatuor campanarum hoc anno . . . . xlvijs.

[Smaller items about the bells, and buying oaks for finishing the tower roof.]

PAGE 135. 32–33 H. VIII. Ⱥ.Ⅎ. 1541–2.

J. HOPKYNS THE ELDER, AND J. HOPKYNS THE YOUNGER, WARDENS.[2]

[The only receipts are from two Ales, two tenants for rent of the bakehouse, pasture in the moor, and for the rent of a little voyd place of ground in the churchyard.]

And for the increase of the holy loffe this year . . . . . . iiijs. iijd.

[The expenses include still, but somewhat irregularly, outlay for wax, for holy taper and trendel, but there have not been any special collections for them since about A.D. 1485.]

PAGE 136.   EXPENSES.

For our new clocke this year bought . . . xxxiijs. iiijd.
It. for the halfe price of the Bible this year bought . vjs. vd.

PAGE 138. 33–34 H. VIII. Ⱥ.Ⅎ. 1542–3.

Same Wardens.

RECEIPTS.

Of the vycary for the chamber in the bakehouse . . . viijd.
Of the increase of the holy loffe . . . . iiijs. iijd.
Of the bequest of Margery Trott for her knell to be rongge . iiijd.

[A new entry.]

PAGE 139.   EXPENSES.

[A new Pascal taper is bought, and the Trendel renewed twice.]

It. for the expenses of the wardens, and others called[3] by the Byssop and his Mynister iij tymes . . . . xviijd.
It. for a chayne to hold the Bible . . . . iijd.
It. a cope and a surplice bought.

---

[1] Called also Bellman. He cast the bells at Chiselborough.
[2] The first account presented wholly in English.
[3] Summoned to testify to Wardens' presentments at Visitation Court, as testes synodales or Sidesmen.

PAGE 141.   1 Ed. VI. **A.D.** 1547–8.
RIC. HOGG AND SYBIL SMYTH, WARDENS.
[The usual entries.]
PAGE 142.   Paid for three visitations.
A cote, undercote, and ijs. is given in alms to J. Bremblecombe.
[A new entry.]
PAGE 143.   Three knells and a burial paid for.

24–25 Hen. VIII. 1533–4.
THOS. AND J. PRYDELL, WARDENS.

25–26 Hen. VIII. 1534–5.
PRYDELL AND J. BAMPTON, WARDENS.

26–27 Hen. VIII. 1535–6.
[No record.]

27–28 Hen. VIII. 1536–7.
[No record.]

[Blank.]

---

38 Hen. VIII and 1 Edw. VI. 1547–8.
RICH. HOGG AND SYBIL SMYTH, WARDENS.

PAGE 143.
ROB. PYCHER AND JOHN DOLLYNG, WARDENS, who follow Hogg and Smyth, 1st of Edw. VI.
[No account.]

JOHN DOLLYNG AND ROGER SERVE.   No date.
[Probably 1557–8.]

PAGE 144. [No date.]
PETER TOWKER AND JOHN DOLLYNG, WARDENS.

Received of Jo. Pryddell and Jo. Stybbs . . . . . . xlvj*s*.
     Balance . . . £x vj*s*.
It from a St. Margaret's ale, a May's ale (*i.e.*, the old SS. Philip and James' ale), the Moor leaze.
It. from T. Bawnton for the Church house . . . . . . viij*s*.
It. of T. Hopkyns for part of the same howse . . . . viij*d*.
It. of my neyghbor Roger for the occupying of the Church howse . . viij*d*.

1558. ROGER SERY AND ROBERT HOSTLER, WARDENS.

1559. NAMES OF WARDENS AND BALANCES.

HOPKYNS AND TUCKER .   lj*s*.

PAGE 145.   [Blank.]

PAGE 146.[1]

11 Eliz. [The Annunciation is the Day of Account.]
W. HOPKYNS AND R. BROWNE, WARDENS.
RECEIPTS.

From two Ales   vj*s*. viij*d*.

EXPENSES.
£vj xiij*s*. ix*d*.
   Balance . . . £xiij xiiij*s*. iij*d*.
   ['The barest summary of totals.]

[1] Irregular entries. No audit sheet till p. 148, in 1568.

Morebath.

The records of this upland parish, lying within the borders of Devon, were selected for publication.

(1). Because extracts from them were presented by the then Vicar, Mr. Berkeley, to the Somerset Archæological Society in 1883, and printed in the Proceedings.

(2). Because the manor and the rectorial tithes formed part of the endowment of the neighbouring Priory of Barlynch in Somerset.

(3). Because of the intrinsic value of the entries, compiled as they were, by one person, viz., the Vicar, Sir Christopher Trychay, who being instituted in 1520, and living till 1574[1], saw *all* the fluctuations, which befell the ritual which he had cherished with the utmost zeal.

(4). Because of the intricacy of the organization and of some peculiar features.

The present Vicar, Mr. Binney, is now engaged in transcribing the whole document, which, being in loose portions greatly needs arrangement, and also annotation from local knowledge. In the belief that he will be able to give the record a more perfect rendering in a separate publication, it has been thought best to produce here, only such extracts as serve to display special features of the

Fiscal System.

The noteworthy features were:—

1. The number of Stores, each in the interest of a separate devotion, supported by an associate body, with a separate balance sheet, audit-day and feast-day, the audit sometimes held by separate Wardens, sometimes by the High-Wardens. There were no less than eight separate accounts.

(1) Of St. George (the patron of the church); (2) Of the Store of Jesus; (3) Of our Lady; (4) St. Sidwell, *i.e.*, S. Ceadwold; (5) St. Antony; (6) The Alms light; (7) The Young Men, sometimes called Gromen, *i.e.*, Grooms; (8) The Maidens.

2. The large amount of sheep belonging to these stores, and the detailed insight into their management.

3. The appointment of a supernumerary body varying in number from three to nine, acting as controllers "for the governance of the Churche Stocke."[2]

---

[1] His burial is recorded at the end of his book. He had resigned some little time earlier.

[2] This body, which is designated by no other name than the 3 men or 4 men, or whatever number it contained for the year, was probably in existence before 1520. It was elected by the parishioners, and accounted to them for the funds received from the various stores, and applied them as may be seen in the printed

4. The resort to Setts[1], *i.e.*, voluntary rates, to clear off debt or to meet voluntary outlays for the benefit of the community, *e.g.*, repair of Ex Bridge and Hucley Bridge.

5. The mode of collecting Peter's pence.

6. The mode of supporting the Parish Clerk.

In other respects, the funds were raised by the usual means, viz., a Churchhouse and ales; gifts and bequests; livestock, such as bees and pigs; special collections for emergencies, once by an Easter play.

The spirit of self-help was very evident. In 1534, when a silver chalice was stolen from the Church, "ye yong men and maydyns of ye parysse dru them selffe togethers and w^t there gyfts and provysyon the bofth (bought) yn another challis w^t owt ony chargis of ye parysse." 81 donors raising 30*s*. In 1538-9, in spite of the warnings of the coming changes a special effort was made to buy a new cope, for which the subscribers paid £3. 6*s*. 8*d*. " and the Churche at no charge."

This spirit was strongly nurtured by the Vicar, who from 1528 onwards, gave his rights of wooltithe accruing from the Church-flock towards the purchase of a suit of black vestments obtained at last at the cost of £6. 5*s*. in 1547.

Owing to the long incumbency of the Vicar, this is one of the most perfect records extant of the ritual revolutions. In most cases the disorder of the times confused the administration of the parish, or made the officers afraid of recording it, or led to the cutting out of pages. Two lists of vestments are printed below, to illustrate the methods employed on the one side by the spoilers, and on the other side by the guardians, of the endangered articles.

The following facts found in the Wardens' Account of 1537 are worthy of note :—

The Priory of Barlynch, with the manor and rectory of Morebath, passed into the hands of Hugh Powlett as lessee. The new Lord saved out of the wreck of the Priory Chapel a window, which he bestowed in its entirety, stone, glass and iron, on Morebath Church, valuing the gift at £3,[2] and bargaining that he should receive in return the prayers of that church. He left the parish to pay the costs of removal.

He seems to have been a close follower of his royal master, in applying the fruits of spoliation to securing for himself the credit of a benefactor and the spiritual benefits which he still believed to be obtainable by bounty to the Church.

N.B.—The language throughout is English with Latin sentences and notes interlarded, as in Leland and other writers who were used to recite Latin offices.

The Editor is obliged to rely on Messrs Berkeley's and Bennett's transcripts, for faithful rendering of the original, which has never been in his hands.

---

account. In the disputes about the Clerkship in 1536, it was accredited by the Visitation Court *pro re nata* but its relation to the High Wardens as well as its original cause of existence is left undefined. Probably the multiplicity of "Stores" with their conflicting claims and interests, led to the appointment of this unusual board.

[1] When the involuntary "Sett" comes in, it is collected not by the Wardens, but by the Civil Officer, the Tything-man. *See* p.   .

[2] The parish valued it at £2.

EXTRACTS.

1. The Bederoll.
2. The High Wardens' Account. 1526-7.
3. The 5 Men's Account. 1526-7.
4. The Alms-light Account. 1526-7.
5. Saint Sonday's Store Account.
6. Settlement of Clerk's Maintenance.
7. Lists of Vestments. 1549 and 1552.

The Bederoff.

Orate pro animabus sequentibus.

N.B.—Mem. that here after schall ye see and knoo how this churche was prevaylyd by the dethe of all those persons that here after ys expressyd by name, the wyche all and synguler gefts was gewyn and bequevyd unto this churche syn y Sir Chrystofer Trychay was made vicar here, the wyche was Anno Domini 1520, 30 die mensis Augusti et in eo anno dextera dominus exaltavit me cujus anime propitietur Deus. Amen.

Primo. A.D. 1520.

JOHN HUCLY and RICHARD WEBBER, was Hye Wardyns of this churche and how this churche was prevaylyd by there wardyng scheppe [Wardenship] and by there tyme now schall ye see.

Jamys Radnynche gave a coppe to this churche for the wyche was ressevyd . xxj*d*.

A.D. 1521.

Was Hye Wardyns of this churche RIC. HUCLY and WYLMOTT AT TYMEWELL, and how this church was prevaylyd by there tyme now schall ye se.

Alsyn Hucly gave to this churche . . , , . viij*d*.
Christina Hurly, ecclesie . . . , . xij*d*.
Dominus Robertus Williams, ecclesie . . . . . . iiij*d*.
Johannes More, filius Galfridi More, ecclesie . . , . . . xx*d*.

John Norman at cowrte payd vj*s*. viij*d*. for hys wyffes grave coram parochianos anno predicto.

A.D. 1522.

Was Hye Wardyns of this church WILLIAM ROBBYNS and THOMAS BORRAGE, and how this church, [&c., as before.]

W. Rumbelow gave to the Store of Sent Jorge a scheppe for the wyche was ressevyd xij*d*.
It. he bequevyd agayn to the almys ly3th another scheppe for the wyche was ressevyd xvj*d*.
It. he gave agayn to the store of owr laydy a scheppe for the wyche was ressevyd . xij*d*.
It. he bequevyd another scheppe to the store of Sent Antoni for the wyche was ressevyd xij*d*.
Thomas Tymwell at hayne gave to the store of owr laydy of this churche a scheppe
    for the wyche was ressevyd . . . . . xvj*d*.

A.D. 1523.

Was Hye Wardyns of this churche JEKYN AT MORE and JAC. TYMEWELL and how this Churche was prevaylyd by the dethe of any man by there tyme now schall ye see.

Margeria Lake gave to this churche in wex	vs.
It. sche gave agayn a awter clothe to Sent Sydwyll ys awter, and a bassyn of latyn to sett ly3th on afore Sent Sydwyll, prise of all	ijs.
Edward Trychay gave to the Churche for his knyll	iiijd.
Johan at yaye . . . for her knyll	iiijd.
William Rowswell gave to the churche to be prayed for	iijs. iiijd.

A.D. 1524.

JOHN MORSE AND HARRY HURLEY, WARDENS, &c., as before.

And yf ye be yn any dowte of any man his gefth loke what [y]ere that ye wyll have and loke apon that acownte and there schall ye a see playnly what proffyth this churche toke by the dethe of any man.

Jekyn at More gave yn to this churche to dress Sent Sydwyll ys awter withall a pere of awter clothys ypayntyd and a bassyn of latyn that the Almys ly3th how doth stonde yn before the hye crosse, all in valew	xiijs. iiijd.
and he lay in the quyr, where for the persson and my patrone[1] ressevyd	vjs. viijd.

A.D. 1525.

JOHN GOODMAN AND THOMAS NORMAN, WARDENS, &c., &c.

Thomas Zaer gave to the store of Sent Jorge of this churche a scheppe for the wyche was ressevyd	xjd.
It. he gave another scheppe to the Almys ly3th for wyche was rec.	xiiijd.
It. he gave agayn another to owr laydys store	xijd.
William Don gave to this churche to be prayed for	xxd.
It. he gave agayn to stande afore owr laydy a taper, prisse of	xijd.
And of this W. Don ys gefte hyt spekyth not of yn John Goodmans acownte	

A.D. 1526.

JOHN WATERUS AND JOHN NORMAN AT COWRTE, WARDENS, &c., &c.

Alicia Oblye servant Thome Zaer (conda conda[2]) gave to the store of Sent Jorge	iiijd.
It. sche gave to the store of Jhu	iiijd.
It. sche dyde bequeffe agayn to the store of Sent Sydwyll	iiijd.
It. sche gave agayn to the Almys ly3th	ijd.
John Holcum gave to this churche a Lent clothe ypayntyd, a Roode clothe ypayntyd, and a sepulture clothe ypayntyd, prisse of all	xs.
Johannes Holcum major filius predicti Johannis Holcum gave to the store of Jhu	iiijd.

---

[1] Barlynch Priory, rector and patron.   [2] Quondam. See below sæpe.

It. he gave agayn to the store of Sent Sydwyll a scheppe, for wyche ressevyd . . xvj*d*
Thomas Holcum filius predicti Johannis Holcum gave unto this Churche a super-alta[1]
    yblessyd, prisse . . . . ijs. iiij*d*
Johan Holcum filia predicti Johannis Holcum gave unto the store of owr laydy . iiij*d*.
John Hurley gave unto the store of Jhu . . . . iiij*d*.
It. he gave agayn unto Sent Sydwyll . . . . viij*d*.
It. he gave to owr laydy . . . . iiij*d*.

Vicar's gifts at divers times.
{ Dominus Christoferus Trychay conda [quondam] istius ecclesie vicarii the
    furst ere that he was made vicar here he gave yn Sent Sydwyll and payd for
    her makyn and gyltyng . . . . xxxiijs. iiij*d*.
It. by thys foresayd wardyns tyme he payd for the glassyng of the sowth west
    wyndow in the quyre . . . . xs.
It. agayn by hys devotion and his peryssen[2] was payd for the tabyllment of
    Sent Sydwyll xl and viijs. iiij*d*. [48s. 4*d*.]
It. agayn this foresayd Sir Christofer payd for on pere [one pair] of the sute of
    white vestments . . . . xiijs. iiij*d*.
And all this foresayd he gave to this churche thoff [though] hyt apear not apon
    the cownte of this ere.

A.D. 1527.

WILLIAM AT POLE AND GEFFERY SMY3TH, WARDENS, &c.

Benefits received by the dethe of any man, or by the quycke.
John Tymewell at Hayne gave to the store of Jhu iij scheppe, prisse . . . iijs.
The wych scheppe was gevyn to this entent to mayntayn ly3th afore the fugar [figure]
    of Jhu and yn this entent the peryssyn [parishioners] hathe ressevyd this scheppe
    and doth entende to fynde [allot] the encressyng of the scheppe to the same
    entent.

A.D. 1528.

MARGYT AT BORSTON AND RICHARD RAW, WARDENS, &c.

torne [turn] over lyffe.
William at Pole vel potter gave his part of beys [bees] that rested with John Morsse
    at his departyn, to the store of Jhu to mayntayn a lamppe barnyg afore the
    fugar of Jhu, and afore Sent Sydwyll every prinssipall feste yn the ere, to barne
    from the furste ensong [evensong] untyll hys masse be don the morow, the wyche
    beys ware yn valure at William at Pole ys departyng . . . . ijs. viij*d*.
It. he gave agayn to the store of Sent Antony a scheppe for wyche was ressevyd . xij*d*.
Also to the store of Jhu a sheep, & . . . . xij*d*.
Also to the Almys light a sheep, & . . . . xij*d*.
  ,, to the store of Owr Laydy a sheep, & . . . . xij*d*.
It. he dyd bequeffe agayn to a new image of owr laydy . . . . vjs. viij*d*.

---

[1] *I.e.*, a slab for a side altar.   [2] Parishioners.

It. for hys grave for he lyeth yn the almatory	vjs. viijd.
Geffery More gave to the store of Jhu a scheppe for wyche was ressevyd	xijd.
It. to the store of owr laydy a sheep, &	xijd.
He bequeathes to the store of S. George a lamb, &	vjd.
He gave to the store of S. Sydwyll ij sheep, &	ijs.

Johan Hyllyer of Bawnton gave to this Churche a banner ypayntyd of Sent Sydwyll in on syde and Sent Jorge yn the other syde, prisse of . . . . . xvjd.

It. sche gave agayn a canstycke of lattyn to stonde afore Sent Sydwyll, prisse . . vjd.

Apon the wyche canstycke sche doth mayntayn a taper before Sent Sydwyll trymmyd with flowrs to borne there every hye and prinscypall fests, this she dothe entende to mayntayne whyll sche lyvyth, gracia divina.

A.D. 1529.

THOMAS BORRAGE AND THOMAS TYMWELL AT COME, &c.

Summa actenus predict. gefts and bequests . . £xj iijs. vjd.

Thomas Trychay of Collumstoke gave unto the store of Jhu, and to the store of Sent Sydwyll a sworme of beys to mayntayne a taper before them, the wyche beys restyth now in John Morsse ys kepyng to halfe mone [money] and John Morsse schall fynde the botts [butts]. It. he payd agayn for on pere of the sute of whytte vestments, prisse of . . . . xiiijs.

Elnor Nicoll gave to the store of Jhu a lytyll sylver crosse perssyll [parcel] gylte of valure . . . . iiijd.

It. sche gave agayn to the store of Sent Sydwyll her weddyng ryng in valure . . viijd. the wyche ryng dyde hylppe make Sent Sydwyll ys scowys [shoes].[1]

Water More[2] a yong man gave to the store of S. Jorge					xxd.
,,	,,	,,	,,	of owr laydy	xxd.
,,	,,		bequeathed to that of Jhu		xxd.
,,	,,		,,	of Sent Sydwyll	xxd.
,,	,		,,	the Almys ly3th	iiijd.
John Tayler, aliter Josse, a yong man gave to the store of Jhu					xxd.
,,	,,	,,	,,	,, of Sent Sydwell	xxd.
,,	,,	,,	he bequethed to the store of owr laydy		viijd.
,,	,,	,,	,,	to the Almys ly3th	iiijd.

Thys ij gefts of Water More and John Tayler apperyth apon the cownte of the v men anno predicto.

---

[1] St. Sydwyll [Ceadwold]'s *shoes*. Compare the following passage from Bishop Hall's Fourth Satire:—
"Whoever gives *a paire of velvet shooes*
To th' *Holy Rood*, or liberally allowes
But a new rope to ring the couvrefeu bell,
But he desires that his great deed may dwell,
Or graven in the chancel window glass,
Or in his lasting tombe of plated brasse."

[2] One of the brotherhood of young men or grooms.

Christina Tymewell bequevyd her best gowne to helppe to bye a new image of owr laydy for the wyche gowne was ressevyd . . . . iiijs.

Johan Rumbelow made this churche her sector[1] to this entent that her goodds that were lefth when sche was brofth yn yerthe schulde be bestowyd apon a new image of owr laydy, so when sche was beryd and every thyng contendyd [settled] the vantage that this churche toke by her dethe was clere to helppe to by a new image . . . . xxjs.

Margarett Holcum gave to this church to helppe to by a new Sent Jorge . . . xxs.

It. sche gave agayn to helppe to new gylte Sent Sydwyll . . . . . vs.

It. for her grave for sche lyeth yn the almatory . . . . . . vjs. viijd.

Thys gefth must cum yn yn this next acownte over leve.

A.D. 1530.

JEKYN ISAAC AND WILLIAM TYMEWELL AT WODE, WARDENS, &c., &c.

Thomas Tymewell at Come to helppe to by the sutte of whytte vestments he gave . . . . xxvjs. viijd.

It. for hys grave for he lyeth yn the Almatory . . . . . . vjs. viijd.

And a scheppe to owr laydy, prisse . . . . xvjd.

He gave agayn to the Almys ly3th a scheppe, prisse . . . . . xxd.

       „   Sent Sonday a scheppe, prisse . . . . . xxd.

A pere of lyne [linen] auter clothys, prisse . . . . . . iiijs. iiijd.

A.D. 1531.

THOMAS RUMBELOW AND JOHN NORMAN AT WODE, WARDENS, &c.

Alsyn Zaer gave unto the store of Sent Sydwyll a pere of beds and a gurdyll for the wyche was ressevyd . . . . viijs. iiijd.

And for this mony was madyn Sent Sydwyll ys showys.

Christina Norman at Wode sche gave unto the store of Sent Jorge . . . xxd.

It. to the store of owr laydy a gurdyll for which rec. . . . . xiijs.

It. a lattyn canstycke of v ly3thys stondyng afore the fugar of Jhu, prisse of viijd. vjd.

It. a kercher to the store of S. Sydwyll, prisse . . . . . viijd.

It. another kercher to owr laydy, prisse . . . . vjd.

Also sche lyeth yn the almatory for the wyche grave there ys payd . . vjs. viijd.

              Summa actenus . . £xx.

William Robbyns a yong man gave to the Churche . . . . . iijs. iiijd.

It. he gave agayn a cotte [coat] for wyche was ressevyd . . . . xijd.

Alsyn Gupworthy gave to this churche . . . . iiijd.

Margytt Chasse   „   „ . . . . iiijd.

Johan Trychay the dofter of Leuys Trychay gave to the new image of owr laydy . iiijd.

---

[1] Executor, meaning legatee also; see in 1531 the like case of Kate Robyns, whose will was administered by the Wardens.

Johan Hucly, puella, and filia Richard Hucly sche gave a canstyke of v ly3thys to stonde afore the new image of owr laydy the wyche cost her fader . . viijs. vd.
And to the Almys ly3th . . . . iiijd.

A.D. 1532.

ROBERT AT HAYNE AND WILLIAM MORSSE, WARDENS, &c., &c.

William Robbyns gave unto thys churche a awter clothe payntyd of Sent Jorge, and a stremer payntyd of Sent Jorge yn bothe sydes. Also he gave a crucifix of Mary and John to make a pax? of. Summa in valure of this hyt cost . . . xvs.
Johan Trychay dyde bequeffe unto the store of Jhu and of Sent Sydwyll a bott of beys the wyche restyth with William Morsse.
Alsyn the dofter of Thomas Tymwell at come sche gave to the store of owr laydy a scheppe, and another to the Almys ly3th all in valur . . . . iijs.
Johan Greneway gave to this churche a corporas with a casse blessyd, yn valur iijs. iiijd.
Keteryn Robbyns gave and bequefyd and by her dethe this churche was v nobylls the better with the pall of satyn that was made yn her behalf [given to the parish after her burial.]

A.D. 1533.

RICHARD WEBBER, WILLIAM NORMAN AT LAWTON, WARDENS, &c., &c.

John Norman at Wode was buryed yn the yle before Sent Sydwyll the viij day of February anno predicto, fer wyche grave was payd . . . . vjs. viijd.
And he gave unto the Churche to help to by a pere of latyn cansticks with the grave mony . . . . xxvjs. viijd

A.D. 1534.

WILLIAM AT TYMWELL AND JOHN TAYLER, WARDENS, &c., &c.

Cecyly Tymwell at Hayne geve and bequeved to the churche her best gowne for the wyche gowne her husband Nicholas at Hayne brostch [brought] yn to this churche a awter clothe of sylke the prisse of xiijs. iiijd., and for his wyfe's grave . vjs. viijd.
Harry Hurly gave yn to Sent Sydwyll ys awter a pere of canstycks of latyn prisse . xxd.
John Don at Exbryge, a yong man, gave and bequeved to this churche a pellow of sylke, prisse of . . . . iijs. iiijd.
Christofer Morsse, filius W. Morsse, bequeved to this church . . . . iiijd.

A.D. 1535.

THOMAS BORRAGE AND WILLIAM LEDDON, WARDENS, &c., &c.

Richard Tymwell gave to the store of Jhu a ramme hogg, prisse of . . xd.

A.D. 1536.

Thomas at Tymwell and William Scely, Wardens, &c., &c.

Sir Edward Nicoll gave unto this churche a sepulture clothe ystaynyd to lay upon the [Easter] sepulture, prisse of . . . . vs. jd.

A.D. 1537.

Harry Hurly and John Hucly, Wardens, &c., &c.

John Webber and Christina Waterus, thys ij persons causyd the sylyng agaynst the syde awter to be madyn to there frendds costs to the savyng of awter clothys [by arresting dust, &c., falling from unceiled roof].

John Tristram at Bawnton, the lawer, gave a borde stoke to this churche, prisse of . xxd.

Annys Tymwell at Hayne gave to this church her gowne and a ryng, prisse of xijs., the whyche mony went to a coppe [cope].

Johan Tymwell at Wode gave to this churche her gowne and her gurdyll, prisse xiijs. iiijd., of the wyche mony ther was bestowyd in the [payntyng, partly crossed out] agaynst the hye awter and for the bords viijs. iiijd., the vs. went to a new cope.

John Morse gave to the tylyng of this churche with the nobyll for his grave . xxvjs. viijd.

John Goodman gave to the tylyng of this churche (what or with) his dofters gefte Christia, viij scheppe, and a lamme, prisse xiiijs. vjd., and this ij gefts payd for all this tylyng of the churche.

M. Hu Powlytt gave to this churche on of the glasse wyndows of Barlych with the yre and stone and all prisse . . . . xls.

William Hucly, the son of Richard Hucly, gave to this churche for his knyll . . iiijd.

A.D. 1538.

Thomas Norman and Richard Hucly, Wardens, &c.

Jone Sawyn gave to this churche to have her knyll rong here . . . iiijd.

Elizabeth Crosse of Cleanger gave to the churche for her knyll . . . . xijd.

Thomas Zaer, a yong man, dyde bequeffe to this churche a ramme scheppe, prisse of xijd.

Jone uxor Ric. Webber condam bequevyd to the churche a gowne and curtyll, yn prisse of xiijs. iiijd., the wyche mony went to a new cope

A.D. 1539.

John Norman at Cowrte and Richarde Robyns, Wardens, &c.

Rycharde Norman dyde bequeffe to this churche vij scheppe and iijs. iiijd. in mony the wyche in the hole was . . . . xs.

And for his grave afore the hye crosse . . . . vjs. viijd.

And all this went to a new coppe.

John Hucly gave and bequefyd to this church for to help to bye a new coppe	xs.
John Swyzth bequeved to this church vs. that went to a awter clothe.	
Harry Tanner gave to this church to have a knell for hys wyffe.	iiijd.
It. of the geft of John Waterus a ramme, prisse	xijd.
Of the bequesth of W. Goodman a scheppe, prisse	xvjd.
Of the bequesth of Eboll Hurly to the black vestments that Harry Hurly hadde	vs.

A.D. 1540.

WILLIAM LEDDON THAT SPELYD[1] JOHN SWYƷTH AND ROBERT AT MORE, WARDENS, &C.

For the knell of Robt. at More his fader yn law	iiijd.
It. of the bequesth of Jone at Pole a banner of sylke and of Sent Jorge, prisse	xs.
„ of the bequesth of Phels Swyƺth, that went to the black vestments	vs.
„ of the bequesth of W. Norman, that went to the stremer	vs.
„ of the bequesth of Eliz Hucly, that went to a new stremer	vs.

Summa totalis gefts actenus ys [this] a kownt (?) respice post in folio lxxxv, a £x.

[A loose page in another hand.]

Hereafter followeth more gifts.

A.D. 1541.

RIC. RAW AND LEUYS TRYCHAY, HIGH WARDENS

Jone at Cowrtleys gave to the church, that went to the streamer	iijs. iiijd.

A.D. 1542.

W. TYMWELL AT COME AND JONE MORSE, HIGH WARDENS.

Tho. Tymwell at Bradford gave	viijd.
Christina Tayler bequeathed an altar cloth, price	iijs. iiijd.

A.D. 1543.

W. TYMWELL AT WODE AND JONE GOODMAN, HIGH WARDENS.

Harry Hurly gave to the black vestments	vjs. viijd.
Edith Raw gave a wether, price	ijs.

A.D. 1544.

HARRY HAYLE AND JOHN GU. . . . .

John Morse, a young man, gave to the black vestments	iijs. iiijd.
The Vicar, Sir Ch. Trychey, gave to the same for Mr. Edward Sydenham his book and vjs. ecclesia habuit.	. .

---

[1] *I.e.*, Supplied the place of—used again in same sense. *See* Glossary.

Edith Tamer (?) gave to the same	v*s.*
Ric. Webber gave to the church	v*s.*

A.D. 1545.

W. Morse and John Norman at Pole, High Wardens.

For the knell of William Kempe	iiij*d.*

A.D. 1546.

John Tayler and J. Tymwell at Borston, High Wardens.

Annys Morse gave a curtle, sold for v*s.*, which went to the black vestments.

A.D. 1547.

W. Leddon and Th. Borrage, High Wardens.

Jone Kymppe gave to the church to be prayed for, to the black vestments	iij*s.* iiij*d.*
Roic. Flyd gave to the church to be prayed for	iij*s.* iiij*d.*
Alsyn Isac gave to the black vestments	iij*s.* iiij*d.*

A.D. 1548.

Luce [Lucy] Scely was High Warden.

[And by her time the church goods was sold away without commission (ut patet postea) and no gifts given to the church, but all from the church; and this it continued from Luce's time to Richard Cruce, and from Cruce unto Ric. Hucly, and from Hucly to Ric. Robyns; from him to Robyn at More, and by all these men's time, which was by the time of King Edward VI, the church ever decayed, and then did the King and Queen Mary Grace succeed; and how the church was restored again by her time hereafter ye shall have knowledge of it. And in the last year of the King, and in the first year of the Queen was Leuys Trychay high warden.]

End of the Bederoll.

HIGH WARDENS' ACCOUNT.

1526–7.

The Cownte of William at Pole and Geffery Smy3th beyng hye wardyns of the goodds and the cattyl [chattels] of the hye store of Sent Georgii the ere of owr kyng and the ere of owr lorde before rehersyd the xxvij day of October madyn.

In primis recets.

Mem. that y William at pole ressevyd at the begynnyng of my wardynscheppe of the wolde wardyns	xxij*s.* j*d.* ob.

It. y ressevyd agayn of John at Cowrte ys cownte . . . . . . v*s*. ij*d*.
It. for the flyes [fleece] of wolle and the talowe of a lamme . . . . . vj*d*.
It. we made frely of owr cherche ale all costs quytte . . . . . iiij marks, v*s*. j*d*.
It. of the gesthe[1] of John at hayne to the store of Jhu iij yowe scheppe of the wyche scheppe John Norman, senior, hath one and John at Cowrte hathe another, and William at pole hathe the wother [other].
It. John Waterus hathe a yowe lamme of the store of Jhu that came from William Tywell this ere.
It. William Robbyns hathe a yowe hogg of the store of Jhu, also that came from W. Tywell this ere.
It. W. Tywell hathe a yowe of the store of Jhu and her lamme of this ere was delivered to Waterus ut predictum est.
Summa of the wolle of this for sayd scheppe is viij pownde, and lamme-towe of one lame not val. (?) pro dec. lame hoc anno et pro dec. ij agnarum debet.
Summa of the scheppe ys v in nomber and a lamme.
Deb. It. John Dore ys in deb. agayn the cherche for the space of his wardynscheppe as yt ij pownde of wex or xvj*d*. for at hys plesure the whyche he will pay to the new wardyn John at Borston agayn Ester [Easter] next commyng of hys fydelite before the paryche promisyd.
deb. It. W. Robbyns ys contentyd for hys debt the whych ys iij*s*. iiij*d*. to bye a new canapy to hong over the sacrament when ye wyll and yff hyt cost more he wyll ley more to hyt and yf hyt cost not so moche ye schall have the reste.
deb. It. William Hurly of Bawnton [Bampton] to this cherche diu deb . . ij*s*. iiij*d*.
Summa totalis receptionis ys . . . . £iiij vj*s*. ij*d*. ob.
      Unde petit allocari pro necessariis Expensis ut sequitur.

Costs.

It. y paid to William Smyrte for fre stone . . . . ix*s*.
„ for vij pownde of wex for the iij tapers afore the hye crosse and the precessional tapers . . . . iiij*s*.
„ for iiij bell ropps . . . . ij*s*. xj*d*.
„ for payntyn of the lente clothe and the rowde [Rood] clothe after the bequysthe of John at Borston . . . . ij*s*.
„ for iiij yerds of lyne[n] clothe for the sepulture with the hemmyng of the same . xv*d*.
„ for makyn of ij gurdylls for the vestments and for mendyng of the coppe . . ij*d*.
„ for mendyng of the bell collers and for thongg . . . . . . ij*d*.
„ for grese for the bells for the hole ere . . . . ij*d*.
„ for settyng yn of the borde to the cherche-howse scev [? seven] fotte and the barys [barrs] of the quire dore . . . . iiij*d*.
„ for vij pownds of wex for the pascall taper and the wyvyn [wives'] taper . iiij*s*. j*d*.
„ for ij yryn bars for the quire dore and a pare of twysts for the hache . . xv*d*.
„ for the cherche ale howse dore loke and for the settyng . . . . viij*d*. ob.
„ for a dirige for the benefactors of this cherche . . . . . . iiij*d*.

---
[1] Quest, or perhaps gefthe = gift.

It. for the cherche howse rente for this ere	iiijd.
„ for mendyng of the ij rachetts for the clerke	ijd.
„ for makyn of the pascall taper	ijd.
„ for makyn of all wother wex all this ere paste that belongyth to the hye wardyns	vjd.
„ for francke and sensse [frankincense] and for wyke yerne for the hole ere	ijd. ob.
„ for iij powndes of wex for the presessonall tapers and for Jhu his taper	xxijd.
„ for the payntyn of the sepulture clothe	xxd.
„ to the plommer for mendyng of the gutter apon the cherche, and the gutter of the towre yn mette and drenke and wage	xxiiijs. ijd.

Not [Notes] the plommer. And here after he to mayntayne and kepe the same gutters and to fynde hemself and the sawder to his own propper coste and charge, exseppte that we doo new caste hyt and he to have for hys fee at lammas of us ijs. if hyt rayne not yn to the cherche thorffe [through] hys defawte.

„ to Andrewe for cuttyng of wode and for caryeng of same	vjd.
„ for nayles to nayle the ledde	vjd.
„ to the raers for rayng the grette stoke in wages	xxjd.
„ for their mette and drenke for that wyke	ijs.
„ for ij pownde of wex	xiiijd.
„ for a sake of lyme caryge and all	xd.
„ for a hylyer[1] to mende the towre and the almatorye[2] yn mette and drenke and wages	xjd.
„ for ij crests for the almatory but a	jd.
„ for wrytyng of this acownte with all wother aconttes of this cherche by the ere	jd.

Summa totalis . . £iij xiijs. iiijd. ob.

Thys aforesayd alowyd here is elyd [yielded] in clere all costs quytte . . xijs. ixd. ob.
And viij powndes of wolle and the wolle of one lamme and apon thys there ys amytted wardyn Margyt at Borston and Ric. Raw and to the wydow Margytt this forsayd mony and the wolle was delyveryd the ere and the day before rehersyd.
In eodem die the cownte of the v men.
Mem. that John Norman, senior, and William Tywell and Robert Tywell and John Norman the yonger, and Richard Hucly thys ere they rescevyd of the yong men stoke xxvjs. viijd. and of owre lady stoke xvs., and of the cherche stoke at the last acownte vijs. iijd. Summa xlviijs. xjd., the wyche resty3th as ytt yn the v men ys handes the ere and the day before rehersyd.

THE COWNTE OF THE V MEN [for 1526-7.]

Mem. that the v men hadde yn ther kepyn this tyme twelmnoth	xlviijs. xjd.
And thereto they have ressevyd agayn this ere of the yong men wardyns v nobyls and of owr laydy ys cownte	xiijs. iiijd.
And this day at this acownte they have received of Margyt at Borston	xxs.

Summa totalis ys now . . . £vj xvs. vijd.
Unde petunt alloc. for expensis.

It. for makyn of the enter closse[3] in part of payment	xxvjs. viijd.

[1] Tiler.   [2] An Aisle, so called.   [3] A partition, probably a Parclose.

Thys alowed, there restyth yt styll yn the v men ys handds £iiij viij*s*. xj*d*., the ere and the day before expressyd.

Summa of all the cownts of this ere with the maydyns acownte the ressets [h]actenus ys . . . . £vj xix*s*. viij*d*.

THE ALMYS LYGTH YS ACOWNT. [1526–7.]

The cownte of William at Lawton beyng Wardyng of the Almys lygth madyn in eodem die of the yong men acownte ut predict. est.

In primis rec.

Mem. that y ressevyd of the wolde wardyn at the begynnyng of my ere	v*d*. ob.
It. for the scheppe of the bequysth of Wat pole	. xij*d*.
It. of the bequyste of John Tayler	. iiij*d*.
It. of the bequyste of Water More	. iiij*d*.

Summa . . ij*s*. j*d*. ob.

Wher of y aske alowance for wex and for makyn for the hole ere yn the basyn . ix*d*. ob]
Thys costs alowyd here ys eclyd [yielded] yn clere all costs quytte . . . . vj*d*.
And apon this ys amytted wardyn for this ere follyng John Tayler and to hem this forsayd mony ys delyveryd the ere and the day before reherseyd.

STORE OF SAINT SONDAY.

1538.

Moreover hereafter followeth ye Count of the store of Sent Sonday, ye which JOHN NORMAN at Court, is yearly warden of.

PRIMO: RECEIPTS.

Mem^m, that this last year then rested in John Norman's hands . . . . xxij*d*.
And to this he hath received for the wool of this year of this foresaid store . j*s*. iiij*d*.
Also he received again for his ewe and her lamb of this year, and for a ram hog that came from Robt. at Hayne, and for Robt. at Hayne his ewe's lamb of this year, for all these iiij he received ij*s*. and iiij*d*.
Also John Norman hath in his keeping as yet, a ewe hog, and a ewe that came from Robt. at Hayne, and as for John at Court's ewe and her lamb, was sold ut predixi —Richard Norman hath a wether in his keeping.
Thomas Borrage a wether is gone I wyne [ween].
Robt. at Hayne's ewe is delivered to John at Court, and her lamb and the ram hog was sold ut predictum est.

Summa totalis Rec. is vere, vij*s*. and vij*d*.

unde, he asketh allowance as hereafter foloweth pro expensis.

PRIMO.

It. for iiij schepyn lesse [leaze] . . . . xij*d*.
It. for wax and wick and making for the whole year . . . . . . vj*d*.
Summa xviij*d*. This cost allowed then resteth still in John Norman's ward clear [one of the iiij men], vj*s*. and j*d*. ann. et die preedic. and for this money the iiij men shall count hereafter, and our lady warden shall count for these sheep and all other sheep concerning the church in future.

NOTE.—Let all the Church sheep in future be put in our lady mark full, what store so ever they be off.

THE CLERKSHIP.

A fresh award made of the clerkship by Mr. John Sydenham, and by 3 men of the parish chosen for the purpose by the parish.

A.D. 1536.

W. Leddon would not pay his stitch[1] of corn to the clerk according to the award of 1531, two others would not pay the iiij*d*. Nor the cots at Exbridge their quarterlage according to that award.

Therefore the vicar would mell [meddle] no more with the clerkship, because he could not have his duty paid without displeasure of the parish.

He therefore gave warning to the parish at Christmas to provide a clerk by Our Lady in Lent following.

For lack of a clerk at the busy time of Easter, the whole parish desired the Vicar to find one until a little after Easter.

When at that time they could not agree about a clerk, 4 honest men were chosen to govern the parish in all causes, concerning the wealth of the church, under orders at Visitation, viz., the Vicar, J. Norman, H. Hurly, and T. Rumbelow (that spelyd John Swyȝth at that time), they to go home and invite Mr. J. Sydenham to join them.

On a day appointed, a Sunday, Mr. J. Sydenham and the summoner asked of every man by name, if they would accept these men who had been chosen by the Ordinary, and their decision. They chose the same, and 26 consented to accept their decision, again 5 dissentients. They could not therefore agree, and there was no clerk at evensong, nor on the morrow which was S. George's Day, wherefore the church was homely served that day. In so much that when upon the morrow of S. George's Day, the Vicar should say Mass for Mark's child at Exbridge. Tho' Mark was glad to go to John at Cowrte to fetch the Church door key, and the challice, and also he fetched old J. Waterus to help the Vicar to Mass before he could have any Mass said for his child, and all was for lack of a clerk. And when Mass was done, we went to William at Tymwell, to the betrothing of Margyd Tymwell and William Tayler, and there all that day we reasoned shamefully about our Clerkship, insomuch that Mark and W. Leddon were almost by the ears for the same cause, because W. Leddon had not brought home his corn before Michaelmas, as well as he did the

---

[1] Stitch, s. Ten sheaves set up on end, elsewhere known as a shock. *Jennings' Som. Dict.*

Tuesday afore the Visitation, the which was half a bushel of rye, and the last pec by hyppe,[1] so in conclusion the parish wholly concluded there and said let us have a fresh day of communication, and we will be ordered every one of us.

Whereupon they desired the Vicar to find them a clerk again till a fresh day of communication, and at the parishioners' desire so did he till the Sunday after Rogation week. And in the mayne space,[2] Mr. Hu Powlytt[3] kept court at Morebath, and he exhorted the foresaid 5 persons, and so did Mr. Hu Stickly also that they should be contented to be ordered as the most part of the parish were, and if they would not, he would order them he said.

So a fresh day was appointed upon all those who would not be ordered by Mr. J. Sydenham and the four men were cited to appear. The day was Sunday before Rogation week. Then was the parish again singularly [one by one] demanded by name if they would accept an order made by Mr. Sydenham, and the 3 of the 4 men (for the fourth man, Robert at Hayne, was sick at that time), and all that were in the church said ye [yea], and there lacked no more that day, but William at Tymwell, and William Leddon, and William Scely. Therefore because they were contented to abide by the order of Mr. Sydenham and the 3 men, the citation was void.

So with Mr. Sydenham's advice, they concluded that henceforth it shall be the clerk's duty by our award, to have whatsoever he hath had afore this, to the intent to have more unity and peace among us, and to have the Church better served. Primo ; he shall have a stetch of clean corn of hevery [every] house, where there is corn upon the bargain as Brochole and wother moo.[4] And he that hath no clean corn shall pay a stetch of wots [oats], and he that hath no corn shall pay the clerk iij$d$. for his stetch, and ij$d$. a coter [cottar], as hyt hath been in times past.

The clerk shall demand his stetch in this manner. Once he shall come for hem, and if he be a redy, and yff not he shall come again, and then if the stetch be not sufficient he shall leave hem till that some of the persons who made the award do see it ; and then if the stetch be sufficient, after their inspection, then the clerk shall fett him, and if he be not sufficient, then the clerk without any business shall fett a stetch with Richard Hucly, and if it be in the west part of the parish ; and if it be in the east part of the parish he must fett his stetch with John Norman at Cowrte, for these two men are surety to the clerk to see all his duty paid truly unto him that these present men have ordered, without any trouble or vexation, and the whole parish hath made their answer unto these two aforesaid men that they will were[5] them harmless, and if any froward fellow will not pay his duty to the clerk according to this award, and also and if the clerk be warned to fet his stetch and peradventure he cannot come for him by and by, then the onner [owner] of the ground shall keep him till he come ; also he shall have jd. a quarter of every householder, and the clerk shall have at every wedding ij$d$. ; also at every corsse [corpse] present, and at every month's end that is sung by note, the clerk shall have ij$d$. ; also the clerk shall be charged with nothing saving only with one challis, and with the church dore key, this for to keep and hide as he will do his own. Also he shall go about the parish once a year with his holy water, when men have shorn their sheep to gather some wool to make him cotts to goo yn [coats to go in] the parish's

---

[1] Heap.   [2] Meanwhile.   [3] Grantee of the Manor.   [4] Other more.
[5] *I.e.*, bear.

livery. And here for the clerk shall help the warden to make up the vestments, and to dress the altars. And also for this year ondly [only] for losing of his duty in times past ; the parish shall help to drienk[1] [drink] him a cost of ale,[2] the Sunday upon Trinity Sunday (et sic factum esset et ibi essent omnes, dumtaxat, Borston, and Scely, Webber and William Norman). Also at every Easter hereafter the clerk shall gather his hire meat, and then the parish shall help to drink him a cost of ale in the Church house.

This is all the [a]ward of Mr. John Sydenham and William Tymwell at Wode, and John Norman at Cowrte, and Richard Hucly, did make upon the clerkship, anno et die predicto, before the perryssin,[3] and John Dyffe, then being bayly [bailiff] there, under Mr. Hu Powlytt[4] and Matthew the sumner [summoner].   In witness whereof, this note was made here upon this account book to testify truly the clerk his duty and our award to avoid all other unconveniens.

1549.

VESTMENTS AND COPES. R. Hucly's Account.

Mem^m that in eodem die there rested with John Norman at Court, a suit of black vestments of Fustain naps, and a cope concerning the same *qd. iterum deliveravit ecclesiæ.*[5]

W^m at Comb habet the suit of white vestments.

Nicolus at Hayne habet the vestment of red velvet and the altar cloth of red satin.

Thomas Rumbelow habet the Lent vestments of blue.

It. the cope of red velvet and the cope of blue satin, *restant nunc in ecclesia.*

John Norman at Pool habet the streamer and the banner rolled in an altar cloth, and the blue vestments, *restant nunc in ecclesia.*

Willm Hurley habet the black pall of satin.

1552.

NOTA BENE.

That, in anno predicto, John at Court, Willm at Come, John at Borston, and Lewis Trickay, did deliver unto Mr. Gawyn Carow[4] [Carew] at Exeter, and to Antony Harvy and Mr. Hache a cope of blue satin, another cope of red velvet with splede egylls of gold, a blue velvet tunicle with splede egylls, a silken tunicle of blue with broncs [*sic*] of gold, a pax of silver of iiij ounces and half parcel gilt, and the paten of the less chalice of ij ounces and half, and this was all the church goods that they had in anno predicto.

END OF MOREBATH ACCOUNTS.

[1] *I.e.*, to brew a special Ale in his benefit.   [2] These were called Clerk-Ales.
[3] Parishioners.   [4] Lessee, or grantee of Barlynch.
[5] The Latin notes in italics were added after the restoration of the hidden articles in Queen Mary's reign.
[6] A similar commission, given to Courtenay and Ford, had in June 1551-2 conveyed the bell-furniture to Sir A. Champernown and Mr. Chichester under Royal grant.
[7] Eagles displayed.

St. Michael's, Bath.

1349–1575.

Wardens' Account Rolls.

••••••••••••••••••••••••

This collection, the most important in the county, was carefully edited by the Rev. Prebendary Pearson in 1878, and printed in the Somerset Archæological Proceedings of that year and the following ones. It is in the hands of most of the members of our Record Society, and therefore not here reprinted beyond a sample of the oldest Roll, giving the normal form, and language and entries of the Accounts. Some of the peculiar words are dealt with in the Glossary.

Its special value for historical purposes lies :—

1. In its early age, 1349, being the earliest Warden's Account known to me.
2. In its comparative continuity, ranging, with small intervals, through 226 years. There are 77 rolls ; 67 in Latin, 10 in English, most of them well preserved.
3. In the complete organization which it represents from the earliest date to the latest, and with very little variation, in spite of vast ritual changes, and ruthless spoliation.
4. In its illustration of the working of the Church in a city parish with a trading burgher-population.

Its Fiscal System

has some peculiar features, viz. :—

1. The occasional Allowance to the Wardens pro stipendio xij$d$. I have never seen elsewhere anything allowed to these officers for discharge of *Duties*, or anything beyond *re*payment for extraordinary demands on time and purse. It was incumbent in foro conscientiæ on every adult member of the church to serve the office, and he or she was compellable in foro externo, *i.e.*, in the spiritual court. The wardens in office were also held to be compellable by penalty to do their duties—see the case in this parish of a fine imposed, 18th Henry VIII.
2. The feasting at audit-time. This was perhaps no rare custom, but it appears in these accounts more undisguisedly than elsewhere.
3. A small flock of sheep, an intractable possession for a town parish. Sometimes their run was paid for, and then the wool and lambs were brought into the Wardens' receipts—sometimes, as in 1536, the flock was let out at a money rent.

4. A continually growing Endowment in land and houses, rising in yearly value from 10s. 9d. in 1349, to £11. 18s. 8d. in 1540. These properties were charged with obituary payments, which indicate the primary motive of the donors. They laid upon the wardens a heavy burden of house-agency. The entries for repairs and management have been duly noted by Prebendary Pearson, but their interest is secular, not ecclesiastical.

5. Partition of duties between the two wardens, one being specially elected as bursar, "portare bursam."

6. The sufficiency of ordinary revenue from endowment, aided by gifts and bequests, for the handsome maintenance of the church, without habitual recourse to the Church-house and its revelries, which formed the mainstay of the country wardens. Ales were relied on, now and then, see 3rd Henry VI, and also gatherings for special objects, see one "inter parochianos ad lapidiodium" in same year, when the Lady Chapel was in rebuilding. The parish seems to have relied wholly upon its own resources.

Church-Wardens' Accounts.

No. 1.

CIVITAS BATHON.

Compotus Thome le Mason et Thome le Tannere procuratorum ecclesie beati Michaelis extra portam borealem ejusdem civitatis a die Dedicationis ecclesie predicto anno Domini Millesimo ccc^{mo} XLIX.

ARRERAGIA.

Idem receperunt de xxiijs. viijd. de arreragiis ultimi compoti precedentis.

REDDITUS.

Idem receperunt de ijs. jd. ob. de redditu mesuagii Matildis Paket per annum.
Et de ijs. de redditu Agnetis la Wode.
Et de vjs. receptis de tenemento Joh^s atte Halle.
Et de xiiijd. receptis de Rogero le Toukere de mesuagio in Froggemerelane.
        Summa   .   . vs. ixd. ob.

NOVUS REDDITUS.

Idem receperunt de vjs. receptis de Rogero Clyware pro tribus terminis. Vid. de terminis Hock', Nativitate Sti Joh^s. Bapt. et Sti Michaelis.
Et de ijs. ixd. de Philippo le Smythe solvendis ad predictos terminos.
Et de receptis de Joh : Gregori.
        Summa   xs. ixd.

PERQUISITA.

Idem receperunt de ij*s*. legatis in testamento Will[1] de Wyke ad unum missale.
Et de ix*d*. ob. de collectionibus contra Natale Domini.
Et de xj*d*. de collectionibus contra Pascha.
Et de xx*s*. de legacione Joh[s]. Michel pro anniversario suo et aliis tenendis per an.
Et de vj*s*. receptis de J. Annatt.
Et de x*d*. de j velamine de cerico [silk] vendito.
Et de v*d*. de j alio velamine de cerico vendito.
Et de xij*d*. de veteribus pannis ad dictam ecclesiam legatis venditis.
Et de xij*d*. de j veteri olla enea de j lagena vendita.
Et de ij*s*. iij*d*. de una olla enea vendita.
Et de ij*s*. vj*d*. de veteri bosco de tenemento Roberti Golde vendito.
Et de vj*s*. de veteri bosco de tenemento Ade Storche vendito.
Et de vj*s*. viij*d*. de lano (sic) vendito ex legacione uxoris Thome Stote.
Et de xij*d*. de herbagio gardini Ade Storche.
Et de iij*d*. de herbagio gardini propinquorum, etc.
Et de j*d*. de candelis venditis Roberto le Doyere.

    Summa . . lij*s*. viij*d*. ob.
    Summa tocius recepte . . iiij*li*. xij*s*. xj*d*.

RESOLUCIO REDDITUM, *i.e.*, Rent-charges payable to the Clergy for obituary offices.

Item computus solutionum pro anniversariis in eadem ecclesia et aliis de veteri per annum . . . . xiij*d*.
It. in Anniversario Ade Storche et aliorum per V vices per annum . . . v*s*. xj*d*.
It. in Anniversario Joh[s]. de Budestone et aliorum per vices . . . . ix*d*.
It. in Anniversario Ricardi Golde . . . . v*d*. ob.
It. in Anniversario Roberti Golde et aliorum . . . . . . v*d*. ob.
It. in Anniversario Thome de Bristolle ij*s*. et omnia hoc anno primo.
It. solut. pro langabulo[1] hoc anno . . . . ij*s*. ob.
It. solut. Coffrario Civitatis Bathonie . . . . xij*d*.
It. solut. procuratori communitatis ij*d*. de tenemento quod fuit Roberti Golde.
It. solut. filio Roberti Golde pro quodam mesuagio ab eis empto jacente juxta dictam ecclesiam . . . . xvj*s*. viij*d*.
It. solut. Rectori[2] dicte ecclesie pro tenemento Roberti Golde a festo Circumcisionis Domini usque festum Sti Michaelis p. xl septimanis . . . . xx*d*.
It. solut. dicto Rectori de tenemento Ade Storche ad festum Sti Michaelis . . vj*d*.
It. solut. pro rudyng[3] tenementum Roberti Golde . . . . . . xviij*d*.
It. solut. procuratori[4] communitatis vj*d*. de mesuagio quod Will[s]. Cubbel tenet de dicta ecclesia.

---

[1] Land-gable. An impost payable in most towns by burgage-tenures to the Crown, or to the Lord, who had to pay the Fee-farm to the Crown. In this case it was payable to the Bishop, as Lord of the borough.

[2] To the rector for obituary services, for discharge whereof the tenements had been bequeathed to the parish.

[3] Ridding, *i.e.*, clearing away of old materials for rebuilding.

[4] The Chamberlain of the City for municipal dues.

It. pro iiij cartis de novo sabendis	ijs.
It. Rectori pro denariis[1] beati Petri	vijd. ob.
In anniverso Joh*. Columbel die Sti Martini	xd.
In coreo empto pro libro missali involvendo [being bound]	ijd.
It. procuratori dicte ecclesie iiijd. de Anniverso Ade Storche.	
Summa xxxviijs. viijd.	

EXPENSA.

In—li cere emptis contra Natale Domⁱ	iiijs. ijd.
In factura ejusdem	vjd.
In lichil empt	jd.
In iiij^{ll} cere emptis contra Pascha	iiijs.
In factura ejusdem	jd. ob.
In dimidia li. cere pro ij torchis emendendis	vjd.
In factura eorundem	iijd.
In jli. cere pro cereo Ade Storche ad pedes Ste Katerine	xijd.
In factura ejusdem	ob.
In oleo empto pro lampade	xd. ob.
In ij cereis de novo factis ad pedes Sti Michaelis	jd.
In Watelrys[2] emptis	xxd.
It. in stipulis emptis	iiijd.
In stipendio clerici ad illuminandum lampadem per annum	jd.
In stipendio js lotricis pro vestimentis et aliis ornamentis lavandis	ijd.
In stipendio procuratoris per annum	iijd.
In parcameno empto pro compoto faciendo	jd.
Solut. pro j^{no} libro missali empto	xlvjs. ijd.
Summa lxs. iijd. ob.	

[On the back.]

STIPENDIUM.

In stipendio clerici pro compoto faciendo	iiijd.
In pane et cervisia emptis pro expensis procuratoris per idem tempus	iijd.
Summa tocius expense iiijli. xixs. vjd. ob.	
Et sic ex [eunt?] vjs. vijd. ob.	

---

[1] Paid to Rector as the channel to forward them through the Archdeacon at Visitation to the Diocesan, who was responsible to the Pope's Collector, under a rescript circa 1200, for the annual payment of £11 5s. in behalf of the diocese. This very ancient impost, the Rom-feoh of Saxon England, once universal, had now come to be leviable from a few houses in each parish.

[2] Withies for wattling. See "rys" in Glossary.

OTHER COLLECTIONS
known to exist in Somerset.
1. Stogursey.
2. Banwell.
3. Bridgwater.

No. 1

Is in the very careful hands of Sir Alex. Acland-Hood, Bt., who inherits it from the Palmers of Fairfield, the chief mansion in the parish of Stogursey. The volume was examined by Mr. Horwood, who describes it in Vol. VI of the Historical MSS. Commission Reports, p. 348–9, and gives its leading features.

It contains 54 leaves (less some gaps) ranging in date from the 18–9th of Hen. VII to the 38th of Hen. VIII. It therefore stops at the eve of the great ritual changes.

It tells very much the same tale as our other records, *e.g.*, a revenue always ample, raised from voluntary sources, *i.e.*, Church-house, and Ales (these the largest items), livestock, bequests and gifts, with small rents accruing from former gifts. There was no recourse to a rate, or any need of it.

The outlay was on the usual objects, purely ecclesiastical.

The language was Latin till 1509, after which are found some English words worth noting, *e.g.*, the "Brethereddyne dirige and mass," f°. 25^b., *i.e.*, the Mass of the United Brotherhoods in behalf of their departed members; the "Holybrede house," *i.e.*, the Church-house where the Holy Loaf was baked; the "Calendar," *i.e.*, the Bederoll or list or commemorated benefactors; a "Taverning" for a Church-ale. One custom is noteworthy, viz., letting out at a rent the "Juells of the Church," *i.e.*, the valuables, whether plate, or adornments.

St. Erasmus and St. George were venerated, besides our Lady, who was represented in painting in the form known as "Our Lady of Pity."

No. 2.

This is a single volume in good condition kept by the wardens in a chest over the Church porch. It begins in the 7th of Henry VIII, 1516, and runs to end of Elizabeth, probably with some gaps. Having had but two hours' examination of its pages, I can only say that the fiscal system which it details does not differ from Yatton in its main features.

The parish had its Church-house and Ales, the house being called both bakehouse and brewhouse in evidence of being fitted for divers entertainments. It had also some landed endowment and live-stock; but the largest income was from the Hogglers. In each account the second item of receipt is headed with slight variation " Venditio et incrementum forinsecum de la Hogeling."

The Hogeling is divided into the Upland and Marshland " in Marisco."

In 1516, the Upland Wardens paid in to the High Wardens £4 7
  „   Marshland „   „   „   „   £4 6
                                      ─────────
                                      £8 13

In the following years similar sums are recorded.

The means whereby such a sum could be realized must be ascertained by further research, which an old man's eyes cannot undertake.

I can only contribute thus much :—

(1.) In 1566 the parish resolved "that the Hoglers of the parish shall yearly make their account and pay their money the Sunday before St. Nicolas, on pain of fines, &c." The Hye Wardens to pay their money (*i.e.*, income from all sources) the Sunday after St Nicolas, *i.e.*, the end of the financial year.

(2.) Hogglers were the lowest class of labourers.

(3.) The terms "Venditio et Incrementum" bid one believe that there was a common stock running on common lands on the hill and in the moor, in which the Church had rights, and that the stock was husbanded, and the rights made productive by a band of working men, who thus made a contribution to the Church funds.

No. 3.

These MSS. are in the hands of the Corporation. I did not know that they contained Churchwardens' Compoti till after the decay of eye-sight had narrowed my powers of inspection. I now give the results of a three hours' survey in May, 1889, granted to me by the courtesy of Mr. Read, the Town Clerk.

I found Rolls of the "Custodes bonorum et luminum Cantariæ B.M." an endowed Chantry with its own Chapel, audited in the 42nd, 43rd, 44th, 45th, 46th of Edward III, and in the 1st and on to the 10th (inc.) of Richard II from Christmas to Christmas.

Of High Wardens accounts (preserved also in rolls) I found one in the 47th of Edward III, and two in Richard II, each running for *two* years, viz, the °7th and °8th, and the °9th and °10th, from Michaelmas to Michaelmas. The same wardens present an account "*in dorso*" as Wardens of the goods and lights of the High Cross, endowed with real property.

In the °2nd, 5th, 6th of Henry V.—In the 19th, 20th, 27th, 28th, 31st, 32nd, 34th 35th, and 46th of Henry VI also one °1447 (no regnal year), and in the 3rd, 4th, and 10th of Edward IV, I found Churchwardens' rolls.

The noteworthy feature in the Fiscal System, is—

The regular Church Rate, "Collecta Assisa," *i.e.*, a Collection by assessment, levied yearly, or once in two years ; as early as 1383.

In 1447-8 it is called " Collecta concessa per parochianos et burgenses ad emendandam Eccl^m £8."

It was laid (apparently *pro ratâ*) on the whole area of the parish in the town and country, and was viewed as a debt, enforceable in the spiritual court. There is one loose membrane,

Those marked ° I examined in detail.

in writing closely approaching to 1447-8, containing a list of defaulters "in *debt* to the Church" each with a rated sum against his name.

This shows that the subsidy was not made up of *gifts*, voluntary in amount. In another account, a citation has been paid for by the Wardens against the "Debtors of the Church," thus bringing the defaulters into the Court Christian.

Three principles are here asserted. (1) The liability in foro conscientiæ of each member of the Church to contribute "quoad res," according to his property. (2) The rating authority of the aggregate body of members, to settle the "how much" and "how often." (3) The authority of the forum externum of the Church to coerce the unwilling.

Being the only case of compulsory church rate before the reign of Elizabeth that I know, I have given the particulars fully.

In consequence of being rate-fed, St. Mary's Parish did not resort to a Church-house or revelries at Hocktide or at other feasts for maintenance. There were gifts and bequests in money and kind, but not very large. Live-stock, if given, was sold, not kept.

The oldest MS. is a detached membrane dated 12th Edward [almost certainly Edward I, and if so, 1284]. It contains a report from a Committee of four empowered by the parish to obtain a bell. They bought the materials, made their mould, and founded the bell on the spot. Its weight was 1781 lbs.

On another sheet 1336-7, William the Tanner, a sole committee, accounts to the parish for the outlay of £143 13s. raised for the "Novum opus ecclesiæ." This sum was paid in 5 instalments to tradesmen, but the items are unrecorded.

A separate bundle is endorsed by Mr. Riley (the Commissioner who reported on the collection to the Hist. MS. Comm.), as transcribed by him in 1871. It contains (*inter alia*) Inventories of Vestments kept in "S. Katrine's Yle," and a rental of the endowed Rode chapel. They are in English, and were printed in Vol. VII, 1858, of the Som. Arch. Pro.

This very interesting collection ought to be thoroughly examined. Together with those of Banwell and Stogursey, it would, if transcribed in extenso, fill a volume, and the examination of contents would probably throw a good deal of needed light upon the history of our churches. One item I will quote as an instance of the timely exercise of the visiting and coercive authority of the Archdeacon.

In the Roll of 9th-11th of Richard II is charged the sum of £4. 6s. 8d. paid to the Vicar "pro emendandis fenestris ad taxam ex assensu parochianorum per coercionem Archid[i]. Tanton." Here is a case of a defect noted by the Archdeacon, the parish ordered to repair up to a given estimate (taxa), the parish complying, and giving the money to the Vicar for the execution of the work. The same roll records the less-pleasing fact of the building of a charnel-house (carnaria) on the north side of the Church.

Church-Wardens' Accounts
OF 15TH OR 16TH CENTURY, BEYOND THE DIOCESE.

Those that have come under my ken are the following :—

No. 1. St. Peter's in the East Oxford, a city parish.
No. 2. Solihull, a large village in Warwickshire.
No. 3. Stanford in the Vale, a Berkshire village.

St. Michael's, Bath, Church-Wardens' Accounts.

No. 1.

These were discovered by myself when Vicar in 1845, in the state of a bundle of loose rolls fast decaying. They are now safely kept in a vaulted room, bound in a volume, and accessible for inspection but not printed. They date from 1444. There are nine before 1500. Then they become more regular and run through the 16th century, but with gaps.

The Fiscal System

Tallies very nearly with that of St. Michael's, Bath, especially in the amount of house property, charged with obits, but in order to eke out this rental, the Wardens—

1. Made collections "inter parochianos' at the great festal processions.
2. Received collections made by the young men and maidens at Hocktide, Monday and Tuesday, each class having one day's possession of the thoroughfares and making the other pay for passing.
3. Made profit by sales of Holy Ale and Holy Loaf, brewed and baked at the Church-house.
4. Kept a stock of players garments and let them out for hire.
5. Let out torches for funerals, especially those of academical students.

The funds were generally ample, the outlay was wholly upon Church objects. The house-property, to escape confiscation in the 16th century, was made over to the Corporation of the City, who till lately, leased it to parish feoffees, in aid of the Wardens' Accounts.

No. 3.

This collection, ranging from 1552–1602, is printed in the Antiquary, four numbers beginning February, 1888.

The following contents are worth noting:—

Inventory of Church goods, as renewed 1° Mariæ by Dame Fettiplace, with a preface touching the order for providing the Holy Loaf.

A fund called "Font-stock" was gathered by two women from the "font-wives," probably for the Font taper at Easter.

There was a gathering for "Crowche (= cross) or paschull money," *i.e.*, for Easter procession. Some allotments of Church-land, a Church-house called also Gildehall, a Whitsun ale, a gathering on Twelfth Even (Eve of Epiphany) for Rood-light called Dawell light, an unexplained receipt from "the encrease of the 40 pences *vs.* vij$d$" (more than once), and for "cheeses gathered for the Church." In 1572 wafer-bread was provided by the parish for Communion for the year.

The usual result followed upon the compulsory imposition of civil charges. The voluntary gifts and bequests died out.

Glossary.

••••••••••••••••••••••••

THE aim of this Glossary is to aid in the understanding of the foregoing accounts and of similar ones. With this view it notices words used in an obsolete or unwonted or local sense, and also some uses peculiar to Wessex. These are marked Z.

Other abbreviations are used, *e.g.* :—

n.s. Noun substantive.
adj. Adjective.
part. Participle.
Z *hod.* Modern Somerset tongue.
v.t. Verb transitive.

C, Y, M, T, P, B, for Croscombe, Yatton, Morebath, Tintinhull, Pilton, and St. Michael's, Bath, the places that have furnished the corpus of the book.

The authorities referred to are Halliwell's Archaic Dictionary, Chambers' English Dictionary, Richardson's Dictionary, Jennings' Somerset Dialect, Parker's Glossary of Architecture, Wright's Prov. Dict.

NOTANDA.

In the use of letters the scribes constantly put V for F, and Z for S according to the spoken sounds. At **P** the letters V and W are quite interchangeable, *e.g.*, Vont (*i.e.*, Font) is written Wont; Wreaths, Vreathes. Sometimes F stands for W, *e.g.*, Freathes for Wreaths, creating doubt about the sound. Y is added as an initial where it has no place, *e.g.*, in "Our" and "Aisle" and dropt elsewhere, *e.g.*, "eeld" for "yield," thus sharing the fate of "h" in other counties. W in like manner is imposed and deposed, *e.g.*, "Wolde" for "Old," "Ood" for "Wood." "At" and "to" are, as in Z *hod*, interchangeable. The use of the Anglo-Saxon participial prefix "ge" represented by "y" or "I" is universal, *e.g.*, y-bought, y-fett, &c.

[1] In "Light," "Draught," &c., our scribes inserted a letter to represent the guttural force, now extinct, of the Anglo-Saxon "G" or "Gh." Sometimes they added it to the "gh," sometimes wrote it instead. It is found also at the beginning of "gate," sounded perhaps more like "y" then "g"—A special type ʒ represents it in our text.

A

Aler, *n.s.* **Y,** *sæpe.* The gallery of the rood-loft. Borrowed from the Alure or gangway of embattled walls, made for the passage to and fro of the defenders, see Solarium.
Ale, *passim, n.s.* An entertainment given in the interests of the parish on a holiday.
Ale-house, *n.s.* **Y,** 201. The Church-house.
Alms light, *n.s.* **M,** *passim.* The light maintained for the souls of the Departed, elsewhere called soul-light, dead-light and Lumen Animarum.
Almatory, *n.s.* Peculiar to Morebath, a portion of the Church, coveted for burial.
An ely, to *v.t.* **Y,** 99. To anoint, *i.e.,* in extreme unction.
Assyon, Y, *adj.* Ashen, made of Ash. **Z** *hod.*
Axsyn, Y, 117, **P,** *n.s.* Ashes. **Z** *hod.*

B

"**Bastyng** the ryng in whyt," **Y,** 172. Something done in the belfry apparently.
Baudries, *n.s. passim,* and diversely spelt. Baldricks, *i.e.,* belts, or pendants of belts, but here used for the handles of bell ropes, and leathern loops in the crown of the bell, from whence the clapper swung.
Bede-roll (diversely spelt), *n.s. sæpe.* The list of Benefactors, claiming the Intercessions of the Church. It was read out by a Bedeman, who might be clerk or sexton or other subordinate, on the Anniversary day when the great Dirige was celebrated at the cost of the parish. See in **M,** p. 210, a sample of a Bede-roll. To be placed on this roll was often a condition stipulated by donors, and always a valued privilege.
Bede-man, *n.s.* The person appointed to read out the Bede-roll and bid the prayers of the congregation. In some cases it was a continuous office, *e.g.,* at Frome, where it has remained in the patronage of the owners of Orchardleigh. See Som. Notes and Queries, 1888, pp. 122 and 135. The modern descendant is the Beadle or Bedel.

The Bedesman was a distinct person, viz., one who was bound in virtue of a benefaction to say intercessory prayers.

Bellatur ⎫ *n.s.* **Y,** 147. Bellfounder.
Bellman ⎭
Blodius, *adj.* Blue.
Borow, *n.s.* **P.** A Guarantor, a man who gives a borow or pledge.
Brand-yre ⎫ *n.s.* **Y,** 26. Andirons for the hearth.
Brondyren ⎭ 56.
Braste, *n.s.* **Y,** 104. Brass.
Burde-Stoke, *n.s.* **Y,** 141, **M.** A board-stock, *i.e.,* a log fit for sawing into board, which is sounded Boord in **Z.**
Burde-nayles, *n.s.* **Y.** Nails suited for joining boards.

C

Capull, *n.s.* Y, 105. A horse.
Carnock, *n.s.* Y, 141. A heap measure applied to lime. Cf. Curnock=Four bushels of corn. Wright's Prov. Dict.
Clavey, *n.s.* Y, 144. A mantelpiece or shelf. Z.
Colas, proper name. St. Nicholas, Y, 101.
Constre-Cowrte, *n.s.* Y. Consistory Court.
Corse, *n.s.* C. The bodice attached to a girdle. Cf. Corselet.
Countes-day, *n.s.* P. Audit-day, Day of Account.
Copps
Copys
Coppsys } *n.s.* {
Coppys
  1. Copes from *Lat.* Capa.
  2. Some kind of Candle-holder, *e.g.*, "the copys that beareth the light." Y, 37.
  3. Generally some kind of cap, finial, topping or coping. In this sense it is akin to German Kopf.
Crese, *n.s.* Increase, the year's addition to a store or stock, *passim*.
Crook
Crowche } *n.s.* { P, *passim*. A portable cross, from *Lat.* Crux, Crucis. At C the High Cross had its own paid keeper. S. Michael also had a "Crook" at C and a Crook-bearer.
Croke-bred, *n.s.*
Croke-money, *n.s.* { C. p. 24, 26 (*bis*) 27. "Croke-money with the vantage of the brede" "and ale." The Holy Loaf and Ale were sold at the great processions, specially Easter, and the profits entered as the Crese of the Crook.

D

Dandy-pratts, *n.s.* Y, 155. A base coin, unauthorized.
Dawbe, *n.s.* See Ryses.
Dayer, *n.s.* P. A dairyman.
Ded-money, *n.s.* C, *sæpe*. A fund kept by wardens for maintaining a light (called in other places dead-light, soul-light, alms-light), on the high beam of the high Cross, and for celebrating an anniversary for the dead, also for torches and tapers at the funerals of the poor. It was fed by bequests and gifts.
Drawle] Y. A sucker or some part of the drawing gear of a pump. Cf. Draw3te Y, 142.
Trawle ∫ Y.
Dyking of the well. Y, 127. Lining it with stone, now called in Z steaning.
Dyking of the Yeo. Y, *sæpe*. Ditching, making good the banks.

E

Ernest-penny] *n.s.* The 1*d*. universally paid down as the evidence of a bargain being
Covenant-penny ∫ struck.
Entreclose, *n.s.* In a dwelling-house a partition-wall, in a church a parclose, or half-open screen.

F

Famels, *n.s.* C, 47. Fanons or maniples.

Femerell. Y. Pierced stonework in belfry for escape of sound, from "Fumariolum," a louvre for escape of smoke.

Ferments. Y, 96 } *n.s.* "Ferramenta," iron work for the steeple windows.
Farments. Y, 100

Fett (oft. y-fett) *passim.* The participle past of "to fetch."

"**Flameolum** de Sypres pro pixide Corp. Xti," B, 1427. A veil of Cyprus silk for the Pyx. Cf. flammula, in low Latin=a banner.

Flaks, *n.s.* Y, 101. Hurdles for scaffolding, also split rods for making hurdles. Cf. Flakes (in Hearn's Jo. Glast. v. 2, p. 321). Wattling for preserving sea walls.

Floryssyng, *part.* Adorning with colour the wax-candles. Y.

Forlock. Y, 149. A carpenter's term.

Freethes, *n.s.* Y, 91=Vreethes or Wreaths, *i.e.*, Wreathen work for dead fencing or for wattle and dab. Cf. Frething and Frether, T, 196, and cum virgis vrydendis T, 178. See Halliwell.

G

Gawds, *n.s.*, *passim.* Bosses or other ornamental attachments to girdles or jewels.

Gemmows, *n.s.*, variably spelt. A pair of hinges [gemelli, twins] including the loop on the door and the hook on the durn.

Glassyn, *adj.* Y. Made of glass.

Grayell, *n.s.*, variously spelt, *sæpe.* Grail. *Lat.* Gradale, an office book.

Grey-cayk, *n.s.* Prob. a pigment, 97.

Groming-wardens, *n.s.* M, 1559. Groomen-wardens, *i.e.*, Wardens of the grooms or young men's guild.

H

Harnest, *p.p.*, applied to a girdle. Garnished, adorned.[1]

Hele, *v.t. passim.* To cover, whence Helyer, a Tiler.

Helme-bought, *n.s.* T. Helm-bōt, *i.e.*, the right of cutting helm [stubble] in a common field. Cf. Fire-bōt, Plough-bōt.

Here, Herys, Here-cloth, *n.s.* Cloth made of hair to cover the stone altar-slabs under a richer cloth.

Hoggler, *n.s.* The lowest class of labourer, including miners, in **Z** *hod.*

Hogling-money, *n.s.* P, 26. The labourers' contribution paid through the lady-wardens.

Hogeling *alias* **Hokeling-light,** *n.s.* A light maintained by a Hoggler's guild, see Preface.

Hopyng, *part.* Y, *sæpe.* Hooping vessels.

---

[1] "Bright-harnest angels sit in order serviceable." Milton's Ode on Christ's Nativity, last line.

Huck-muckes, *n.s.* **Y**, 28. Something for wiping the feet upon, often renewed, probably of brushwood, Jenn. Z. Dict. gives the word=A strainer retaining the dregs of a mash-tub.

Husselling-Cloth. **Y**, 14. A cloth used in Houseling, *i.e.*, in administering the Holy Sacrament of the Body.

J

Jettyn, *adj.* **C**, 1499. Made of Jet.

Jornale, *n.s.* **B**, 1370. A wax candle "j cereo empto ad jornale."

Judas. **Y** and **T**, *sæpe*. A light or series of lights, or of light holders, ranged along the rood-loft, casting up their glare on the Rood. At **T** there were 40 such light-holders of wood, p. 185.

K

Key, Kye, *n.s.* **P**, *passim*, for plural of cow. Hence Key-wardens.

Kreys-cloth ⎫ *n.s., passim*. Linen cloth applied to divers uses in Church and
Cresse and **Creste-cloth** ⎭ Church-house.

Kyve, *n.s.* **Y**, *sæpe*. A large tub. Cf. keeve in Devon *hod*.

L

Lamb-tow, *n.s.* **M**, *passim*. Wool of young lambs.

Latten, *n.s., sæpe*. A mixed metal, still used.

Lege-bell, *n.s.* **Y**, 90. Possibly a Lyche-bell.

Legent, *n.s.* **C**, p. 5. A book of Legenda or Lections.

Leverys, *n.s.* **T**, 186. Some kind of grain-crop "segetes."

Liernes, *n.s.* **T**, 184. Oaken ribs under the projecting gallery of the rood-loft. (Walcott's Sacred Archæo.)

Light-men, *n.s.* Gatherers for the maintenance of lights in the east and west parts of **Y**.

Lugs to the banners, *passim*. Strings to hold the banners in place.

Lyche-rest, *n.s.* **Y**, 1559. A privilege of being buried in the Church, including probably the lying in the Church with tapers, &c., before burial. The term is very shortlived.

M

Maser, *n.s.* **P**, 51. A wooden bowl provided for the office of Holy Matrimony. See note at end.

Mell, *v.n.* To meddle. **M**. Z *hod*.

Mese ⎫ *n.s.* Moss. ⎧ **Y**, 94. Cf. Mesh Z *hod*. Moss was largely used to lay under the
Muse ⎭ ⎩ **B**, 1376. sheets of lead in roofs.

Mind ⎫ *n.s.* A commemoration of the dead, at the end of a month or year, sometimes
Mynde ⎭ endowed for a term of years, or in perpetuity.

Mynells, *n.s.* **Y**, 129. Mullions. Cf. *Fr.* Menaux ; *Eng.* Moynells.

Myster, *n.s.* **Y**, 142. Some chest or locker built by the wardens in Church house.

N

Nelme, *n.s.* An Elm by transfer of the "n" from the article. By like transfer an oak, an ewe, become noak and newe.

Numerale, *n.s.* A bracelet or similar ornament, the beads perhaps arranged in tens to aid in counting. T, 192.

O

Orphrey, *n.s.*, variably spelt. A band of gold or embroidery set on vestments. *Lat.* Aurifrigia.

Oriscopium, *n.s.* T, *sæpe.* A clock, meant for horologium, a word still extant in Z in the form of "horloge."

P

Par, *n.s.* Strictly a pair, but used for a suit or set, *e.g.*, "par vestimentorum" "par precularum."

Parcella, *n.s.*, in T. A Bill of parcels or details presented by the Wardens in addition to the audit-sheet. Two samples are extant.

Pax } *n.s., sæpe.* The small metal plate serving for the Kiss of Peace in the Liturgy.
Paks

Paxbrede, *n.s.* Y, 30. The plate apart from the Foot of the Pax. Brede=Breadth.

Pelow, *n.s.* A Pillow, whence Pelow-tow, *i.e.*, stuffing for pillows.

Peyse, *n.s.* A weight, used either for a clock—or organ bellows.

Plocks, *n.s.* Blocks of wood. Y, 1–7–9, "ligno voc. plocks."

Portass } *n.s. sæpe.* The office-book called in *Lat.* Portiforium.
Portoce

Posenett, *n.s.* A litttle pot. (Halliwell.) Y, 1466.

Preculæ, *n.s.* Beads for use in prayer. T, 1512–3, par precularum, a set of beads.

Pricket } *n.s. sæpe.* A tall candle, elevated on a spike.
Prekyt

Procurator } *n.s. passim.* A warden, steward, manager or other accredited person.
Proctor

Putteful, *n.s.* P, 10. Cartload. A two-wheeled cart is still a Putt in Z.

Pye, *n.s.* Y. The ritual directory or ordinale, see Preface to Book of Common Prayer.

Pyggesfote, *i.e.*, Pigsfote, *n.s.* Y, 105. A vessel used in Y Church-house for bearing coals.

Pynowne, *adj.* Pointing or gable end. Z *hod*, pronounced "pwinen" Y, 56.

Perrson, *n.s.* M, 211. The rector impropriate, *i.e.*, Barlynch Priory. The term was in strictness limited to the rector, as "persona ecclesiæ."

Q

Quetin, *n.s.* P. *Prob.* Cushion.

R

Range, *n.s.* A sieve, Z *hod.* Y, 128. A cleansing range.
Rather, *adj.* Earlier, preceding—the comparative of rathe, *i.e.*, early. Z *hod.*—Y *sæpe* "the rather wardens."
Ray, *n.s.* Striped cloth.
Ray-corse, *n.s.* The striped bodice of a girdle.
Rayer, *adj.* Rear, *i.e.*, the preceding year. Y, 99, or, if the "y" stands for "th," the *rather* year would mean the same.
Rede, *n.s.* Reed, *i.e.*, in Z, straw severed from the ears before thrashing, and dressed for the thatcher, see Y, 53, "reaping rede."
Rele, *n.s. Lat.* Rota. Reel or corona, hung to carry a circle of lights, Y, 23, "wax to fulfill ye rele" "gylding the rele." See Trendell, which is sometimes used in same sense.
Rest, *n.s.* C, *passim.* The balance of an audited account.
Ridding, *part., passim.* Clearing out dirt or rubbish.
Ryses, *n.s.* Y. "Ryses to the dawbes." Hurdlework daubed with clay to form partitions, or to fill panels in a timber frame—called Z *hod*, "Wattle and dab." Rys = Twig [Mayhew and Skeat]. Anglo-Saxon Hris.

S

Seges } *n.s., passim.* Seats, *Fr.* Siége.
Seggs
Seme or **Zeme,** *n.s.* A long measure, *e.g.*, of boards, Y, 100, also a heap-measure as of lime. Cf. "Seme of wheat." (Piers Plowman.)
Semys, *n.s.* Y, 90. "Scouring of the great semys."
Shudde
Shyde } *n.s.* Variously spelt, *passim.* The small wood of timber trees, or the top and lop of pollards—called Shrouds, Z *hod.*
Schryde
Servy or **Sarvy,** *v.n.* Y, *sæpe.* To serve for a regular purpose, see note on letter Y.
Shere-Thursday, *n.s.* Y, 60. Maunday Thursday.
Smygma, *n.s.* T, *sæpe.* An ointment. See Migma. Ducange.
Solarium, *n.s.* Y, *sæpe.* The Aler or gallery of Roodloft. In its other sense of a sun-dial or clock, it is not used.
Sommar, *n.s.* Y, 116. A somerstone, *i.e.*, the headstone of a coign, corbelled out to support the coping of the gable. The term "somer" is also applied to corbel-beams. (Parker's Glossary.)
Somner, *n.s.* Summoner, an apparitor of Consistory Court. Y, 149.
Spelyd, *v., past tense.* M, 217. Served the place of. A.S. spelian, to take a spell or turn of duty. (Chambers' Eng. Dict.)
Sprangs, or **Spronges,** to a ladder, *n.s.* Rungs. (Wright.)
Stansile, *n.s.* T, 191. A style, an error for "scansile" from scando, to climb.

Strekyng, *part.* (1) colouring wall with lines or patterns, perhaps stencilling.
(2) colouring walls plain, within and without. **Y,** 37, *et passim.*

[The use of plaster and of lime-washes on church walls inside and out, was very common.]

Syler, *n.s.* A ceiler, *i.e.*, a decorator, who did both the woodwork, and colouring of the highly adorned canopies, formed in the roof over Altars, and called ceilings. *Lat.* celatura, sylatura.

Syntorne. Y, 118. Centering for turning an arch.

Synt ⎫ *n.s.* Saint. The spelling is phonetic, and shows how St. John, St. Leger, St. Maur,
Syn ⎭ came to be pronounced Sinjohn, Silleger, Seymour.

St. Sonday. M. See note at end.

T

Tablement, *n.s.* **Y,** *sæpe.* A representation in painting or carving.
Tak, *n.s.* **Y,** 1490. Iron gear attached to a wagon. "Two takys." **Y,** 1446-7.
Trawle, *n.s.* **Y,** 140, see Drawle.
Threddyn, *adj.* **C,** 1499. Made of thread.

Token ⎫
Tocking ⎬ girdle. **Y,** 47; **C,** 5. A girdle suited for Tucker's work, or for tucking up the
Tucking ⎭ petticoats.

Tornelle, *n.s.* A turret. **Y,** 147, "for poynting a tornelle of Ch." (Gloss. of Arch.)
Trayle, *n.s.* The running vine-pattern common on cornices of rood screens, p. 27. Cf. Trellis.
Treyn, *adj.* Made of wood, **Y,** 150, applied to a platter.
Trendyll, *n.s.* (1) A hanging corona or hoop for bearing lights. Reel and Rota.
(2) A tub. (Halliwell.) **Y.** Inventory of Church-house "21, Trendylls."
(3) Rarely. The candles used in the Corona.
Like trundle, the word is derived from "turn" as treadle from tread.
Trussing (bells), *n.s.* Strengthening the timbers of the bell-cage by a diagonal brace.
Tynnell, *n.s.* A tunnel or funnell called in **Z** *hod.* "Tunnegar."
Tynnyng, *part.* Tending. **Y,** *sæpe,* "Tynning the lights."

V

Vestment, *n.s.* The Chasuble—sometimes, when in plural, including minor articles. **Y,** 67
A vestment is made out of an old cope.
Vicary, *n.s. passim.* A vicar, formed direct from Latin vicarius, like notary.
Vyse, also **Fyce,** *n.s.* A winding staircase. **Y,** *sæpe.* Also Vyse-door.

W

Walshe-bord, *n.s.* **Y,** 23. Foreign wainscot. Welsh in **Z,** as in German = foreign.
Wardenwick, *n.s.* **P,** *sæpe.* Wardenship, like Bailiwick, &c.
Want ⎫
Vont ⎬ *n.s.* Font. **P,** *sæpe.* N.B. Vaute, a spelling of Vault is often difficult to discriminate from the versions of font.
Vout ⎭
Whirligoge, *n.s.* A turnstile. **T,** 49, 183.
Wrestys [for door], *n.s.* Perhaps Twysts, *i.e.*, the iron loops, fitted to the hooks of the hinge.

Y

Yeo, *n.s.* The main drain of a level **Z.** In the case of the rivers Ivel and Wring, the term has superseded the ancient river-name.
Yere, *n.s.* A sluice-gate. See in ordnance map of **Z,** "Hook year," "New Yar," on the Yeo, perhaps a **Z** pronunciation of "Weir," dropping the "w."
Yncull, *n.s.* Broad linen tape for girdles, for an amice, for a book covering; now spelt inkle, see Shakespeare's Pericles. **V,** 1.

N.B.—**Y** in modern **Z** is added to the end of a verb to make it frequentative, *e.g.*, to sewy = to sew for a livelihood; to glovy, to make gloves, as a trade. In the **Y** accounts there are several instances of this use.

Z

Zitter, *n.s.* Guitar, from Cithara. **P,** 25.

NON SOLUTA.

The following words or phrases have as yet defied solution, some of them are perhaps disguised by mispelling, or by decay—others it is hoped may find an interpreter :—

Taratantaryatione unius ligni. **T,** 194.	**Whyt mother.** **Y,** 160. (?) Godmother.
Dipote or **dipoce** and **Poyntell.** **T,** 187.	**Haffe.** **Y,** 166.
Cloths staffyng. **Y,** 167.	**Ewell.** 198.
Jaole. **T,** 196.	**Clogill.** 187, 9.
Quyrbys. 154.	**Walete.** 195.
Prelubkys. **Y,** 84.	**Bastyng the ryne in Whyt.** 172.
Dawell-light. 324.	**Lyche of a rope.** 76.
Pokysy. **Y,** A°. 1452.	**A cenne of ye vestments.** 117.
Swystyng gyrdyll. **Y,** 130.	

NOTES EXPLANATORY.

MASER.—"A stonding maser to serve for brides at their weddyng" is found at Pilton. This was in compliance with the Rubric of the Sarum Manual. "Post Missam benedicatur panis et vinum vel aliud quid potabile *in vasculo*, et gustent in nomine Domini sacerdote dicente Dom Vobiscum. Oremus." The Collect that followed refers to the marriage of Cana &c. In the same Inventory is another Maser with a bande of sylver.

ST. SONDAY.—She is found to be a female Saint reverenced at **M** (where she had a "Store" and a warden, see p. 222) and at **Y**, and also in West Somerset and Devon, *e.g.*, at Cutcombe and Brompton Regis, also in Yorks (Test Ebor, **V**, 299). The name has lately been much discussed. It is now supposed by good authorities to be a translation of Dominica, who is stated in Stanton's Menology, p. 202, to have been a hermitess at Shapwick with her brother S. Indractus, and to have shared his violent death, and canonization. The sainted remains were removed by King Ina in the 8th century to the neighbouring Abbey of Glastonbury, where S. Indractus was a recorded name in the time of the chronicler Ad. de Domerham.

ST. DOMINICA gives name to the Church of S. Dominic, Cornwall, dedicated to her by Bishop Bronscombe in 1263. She was invoked in an Exeter Litany of the 11th century. The vernacular version of her name may be due to the difficulty of differencing her from the great founder of the Dominican Order, canonized in 1234, the English tongue failing to distinguish the male from the female name.

END OF GLOSSARY.

Appendix A.

LIST OF CHURCH GOODS, "SUPELLEX," REQUIRED BY ARCHBISHOP WINCHELSEA'S CONSTITUTION, 1305, TO BE FOUND BY PARISHIONERS.

[*See* Lyndwood's "Provinciale," Lib. III, Tit. 27, and Johnson's "Canons," Vol. II, p. 319. Ed. 1851.]

Books.

1. Legenda.
2. Antiphonarium.
3. Gradale.
4. Psalterium.
5. Troperium.
6. Ordinale.
7. Missale.
8. Manuale.

Notes from Lyndwood and Johnson's Canons.

1. A lectionary of lessons from Holy Writ, or from Lives of Saints or Homilies.
2. Containing whatever was sung at the canonical hours, save the Psalter.
3. Or Grail, containing all that pertains to the Choir at celebration of Mass.
4. The Psalter noted.
5. Containing the sequences sung after the epistle at Mass.
6. Or Pie. A directory of Divine Service.
7. Containing the whole office of the Mass.
8. A Handbook of various offices, *e.g.*, baptisms, benedictions, processions.

Notes from Lyndwood.

Calix	Chalice, including the Paten which formed its cover.
Vestimentum principale cum casula	Casula, the chasuble, the chief robe of a set of vestments, and indispensable for celebration.
Tunica	The subdeacon's robe.
Dalmatica	Robe for Priest or Deacon.
Capa in choro (*i.e.*, not at side altars)	Used at other priestly offices than the Mass
Cum appendiciis	*E.g.*, Amice, with girdles, maniples, stoles.
Frontale ad magnum Altare	Also called the Pall (Palla).
Cum iij tuellis	Two veils or cloths, to be placed under the corporal, one for hand-washing.

Appendix.

Tria Superpellicia	For use of Priest, Deacon, Sub-deacon.
Rochetum.	Linen robe without the sleeves of surplice, used by priest's assistant.
Crux processionalis.	
Crux pro mortuis.	
Thuribulum	Thurible or Censer.
Lucerna.	
Tintinnabulum ad deferendum coram Corp. Xti., in Visitatione	Used in visitation of sick to warn passers-by to venerate the Holy Eucharist.
Pyxis pro Corpore Xti	Pyx cum clausura, *i.e.*, a decent outside case of ivory or silver.
Velum quadragesimale	To veil the images in Lent.
Vexilla pro Rogationibus	Banners for Intercessory processions on the Gang-days.
Campanæ cum chordis.	
Feretrum pro defunctis.	
Vas pro aquâ benedictâ	Portable vessel with its Sprinkler.
Osculatorium	The Pax, to receive the Kiss of Peace from the faithful at Mass.
Candelabrum pro cereo paschali	The Easter taper was also to be provided by parish, by special collection, at the Easter procession.
Fons cum serurâ	Fonts were locked to preserve the stock of blest water, which was renewed at intervals.
Imagines in Ecclesiâ.	*I.e.*—In the Nave, not those in side chapels.
Imago principalis in cancello	*I.e.*—generally of the Patron Saint.

Reparationes.

Navis Eccl^æ, intra et extra, tam in imaginibus quam in fenestris vitreis.
Librorum.
Vestimentorum.

Cetera contingunt Rectoribus, Vicariis, et aliis secundum loci consuetudinem.[2]

---

[1] Including new work when needed.
[2] Custom, says Lyndwood, is held to modify any of the above liabilities.

Appendix B.

CHURCH ALES, WAKES, &c., BEFORE THEIR ABOLITION.

In the reign of Elizabeth Chief Justice Popham made some orders to the Justices of the Shire for the restraint of these revels [Fuller's Church History, vol. II, p. 147].

In 1631 Judge Richardson repeated the orders, with concurrence of the Justices who petitioned the King through the Lord Lieutenant to suppress wakes [*ib.*].

The King then desired the Archbishop to procure evidence from the clergy touching the alleged abuses. The Bishop of this Diocese, Piers, procured the evidence by citing 72 incumbents from various quarters. Bishop Piers' Return to the Archbishop, Nov. 3, 1633, is as follows :—

(1.) These dedication feasts have been in all these (72) parishes, not only this last year, but also for many years, without any disorders.

(2.) Upon the Feast days (for the most part Sundays) the service of the Church hath been more solemnly performed, and the Church better frequented, forenoon and afternoon, than on any other Sunday.

(3.) They have not known nor heard of any disorders in the neighbouring towns, where the like feasts are kept.

(4.) The people do very much desire the continuance of these feasts.

(5.) It is fit, in the opinion of all these Ministers, to continue them as a memorial of the dedication of their Churches, for the civilizing of the people, for their lawful recreations, for the composing of differences by occasion of meeting of friends, for the increase of love and amity, as being feasts of charity for the relief of the poor, the richer sort keeping then, in a manner, open house, and for many other reasons.

In addition to this return, which Bishop Piers believed would be endorsed by a hundred more of his clergy, he subjoins his own observations.

"I find that there are not only feasts of dedication, but in many places, Church-ales, Clerks' ales, and Bid-ales. The dedication feasts are more general, and generally they are called feast-days, though sometimes revel-days, they are not known to the ignorant people as feasts of dedication, but they are so, for the churches dedicated to the Holy Trinity keep their feast on Trinity Sunday; most that are dedicated to Saints keep their feast on the Sundays before or after the Saints' day. I find that almost all are kept in the summer time because that time is convenient for meeting of friends from all places, in some places they have solemn sermons, preached by Divines of good note, and also communions; in one place the parish holds lands by its feast. One of the Ministers notes in his answer that in the reformed Churches of Switzerland these feasts are kept.

I find that the people, hearing two years ago that the judges would put down their feasts, thought that it was very hard if they could not entertain their kindred and friends once a year, to praise God for His blessings, and to pray for the King's Majesty, under whose happy government they enjoyed peace and quietness, and they would endure the judges' penalties rather than break off their feasts. It is found also that many suits in law have been taken up at these feasts by mediation of friends, which could not have been so soon ended in Westminster Hall.

Moreover, I find that the chiefest cause of the dislike of these feasts among the preciser sort is because they are kept on Sundays, which they never call but Sabbath days, upon which they would have no manner of recreation, nay neither roast nor sod; and some of the Ministers who were with me, have ingeniously [ingenuously] confessed that if the people should not have their honest and lawful recreations on Sundays after evening prayer, they would go either into tippling-houses, and there upon their ale-benches talk of matters of Church and State, or else into conventicles.

Concerning Church-ales I find that in some places the people have been persuaded to leave them off, in others they have been put down by Judges and Justices, so that now there are few of them left; but yet I find that by Church-ales heretofore many poor parishes have cast their bells, repaired their towers, beautified their churches, and raised stocks for the poor; and not by the sins of the people (as some humourists say) but by the benevolence of people at their honest and harmless sports and pastimes, at which there hath not been observed so much disorder as is commonly at fairs and markets.

Touching Clerks'-ales (which are lesser Church-ales) for the better maintenance of parish clerks, they have been used (until of late) in divers places, and there was good reason for them; for in poor country parishes, where clerks' wages are small, the people thinking it unfit that the Clerk should duly attend Church and lose by his office, were wont to send him in provision, and then feast with him, and give him more liberally than their quarterly payments should amount to in many years. And since these have been put down, some Ministers fear they shall have no parish-clerk, for want of maintenance.

There is another kind of meeting called a Bid-ale, when an honest man, decayed in his estate, is set up again by the liberal benevolence and contributions of friends at a feast; but this is laid aside in almost every place.

* * * * *

Your Grace's ever to be commanded,
GUIL., BATH AND WELLS.

Wells, Nov. 5° 1633.

Within the original is folded the following order, but whether issued or not, *non constat*.

Somerset. Whereas divers orders have heretofore been made by Judges of Assize for the suppression of Church-ales, Clerks'-ales, Wakes, Revels, and such like, by reason of disorders, &c.

It is now ordered by his Lordship[1] that all such orders be revoked [as much as in him lieth] and made utterly void; and that it may be lawful for all persons freely to use any lawful recreation or exercise at such meetings, but with this advice, that they be careful that no misdemeanours commonly arising at such feasts be done or committed."

There is also in the State Paper Office a Draft of a Letter from the King, May 2, 1633, to three Justices, requiring them to certify (1) what orders had been given by any Judges of Assize for suppression of Wakes, *i.e.*, dedication feasts; and (2) what orders C. J. Richardson had given at the last assizes for recalling, pursuant to the King's command through the Lord Keeper, the prohibitions of such feasts, the King wishing that people should enjoy lawful recreations after evening prayer, the Justices repressing excesses, and all profaning of the Lord's Day.

ADDENDUM TO APPENDIX B.

I add a document which helps to track the fate of Church-houses after their first uses failed.

It is a Petition to Archbishop Laud, extracted from the State Papers by my father when Keeper of the S. P. Office. (See Hadspen MSS. v. x. 71.)

Antony Earbury, Vicar of Weston Zoyland, states in Petition that the Parishioners had at their own charge built a fair Church-house, and employed it for 100 years for benefit of the Church, that Sir Edward Powell,[2] Kt., had lately taken possession thereof and built a common bakehouse for his own benefit, which was presented at the Archbishop's Visitation, that for this presentment Sir. E. P. has questioned the Petitioner, Church-wardens and Sidesmen in the Wells Court.

The Archbishop, therefore, desires Sir John Lambe (who was Dean of Arches) to issue inhibition to the Court at Wells, and to advise as to future course.

[1] *Qy.*, the Lord Keeper?
[2] He was Patron, and probably also represented the Grantee of this old Glastonbury Manor. The Abbey seems to have favoured the establishment of Church-houses on their Manors by granting leases of sites. Many of them are specified in Abbot Beere's Terrier, 1517.

Appendix C.

RETURN OF ELEEMOSYNARY ENDOWMENTS HELD BY ECCLESIASTICAL BODIES IN DIOCESE OF BATH AND WELLS, COMPILED FROM HENRY VIII's VALOR, 1537.

	£	s.	d.
Glastonbury Abbey	140	16	8
Wells Cathedral—no charge on corporate funds—but there were many doles to the poor in connection with obituary services		Nil.	
[returned A° 1 Edward VI to the Chantry Commissioners at, £21 16s. 6d.]			
Wells—St. John's Hospital at Founders' anniversaries	3	6	8
Bruton Abbey—daily, and on Maunday Thursday	16	6	8
Taunton Priory—including 4 Almsmen at Stavordale	41	9	0
Keynsham „	10	15	0
Worspring „	8	0	0
Bath „	10	2	6
Muchelney Abbey—4 Almsmen, 7 poor men occasionally	11	3	0
Montacute Priory—7 Almsmen, others occasionally	23	8	6
Athelney Abbey—charged on divers[1] estates	22	18	2
Cleeve „ „ „ „	26	18	4
Barlynch Priory „ „ „	8	1	0
Dunster „ „ „ „	0	14	8
Bridgwater—St. John's Hospital	32	6	8
two estates charged by Bishop Burnell with maintenance of thirteen boys—another with maintaining seven Almsmen, leaving only £1 13s. for distribution.			
Bath—Hospital of St. John	0	8	0
	£356	14	10

The houses at Hinton and Witham, Barrow, Buckland and Templecombe return nothing.

---

[1] The Manor of Sutton was charged with £11 4s. for eleven Bedesmen to pray for the soul of King Alfred, the founder of Athelne

REMARKS.

The abatements allowed by the King's valuers were, I conceive, only such as could be proved "ut patet per chartas" to be *fixed* charges, "doles by tenure," and so to form no part of the available corporate income which was taxable, when subsidies to the King were voted by Convocation.

There was no doubt much besides of ungauged benefaction flowing from the convents, though varying in each place, fluctuating and arbitrary, *e.g.*—(1) Relief to the wayfarer, (2) Broken meat, (3) Treatment of the Sick; for though the conventual Infirmaries were designed for the inmates of the house, yet inasmuch as they were the only infirmaries of the land, probably their benefits were sometimes extended if not to in-patients, at least to out-patients.

There were also, besides the Doles by tenure, many occasional gifts to the poor from great visitors lodging at the convent, and from pilgrims.

At Glastonbury there were *two* Almshouses, with their own special endowments, which survive to this day.

In the way of popular education, I cannot find any trace of the convents conferring any benefits. We look in vain through the chroniclers of Glastonbury, and whilst we read of many benefactions of the better Abbots of the 14th, 15th, and 16th Centuries, we read of no educational ones either inside or outside the walls, available for the people.

The abbey held an endowment[1] for maintenance of 10 scholars at Oxford, and also contributed to the maintenance of the Oxford House (now Worcester College), which educated the Novices of the Benedictine Order; but this education was academical, not popular.

After all, I suppose that the most sensible loss accruing to the neighbourhood, and especially to the abbey estates, arose from the fact, that the novices were chosen from those estates, that they rose to hold endowed monastic offices, and being allowed the private use of that earned income (though as *monks* sworn to poverty) they were able to pour their bounty into the laps of needy kinsfolk, and also to confer on them such appointments as reeves, woodmen, &c. In these indirect ways the dissolution made itself felt more than by the loss of doles at the Abbey Gate.

It must not be forgotten that endowed chantries were frequently charged with doles to the poor to be made on the day of obit.

The commission in 1st Edward VI reports the following:—Porlock 13s. besides maintenance of two Bedesmen at £3 0s. 8d per annum; Greinton, 2d.; Wedmore, 12d.; Shepton Malet, £1 10s. 8d.; Trent, 10s. 8d.; Wells Cathedral, £21 16s. 8d.

The wills in the Wells Probate Registry show likewise that the pilgrims remembered the duty of Almsgiving at the shrine which they sought. See Sir R. Playce's Will, 1534, in which he leaves money for pilgrimages to be made for the benefit of his soul "to Joseph Abarmathia," *i.e.*, Glastonbury, and to "Our Lady of Cleve," and in each case v*d*. to be given to poor people. The same motives may be assumed to have operated at the time of celebrating obituary services in village churches, and to have kept alive a sense of the duty of remembering the poor, which was fruitful in other ways and at other seasons.

---

[1] Charged on the Manor of Camely by John Byconell, and amounting to £36 6s. 8d. It shared the fate of the other revenues at the Attainder, 1539

BISHOP DROKENSFORD'S DAILY AND YEARLY ALMS, FROM 1313 TO HIS DEATH 1329.

See Reg. Drok., fo. 141, a, b.

The estates being divided into 6 Bailiwicks, the Bailiff of each was ordered to deliver to 40 of the poorest persons daily a silver farthing, or its value in food.

At Michaelmas the survivors of the 40 were to receive 4s. for a cloak and shoes.

The Incumbents of the benefited parishes were to oversee the Bailiffs (*i.e.*, to secure fitting selection of recipients). Worn-out priests admissible; but preference was to be given to such of the Bishop's serfs, or widows as had been driven by poverty to throw up their holdings and to beg.

The complement of persons thus relieved was 240.

RECTORIAL TITHES
As a Source of Relief to Poverty.

Relief of the poor is often enumerated in formal documents as one of the "onera" of rectorial income. The obligation and its extent was of necessity left, in most cases, to the rector's conscience, but where the administration of the income fell into the Bishop's hands by sequestration, the registers show that the "onus" was remembered, and sometimes defined. In some cases the sequestrator was instructed to administer relief to the poor out of the revenues in his hands. See Reg. Drok., fo. 75 (*et alibi*) and *ibid.*, fo. 214, the Bishop's complaint that non-residence of rectors, which he had too freely sanctioned, had robbed the poor of their due. Owing to this evil and to the increase of tithe-appropriation, which ensured perpetual non-residence, the relief of the poor flowing from the Rectory, must have been very intermittent, and in many large areas wholly drained away. The loss of this relief was in fact great enough to induce the King and Parliament in the 15th of Richard II, and again in 4th of Henry IV, to require that a convenient (*i.e.*, proportionate) sum of money should be set apart out of the fruits of each benefice thenceforth appropriated, and bestowed on poor parishioners. The Second Statute added the penalty of disappropriation in case of neglect, thereby attesting the fact that the requirements had been evaded. Whatever benefits flowed into the parish from the resident and conscientious rector, none can be reckoned on as a source of standing relief after the bane of appropriation had impoverished the benefice.

Appendix D.

THE HOGGLERS.

The existence of this class of men, of their name and of the share assigned to them in the life of the parish is so novel to me, and to all whom I confer with, that I deem it expedient to put on record all I know about them, in hope that their place and function in the Village Church community may be cleared up fully hereafter.

I offer the following helps:—

There were Hogglers and Hoggling lights maintained in the Church at T, at P, at Y, at M. At C, they were a Guild with Wardens, bringing their surplus, after Guild-expenses paid, to the Church-Warden's audit, like the other Guilds.

At Banwell they made a much more important contribution, see p. 229, under the name of "le Hogeling," apparently by taking charge of common lands and cattle running on them, and bringing the profits to the parish audit.

At Banwell, the Hogglers continued to bring their subsidy in Elizabeth's reign. At Cheddar, Hogeling money is found an item of receipt up to 1630, but whence it accrued, is unexplained.

The class was the lowest order of labourer with spade or pick, in tillage or in minerals. The word still survives in the Mendip villages, though not a class-name, as it was in the days of Hannah More, when her sister Patty, 1795, addressed a Provident Club thus:[1] "let the men of Shipham and Rowberrow become honest and good graziers and *Hoglers*. They are placed on this spot by Almighty God. The very ground you walk upon points out your daily labour (*i.e.*, by its richness in minerals). Excel in that. An honest Hogler is as good in the Almighty's eyes as an honest squire. Do your duty in the state of life where God has placed you." Again p. 111: "The instances are rare when you have not a moment to beg God's blessing. 'Tis presumptuous to enter on the matters of the world without asking it. A prayer put up to God at *Hogling* or at Haymaking will be as acceptable to Him," &c., &c.

The word has now fallen in use to describe not the lowest class of workman but the lowest class of *work* and *workmanship*. "You might hoggle them potatoes, but you can't dig them, *i.e.*, properly," was said in scorn to a young inexpert girl in 1889 in Churchill. "A hoggling job;" "He has been and hoggled my potatoes;" are current expressions in Cheddar and Priddy, used to discredit the *manner* of work.

For our purpose the sense of the now-dying-out word is clear enough, and the social and other facts we gain from the records are important.

The lowest class of hand-worker in our villages, whether in field or in minery was called by the name of Hoggler. It was the lowest in the social rank and in means. It must have included the serf, and yet it was allowed to take its place amongst other classes in organized

---

[1] "Mendip Annals," by Rev. A. Roberts, p. 145. Nisbet & Co., 1859.

aid to the church; and poor as it was, it was willing to bring its continual contribution if not in money to the Church Wardens' coffer, at least to the maintenance of a light, one of the continuous devotions of the sanctuary. Moreover its acceptance as an organized Guild implies an acknowledgment of its being in matters spiritual on an even level with the rest, and the effect of acting in a Guild must have been to elevate its members in capacity for orderly management and control, and also in self-respect.

These facts all tend to show that the Church did not know of any degradation in poverty or even in serfdom, and that the villagers of all ranks were in the habit of meeting the bondsmen of their community under the sacred roof as Brethren in the family of Christ. The silent teaching of these facts must have been powerful to soften the dividing lines of the body social.

In immediate connexion herewith, I now offer some proofs of the softening of the social barriers, and even of the legal ones which in their original rigour deprived the serf of political rights.

In the episcopal and capitular registers of Wells and Lichfield of the 14th and 15th Centuries the work of manumission is found to be continually going on. Even before the great changes wrought by the Black Death of 1349, *et seq.*, which raised the value of labour, the ecclesiastical landlords were largely releasing their human property "a vinculo Nayvitatis." In many cases, Bishop Drokensford tonsured the manumitted youth on the day of his release, proving that he had been selected with the view of elevation to the ministry, and that he must already have had by favour of his patron some education to bring his capacity to proof. The effect of serf-born men being thus elevated by patrons must have been very powerful in abating the scorn which free classes commonly feel towards the servile ones around them.

In my college of Merton in 14th Century, there were recorded cases of youths born in serfdom obtaining fellowships, and producing their manumission from their Lord (Kellaw, Bishop of Durham, 1311–8) to enable them to hold their fellowships. In a communer's roll 1394-5 of Wells Chapter is recorded the fact that Henry Grey a serf (nativus) had impleaded his masters the Dean and Chapter in the King's Court for unjust imprisonment and loss of goods, that the court had allowed his civil right to plead as an owner of goods, that the Chapter had been obliged to acknowledge that right, and to appear by attorney before the King's Justices at York, where they compromised by making fine.

This recognition of rights of ownership and of legal action must have been unknown to the legists, for Littleton, sec. 177, as quoted by Blackstone, Comm. Bk. II, 6, lays down that " A Villein (meaning a serf) cannot acquire lands or goods, but if he purchased either, the Lord might seize them to his own use." Littleton wrote in Edward IV's reign, 1464-82. He was recording no doubt what was the common law as laid down by the earlier writers, and not taking notice of the modifications of its stringency, which were happily growing up through the welding influences of Christian fellowship and teaching. One more documentary proof I am enabled to give by the kindness of J. F. S. Horner, Esq., of Mells, who possesses a "Terrier and perambulation of the Manor of Doulting" made by his ancestor John Horner (in 8th of Henry VIII, 1516) who was then Bailiff of the manor of D, under the Abbot (Beere) of Glastonbury, the Sub-prior and other sworn men, tenants of the manor, being present. The terrier shows that the demesne lands were no longer tilled by serf labour but divided into farms and leased out to renting tenants, who paid fines on entry. The chief lessee of demesne lands, John Whyte, is described as a serf "nativus domini."

As such he was legally incapable of owning goods, yet he is found renting from his masters at a rent of £8 16s. 8d., after paying a sum down for entry on the lease. At the end, the Terrier sums up the human property of the manor in a list of 16 " nativi domini per capita," which, on comparison with the names of the farm-tenants, reveals the facts that these serfs had been allowed to acquire property and responsible position, enabling them to pay fines, and rents. "Per capita" adverts to the legal fact that not only the heads of the servile families belonged to the Lord, but also all their "sequelæ," *i.e.*, all that followed them, wives, children, goods.

It is evident that the bulk of the yeoman class of the parish consisted of serfs, and that the parish offices must have been filled by them, and also, that the yoke of serfdom sat so lightly, and was so slight a social disparagement, that they did not think it worth while to purchase their manumission, which, as the records show, could always be done at a fixed cost.

In the Terrier, made out by the Crown officers in 1539 immediately after the Attainder of the Abbey, the serfs were dropped altogether at Doulting, though returned in neighbouring estates as "bondmen dependent on the King's pleasure for body and goods." These bondmen were reduced at Mells and at Godney to an unit, but at Pilton reached twenty-two. The Doulting serfs had probably purchased their freedom of their kind master, the Abbot, before lapsing into the hands of the King.

Index.

A.

Account books, 2, 50, 81, 84, 86, 139, 154, 166, 176, 177, 230, 231.
——————— inspected at Visitation, 167.
——————— language of, xxiii, 80, 174, 210, 225, 229, 231.
——————— payment for, 186.
——————— writing, xxii, 61, 62, 76, 86, 186, 221.
Account Day, 1, 2, 43, 167. *See* "Audits."
Account of Our Lady, 220. *See* "Our Lady's Wardens."
Account of the "Five Men," 214, 220.
Aghadoe, James, Bishop of, 95 (*n*).
Aisle, south, repaired, 103.
Alabaster-man, 185, 186.
Alabaster-slab for the High Altar, 183, 185, 186.
Albs, 71, 88, 99, 102, 124, 135, 149, 183.
Ale allowed, 66, 84, 89, 98, 104.
—— days, 140, 159.
—— givers of, 93, 94 (*n*), 98.
—— St. George's. *See* "St. George."
—— holy. *See* "Holy."
—— house, 201, 220.
——————— vessels of, repaired, 199.
—— money, 43, 224.
—— Scot, 80, 173.
Aler, (alure and alle), 79, 86, 88, 90, 92, 93, 95, 98, 100, 234.
Ales, Church, 179, 181, 182, 195, 196, 200, 227, 230, 231, 233.
—— interparochial, xx, 80, 86, 132, 135, 148 (*n*), 149, 151, 155.
—— at Michaelmas, 92.
—— at Whitsuntide, xxii, 44, 84, 87, 89, 92, 94, 128, 130, 158, 159.
Allhallowmass, 163.
Allhallowtide, 170, 172.
Allowance claimed for expenses, 221, 222.
——————— to Wardens *pro stipendio*, 225, 226.

Almatory, 213, 220, 234.
——————— grave in, 214, 215.
——————— repaired, 220.
Alms-box, xxv.
—— giving, 249.
—— light, 208, &c.
—— account, 209, 221.
—— gifts to the store, 210, 211, 212, 213, 214.
Altar, building of, 164.
—— High. *See* "High Altar."
—— iron set over, 165.
—— made, 129.
—— painted, 201.
—— table, 110.
—— taken down, 172.
Altarage (Altelage), xxv.
Altars dressed, 162.
—— two made, 86.
—— side, 148.
—— washing of, 88.
Altar-cloths, 2, 3, 31, 53, 91, 134, 149, 150, 151, 197, 198, 214, 217, 218.
——————— bought, 92, 142.
——————— blessed, 60, 129, 142, 154.
——————— crooks to, 148.
——————— new, 149.
——————— painted, 215.
——————— red satin, 225.
——————— silk, 216.
——————— washed, 178.
Amber-beads, 64, 65.
Amusements, popular, xiii, xx.
"Amys," 113, 135, 147, 149, 159.
"An ely [anneal] a sick man," 99.
Angel gilded, 96.
—— St. Katherine stands on, 126.
"Anniversary," 195. *See* "Obit" and "Mynd."
Antiphonale, 188.
Antiphoners, 52.
Antony's (St.) Store, 208, 210.
"Apparel" of the Altar, 35, 118.

"Apparel" of Chasubles, 183.
Appendices, 243, 245, 248, 251.
Apportionment to Vicars, xii and *n*.
Appropriation, Act of, 152, 204 (*n*).
Aprons, 106, 113, 130, 133, 136, 140.
"Aquæ bajulus," xviii, 188, 189, 191, 192.
Arch at chancel door repaired, 199.
Archbishop of Canterbury's Visitation, 168, 181.
Archdeacon of Tanton, his coercive authority, 231.
—————————— his visitation, 178.
Arches, closing of, 112.
Arrearages, 175, 176, 178, 186, 226.
Assessments, xii.
"Asyon" (ashen), 146.
Audits, xxiii, 1, 2, 167, 225, 226.
Axbridge, 138, 139, 161, 162.
"Axsyn," 117, 119, 234. *See* also under "Lead."

B.

Backwell, 83, 130 (*n*), 143 (*n*), 151 and *n*.
Bakehouse, xxi, 173, 177, 178, 183, 186, 187, 188, 194, 195, 231.
—————— covered, 187.
—————— rent of, 178, 179, 181, 196, 203, 205.
—————— thatched, 179.
—————— chamber in it rented, 188, 203, 205.
—————— the old, rent of, 196.
—————— repaired, *ib.*
Baker's land at Bristol, 138.
Baking for the Church, allowance for, 197.
Balance beam, 182.
Bale and Bayle (bailiff), 94, 132.
—————————— payment to for bakehouse, 197.
—————————— for Church-house, 198.
"Bales,' (bellows) 149.
Baltsborow, 199.
Banner bought, 155, 183.
—————— carried, 44, 174, 188, 189, 190, 191, 197, 203.
—————— cloths, 52.
—————— of St. Katherine, 112.
—————— of our Lady, 59.
—————— made or set up, 88, 107, 125.
—————— paid for, 135.
—————— recovered, 46.
—————— of St. Sidwell, 213.
—————— of silk (St. George), 217.
—————— and streamer rolled in an altar-cloth, 224.
Banwell, x, 92, 98, 122, 149, 161, 168, 229, 230, 231, 251.

Bargain, 142, 146, 151, 152.
Barley, gift of, 85, 87, 100, 127.
Barlinch Priory, 208, 209, 211 (*n*).
——————— lessee of, 209.
——————— window of, 209, 216.
——————— wrecked, 209.
Barlow, Bishop, 78.
Bartholomew, Friar, legacy from, 184.
Bartin wall, 203.
Basket for carrying the *Panis benedictus*, 192.
Bason, 39, 53, 80, 83, 210, 211.
—— and laver, 82.
—— recovered, 46.
—— wooden, 183.
"Bastyng the ryng,' 172.
Batell, Sir John, 147, 151.
Bath, riding to, 141.
—— St. Michael's, ix, xvi, 225, 226, 227, 228.
—— historical value of the accounts of, 225.
Battlement, 100, 101, 118.
Bawdrickes for bells, &c., 55, 57, 58, 61, 62, 68, 70, 71, 72, 74, 124, 178, 203, 213, 234.
—————— buckle for, 62, 83.
—————— for a Cope, 52.
Bawnton (Bampton), 213, 216, 219.
Beads, pairs of, 21, 35, 36, 56, 59, 69, 71, 72, 199, 215.
—— amber, 64, 65, 89.
—— coral, 22, 25, 27, 29.
—— jet, 23, 28, 36, 53, 56, 64, 65.
Beam before the High Altar, 155.
—— the High Cross, 192.
Beans, legacy of, 181.
Beckham, Canon, 140 and *n*.
Beckington, Bishop, 7, 95 (*n*), 103 (*n*),181 (*n*).
Bede-man, xiii.
Bede-roll, xiii, 175 (*n*), 192, 210, 229, 234.
Bedminster, Archbishop's visitation, 168, 169.
—————— King's visitation, 160, 161.
Beere, Abbot, 247 (*n*), 252.
Bees, 209, 213.
—— a "bott" of, 215.
—— a swarm of, xiii, 213.
"Bellator," 146, 147, 148, 205 and *n*.
Bell-ropes, 44, 57, 58, 66, 70, 72, 73, 76, 176, 203, 220.
Bells bought, 204.
—— cage for, 76, 204.
—— carriage of, 92, 114, 125.
—— casting, 61, 88.
—— collars, 219.
—— consecration of, 95, 198.
—— cost of do., 198.
—— contract for casting at Bristol, 125.

Index.

Bells, cost of, 79, 90, 105.
—— founded on the spot, 231.
—— frame for, 44 and *n*.
—— gifts to, 23, 25, 33, 34, 67.
—— the great, 92, 146.
—— "hoisting down," 125.
—— iron work for, 84.
—— keeping, 86, 88, 103, 123, 163, 165.
—— knells on. *See* "Knell."
—— leather for, 176.
—— the little, casting, 169.
—— maker, 144, 145.
—— "man," (*i.e.*, founder), 92, 105.
—— metal sold, 204.
—— money gathered for, 125
—— rung for a Monk, 85.
—— old and new, expenses of, 92, 93.
—— poor man's bequest to, 67.
—— pully for, 92.
—— recasting, 127, 173
—— repairs to, 48, 60, 61, 68, 69, 70, 71, 76, 90, 103, 106, 124, 129, 167, 183, 205.
—— Sacring. *See* "Sacring."
—— subscribers to, 204.
—— trimming, 172.
—— trussing, 88.
—— the warning, 61.
—— weighing, 92.
"Bellyn," 106 and *n*.
Bench in Church, 61.
Benches of carved-oak, 173.
Benefactors, dirige and mass for, 55, 56, 57, 59, 60, 62, 68, 76.
Bennett, Rev. J. A., ix, xxvi.
Beryngton, 116.
Bible, 47, 152, 161.
—— bought, 205.
—— chain for, 153.
Bid-Ales, 246.
Bier, 45, 57, 58, 59, 69, 70.
Bishop Drokensford's daily and yearly Alms, 250.
—— Piers, xxii.
—— Richard, Vicar of Y, 85 and *n*.
Bishop's counsel asked, 168.
———— receiver, 87 (*n*.).
———— visitation, 181, 205.
———— visitation court, 205 and *n*.
Blessing of bells, vessels, vestments, &c., 60, 67, 71, 79, 95, 110 (*n*.), 112, 113, 123, 126, 129, 136, 138, 142, 149, 154, 197, 198, 201, 215.
Bluett, family, 94 and *n*.
"Bocher," 138.
Bolen, Thos., 52.
"Bona Ecclesiæ," 188

Bonfire, 44 (*n*.).
Book, gift of, to the Church, 35.
—— of the High Wardens, 121, 122.
Bookbinder, 116, 124, 151, 152, 186, 187.
Book for the procession, 44.
—— maker, 114.
—— for the Communion, 163.
—— of accounts for St. James' Chapel, 139.
Books of the Church, 50, 52.
—— binding of, 93, 100, 112.
—— bought by the Priest, 73, 143, 152.
"Borow" (security), 49, 63.
Boss, iron, 181.
Bottle, glass, to keep wine for the Communion, &c., 172, 197.
"Botts" for bees, 213.
Bowls for the Church-house, 114, 130, 142, 165, 171.
Box of copper "for the sacrament," 46.
—— for Deeds, 62.
—— of silver gilt, 53.
Boxes for money, 47.
Brandiron, 53, 145.
"Brasina," 173, 186, 188, 191, 196.
Brass, 35.
—— casting, 104.
—— of old candlesticks, 163.
Bread and Wine for the Holy Communion, 48, 163, 168, 172.
"Brethereddyne dirige and mass," 229.
Brewhouse, 173, 181, 182, 231.
Brewing, xxi, 83, 113, 122, 130, 159, 173, 175, 182, 186, 188, 195, 196, 197, 201.
Brides, Maser for, 51, 242.
Bridge near Churchyard stile, 188, 191.
Bridgewater, ix (*n*.), x, xii, xiii, xiv, xvi (*n*.), 229, 230.
Briefs, 102, 171.
Brimstone, 178, 187.
Bristol, 114, 123, 144, 153, 169.
—— to Bellator at, 146, 147, 148.
—— bells at, paid for, 92, 144.
—— bells recast at, 105, 125, 146.
—— cross from, 153.
—— embroiderer at, 149.
—— lands at, 138.
—— organ maker, 142, 143.
—— painted cloth from, 167.
—— painter at, 161.
—— Priest from, 153.
—— Smith of, 155.
—— vestments from, 113.
—— visitation charges at, 171.
—— wainscot boards from, 88.

2 L

Bristol, wax bought at, 94.
"Broches" (spits), 53, 142.
"Brochys" (brooches), ornamental, 64.
Brockley 83.
Broiderer, 157.
Broken money, 155.
——— silver, 156.
Brompton Regis, 242.
Bronscombe, Bishop, 242.
Brotherhood of St. Mary, 174, 181.
Bruges, satin and silk, 46, 47, 143.
Bruton, xviii, 44.
"Brymbylls," 141.
Brytell, Syr Thomas (chaplain), 178.
Buckles, silver, 65, 83.
——— with pendant, 54.
Buckram, 112, 130, 142, 189.
Bull, killed and distributed, xiv, 83.
——— red, 180, 181, 182, 183.
Bulls, papal, 167.
"Burdestock,' 141.
Burials in the Church, 47, 79, 166, 200.
——— in the aisle before St. Sidwell, 215.
——— in the Chapel, do.
——— mending pavement of the Church after, 105.
Burying fee, 38, 47, 54, 79, 155 (*n.*), 206.
——— ——— debt for, 152.
——— ——— gift at, 169.
Butcher, 183.
Butterton chapelry, xvi.
Button (*al.* Bitton), 86.
Butts (Archery), xx.

C.

Cadbury, north, xviii (*n.*).
Cage to belfry, 204, 205.
Calendar, 229
Camel, Sir John, 17.
"Canan, bokys of," 36.
Candles sold, 175, 176, 178, 190.
——— for the visitation of the sick, 164, 167, 168, 171.
Canons of 1603, xvii.
Canopy, 74, 83, 84, 131, 133, 138, chain to do., *ib.*, 148.
——— a band to support, 194.
——— cord to, 99, 192.
——— of High Altar, 194.
——— lace and thongs for, 141.
——— to hang over the Sacrament, 219.

Canopy for Sepulchre, 75.
Canvas, 95, 171.
Capel, Sir Giles, 78.
——— Master, 145.
Capellanus, xviii, 175, 176, 177, 178, 179, 191
Capul, 105, 235.
"Carchow," &c. *See* "Kerchief."
Carnocke, 141 and *n.*, 143, 235.
Carter, Mason of Exeter, 2, 29.
Carver, 74, 145, 149, 150.
Castle of Montacute, 200.
Causey, 186, 193.
Cave (Easter), 117
Ceiling of the High Cross, 194, 195.
"Cena Domini," 167.
"Cenne," of the vestments, 117.
Censer, 47, 90, 102, 106, 149, 165, 194.
Chain for Bible, 153, 205.
Chalices, 51, 176, 178, 198.
——— bequest of, 118.
——— blessed, 60, 71, 103, 112, 122, 123, 136.
——— bought, 103, 177, 178.
——— carchawe for, 101.
——— case for, 103, 136.
——— changed, 112.
——— cloth for, 82, 127.
——— collection for new one, 122.
——— gift of, 35, &c.
——— mended, 70, 73, 124, 136, 151.
——— new cast, 136.
——— stolen, 115, 209.
Chamber in bakehouse rented, 188.
Chamberlain, 227, 230.
Chancel repaired, 140, 141.
"Chandeler" (Chandelier), 98.
"Chanon," 135.
Chantries, xvii, xviii, 249.
Chantry of B.V.M., 230.
——— Commissioners, xviii, 162 and *n.*
——— endowments, xviii.
——— seized, 45 (*n.*).
——— founded, 143 (*n.*).
——— wardens, xvii.
Chapel Priest, 135, 136, 156 and *n.*
——— wardens, xvii
Chaplain, 175, 176, 179.
Chapman, 105.
Chapter of Wells, Consistorial Court of, 91 and *n.*, 94 and *n.*, 150
Charcoal, 98.
Chard, x.
Chard, Thos., Prior of Montacute, 204 (*n.*).
Charnel house built, 231.

Charlton, visitation at, 158.
Chasubles, made of old cope, 156, 183.
—————— white and silver, 52.
Chaworth, Lady Elizabeth, 143 (*n.*), 151 (*n.*).
Cheese for the Croke procession, 21, 24, 28, 29, 30, 31, 33, 34, 42, 108.
—————— gathered for the Church, 232.
Chelvey, 96.
Chest, 162.
—————— key for, 165.
"Chestremede," 184.
Chew, visitation at, 160.
Chewton, lime at, 152.
Chief-rent, 20 and *n.*, 38 (*n.*).
Children, bequest for, 107, 110, 115,
—————— surplices for, 94.
Chilthorn, 173, 202.
Chiselborough bells, 205 (*n.*).
Choward, "Master," 151.
Chramore, 168.
Christmas play, xiv, 184.
Christmastide sport, 3.
Christopher, Saint, painted, 104, 105.
—————— Sir, of Kynston, 159.
Church ales, xiii, 89, 177, 181, 186, 201, 204, 205, 207, 209, 219, 245, 246.
—————— blending force of the, xxi, 252.
—————— books of, 50, 52.
—————— costs of, 34.
—————— fabric of, 2, 50, 79, 146, 173, 180, &c.
—————— goods, 123.
—————— heifer, 129.
—————— hey, 55, 59.
—————— house, xiv, xx, xxi, xxii, xxiii; 9, 10, 79, 80, 81, 82, 107, 109, 119, 173, 209, 219, 229, 231, 232, 247 (*n.*).
—————— —————— completed, 204.
—————— —————— hire of, 204, 108, 110, 111.
—————— —————— hire of a chamber in, 108.
—————— —————— rent of, 122, 162, 163 and *n.*, 164, 165, 166, 207, 220.
—————— —————— rent of the old house, 212.
—————— —————— do. of new, *ib.*
—————— —————— special contributions towards, 201.
—————— —————— ultimate fate of, 247.
Church land, 33, 34, 39, 70, 232.
Church lead, 67.
Church loaf, 193. *See also* "Holy Loaf," and "Panis Benedictus."
Church-rent, 75.
Church stock, governance of, 208.
Church-warden's accounts, 50, &c.
—————— —————— examined, 167.

Church-wardens examined beyond the diocese of B. and W., 233.
Churchyard, consecrated, 113, 116.
—————— cross, 79, 140, 141.
—————— enlarged, &c., 79.
—————— gate, key of, 121.
—————— rent of, "little voyd place of ground" in, 205.
—————— wall, 66, 72, 75, 107, 183.
Citations, 106, 127.
"Citula," 191.
Civil charges imposed, 80.
—————— result of, 232.
Claram (Claverham), 78, 87, 92, 93, 94, 95, 113, 127, 156, 162 (*n.*).
—————— chapel, 162 and *n.*
—————— court, 79.
—————— cross, 127.
Claret wine, 168.
Clasps to books, 51, 91, 187.
—————— to cope, 150.
"Clavey," 144, 235.
"Cleancorn," 224.
"Clericus Parochialis," xviii.
Clerk ales, 224 and *n.*, 246.
—————— bearing banner, 188, 189, 191, 192, 197.
—————— folding vestments, 162, 172.
—————— keeping the book, 172.
—————— lack of, 222.
—————— making the account, 160, 228.
—————— maintenance, settlement of, 209.
—————— payments to, and wages of, 41, 73, 74, 76, 79, 115, 119, 153, 155, 160, 172, 230.
Clerk of Axbridge, 138, 139.
Clerkship, fresh award of, 222, 224.
Cleve, 92, 93, 95, 99.
—————— Our Lady of, 249.
Clevedon, 172.
—————— The Lady of, 106.
Clifton, Sir Gervase, 33 (*n.*).
Clipped money, 55, 59, 127.
Clock, 13, 79.
—————— and chime, 150.
—————— cord for clock-weight, 183.
—————— cost of, 60, 153.
—————— keeping, 14, 16, 17, 48, 62, 69, 70, 71, 76, 152, 155, 166.
—————— maker, 150, 153.
—————— new, 205.
—————— old one taken down, 153.
—————— repaired, 44, 61, 70, 72, 74, 159, 179, 184.
—————— rope to, 76.
—————— the village, 176.
—————— washing and scouring, 20.

Clock-house, 151, 152.
Cloghill, 187, 189.
Closes, our Lady's, 38 (*n*.).
"Closing" of arches, &c., 112, 114, 120.
Cloth (linen, &c.,) for the High Altar, 90, 144, 191, 195.
—— do. painted, 167.
—— for low Altars, 202.
—— to mend low altar cloths, 202.
—— for two altar cloths, 197.
—— painted at Bristol, 167.
—— for the High Beam, 132.
—— for the chalice, 82, 126.
—— for the corporas, 197.
—— the "Hussylyng," 147.
—— before our Lady, 75, 106, 198.
—— before our Lord, 105.
—— over the Pyx, 165.
—— of the Rood, 153, 167, 212, 219.
—— before the Rood-loft, 133.
—— for the Sepulchre, 153, 212, 216, 219, 220.
—— before the Table, 88, 90.
Cloths, Church, 58, 62, 66, 69, 70, 71, 73, 74, 76, 83, 84, 88, 90.
—— washed, 183, 186, 189.
—— old, sold, 227.
—— in the Chapel taken down, 161.
Clouting leather, 177.
"Clovys," 92.
Clowesworth, old bells sold to, 204.
Cluniac Priory, 173.
Coal, 107, 117, 118, 126.
Coat, 215.
Coats (grey), 73.
Coercive authority, 232.
Coffers, 73, 113, 121, 124, 129, 152, 198.
—— given, 57.
—— mended, 150, 153.
—— the Register, 153.
"Coffrarius," 227.
Cokke, Agnes, xxi, 203.
"Collecta assisa," 230.
Collection book, 169.
———— for Christmas, 228.
———— for Easter, *ib*.
———— interparochial, 233.
Collectors, the King's, 157.
Collumstoke, 213.
Comb, Sir John, 17, 18.
Commission, the King's. *See* Edw. VI, and Hen. VIII.
———— of spoliation, 224 and *n*.
———— Chantry, Report of, xviii.

Commissioners of Edward VI, 11 and *n*., 45 (*n*.), 80, 161, 162 and *n*., 163.
———— of Henry VIII, 156.
———— of Sewers, 80 and *n*., 160 and *n*.
Common Prayer, Book of, 171.
"Compassion," payment for, 84.
Composition, paid for the, 135.
Compulsory church-rate, 231.
"Concordantia," 188.
Congresbury, xviii, 80, 84, 86, 92, 128, 132, 138, 148, 149, 151, 154, 158.
Consecration of a bell, 95. *See also* "Blessing."
Consistory Court, 127.
———— suit withdrawn from, 150.
Constable, 80, 133.
Constitutions of Bishop Winchelsea, 243.
"Continuance of Mary and John," 170 and *n*.
Contract for casting bell, 125.
Copes, 21, 44, 51, 101.
—— black, 129.
—— blue, 164.
—— blue satin, 225.
—— blue velvet, 47.
—— bought, 205, 209, 216, 217
—— clasps to, 150.
—— earnest for, 148.
—— given, 210.
—— green, 52, 64.
—— mending, 57, 76, 91, 135, 159, 170, 189, 220.
—— red, "with green bawderyck," 52.
—— red velvet, 52, 225.
—— repaired and new, coloured, 202.
—— white, 51.
"Coppys," 106, 121.
"Copysys," 145.
Corbel stones of the Aler, 98.
Corn, 157 and *n*.
Corporal, 92, 197.
Corporas, 38 and *n*., 106, 153, 157, 165, 197, 215.
———— case for, 53, 215.
———— washing, 58, 62, 76.
Corpus Christi day, 52.
Corscomb, 4, 5, 6, 7, 8, &c.
"Corse, a blew," 20.
"Costagiys," 98 (*n*.), 203.
Costrell, Sir Wm., 13.
Cote and under-cote, given in alms, 206.
"Cotes of fence," 171.
Cottage, rent of, 203.
Counsel's opinion, 123.
Court, Archdeacon's, xii, xiv.
Court-day, the bishop's, 87 and *n*.
Court de Wyke, 78.
Court-house, 80.

Court, Rolls, xxiii, *n*.
—— the Spiritual, 166 and *n*.
—— the Visitation, 188 (*n*.).
"Courtesy" to workmen, 114
Coverlet, 94, 190.
Cow, 10, 12, 13, 14, 15, 63, 82, 87.
—— given, bought, hired, or sold, 178, 179, 180, 183, 185, 193, 194, 198, 199
—— stock, 182.
Cradle, 164.
Crane, 118, 120.
"Crest" of the High Altar, 122.
Crewkerne, lime from, 189.
Croke (the processional cross), 1.
—— box, 31, 33.
—— box, key of, 34.
—— bread, 24, 235.
—— keeping, 4, 5, 6, 7, 8, 10, 12, 16, 17, 20, 24, 25, 26, 28.
—— money, 1, 4, 5, 6, 8, 9, 10, 11, 12, 14, 15, 17, 18, 19, 20, 21, 22, 23, 24, 25, 26, 27, 28, 29, 30, 31, 32, 33, 34, 39, 40, 44, 76.
—— payment for carrying, 125.
Crops in the Marsh sold, 180, 185.
"Cropys" (cramps), 98.
Croscombe, xi, xiii, 1, 20, 29, &c.
Cross bought, 177.
—— brought from Bristol, 153
—— copper gilt, 51, 178.
—— the High. *See* "High.
—— latten, 100.
—— made, 101.
—— new, 84.
—— the old mended, 159.
—— payment for, 166, 167.
—— the processional, 79 (*n*.).
—— recovered, 47.
—— silver, sold, 160, 172.
—— sum paid for, 167 and *n*.
—— wood and silver, 51.
—— at St. James's Tide, 149
—— near Axbridge, 83.
Cross-bow, legacy of, 125.
Crosse, the Carver, xx.
"Crowche" money, 232, 235.
Crowns to the B. V. M., 25.
Crucifix, 21, 52, 53, 54, 59, 215.
—— housing over, 59.
Cruets, 37, 103, 117, 199, 201
—— exchanged, 121, 181.
Cups, 111, 114, 165.
—— "asyon" (ashen), 146.
Curfew, 7, 9, 11 (*n*.).
Curtain, gift of, 31, 37, 38, 52, 118.

Curtain, fringe to, 103.
—— rons to hang, 121.
—— rings to, 103.
—— "steyned," 52.
Curtle, 218.
"Curtyll," 216.
Cushion, 148.
Custodes bonorum, xv.
"Custom" (*i.e.*, toll) at Bristol, 92, 114.
Custumalia, x.
Cutcombe, 117 (*n*.).
"Cytte" (*seat*), 165.

D.

Damask suit, 51.
"Dandépratts," 155, 235.1
Danyell, Sir John, 158, 159.
"Danys yere," 157, 160.
Darshill, 41.
Daub and wallet, 196.
Davy, Sir, 137, 145.
"Dawbs," 82, 110.
"Dawell" light, 232.
"Dayer" (dairy-man), 58 and *n*.
Dead-money, 1, 4, 5, 6, 7, 8, 9, 11, 13, 235.
Debts to the Church, 64, 67, 70, 82, 131, 137 140, 152, 156, 165, 171, 172, 220, 230.
Dedication Day, xx, 55, 57, 58, 61, 62, 66, 72, 173 226.
"Defawte in service of Yatton," 158.
"Deffawt of apparance of neybars," 201.
Demission of the Court, 166 and *n*., 169.
Desk, 150, 198.
—— cloth, 93, 133, 142, 183.
Diaper for altar-cloth, 149.
"Dipote," 187, 241.
Dirige and Mass, for benefactors, 55, 56, 57, 59, 60, 62, 66, 68, 70, 71, 72, 74, 76, 175, 181, 193, 211, 219.
—————— for Lady Mayow, 66.
—————— for Sir William, 74.
Dishes, 142, 146, 171.
—— brass, 192, 195.
Dissolution of the Monasteries, 249.
Distraint, 38 and *n*.
Ditch or dyke on the Moor, 188.
Doeskin, 187.
Doles at Glastonbury, xxiv.
—— Wells, *ib*.
Door, old Church, sold, 184.
"Dornes" and "Dorneys," 127, 179.
Doulting, xxi, 252, 253.
Dowlas, 170, 171.

Drokensford, bishop, his alms, 250.
——— elevation of serfs, 252.
——— his Register, x.
Dundry, 118, 137.
——— stone, 98.
Dusters, 117.
Dyking at the Parsonage, 152.
——— of stones, 118.
——— of the well, 109, 165, 235.
——— of the Yeo, 139, 165 and *n.*, 170.

E.

Eagles displayed, 224.
Earbury, A., 247.
Earnest, 8, 20, 55, 72, 95, 98, 100, 137, 148, 149, 150, 165.
Easter light or taper, 54, 57, 59, 60, 65, 66, 67, 68, 69, 70, 72, 73, 74, 76, 82, 84, 85, 87, 88, 90, 130.
——— play, 209.
——— Procession, 234.
——— Sepulchre, 84, 216.
Easton-in-Gordano, 86.
Edmonds, Sir Stevin, 36.
Edmund, " my lorde," Chan. of Wells, 52.
Edward, Sir, 111.
Edward VI, xv, xviii, xxiii, 2, 46, 64 (*n.*), 218, 249.
——— his Commissioners, 11 and *n.*, 45 (*n.*), 80, 161, 162 and *n.*
Eleemosynary endowments, 248.
Embroider, 149, 157, 164.
English, first account presented wholly in, 206.
Enterclose, 220, 235.
Endowment in land and houses, 226.
Erasmus, D., 161.
——— his paraphrase, 45 (*n.*), 161.
——— Saint, 229.
"Ereabull" ground, 156.
Estates, monastic, how managed, xxi.
Ewell, 198.
Ewes, 36, 37, &c.
Exbridge, 209, 216, 223.
Executors of Bp. Beckington, 27, 95 (*n.*).
Exeter Litany, 242.
——— mason from, xiv, 2, 29, 30, 32 (*n.*).

F.

Fabric of the Church, 2, 3, 79, 94 (*n.*).
Fair, the, 92, 102.
Fall of money, 162.

Fall, allowance for, 172.
——— loss by, 172.
Famels, 47, 236.
Fees for burial, 38 and *n.*
" Felewote," 17.
Felton, 140.
——— stone from, 141.
Femerell, 84.
Ferments, 84 and *n.*, 100.
Festival (book for Feasts), 52.
——— ale, 128 and *n.*
Fettiplace, Dame, 232.
Fifteenth paid to ye King, 184.
——— collector of, 184, 185.
Fine for admission to Manor tenancy, 113 and *n.*
——— imposed on Warden, 226.
Fines levied, 44.
Finials, 139.
Fiscal system, 1, 2, 49, 78, 173, 208, 225, 230, 232, 233.
Fitz-James, 41, 75, 107, 123 and *n.*
" Five Men," the, xviii, 208, 223.
——— their account, 209, 220.
" Flakys," 101, 236.
Fleece, 181.
Floor (middle) of belfry opened, 167.
" Floryssyng " wax, 132.
Flowers to trim the taper, 213.
" Flowre " (floor of belfry?), 172.
" Flowrs " to Rood-loft, 132.
Folding the vestments, 119, 162, 165, 166, 170.
Font cover, 90.
——— mended, 148, 151.
——— line to, 90.
——— lock to, 128, 153.
——— lock and key, 151, 159.
——— ring and staple to, 148.
——— stock, 232.
——— taper, 2, 3, 4, 7, 12, 13, 79, 92, 99, 157, 158, 161, 168, 169, 192, 232.
——— " wives," 232.
Forks and forlocks, 149.
" Formula," 180.
Forms in the Church, 163.
" Forty-pences," &c., 232.
Frankincense, 48, 120, 166, 167, 171, 187, 203, 220.
" Frary Clark," 66, 69, 70, 72, 73.
——— the old, 114.
Freemason, 140, 141.
Freestone, 165, 183, 185, 220.
" Frette " (freight), 119.
Friar, xxvi.
——— of Ilchester, *ib.*
Fringe to altar table, 164.

Fringe to banner, 112.
——— to curtains, 103.
——— to hangings of the altar, 121.
——— to kerchief " to hang over the sacrament," 198.
"Froggemere lane," 226.
"Front," over the High Altar, 148.
——— to altar-cloths, *ib*
——— to side-altars, *ib*.
Frontlet, 33 and *n*.
"Fundament," the, 107, 118.
Funds, sources of, 173.
Furnace of Church-house, 154 and *n*., 177
Fustian naps, vestments of, 225.
Fyce. *See* "Vyse."
Fyllocks, 3, 4, 5, 6, 8, 9, 10, 11, 12, 13, 15, 16, 17.
"Fysche and flesche and chese" allowed, 84.
Fysscher, skilled Mason, 119.

G.

"Gake-house," 179.
Gargoyles, 125, 146.
Garlantte, Sir Nycolas, 40.
Gathering-book, 165.
Gawds, 21, 22, 25, 53, 64, 65.
"ʒe," a, in the Treasure-house, 106.
——— in the vestments, 106.
Gear of the Church, 13, 14, 15, &c.
Gemmowys, 72, 73, 142, 168, 236.
George, St., xxiii.
——— statue of, 2, 30.
——— cost of, 32 and *n*.
——— new image of, 214.
——— maker, 2, 29, 30.
——— ale, 36, 38, 39, 40, 43.
——— altar-cloth of, painted, 215.
——— banner of silk, 217.
——— chapel, xiv, 2.
——— day, 223.
——— increase of, 41.
——— light, 34.
——— money, 34.
——— setting the plate before, 152.
——— store, 208, 210, 214, 218.
"ʒete" (gate), 106.
Gibbes, Davy, 80, 122 (*n*.), 123, 124.
——— cost of his suit, 123.
Gilder of Bristol, 155.
Gilding, 132, 133, 134, 137, 141, 142, 144, 147, 151, 155, 161, 198.

Girdles, 21, 22, 25, 111, 158, 191, 215, 216.
——— with buckles and pendants, 25, 54, 199.
——— for the Chaplain, 191.
——— of green silk and silver, 181
——— harnest. *See* "Harnest."
——— silver studs of, 151.
——— a "Swystyng," 130.
——— tucking, 5, 61, 126, 130, 133.
——— to the vestments, 83, 95, 103, 219.
——— for the Vicar, 85.
Giso, bishop, 78.
"Glasyng" of the Church windows, 62, 72, 97, 124, 127, 134, 143, 156, 168, 190, 212.
Glass mending, 97.
Glastonbury Abbey, 49, 242, 247, 249.
——————— Abbot of, 49, 53, 74.
——————— doles at, xxiv.
——————— Manor, 247.
Glossary, 233.
Gloves, 96.
Glue and gum, 90, 93, 187.
Goatskins, 110.
Godney, 253.
Gold paint, 96.
"Good-doers," 43 and *n*.
"Goody," 65.
Gown, gift of, 19, 85, 87, 115, 191, 193, 198, 214, 216.
——— and curtle, 217.
——— and girdle, 216.
——— green, 5, 7.
——— and ring, 211.
——— sale of, 91.
——— violet ingrain, 6.
"Gownte," 144 and *n*.
"Gowte," 168.
Grave, fee for, 21, 210.
——— in the aisle before St. Sidwell, 215.
——— before the High Cross, 217.
Grayle, 22, 52, 101, 199.
"Grey cake," 97, 236.
Groat, 199.
Gromen, 208.
"Grotes," Irish, 155.
"Grotes cryppe," 55, 59, 127.
Gudgeon of the bells, 103.
Guildhall at Stanford, xxii, 232.
Guild of St. John Bapt., 49.
Guilds, system of, xiii, xvii, xxiv.
——— secular successors of xvii.
Gutters of the Church, 125.
Gyngylls, silver, 25.

H.

Hall, Bishop, 214 (*n*.).
Halowntyde, 155.
Hamdon, stones from, 183, 188, 191.
Hardington, 203.
Harness, purple silk, with silver, 51.
―――― scoured, 172.
Harneyste gurdle, 111, 151, 182, 236.
Healing, 170.
Heifer, 82, 85, &c.
Hele (ceil), 120.
"Helmebought," 178, 236.
Helyng (tiling), 22, 94, 166.
Henbere, 161.
Henry VIII, xxi, xxiii, xxiv.
Henry's Commissioners, 156.
Herdewyke, Robt., 60.
Here, 121, 129, 236.
Here-cloth, 153, 202.
Herryherte, 88.
"Heryng-barells," 147.
Herys, 121, 125.
Heyward, xvi, 138.
High Altar,
―――― beam before, 155.
―――― cloth before, 90.
―――― crest of, 122.
―――― hanging of, 121.
―――― painted cloth to, 144.
―――― rings to, 90.
―――― washing, 133.
―――― two wings of silk for, 90.
High beam, 132.
―――― cloth for, 132.
―――― iron for, 133.
"High Book" (viz. : the High Wardens' account book), 121 and *n*.
High Chamber, 110.
High Cross, 132, 185.
―――― cloth hung before, 191.
―――― repaired, 132.
―――― Beam, 192.
―――― Light, 60, 62, 63, 67, 71, 133.
―――― endowment of, xiv, 232
―――― keeping of, 67.
―――― Wardens of, 49, 58, 63, 64 (*n*.), 69.
―――― sum owing to, 61.
High Warden's account, 209, 218, 230.
Hinton Bluet, 94 (*n*.).
Hock-day, xx and *n*., 132, 146, 159.

Hocktide, 228, 233.
Hody, Sir John, Kt., 180.
Hoglers, xx, 1 and *n*., 3, 4, 7, 9, 10, 11, 12, 13, 14, 15, 16, 17, 18, 19, 20, 21, 22, 23, 24, 25, 26, 27, 28, 29, 30, 31, 32, 33, 34, 35, 36, 37, 38, 40, 49, 174, 230, 236, 251.
―――― light, 34, 57, 60, 63, 181, 190.
―――― money received from our Lady Wardens, 65.
―――― stoke, 33.
Hogeling (and Hokelyng), 58, 229.
―――― Marsland and Upland, 229, 230.
Holmes, Rev. T. S., ix, xxvi.
Holy Ale, xxi, 173, 232.
―――― brede-house, 229.
―――― day and holiday, xxi.
―――― loaf, xxi, 24, 205, 229, 232.
―――― wafer, xxi.
Holy water pot, 170.
―――― stock, 136.
―――― stone, 93.
Hood, Sir Alexander, 229.
―――― Robin. *See* "Robin Hood."
Horington, free Chapel at, 11 (*n*.), 45 (*n*.).
―――― lands at, 45 (*n*.).
―――― money, 13.
Horn of the Church, 38, 84.
Horner, J. F., Esq., 252.
Horse-lock, 145.
―――― "mete," 84, 123.
Horwood, Mr., 229.
House-property in Oxford, 232.
"Howsing of our Lady," 199.
"Huckmucks," 108, 135, 146, 237.
Hucley Bridge, 209.
Huntspill, 95.
Hurdwyche, 85, 87, 94, 108.
"Hussyllyng cloth," 147, 237.
"Hylyer," 220, 236.
Hymnals, 138.
"Hyppe, by," 223.
"Hyve" for bees, 188.

I.

"I. H. S.," 52, 145, 148, 150, 157, 159.
Ilchester, 178, 191, 192
"Ill-deed done," 161.
Illuminated book, 24, 199
Images, 53, 97, 98, 99, 100.
―――― gilded, 161, 214
―――― makers of, 98.

Images plucked down, 160, 171.
——— of Roodloft, 170 (n.).
Incense, 121, 183.
Incull, 155, 159 (ynkle, 170).
Indictment, bill of, 122, 154.
Indractus, S., 242.
Injunctions, 160, 162.
——— book of, 171.
Inscriptions on account books, 154, 210.
"Institution of a Christian Man," 157 (n.).
Interdict, episcopal, xvii.
Inventories of Church goods, 50, 51, 64, 119, 163, 171, 197, 199, 232.
——— of Vestments kept in St. Katrine's Yle, 231.
Irish cloth, 121, 147.
Iron gear before Our Lady, 120.

J.

James', St., ale, 130.
——— chapel, 88, 115, 122, 123, 124, 125, 126.
——— bell of, 128.
——— book for (very costly), 155 and n.
——— cleaning, 100.
——— debt of the chapel, 139.
——— gilding, 144.
——— helyny, 94.
——— purging, 126.
——— timber taken down, 94.
——— timber work, ib.
——— walls made, ib.
——— Day, 144, 146.
——— proctors, 124.
——— shell, 51, 53, 64.
Jeferes of Bristol " bellatur," 148.
Jesu, store of, 208. See under " Store."
— – his taper, 220.
John, St., fraternity of, 49, 55, 57, 59, 62, 76.
——— proctor of, 57, 58.
——— iron gear for, 151.
——— his light, 59.
——— scaffold to, 151.
——— tapers before, 73.
John, Sir (Priest), 124, 137.
Johnson, Sir Umefry, 36.
Joists sold, 184.
"Jorge, the." See " St. George."
Jornale, 237.
"Judas," 99, 185.
Judges at Wells, 123.
"Juells of the Church," let out, 229.

K.

Kalendar, writing of, xiii, 199.
Katherine, St.
——————— her altar, 126.
——————— altar stone, 126.
——————— angel on which she stands, 126.
——————— banner of, 112.
——————— image of, 126, 135.
——————— light, 120, 124.
——————— pricket for lights before, 135.
——————— wax for, 111, 124.
——————— Yle, 231.
Kellaw, Bp., 252.
Ken, ale at, 80, 131, 132, 135, 151.
Ken, Robert, legacy from, 94.
——— obit for, ib.
Kenston, 155.
Kerchiefs, gifts of, 36, 37, 39, 41, 53, 69, 71.
——— of the canopy, 58.
——— to the chalice, 101.
——— for the Images, 53, 178.
——— to Our Lady, 65.
——— "lawnde," 30, 37, 39.
——— recovered, 46.
——— washing, 59.
Ket, Nycholas (Scrivener), 114, 115.
Kettle of the Church-house, 82, 83, 108, 112, 119, 121, 122, 149, 154, 170.
Keve, 83.
" Key " (cows), 49, 58, 60, 61, 63, 64, 237.
——— wardens, xiv, 49, 50, 54, 63, 64.
" Key-Whyt," 54 and n.
Keynsham, ale at, 80, 149, 151.
——————— summons to visitation at, 149.
Keys to lock, 170.
King, Bishop, 197.
—— the play king of Montacute, 183 and n.
King's Arms, the, 155.
——— Bere, 157, 158.
——— Book, 157 (n.).
——— Collectors, 157.
——— Commissioners. See "Commissioners," "Edward VI" and " Henry VIII."
——— Crown painted on an image, 202.
——— Revel, 3 and n., 5, 6, 27, 158.
——— silver, 44.
——— Subsidy, 156, 158, 159, 160.
——————— making a bill for, 157, 170.
——— Visitation, 161.
——— Visitors, 159, 161

King's Wood, 149.
Kingsbury, 184, 197, 199.
Kingston Seymour, ale at, 55, 112.
—————— Parson of, 121.
Knells, 14 and *n.*, 15, 17, 24, 26, 43, 92, 141, 165, 205, 206, 211, 216, 217, 218.
Knives, gift of, 136.
"Kynter-kynnys," 146.
Kyve, 109, 119, 130, 237.

L.

Ladder for the belfry, 180.
Ladle for Church-house, 142.
Lady, Our, account of, 220.
—————— candlestick with five lights before, 215.
—————— Chapel, xiv, 174.
—————————— rebuilt, 227.
—————— gilding, 144.
—————— image in chancel taken down, 169.
—————— new image of, 213, 214, 215.
——————'s light, 60, 67, 71, 75.
——————'s mark, 222.
—————— of Pity, 229.
—————— stores. *See* "Store."
—————— taper to stand before, 211.
—————— wardens of, 54, 55, 56, 57, 59, 60, 62, 64, 65, 66, 68, 69, 72, 73, 74, 75.
—————— increase of their ale, 71.
Lady Wardens. *See* "Women wardens."
"Lamme-towe," 219, 237.
Lamp hung in the Chancel, 136, 153.
—————— before the figure of Jhu, 213.
—————— before St. Sidwell, 213.
Lamp-yarn, 89.
—————— payment to clerk for lighting, 228.
Land, Church, 33, 34.
—————— increase of, 39.
Langabulum, 227 and *n*
Langmede, 156.
Language of the accounts, xxiii, 231.
"Lasyng" (lace), 147.
"Latham," 183.
Latten basons, 211.
—————— candlesticks, 215, 216.
Latin, xxiii, 80, 88, 98, 210, 229, 231.
Laud, Archbishop, 247.
Laundresses, 183, 186, 230.
Lavender, the, 116.
Laver, gift of, 53, 82.
"Lawer" (lawyer), 216.

"Lawfull money of Engelonde," 118.
"Lawnde" (lawn), 30, 37, 39, 134 (black).
Lead, 38, 42, 67, 69, 100, 116, 119, 121, 138, 181, 182.
—— casting, 63, 121, 138.
—— of Church repaired, 203.
—— for Holy Water Stone, 93.
—— for St. Mary's House, 56, 63.
—— from Mendip, 68, 69.
—— rent for, 65.
Leadmining, 3.
Lease of sheep, 37, 38, 40.
Leather, 187.
—————— of horse skin, *ib.*
Leazes, 199 (*n.*).
Lebetina, 180 and *n.*
"Leddehaxyn," 68, 117, 119, 121.
—————— to Chewton, 68.
"Lege-bell," 90, 237.
Legend, 4.
Leger, 22, 79 (*n.*), 112 and *n.*, 115.
"Leggs in the More," 199 and *n.*, 200.
Leigh, xviii.
Leland, 210.
Lent cloth, 58, 74, 95, 124, 130, 176.
—————— cord for suspending, 182.
—————— painted, 212, 220.
—————— vestment, 52.
Lett, Humfrey, Parish Clerk, 153.
Leverys in the Marsh, 186.
Levys to windows, 104, 145.
Liability of parishioners, xii, xvi, xvii, 231.
Liber obitalis, xiii.
Lichfield episcopal registers, xvi, 252.
"Liernes" of Roodloft, 184.
Life of a Parish, xx.
—— in what lacking, xxiii.
Lights, not defined, xiii, 34, 73, 87.
—— before the Cross, 99.
—— for Dedication Day, 72.
—— for the Departed, 1, &c.
—— Easter, 54, 57, 59, 60, &c. *See* "Paschal Taper."
—— The High Cross. *See* "High Cross."
—— Hokelyng, 57.
—— before the figure of Jesu, 212.
—— keeping, 25. *See* also "tynnyng."
—— Our Lady's, 60, &c.
—— at the Nativity, 59.
—— for Visitation of the Sick, 164.
—— Wardens of the, 95.
—— for Whitsuntide, 72.
"Lightmanship," 148.
Light-men, 84, 85, 89, 91, 92, 93, 94, 95, 97, 99.

Light-men, East, 79, 141, 159, 165, 166, 170, 172.
——— North side, 99.
——— West side, 79, 113, 141, 159, 165, 166, 170.
Lily-pots, 160.
Lime at Chewton, 152.
——— for the Church, 167.
——— for pulpit and altars, 86.
——— for the Windows, 66, 189.
Linen for Lent-cloth, 130.
——— cloth for Rood, 167.
——— to mend Albs, 183.
——— painting Lent and Rood cloths, 220.
——— for the Sepulchre, 220.
Little John, 1, 24.
Littleton, 252.
Live-stock, xiii, 173, 179, 209, 231.
"Loaf of the Church," 24.
——— the Holy, xxi, 24 and *n.*, 173, 205, 231, 233.
Lock and "gemmulls," 168.
Lord of the Manor, 170 and *n.*
Luggs for banners, 46 and *n.*; 88 and *n.*; 125; 165.
"Lyche-rest," 76, 170, 171, 172.
——— of a rope, 76.
Lying in the Chapel, 139, 158, 166.
——— in the Church, 32, 35, 134, 136, 137, 145, 158, 161, 165.
Lyme Ryge, 112.
Lynch, John, Minstrel, 155.
Lyndwood, 243, 244 (*n.*).

M.

Maidens, the, 1, 4, 5, 7, 8, 9, 10, 11, 12, 13, 14, 15, 16, 17, 18, 19, 20, 21, 22, 23, 25, 26, 27, 28, 29, 30, 31, 32, 33, 34, 35, 36, 37, 38, 40, 43, 208.
——— account of, 221.
——— ale, 44.
——— light, 21.
Malet, "Master," 123 and *n.*
Maniples, 47 (*n.*).
Manor Court Rolls, xx, xxiii and *n.*
Mantle of B.V.M., 64.
——— with rings, *ib.*
——— blue velvet, 52.
——— purple velvet, 52.
Manual, 25, 52, 120, 142, 16
——— a manual book printed, 52.

Manumission of serfs, 252.
Manuscript, old, 232.
Margaret, St., 173.
——— ale, 177, 182, 188.
——— chapel, 182.
——— Day, 182.
——— Dedication Day, 173.
——— feast, 186, 193.
Marks, payment of, 93, 115, 116, 219
Marsh, the, 177.
Martilege, xiii.
Mary St. (the B.V.), cloth before, 106.
——— painting of, 104.
——— goods of, 178.
——— House, lead for, 56.
——— cost of repairing, 63.
——— figure of, with St. John on a cross, 51.
Mary Magdalene, St., 160.
Mary Magdalene's Day, 179, 180, 182.
Mary, Queen, 164, 219, 231.
Masday, Sir John, 138.
Maser, 17, 31, 51, 53, 242.
Mason's wages for Turret-staircase, 202.
Mass-book, 24, 36, 52, 124, 129, 199.
——— in English, 161.
Mat for the table, 163.
Mawdley, 27.
May's Ale, 207.
Mayfield Church, xvi.
Mayow family, 8, 9, 10, 11, 23.
——— endowment for a light, 41, 42.
——— Lady M. of Croscombe, 65.
——— her Dirige, 66.
Meadowland, 184.
Mells, xviii, 253.
Mendip, lead from, 68, 69.
——— "riding to," 138.
"Mere," 156 and *n.*
Merton College, Oxford, 252.
"Mese" (and "Muse"), 116, 119, 194 and *n.*
Metecloth, 122, 135.
Michael's, St., Bath.
——— Croke, 2, 14, 23, 24, 25, 26, 27.
——— increase of, 36.
——— light, 4, 7, 9.
——— money, 3, 5, 10, 11, 16,
Michaelmas, Tavern of Ale at, 92.
Middle-floor, 148.
Mill Blewett, 94.
Minstrels, xxii, xxiii, 79, 138 and *n.*, 144, 145, 146, 148, 150, 151, 152, 154, 155, 157, 159, 160, 167, 169, 171.
Missal, 165, 180, 183, 228, 229, 230.

Money, broken, 155.
——— fall in value of. *See* "Fall."
——— collected on the Vigil of the Epiphany, 202.
——— suit for recovery of, 106.
Monitions, xii, xvi.
Monk, bell rung for, 85.
——— paid for carrying altar cloth to Wells, 129.
——— his " wages," 129.
Montacute, benefice appropriated, 173.
——————— charged with Vicar's Stipend, 173.
——————— secularized, *ib.*
——————— Castle, 200.
——————— Church Ale, 202.
——————— king of, 183 and *n.*
——————— Parishioners of, 173.
——————— Prior of, 178, 183, 201.
——————— Priory, 173.
——————— Surplice bought at, 186.
——————— W., 188.
Moor (or Marsh).
——— corn and beans from, 182.
Moorland, 173.
Moorlease, 207.
More, Patty, 251.
Morebath Church, ix, 209.
——————— court at, 223.
——————— manor and rectory, 209.
——————— Parish, 208.
"Morelese," 196.
Morris dance, xxiii.
Mortice for Beam of the Cross, 194.
Mould for casting lead, 138.
Muster of soldiers, 161.
——— bill of, 169, 170.
Mynd, 86 and *n.*; 88, 90, 98, 99, 104.
Mynells, 129, 130.
"Myster" to Church-house, 142.
——————— locks and rings to, *ib.*

N.

Nails, "five-stroke," 180.
Nailsea, 94, 165.
Navicula, Navis, 95 and *n.*
"Necessary Doctrine," 157 (*n.*).
Net, 133.
Newton, Sir John, Knt., 114, 115 and *n.*
——— family, 78 (*n.*), 79. 114.
——— Isabel, Lady N., 79, 116, 120, 121, 146.
——— Philippa, the lady of Court de Wyke, 92, 95, 103, 105.
"Neybor Roger," 207.

Nicholas, St., Altar, 3, 173.
——————— gatherers of, 3.
——————— steyned cloth for, 101.
——————— feast of, 231.
——————— light, 6.
——————— painted, 202.
——————— his staff, 55.
Nicoll, Sir Edward, 216.
Nobles, payment of, 23, 35, 51, 67, 68, 97, 125, 215, 216, 220.
Norbury, Roger de, his Register, xvi.
Notary, 123 and *n.*
"Numerale," 192.

O.

Oaks in the King's Wood, 149.
Oats, 176, 188.
"Obligation," 123, 126.
——————— box to hold, 126.
Obits, xiii, 43, 190, 211.
Obituary payments and services, xviii, 43 and *n.*, 89, 175, 178, 179, 181, 184, 187, 190, 194, 227, 229.
Offertory, no mention of, xxv.
"Official master, costs at his visitation, 69, 73.
Oil, 175.
——— box, 165.
——— for clock, 176.
——— for lamp, 168, 229.
Oil-vat, 198.
——— vessels, 23, 53.
"Omelys," 160.
"Onera," xii.
Ordinal, The, 52.
——————— binding, 175.
"Ordinatio vicariæ," xli.
Organ, xix, 79.
——— "fote" to, 142.
——— maker, 142, 143, 149, 170.
——— mending, 101, 110, 128, 156.
——— playing, 17, 112 and *n.*, 143.
——— tuning, 149.
Organist, xix, 19, 79, 142, 143.
——————— his grave, 129.
Orphrey, 101, 129.
Osburne (maker of clock-house), 152.
Our Lady's aisle, 66, 73, 76.
——————— light, 75, 121.
Oven in Church-house, xxi, 145, 166, 188, 193.
Ox sold, 176.
——— brought for Church store, 178.
Oxford, riding to, 122.
Oyster shells, 98

P.

Painting the Altar, 201.
—— a cloth, 195.
Pall, 43, 46, 76, 154, 215, 225.
—— cloth, 156, 167.
Palton chantry, xiv, 11 (*n.*).
Palton family, 3, 11 (*n.*).
Pan, 199.
"Pandoxaterium," 173, 186, 195, 196, 197.
"Panell," 123.
"Panis benedictus," 24, 25, 102, 190, 191, 192, 194, 195, 197, 204.
—— ecclesiasticus, 196.
Parapet, 126.
"Paraphrase," 45 and *n.*, 161.
"Parcels," 82, 89, 119, 177, 180, 186.
Parchment, 187, 230.
Parclose, 112, 114 and *n.*, 120.
Pargetting, 56, 76, 185.
Parging, 126.
Parish, life of, xx.
—— organization of, xi.
—— personnel of, xviii.
Parish Clerk, 209.
Parson, 7, 9, 10, 11, 17, 45, 121, 163.
Parsonage, 129, 138, 152.
Parvise, 102.
Paschal money, 6, 15, 16, 17, 18, 19, 21, 22, 23, 24, 25, 26, 28, 29, 33, 34, 35, 40, 41, 43, 48, 234.
—— increase of, 12.
—— Taper, 2, 7, 12, 13, 29, 30, 31, 32, 43, 44, 79, 89, 91, 93, 97, 99, 103, 150, 179, 180, 188, 203, 205.
Paschal Font Taper, 57, &c.
—— Towel, 95.
Passion, emblems of The, on a banner, 52, 53.
Pasture for Church-house, 197.
—— in the Moor, 205.
Paten, 70, 153, 225.
Pauper, payment for, 114.
Paving of the Church, 100, 134, 163, 201.
—— repaired, 101, 105, 106.
Pax, 24, 114, 115, 117, 158, 165, 190, 215.
—— the great, 71.
—— silver, 225.
"Pax-brede," 51, 111.
"Pecas" (pick-axe), 120.
"Pelewe," a brazen, 84.
Penance, 166.
Pendant, 22, 54.

Penford, 168.
Pennard, 51.
Pennysford, 157.
Pension, 94, 95.
Percival, "Master," 150.
Personnel of the Parish, xviii.
Peter's, St., in the East, Oxford, xx (*n.*), 233.
—— 's Pence; 209, 229.
Pewter vessels of the Church-house, 40, 41, 42, 43.
Piers, Bishop, xxii, 53, 245.
Pigs, 209.
Pilgrimages, 249.
Pillows, 52, 56, 150, 151, 157, 216.
Pilton Church, 49.
—— guilds, *ib.*
—— Our Lady's house at, xxii.
—— Vicar of, 23.
Pinnacle "to the best cross," 132, 133, 151, 158.
—— repaired, 112, 118.
Pistrina, 173, 191.
"Plake," 18 and *n.*
Plate double, 155.
—— set before St. George, 152.
—— sold, 45, 172.
Platters, 35, 36, 37, 39, 130, 133, 162, 165.
Play, Autumn, xiv.
—— Christmas, xiv, xxii, xxiv, 184.
—— Easter, xiv, 209.
—— Kings, xiv, xxii.
—— Summer, xiv, 183.
Players' garments, xiv, 232.
"Plegge" (security), 49, 61, 63.
"Plumpe" maker, 136, 139, 140, 142.
Pogger, 36.
Pointing, 147.
"Pokysy," 114, 241.
Poor Law of 1834, xxii.
Poor man's bequest to the bells, 67.
—— box, xv.
—— men of the Parish, 161.
—— woman, bequest from, 152.
—— Relief, xv, xxiii, 80, 250.
Poore, Sir Nicholas, 161.
Pope of Rome, 167.
Porch, covering for, 203.
—— laths for, *ib.*
Portiforium, 180.
Portuas (Portoce), 22, 52, 100, 165, 199.
—— "a great p. of Prynte," 52.
—— "a holle portas," 165.
"Posenett," 104, 238.
Pot, for Holy water, 170.

Pots, brass, &c.; 31, 53, 54, 87, 91, 92, 163, 182, 185.
—— old ones sold, 82, 229.
"Pothynger," 118.
Pound, the, xvi.
Powches, 17.
Powell, Sir Edw., 247.
Powlett, "*Hu*," 209, 216, 223, 224.
—— his bailiff, 224.
"Poyntell," 187.
Precept, 163.
"Precul," 72.
"Prelubkys," 84.
"Prevaylyd," peculiar use of the word, 210, 211.
Prickets, 88, 142, 143, 188, 191.
Priest, payment to, 73, 153, 156, 157. *See also* "Sir Richard Yorke," and "Chapel Priest."
Prior of Montacute, 183, 201.
Priory church of Barlinch wrecked, 209.
—— window saved, *ib*.
Processional book, 22, 52, 94, 121, 132, 165, 183.
———————— a new one printed, 62.
———————— do. in English, 179.
—————— - cross, 79 and *n*.
—————— keepers of, xviii.
—————— - Taper, 220.
Proclamations, 161, 167.
Proctors (wardens), 62, 108, 118, 124, 192.
"Procuratores ecclesiæ," xv.
"Profession, book of our," 157.
"Propters," 124, 125.
"Pryckyng, wrytyng and lymynyng" a greyll, 199.
Psalters, 11, 14, 112, 171.
Pulpit, making of, 86.
—— mending, 101.
—— setting an iron in, 160.
Purlins, 183.
Purse to hold keys, 167.
"Putts" of stone, 193.
Pye, 129.
Pyers (Dr.), 53.
"Pyggswote," 105, 108, 120.
Pylle, 57.
Pyns, 48 and *n*.
Pynon, 126.
Pype for bell-rope, 139.
—— with wood, 32.
—— (*i.e.*, spout), 146.
Pypes, 114.
Pytte, 21, 23, 129.
—— sawpit, 150, 151.
Pyx, 51, 93, 102, 143, 166, 167, 178.
—— of latten, 175.
—— netcloth over, 165.

Q.

Queen Mary, 2, 46, 164.
Quire, 128.
—— burial in, 211.
—— door, iron bar for, 220.
Quit-rent for the Church-house, xxi, 197.
"Quyrbys," 154.

R.

"Rage of the salte-water," 160.
—— of the sea, 162 (*n*.).
Rate, compulsory, 230.
—— by assessment, 232.
—— voluntary, 209.
Rate-book, 166 (*n*.).
"Rather," Proctors, the, 108, 109.
Rates, Church, xvi.
—— voluntary and involuntary, ix (*n*.), xii, xiii.
Rating authority, 232.
Ray-corse, 13.
"Rayer" year, 99.
Re-casting bells, 105, 114, 127.
Receiver, the bishop's, 84 and *n*., 87 and *n*
"Reconciliation" of the people, 167.
Recovery of Church-goods, 46.
Rector paid for obits, 179, 184, 187, 228.
—— for Peter's Pence, 229.
—— of Tintinhull, 204 (*n*.).
—— his Dirige, 187.
Rectorial Tithes, a source of relief to poverty, 250.
Rectory, 80.
Redcliffe, bell taken to, 92.
———— St. Mary, 171 (*n*.).
———— Visitation at, 171.
"Rede," 63, 141.
Reeds for thatching, 195.
Reeve, the bishop's, 80, 132.
"Refows" (refuse or broken) money, 26.
Regnal year noted, 30, 40, 46, 64, 65.
Regyl (rail), 100.
"Rele," 85, 89, 90, 101, 108, 111, 113, 132, 134, 135, 137, 138, 153, 159.
Relics of St. Thomas of Canterbury, 35.
Relief of the poor, x, xiii, xxiii, 80, 250.
Religious Plays, xiv.
"Fenge," 128.

Rent of Bakehouse, 194.
—— of cottage, 203.
Rental of endowed "Rode-chapel," 232.
Repairs of Church and Brew-house, 193.
——— of St. James's Chapel, 130.
——— of Tower, 112, 118, 145, 221.
Reste, 1, 55, 57, 58, 64.
Revel, the King's, 3 and *n.*, 5, 6, 27, 158.
——— the wives', 1, 12.
Revelry, xxii.
"Reward" (gratuity), 143 and *n.*, 145.
Rings, xiii and *n.*, 2, 12, 14, 21, 27, 31, 42, 45, 50, 51, 53, 54, 58, 61, 62, 65, 75, 87, 111, 112, 122, 136, 151, 158 [7½ ounces], 194, 199.
——— enamelled, 23.
——— gilt, 5.
——— gold, 6, 8, 10, 13, 21, 23, 24, 25, 27, 28, 29, 30, 31, 32, 33, 34, 35, 36, 37, 38, 39, 97.
——— over gilt, 23.
——— signet, 17, 25.
——— silver, 4, 8, 10, 13, 14, 15, 16, 19, 20, 23, 24, 25, 26, 28, 29, 30, 31, 32, 33, 34, 36, 37, 38, 39, 41, 42, 120, 189, 192.
——— silver and gilt, 5, 21, 23, 25, 27, 28, 29, 30, 32, 33, 34, 35, 36, 38, 39, 40, 41, 42, 51, 71, 187.
——— wedding, 22 and *n.*, 27 (gilt).
——— to our Lady, 26, 27.
Rings for cloth to the High Beam, 132.
——— for curtains, 103.
Ringers, 60, 73, 74, 76, 98, 164, 168.
Ringing the bell, payment for, 84, 87, 92.
"Ryses for the dawbes," 82.
Robin Hood, xiv, xx, 1, 2, 4, 10, 11, 12, 14, 16, 18, 20, 24, 26, 28, 29, 30, 31, 38.
——————'s ale, 200.
Rochets, 32, 71, 73, 75, 86, 106, 112, 142, 149, 154, 162, 220.
Rodney family, 78 and *n.*
——— Sir John, 38, 123 and *n.*
——— Lady Elizabeth, 39, 143.
——— Sir Walter, 143 (*n.*), 151 (*n.*).
Rogers, Sir Thomas (Priest), 39.
Roller, 198.
"Rom-feoh," 227 (*n.*).
Rood, 173.
——— buckram, for, 130.
——— cloth, 130, 153, 167.
——— gift to, 24.
——— made and set up, 169.
——— painted, 153, 202, 220.
——— rings for, 130.
——— taken down, 171.

Rood-light, 234.
Rood-loft, 16, 54, 55, 79 (*n.*), 90, 91, 97, 98, 100, 107, 122, 132, 133, 151 (*n.*), 160.
——— cleaning, 156.
——— covering of, 54.
——— images on, 170 (*n.*).
——— iron for, 96.
——— "liernes" of, 184.
——— new, 173, 185.
——— cost of, 185.
——— old one pulled down, 98, 185.
——— painting, 55, 100, 188, 189.
——— washing, 170.
Rope for bell, 114.
——— for clock, 76.
——— for clockweights, 61.
——— for sacring bell, 90.
——— to Trendell, 76.
Rosin, 84, 89, 119, 157, 180
Ruby ring, 10.
"Runs" of match-yarn, 180.
Rushes, 120.
Ryndyn, 82 and *n.*
"Ryng, basting the," 172.
——— making do., *ib.*

S.

Sack-wire, 168.
Sacrament, drawer for, 198.
——— over the High Altar, 147.
Sacring bell, 99, 103, 125, 143, 165, 195.
——— repaired, 149, 199.
——— rope for, 90.
Saints, covering for "at Lent," 70, 76.
Salt-cellars, 146.
Satin of Bruges, 143.
Saucers, 37, 118.
"Sauter" (Psalter), 11, 14.
Savaric, Bishop, 49.
Saye, red, 53.
"Scapha" (censer), 102.
Scely, Lucy, xv, 219.
Schefton, Lady, 10.
Schepton, Lady, 2, 3, 33, 34.
"Schere Thursday," 152.
Scholars, 162 and *n.*
Scholastica, St., feast of, 93.
School and schooling, want of, xxii.
"Schot," 128.
Screen (stone), 173.
"Scrinium," 191.

Scriptures written on cloth, 167.
Scrivener, 114, 115.
Sea, 162 (*n.*).
—— bank, 144 (*n.*).
—— walls, 80.
Seat, 149, 161.
Seats in the Church, made, 89, 200.
—— old, 200.
—— sawing timber for new ones, 199.
"Sege" in chancel, 145.
—— in the Church, 149, 150.
—— in the Church-house, 136.
—— ends, cutting of, 163 and *n.*
Segg for thatching, 179.
"Segys" in Church, 86, 96, 134.
Self-government of the community, xvi.
Selwood forest, 86 and *n.*
"Selyng," 112.
"Semys," 90, 119.
Sepulchre, 53, 79, 84, 90, 103, 105, 107, 117, 138, 152, 165, 179.
—— canopy for, 75.
—— cloth for, 86, 101, 153.
—— cloth painted, 212.
—— "ystaynyd," 216.
—— taper, 64, 71.
—— "tree," 90.
Sepulture, fee for, 54, 63.
Serel, Mr. Thos., x (*n.*).
Serf, pleads successfully against the D. and C. of Wells, 252.
Serfdom, xxi.
Serfs, xx.
Service books, 79 (*n.*).
Sessions at Ilchester, 122, 124, 154.
—— at Wells, 154.
"Sett, a" (probably of beads), 28, 30.
"Setts," voluntary and involuntary rates, xii, 169 and *n.*, 209 and *n.*
Sewers, Commissioners of, xv. *See* "Commissioners."
Sexton, xviii, 79, 103, 106, 136, 152.
Sheep, 226.
—— gift of, 42, 97, &c.
—— lease, 37, 38, 40.
—— "leaze," 222.
—— legacy of, 181, &c.
—— skins, 135, 187.
—— sold, 188, &c.
—— of the stores, 205, 208, 211, 212, 213, 215.
—— tithe, 220.
Shells of St. James, 51, 53, 64.
Shoes, St. Sidwell's, 213, 214.

Sick person annealed, 99.
—— gift to, 171.
—— person helped, 169.
—— —— keeping, 169.
Sidesmen, xvii, xviii, 205 (*n.*).
Sidwell, St., 208.
—— aisle before, 215.
—— altar cloth, 211.
—— basin of latten, *ib.*
—— candlesticks of latten, 216.
—— candlestick and taper before, 213.
—— image of, 117 (*n.*), 212.
—— do. gilded, 214.
—— lamp before, 213.
—— shoes, 213, 214.
—— tabylment of, 212. *See* also "Store of St. S."
Silarium, 204.
Singers' fee, 72.
Singing the service, 114.
Sir John Batell, 147, 151.
Sir Thos. Brytell, 178.
Sir John Camell, 17.
Sir Giles Capel, 78 (*n.*).
Sir Cristover, 159.
Sir Robt. Cocke, 153.
Sir John Comb, 17.
Sir Wm. Costrell, 13.
Sir John Danyell, 157.
Sir Davy, 137, 145.
Sir Stevin Edmonds, 36.
Sir John Frenshman, 154.
Sir Harry, 151, 152.
Sir John, 124, 137.
Sir Umfrey Johnson, 36.
Sir John Masday, 138.
Sir Nicholas Poore, 161.
Sir Richard (priest), 149.
Sir Robert, 150.
Sir Robert's brother, 165.
Sir Walter Rodney, 151 (*n.*).
Sir Thos. Rogers, 39.
Sir John Smyth, 162, 163, 166, 167, 168.
Sir Smyth (*sic*), 47.
Sir Thomas, 33, 169.
—— his bequest of a cross-bow, 125.
Sir Christopher Trychay, 208, 210, 212.
Sir Thos. Vox, 34.
Sir Thos. Wade, 52.
Sir William, 74, 137.
—— 's "Moder knell," 141.
Sir John Wullner, 52.
Sir Richard Yorke, 129 (*n.*), 130, 131, 135.
Skynner, 199.

"Skyppe," 176.
Sluices, 157 (*n.*), 160 ("sklusse"), 162 (*n.*), 165 (*n.*).
———— gate, 80.
Smigma, 178, 189.
Snow, 66, 71.
Solarium, 85, 88, 90, 95, 97.
———— under the Roodloft, 185
Solder and lead, 193.
Soldiers, 159, 161, 169.
Soler, 98.
Solihull, 233.
Solubrensis episcopus, 204.
"Sommar," 116.
Sonday, St., 117, 242.
———— store, account of, 209, 214, 221
"Sonnynge" (sun-drying), xx, 71
Sope, 203.
Sores, de la, 78 (*n.*).
"Sowtheampton," 96.
Sowthmore, Rich., 5, 6, 8, 9, 10, 11, 12, 13, 15, 16, 17.
———— John, 38.
Spades, 186.
Spars, 188.
"Spell," 217 and *n.*, 222.
Sperak the Carver, 149.
Spire, 98, 100, 118, 130, 164.
"Splede egylls," 225.
Spoons, 15, 53, 81.
"Sprangs" of ladder, 143.
"Spruc," a, 54.
"Stablyng" of stones, 107.
Staff, copper gilt, 51.
———— of St. Nicholas, 55.
Stair in the Church-house, 132, 153, 166.
———— to the tower, 173.
Stanford in the Vale, xxii, 231.
"Stang," 189.
———— bought for the Church-windows, 189.
Statute of Labourers, xv (*n.*).
Staverdale, canon of, 97.
———— monk of, 85.
Stentyate, 178.
Steeple, battlement of, 100.
———— repaired, 112.
———— window in, 98.
Steward of Hoglers, 174.
———— of St. Mary's Brotherhood, *ib.*
Stickly, Mr. Hu, 223.
Stile, churchyard, 107, 182, 183, 205.
Stillington, Bishop, 113 (*n.*).
"Stitch" (stetch), of corn, 222 and *n.*, 223.
Stock, 1, 2, 33, 151

Stogursey, 230, 233.
Stoke, Church-ale at, 202.
———— Parish, 173.
Stoles made, 101.
———— recovered, 47.
Stoke Michael, al. Stoke Lane, 38.
Stone in Chancel (tombstone?), 161.
———— behind a tomb, 162.
———— bought at Hamden, 188.
———— bought at Stenteyate, 178.
———— for Chapel window, 146.
———— for a Cross, 140.
———— for a monument, 140.
———— for the porch, 203.
———— for the store, 203.
———— of window sold, 189.
Stones, precious, with silver, and gilt setting, 17, 29, 40.
"Stonyn door," 173, 200 and *n.*
Store of St. Antony, 208, 210, 213.
———— of St. George, 208, 210, 211, 212, 213, 214, 215, 219.
———— of Jesu, 208, 212, 213, 214, 216, 219.
———— a little cross of silver given to, 213.
———— of Our Lady, 208, 210, 211, 212, 213, 214, 215.
———— of St. Sidwell, 208, 210, 212, 213, 214, 215.
———— of Sonday, 208, 209, 214, 222.
Stores, 208, 209, &c.
———— of the alms-light, 208, 210, 211, 212, 213, 214, 215, 221.
Straw, 188, 192.
Streamer, 135, 217, 218.
———— "painted of S. George," 215.
———— recovered, 46.
Stubble, 183, 186, 230.
Studs, 22, 25, &c.
———— of girdle, 151.
Subsidy, 50, 159.
———— bill for, 162, 170.
———— on the whole Parish, 232.
Suffragan Bishop, 95, 113 (*n.*).
———— service, 204 (*n.*).
Sugar, Alsun, 21, 22.
———— Edward, 42.
———— Elynor, 36.
———— Richard, 18, 20.
———— Dr. Thos., 52.
———— William, 43.
Suit in ecclesiastical court, 91. 94 and *n.*
———— a "free," 44 and *n.*
"Sumnar" (summoner), 149.
Super-altar, 212 and *n.*
———— blessed, *ib.*

2 N

Sureties delivered, 137.
Surplices, xix, 13, 18, 30, 34, 48, 53, 60, 62, 73, 74, 84, 86, 89, 95, 103, 121, 124, 129, 132, 147, 157, 162, 170, 171, 176, 186, 192, 205.
────── for children, 94.
────── for clerk, 92, 170, 192.
"Swystyng" girdle, 130.
Sydenham, Mr. John, 222, 223, 224.
────── Mr. Edw., 217.
Syle, 120, 128.
Syler, 96, 98.
Sylyng of the Church, 195.
────── against side-altar, 216.
"Syntorne," 118.
Sypers, 6.

T.

Taberna, xxii.
Tabernacle made, 168.
────── washed, 130.
────── of St. Thomas, 145.
Table of High Altar, 90, 95.
────── and forms for Holy Communion, 171.
────── fringe about, 164.
────── mat for, 163.
Table-board, 162.
Table-cloths, 53, 171, 172.
────── for Church-house, 114, 132
Tablyng, 164.
Tabylment, 86 and *n*., 135, 140, 14
"Talwe" (tallow), candle, 84.
Taper for High Altar, 74, 76.
────── before High Cross, 202, 220.
────── against Candlemas, 73.
────── for funerals, 144, 169.
────── Holy, 175, 176, 178, 180, 205.
────── before St. John, 73.
────── before St. Katherine, 229.
────── before St. Michael, 230.
────── on North Altar, 91.
────── Processional, 220. *See* also "Font-taper," and "Paschal-tapier."
"Taratantaryatio ligni," 194.
Tassels, 166.
"Taverning," 231.
Taverns of Ale, xxi, 82, 87, 92, 93, 94, 95, 97, 99, 118, 122, 130, 132, 158, 159, 169, 193, 195.
────── at the Church-house, 115.
────── at Hocktide, Midsummer, and Whitsuntide, 159.
Tending the light, 22, 24.

Terrier of Doulting Manor, 252, 253.
"Testes synodales" (Sidesmen), xvii, 205 (*n*.).
Thatching, 188.
Thomas (chaplain), 176, 177.
────── St., of Canterbury, 35, 134.
────── gilding and setting up, 134
────── tabernacle of, 145.
Thongs for bells, 220.
Thrawll for the well, 129.
────── for pump, 140.
Thread "de abisso," 189.
"Threehewgll" (threshold), 98.
Thubbewyll, 85, 86.
Thurible, 95, 102, 194.
Tickenham, 93.
────── Court, 150 and *n*.
Tiles, 165, 166.
────── to mend Tower, 221.
Tiling of the Church, 216.
Timber, 42, 46, 106, 112, 119, 123, 150, 153, 191.
────── for clock-house, 151.
────── for the "Vawte" of the Church, 172.
Tinker, 135, 136.
Tintinhull, ix, xviii, 173, 183.
────── benefice, 173.
────── church, *ib.*
────── manor, *ib.*
────── manor-house, *ib.*
────── moor, 187.
────── tenants, 177.
"Tokyng gyrdyll," 5, 61, 126, 130, 133.
Tombs, 101.
────── repaired, 171.
────── stones, erected, 140, 170.
"Torcas" (turquoise), 6.
Torches, 35, 92, 94, 95, 100, 103, 105, 121, 138, 144, 180, 228.
────── coffer for, 129.
────── let out, 233.
────── repaired, 229.
"Torfft" (taffeta), 8.
Towels, Paschal, &c., 17, 21, 27, 42, 95, 147, 190.
────── recovered, 46, 47.
Tower raised, 173.
────── repaired, 112, 118, 145, 221.
────── staircase to, 173.
────── oak for roof, 205.
────── to St. James' Chapel, 30.
Trayle under the Roodloft, 66.
Treasure-house, 2, 35, 104, 106, 169.
Treasury, 102.
Trenchers, 35, 142, 146, 165.

Trendell, 2, 3, 4, 55, 57, 61, 66, 70, 73, 74, 83, 100, 110, 119, 135, 163, 175, 176, 179, 180, 183, 191, 192, 193, 203, 205.
———— new, 182, 190, 205.
———— rope for, 57, 76, 179.
Trestell, 98, 109.
"Treyn," 130, 133.
Trimming the bells, 172.
Trussing the bells, 88.
———— the cross, 96.
Trychay, Sir Christopher, 208, 210, 212.
———— John, 215.
———— Lewis, 218, 224.
———— Thomas, 213.
Tuckers, 1, 3, 4, 5, 7, 13, 14, 15, 16, 17, 18, 19, 20, 21, 22, 23, 24, 25, 26, 27, 28, 29, 30, 31, 32, 33, 34, 35, 36, 37, 38, 40.
———— light, 17, 34.
Tunicles, the best, 131.
———— blue silk, 225.
———— blue velvet, ib.
Twelfth Even, 234.
Twysts, 181.
"Tynnyng" the light, 22, 23, 24, 26, 43, 45.
Tything man, xvi, 133.

U.

Unguent for Torch-maker, 180.
Uphill, 154.

V.

Vagabonds, Act against, xv (n.).
"Vanteg of the brede," 24, 25, 26, 27, 28, 43.
"Varmynge," 130.
Vases, 103.
Vat for oil, 53, 198
Vautte, 198.
Veils, 167, 175, 176, 187, 188.
——— silk, sold, 229.
"Vele and lome," 114.
Vellum, 199.
"Venditio et Incrementum," 229, 230.
Verdigris, 110.
"Vessels," 39, 114, 130.
———— hired, 40, 41, 42, 43.
Vestments, 157, 160.
———— black suit, 209, 217, 218, 219, 225.
———— with cope, 225.

Vestments, folding of, 162, 165, 166, 170, 171.
———— of fustian, 225.
———— Lent vestments of blue, 225.
———— list of, 209.
———— made of the old cope, 137.
———— maker, 156.
———— mended, 189.
———— red velvet, 225.
———— from Wells, 190.
———— white, 225.
———— (a) presented to the Church, 35, 118.
———— of black, 52.
———— of blue damask, 57.
———— of blue and red Bruges satin, 47.
———— of flowery satin, 52.
———— of green, 52.
———— of green velvet, 57.
———— red, 129.
———— red velvet, 52, 53.
———— white, 52, 212, 213.
———— white damask, 53.
———— white for Lent, 52.
———— white with scallop shells, 52.
———— white and silver, ib.
———— (b) belonging to the Church.
———— blue, 64.
———— blue damask with cope, 64.
———— green, 51.
———— green with cope, 64.
———— plain damask, 51.
———— white damask, 4.
———— suit with cope, 148.
———— "whole suit," 149.
———— girdles to, 83.
———— loan of, 143.
———— payment for, 153.
———— recovered, 46, 47.
———— setting on a "cenne" of the vestments, 117.
———— setting a "Ze" in them, 106.
———— sums expended on them, 79 (n.), 113.
Vestry, xi, xv, xvi, 2, 31 and n.
Vicar, 74, 76, 84, 92, 93, 94, 95, 100, 102, 205 223, 233.
Vicarage, 80, 98, 121.
Vine in Roodloft, 107.
Virgin, The Blessed, 113, 126, 138, 149.
———— her closes, 38 and n.
———— gifts to, 22, 23, 24, &c.
Visitations, 44, 48, 69, 70, 71, 73, 75, 137, 140, 158, 160, 167, 174, 175, 177.
———— Archbishop's, 181.
———— Archdeacon's, 178.
———— at Bedminster, 169.

Visitations, the Bishop's, 181, 205.
——— at Bristol, 171.
——— costs at, 70, 168, 203.
——— at Wells, 161.
——— the King's, 159, 160, 161.
——— of the B.V.M., picture of, 194.
——— of the sick, 99, 164, 167, 168, 171.
Visitors, the King's, 159, 161.
Voluntary funds, diversion of, xxiii.
——— rates, ix (*n*.), xii.
"Voupp," 119.
Vox, Sir Thos., 34.
"Vrinakull," 25.
Vyse, 83, 125.
——— door, 96, 148.
——— lock to, 170.

W.

"Wadling" (wattling), 145.
Wafer-bread, xxi, 234.
Wages to Priest, 111, 129, 137, 157, 158.
——— to Parish Clerk, 167.
"Waggs" (wages), 167, &c.
Wainscot, 87, 88, 180, 185.
"Waking of the Sepulchre," 79, 103, 104, 105, 107, 138 and *n*.
Walker, Master Morris, priest, 39
Wall of Church, 155, 182.
——— of Churchyard, 177, 200.
——— of Rood-loft, 185.
"Walsche-bord," 100, 119.
"Wante," 52.
Wardens, Church or High, xiv, xviii.
——— chantry and chapel do., xvii.
——— attend Visitation, 174.
——— election of, xi, 1, 173.
——— of guilds, xvii, xviii.
——— language of their accounts, xxii, xxiii, 174.
——— partition of their duties, 227.
——— stipend, 230.
Washing of Church cloths, 16, 183
——— "of the Church gear," 13, 14, 15.
——— of High Altar, 36.
——— of surplices and vestments, 8, 186, 228.
Watching oxen, 169.
"Watelrys," 230
Water, holy, xxi, 93, 136.
——— "the salt," 160.
——— of sluice, 144 and *n*.

Wattling, 178, 179.
Wax "floryssyng," 132.
——— of High Cross, "borrowed of the wardens," 73.
——— "row," 117.
Ways and means, xii.
Weaver, Rev. F. W., xii (*n*.).
Webb, 130.
Webbers, xx, 1.
Webers, 1, 3, 5, 7, 9, 13, 15, 16, 17, 18.
Weights, 182 and *n*.
Well, 109, 112, 134.
——— wall for, 129.
"Well berow" (wheel barrow), 107.
"Well-willed," 98.
Wells, x, and *n*, 37, 39, 42, 52, 62, 71, 78, 91, 94, 95, 106, 110, 114, 122, 123, 129, 137, 140, 149, 153, 154, 161, 162, 167, 176, 190, 247, 252.
Wembdon, defaulters at, xiii (*n*.), xvi.
"Wene," 105 and *n*.
Weston, the Parson of, 163.
Whatley, xviii.
Wheat, 37, 81, 85, 87, 160, 176, 177, 181, 188, 194, 199.
Wheels for bells, 44, 165.
Whirligig, 48, 183.
White Cross, 107.
Whitsun ale, xxii, 234 (*n*.).
"Whyche," a, 85.
"Whyt-mother," 158.
Wick-yarn, 144 and *n*.
William, Dan, Monk, 129.
William, Sir, 118.
Wimberham, 144, 160.
Winchelsea, Archbishop, his constitutions, xii, 243.
Windows of the Church, 233.
——— parish ordered to repair, *ib*.
——— expenses of setting, 81.
——— iron work for, 92.
——— new, 129.
——— repaired, 20, 73, 101, 126, 140.
——— west, enlarged, 173.
——— west window in tower, 202.
——— of the Aler, 98.
——— of Barlynch given to Morebath, 216.
——— of Church-house, levys to, 104, 145.
Wine for Holy Communion, 163, 164.
——— for organ tuners, 149.
Wings of ray silk for the High Altar, 90.
Winnowing malt, 98.
"Wintering and summering" cattle, 193.
Wives' guild, 1, 12.

Wives, gift of malt from, 176.
——— revel, 12.
——— taper, 219.
Women Wardens, xiv, xv, 120, 219.
Wood, the King's, 149.
——— old, sold, 184, 227.
——— do., portions of the rood-loft, 184.
Wookey, 103.
Wool, 219, 221, 222, 226.
——— sold, 229.
——— stock, 182.
——— tithe, 209.
Wootton, North.
——————— chapel, 49, 50.
——————— endowment of light confiscated, 50.
——————— received from, for Easter Taper, 58, 65, 66, 67, 75, 76.
——————— for High Cross light, 60.
——————— Wardens of, 50, 57, 58, 60, 62, 69, 75.
Workhouse, xxii.
Worle, 89.
Worspring, 135 (*n*.).
Wrington, 80, 95, 105, 108.
Wyke, Court de, 78, 92.
——— St. Lawrence, xvii.
"Wyllyng of the walete," 195.
"Wymmynge" (winnowing), 98.
"Wyntering and Summeryng," 193.

Y.

"Yatt" and "Yatte," 145.
Yatton, chapels in, 78.

Yatton, D. Gybbes brought from Bristol to Y., 123.
——— lightmen of, 130.
——— Manor, 78.
——— parishioners of, 162 (*n*.).
——— Priest from Bristol to serve Y., 153.
——— surrendered, 78.
"Ye," a new, to the bell-clapper, 129.
"Yeere," to cowl of Church-house, 143.
Yelchester (Yevelchester and Yvelchester), 122, 181, 189, 190, 204.
Yeo (Sluice), xv (*n*.), 80, 139 (*n*.), 144, 157 (*n*.), 160, 170.
Yere, 139 (*n*.), 157, 160, 162, 165.
——— new, door to, 171, 172.
Yew (main drain), 139, 157.
"Yncull" (Ynkle), 155, 159, 170.
"Yonglens," 9.
Yongling light, 68.
Yorke, Sir Richard, 129 (*n*.), 130, 131, 135, and *n*.
Young men, 1, 3, 4, 7, 10, 12, 13, 15, 16, 17, 18, 19, 20, 22, 23, 24, 25, 26, 27, 28, 29, 30, 31, 32, 33, 34, 35, 36, 37, 38, 40, 67, 208, 214, 215, 216, 217.
Young men's light, 31, 56, 58, 65, 71, 76.
——————— stock, 221.
——————— Wardens, 67, 69.
Yowe (Yeo), 168.

Z.

"Zeme," 100, 239.
"Zetter," 65, 241.

HARRISON AND SONS,
PRINTERS IN ORDINARY TO HER MAJESTY,
ST. MARTIN'S LANE, LONDON.

www.ingramcontent.com/pod-product-compliance
Lightning Source LLC
Chambersburg PA
CBHW022102230426
43672CB00008B/1249